OXFORD SYMPOSIUM ON FOOD & COOKERY 1990

Feasting and Fasting

Proceedings

The Coronation Banquet of King Karl IV of Hungary, Budapest, 1916
A feast and a fast
Described by Louis Szathmary, p 205

OXFORD SYMPOSIUM ON FOOD & COOKERY 1990

Feasting and Fasting

Proceedings

PROSPECT BOOKS
1990

Introduction

This volume of papers presented to the Oxford Symposium on Food and Cookery at Saint Antony's College, Oxford, under the Joint chairmanship of Dr. Theodore Zeldin and Alan Davidson in June 1990 follows the pattern of previous collections. The first four papers were given in plenary session and the others follow in alphabetical order by author.

Emphasising the close and friendly relationship with the Australian Symposium, two papers given there in 1988 had been circulated to all symposiasts in advance of the meeting. These were 'Metamorphoses of the Banquet' by Barbara Santich and extracts from 'In Search of the Opera Gastronomica' by Graham Pont. At our opening plenary session Alan Davidson read extracts and spoke about them. The subsequent discussion provided an appropriate introduction to our deliberations.

As always the staff of the college gave every possible help with our sometimes bizarre needs and fancies. Our Saturday bring-it-yourself lunch in particular must have taxed the patience of the kitchen staff, but again it was interesting, surprising and enjoyable.

On Saturday evening, Mark Walker, the chef at the college, cooked us an English dinner. Details of this meal and the sources for the various dishes are given on page 225.

A Welsh lunch was organised by Gilli Davies on Sunday. It consisted of bread, butter and a splendid selection of cheeses with Welsh water in beautiful blue bottles and Welsh beer. Details are shown on page 230.

We are very grateful to Foods from Spain who made a grant towards the cost of reproducing the papers for circulation before the symposium. This in turn greatly facilitated the production of this volume.

Harlan Walker
June, 1991

FRONT and BACK COVERS: Illustrations by Lupe Rios to Alicia Rios' paper.

FRONTISPIECE: Illustration by József Bató to Dr. Louis Szathmary's paper.

ISBN 0 907325 46 7
© 1991, as a collection, Prospect Books Ltd. (but © 1990, in the individual articles, rests with the authors).

Editor: Harlan Walker
Published by Prospect Books Ltd. 45 Lamont Road, London, SW10 0HU.
Type-set by Armorel Productions, 27 Green Lane, Coleshill, Warwickshire B46 3NE.
Printed by Antony Rowe Ltd., Bumper's Farm, Chippenham, Wiltshire SN14 6QA.

CONTENTS

	Page
FASTS & FEASTS - AN INTRODUCTION Theodore Zeldin	*1*
TRADITIONAL FOODWAYS, FAST AND FEAST Astri Riddervold	*2*
THREE WHOLE DAYS TO AN END. THE NORWEGIAN PEASANT WEDDING FEAST AS A SOCIAL MIRROR Bjorn Fjellheim	*7*
FROM EVERYDAY DIET TO FEAST FOOD: AN EXAMPLE FROM THE HEMSEDAL COUNTRY DISTRICT IN NORWAY Marit Ekne Ruud	*11*
THE WAY THE CONTEMPORARY WESTERN ASSYRIANS IN THE MIDDLE EAST TAKE FOOD DURING FASTS AND CHURCH HOLIDAYS Michael Abdalla	*15*
THE FESTIVAL OF CHRISTMAS Joan P. Alcock	*27*
EMMA'S WEDDING FEAST - A GLANCE AT FLAUBERT'S MADAME BOVARY Rose Arnold	*49*
KALACH, KOLATCH, KULITCH - CHALLAH? Josephine Bacon	*53*
THE BLACK OR HELL BANQUET Professor Phyllis P. Bober	*55*
THE BAYEUX TAPESTRY SHISH KEBAB MYSTERY Robert Chenciner	*58*
IGUANAS, CHOCOLATE, MUSKRATS, AND A GLIMPSE AT COCHINEAL Dr. Sophie D. Coe	*65*
ON THE EDGE OF THE FEAST. OUTSIDERS IN EARLY GREECE Andrew Dalby	*69*
TRADITION AND INNOVATION IN THE PACIFIC NORTHWEST OUTDOOR FEAST John Doerper	*73*
BELOW-THE-SALT COOKERY Christopher Driver	*78*
FEASTS OF THE FUR TRADERS Dorothy Duncan	*79*
BUTTER BEFORE GUNS Hugo Dunn-Meynell	*81*
FOOD FOR FAMILY AND FRIENDS FROM SHROVE TIDE TO EASTER Dr. Johanna M. P. Edema with Mrs. Katinka Hermans	*85*
THE POLITICS AND SOCIAL IMPLICATIONS OF TABLEWARE FOR FEASTING Elizabeth Gabay	*99*
WHITE FOODS IN ANATOLIAN FEASTS Nevin Halici	*104*
TEXAS BARBECUE: A FEAST FOR ALL CLASSES Sharon Hudgins	*106*
NOTES ON FASTING AND FEASTING IN THAILAND Philip Iddison	*121*

FASTING AND FEASTING AMONG OREGON'S RUSSIAN OLD BELIEVERS Mary Wallace Kelsey	*124*
FASTING ON RUMFORDSCHE SUPPE (CIRCA 1791) AND WOOLTON PIE (CIRCA 1941). FEASTING IN OXFORD, CAPENHURST AND HAMMERSMITH. Nicholas Kurti	*129*
ROYAL FEASTS Janet Laurence	*138*
FEASTING AFTER FASTING IN ARCHIB VILLAGE, DAGESTAN Dr. Magomedkhan Magomedkhanov	*152*
THE ST. JOSEPH DAY ALTARS OF NEW ORLEANS Richard C. Mieli	*155*
DUTCH TREATS OR FESTIVE FOOD IN AN AFFLUENT SOCIETY Ileen Montijn	*158*
ELEMENTS OF ARAB FEASTING Charles Perry	*162*
L'ORDRE DE BON TEMPS - GOOD CHEER AS THE ANSWER Jo Marie Powers	*164*
BEANS FOR THE DEAD Gillian Riley	*173*
THE FIRST COMMUNION BANQUET Alicia Rios	*175*
A PERFECT FEAST? PREVENTATIVE MEDICINE AND DIET IN MEDIEVAL FRANCE Brenda S. Rose	*183*
SERENDIPITY Alice Wooledge Salmon	*191*
THE GOLDEN SPICE FROM ANCIENT PERSIA Margaret Shaida	*194*
FEASTS IN THE ARCHAEOLOGICAL RECORD Paul Stokes	*198*
FEASTS & FASTS. AS DESCRIBED, DOCUMENTED AND ILLUSTRATED IN THE JOHNSON & WALES UNIVERSITY CULINARY ARCHIVES AND MUSEUM, PROVIDENCE, RHODE ISLAND Louis I. Szathmary	*202*
'TWELFTH NIGHT' Greta Verdin	*207*
FEASTS IN JORDAN AND THE TRANSKEI Kathie Webber	*208*
OF SUGAR AND PORCELAIN. TABLE DECORATION IN THE NETHERLANDS IN THE 18TH CENTURY Joop Witteveen	*212*
RAMADHAN: FASTING AND FEASTING Sami Zubaida	*222*
DINNER ON SATURDAY EVENING - MENU AND RECIPES Lisa Chaney and Harlan Walker	*225*
WELSH FOODS AND DRINKS OFFERED AT LUNCH ON 23RD SEPTEMBER Gilli Davies	*230*

A List of Participants

A brief description of the profession or particular interest of symposiasts is shown when this information has been given to us.

Michael Abdalla, ul. Szydlowska 53/10, 60-656 Poznan, POLAND
Dr. Joan P. Alcock, 24 Queensthorpe Road, Sydenham, London SE26 4PH
Darina & Myrtle Allen, Ballymaloe Cookery School, Shanagarry, Midleton, Co. Cork, EIRE
Alice Arndt, The Life of Spice, 2628 Albans, Suite A, Houston, Texas 77005-1308, USA
Rose Arnold, 10 Braxfield Row, New Lanark, Lanarkshire ML11 9BP
        Interface between literature and food history
Josephine Bacon, 82 Stonebridge Road, London N15 5PA
Mrs. Anna Bamborough, 40 St. Giles, Oxford
Ann Barr, 36 Linton House, 11 Holland Park Avenue, London W11 3RL
Nancy Barr, 109 Williams Street, Providence, RI 02906, USA
Suzy Benghiat, 93-95 ave du General Leclerc, Batiment B, 75014 Paris, FRANCE
        Evolution of food habits and taste
Sven-Erik Bergh, Bergh & Bergh Verlagsanstalt GmbH, Postfach 78, CH-6314 Unteraegeri (Zug), SWITZERLAND
        Publisher.
Michelle Berriedale-Johnson, 5 Lawn Road, London NW3 2XS
        Food writer & historian. Tofu ice cream manufacturer.
Maggie Black, 167 Putney Bridge Road, London SW15 2NZ
Prof. Phyllis P. Bober, Bryn Mawr College, Bryn Mawr, PA 19010, USA
        History of cuisine - especially ancient and renaissance
Mrs. Rita Brodie, 3 Greenaway Gardens, Hampstead, London NW3 7DJ
Catherine Brown, 13 Kirklee Terrace, Glasgow G12 0TH
        Food writer.
Penelope Carew Hunt, Cowleaze, Edington, Westbury, Wilts BA13 4PJ
Mollie Chadsey, 19 Finlay House, Phyllis Court Drive, Henley on Thames RG9 2H
        Cookery book collector.
Lisa Chaney, 40 Southfield Road, Oxford OX4 1NZ
Robert Chenciner, 5a Shepherd's Market, London W1
Julia Child, 103 Irving Street, Cambridge, MA 02138, USA
        Cookbook author and teacher
Janet Clarke, 3 Woodside Cottages, Freshford, Bath BA3 6EJ
Dr. Sophie D. Coe, 376 St. Ronan Street, New Haven, Connecticut 06511, USA
        Pre- Columbian cuisine
Andrew Dalby, 5 Primrose Way, Linton, Cambridge, CB1 6UD
        Librarian
Alan & Jane Davidson, 45 Lamont Road, London SW10 0XU
Caroline Davidson, 5 Queen Anne's Gardens, London W4 1TU
        Literary agent. Director of Prospect Books.
Gilli Davies, 11 Queen Anne Square, Cardiff CF6 3ED
Joy Davies, Flat 1, 125 Fordwick Road, London NW2 3NJ
Anna Del Conte, 93 Elm Bank Gardens, London SW13 ONX
Janny de Moor, Burg V. de Vriesweg 29, 8084 AR 't Harde, NETHERLANDS
John Doerper, 111 Old Mill Village, Bellingham, WA 98226, USA
        Food editor and publisher
Anne Dolamore, 10 Chivalry Road, London SW11 1HT
Christopher Driver, 6 Church Road, London N6 4QT
        Writer and editor
Dorothy Duncan, The Ontario Historical Society, 5151 Yonge Street, Willowdale, Ontario M2N 5P5, CANADA
Hugo Dunn-Meynell, The International Wine & Food Society, 108 Old Brompton Road, London SW7 3RA
        Writer. Director of International Wine & Food Society
Sarah Edington, c/o Margaret Willes, 17 Appleby Road, London E8 3ET
        Author
Dr. Johanna M. P. Edema, Emmalaan 18A, 6721 EV Bennekom, NETHERLANDS
        Sociologist of food and nutrition. Consultant.
J. Audrey Ellison, 135 Stevenage Road, Fulham, London SW6 6PB
        Food consultant and writer.
Meryle Evans, 325 E 52nd Street, New York, NY 10022, USA
Rachael Evans, Kiln Cottage, Culham, Abingdon, Oxon OX14 4NE
Sarah Jane Evans, Crescent Wood Cottage, 6 Crescent Wood Road, London SE26 6RU
        Interest in Spanish foods. Marketing of foods.

Clare Ferguson, 5 Colville Terrace, London W11 2BE
Bjorn Fjellheim, Kystmuseet i sogn og fjordane, Postboks 94, 6901 Floro, NORWAY
Jean Freemantle, Ongar Hill Farm, Magpie Lane, Coleshill, Amersham, Bucks
Dr. Robert Frey, 194 Sutherland Avenue, London, N9 1RX
Susan Friedland, Harper & Row Publishers Inc. 10 East 53rd Street, New York, New York 10022, USA.
    Senior editor - Harper & Row
Elizabeth Gabay, 25 Cottenham Drive, London SW20 0TD
    Wine merchant
Anne & Patrick Gibbins, The Lodge, 56a Nightingale Lane, London SW12 8NY
Richard Grant, 68 Grove Hill, Caversham, Reading, Berks RG4 8PR
Henrietta Green, Rich & Green Ltd., 15a Pembridge Crescent, London W11 3DX
Rosalind Green, Underhills Garden, Clanfield, Oxon OX8 2SP
Nevin Halici, P.g. 88 Nalcaci, 42005 Konya, TURKEY
Elaine Hallgarten, 14 Antrim Grove, London NW3 4XR
    Food & cookery writer
Mrs. C. Hermans, Dommelrodelaan 71, 5492 GH St. Oedenrode, NETHERLANDS
    Teacher - food, nutrition and cooking
Gwenda V. Hill, Blaysworth Manor, Colmworth, Bedford MK44 2LD
Caroline Hobhouse, 5a Inverness Gardens, London W8 4RN
    Publisher
Kate Holland, c/c Castle Veterinary Surgery, 1 Tilehurst Road, Reading, Berkshire
Geraldene Holt, Clyst William Barton, Plymtree, Cullompton, Devon EX15 2LG
    Food writer
Sharon Hudgins, University of Maryland, Munich Campus, Postfach 900 760, 8000 Muenchen 90, GERMANY
    Food writer, editor, correspondent
Claire Hudson, 14 Frederica Road, Chingford, London E4 7AL
Philip Iddison, 3 Upper Grotto Road, Twickenham, Middlesex TW1 4NG
Barbara Inskip, 43 Periwinkle Lane, Hitchin, Herts SG4
    Translator of German & French cookery texts.
Rosalind Irwin, 23 Vale Court, Mallord Street, London SW3 6AL
    Journalist - food history and sociology
Elaine Johnson, 23 Chartfield Avenue, Putney, London SW15 6DZ
Corinne Julius, 15 Camden Square, London NW1 9UY
Dr. Brigid Keane, c/o Olive Portnoy, Oaktrees, Woodman Lane, Sewardstonebury, London E4 7QR
Ruth Keene, 51 Nina Street, Toronto, Ontario MSR 1Z5, CANADA
Mary Wallace Kelsey, Nutrition & Food Management Department, College of Home Economics, Oregon State University, Corvallis, OR 97330, USA
    Teaching speciality - cultural aspects of food
Giana & Nicholas Kurti, 38 Blandford Avenue, Oxford OX2 8DZ
    Nicholas - Emeritus professor of physics
Janet Laurence, The Grooms, East Lydford, Somerton, Somerset TA11 7HD
    Freelance writer on food
Beverly Le Blanc, Top Flat, 128 Shirland Road, London W9 2BT
Paul Levy, The Observer Magazine, Chelsea Bridge House, Queenstown Road, London SW8 4NN
    Journalist
Valerie Lis, c/o Mrs Rita Brodie, 3 Greenaway Gardens, Hampstead, London NW3 7DJ
Sandy Littman, 69 Harberton Road, London N19 3JT
Jenny Macarthur, 13 Wavell Road, Maidenhead, Berkshire, SL6 5AB
    Etymology, food names, migration of foodstuffs
Carolyn McCrum, 57 Oakthorpe Road, Oxford OX2 7BD
Frances McCullough, 117 Villard House, Hastings-on-Hudson, NY 10706, USA
Mike & Tessa McKirdy, Cooks Books, 34 Marine Drive, Rottingdean, Sussex BN2 7HQ
    Cook books
Dr. Magomedkhan Magomedkhanov, 367012 Dagestan ASSR, Makhachkala, Prospect Kalinina 77B Kv.19, USSR
Gerald & Valerie Mars, 53 Nassington Road, London NW3 2TY
    Gerald - anthropologist.
    Valerie - Research on Victorian dining.
Richard C. Mieli, 4 Longfellow Place #1703, Boston, Ma 02114,
Marie-Pierre Moine, 22 Arundel Gardens, London W11 2LB
Mrs. I. H. Montijn, Stationstraat 17, 1391 GL Abcoude, NETHERLANDS
    Writing book on Dutch food
Dr. H. & Mrs. Morrow Brown, Highfield House, Highfield Gardens, Derby DE3 1HT
    Dr. H. - consultant physician and allergist

Betsy Newell, 3 St. James Gardens, London W11 4RB
        Cookery teacher
Jill Norman, 1 Rosslyn Hill, London NW3 5UL
Sri & Roger Owen, 96 High Street Mews, London SW19 7RG
Victoria O'Neill, The Gate Cottage, Bampton, Oxford OX8 2JW
        Cook
Helen Peacocke, Rose Cottage, 43 Acre End Street, Eynsham, Oxford
Charles Perry, 12912 El Dorado Avenue, Sylmar, CA 91342, USA
        Historian of Islamic world food
Karin Perry, The Lawns, 16 South Grove, Highgate, London N6 6BJ
Olive Portnoy, Oaktrees, Woodman Lane, Sewardstonebury, London E4 7QR
Jo Marie Powers, University of Guelph, Hotel & Food Administration, Guelph, Ontario, N1G 2W1, CANADA
Iris Raven, 94 Farnham Avenue Apt 3, Toronto, Ontario M4V 1H4, CANADA
        Food writer
Dr. Astri Riddervold, Dyrlandsvei 9, 0875 Oslo 8, NORWAY
        Scientist, cook and writer
Gillian Riley, 11 Kersley Road, Stoke Newington, London N16 0NP
        History of Italian food and cookery
Alicia Rios, Avenida General Peron 19-8°C, Madrid 28020, SPAIN
Cherry Ripe, 1 Tivoli Street, Paddington 2021, NSW, AUSTRALIA
Claudia Roden, 8 Wild Eatch, London NW11 7LD
Dr. B. S. & Mrs. Brenda S. Rose, 626 London Road, Davenham, Northwich, Cheshire CW9 8LG
        Brenda - French medieval cookery
Owen Rossan, Epworth, Antrim Road, London NW3 4XN
        Sociologist
Marit Ekne Ruud, Grabrodreveien 8, 0379 Oslo 3, NORWAY
Rena Salaman, 145 Tufnell Park Road, London N7 0PU
Alice Wooledge Salmon, 125 Mount Street, London W1Y 5HA
        Writer
Tugrul Savkay Bay, Amiral Fahri Engin Sk., Vaizoglu Ap. Daire 7, Rumelihisari-Istanbul, TURKEY
Philippa Scott, 30 Elgin Crescent, London W11 2JR
        Author
Maria Jose Sevilla Taylor, 72 Brisbane Road, Ilford, Essex IG1 4SL
Margaret Shaida, Della Ra, Harpsden Way, Henley-on-Thames, Oxfordshire RG9 1NL
        Persian cuisine
Jenny Sheridan, The Wolfson Medical Rehabilitation Centre, Atkinson Morley's Hospital, Copse Lane, Wimbledon, London SW20 0NQ
        Speech therapist. General interest
Roy Shipperbottom, 9 Southgate, off Heathfield Avenue, Heaton Chapel, Stockport SK4 4QL
Ralph & Kate Shirley, The Studio, 39 Uttoxeter Road, Foston, Derby DE6 5PX
        Ralph - Vice-chairman of Environmental Health committee, South Derbyshire
Kay Staniland, Dept. of Costume & Textiles, The Museum of London, London Wall, London EC2Y 5HN
        Keeper of Costume and Textiles
Rosemary Stark, 6 Chamberlain Street, London NW1 8XB
        Freelance food writer
Jeffrey L. Steingarten, 29 West 17th Street, New York, NY 10011, USA
Paul Stokes, 32 Manor Way, Bagshot, Surrey GU19 5JZ
        Archaeologist. Retired chef lecturer
Dr. & Mrs. L. Szathmary, 630 West Webster Avenue, Chicago, ILL 60614, USA
        Louis - Chef laureate of Johnson & Wales University. Retired restaurateur
Ms. Anna-Maija Tanttu, POB 240, 00101 Helsinki, FINLAND
        Food writer and consultant
Malcolm Thick, 8 Buckingham Close, Didcot, Oxfordshire
        Historian, especially market gardening and vegetables
Jill Tilsley-Benham, 12a Upper Mulgrave Road, Cheam, Surrey SM2 7AZ
        Freelance writer - Middle Eastern food and travel
Professor. C. & Mrs. R. P. Tyler, 22 Belle Avenue, Reading, Berks RG6 2BL
        C. Tyler - Professor Emeritus - physiology and biochemistry
Greta Verdin, The Cherwell Boathouse, Bardwell Road, Oxford OX2 6SR
        Tutor in English literature
Harlan Walker, 294 Hagley Road, Birmingham B17 8DJ
Jennifer Walker, 10 Whitley Park Lane, Reading, Berks
Conal Walsh, 36 Great Queen Street, London WC2B 5AA

Ann Watson, The Forge, High Street, Barford, Warwick CV35 8BU
    Cookery consultant and nutritional analyst
Kathie Webber, Stoke Green Farmhouse, Stoke Green, Stoke Poges, Bucks. SL2 4HN
    Journalist.
Suzanne Webber, BBC Enterprises, Woodlands, 80 Wood Lane, London W12 0TP
    Senior Commissioning Editor - cookery books, BBC
Robin Weir, 104 Iffley Road, London W6
    Condiments, ice cream, flavours
Barbara K. Wheaton, 268 Elm Street, Concord, MASS 01742, USA
    19th century French culinary history
Rosemary Wilkinson, 30 Blackroot Road, Sutton Coldfield, B74 2QP
Margaret Willes, 17 Appleby Road, London E8 3ET
    Publisher
Anne Williams, Top Flat, 41 Devonport Road, London W12 8NZ
    Journalist
Joop Witteveen, Tweede Oosterparkstraat 261, 1092 BN Amsterdam, NETHERLANDS
    Culinary historian
Georgina Wood, c/o Karin Perry, The Lawns, 16 South Grove, Highgate, London N6 6BJ
Dr. & Mrs. John A. Yena, Johnson & Wales University, Providence, Rhode Island, USA
    Dr. Yena - President of Johnson & Wales University
Dr. Theodore Zeldin, Tumbledown House, Cumnor, Oxford OX2 9QE
Sami Zubaida, 2 Avenue House, Belsize Park Gardens, London NW3 4LA
    Sociologist

In addition the following special guests attended our dinner on Saturday evening:
Mark Cherniavsky & Anne Willan, 1613 30th Street, N.W., Washington, DC, 20007, USA
Julia Child, 103 Irving Street, Cambridge, MA 02138, USA
Barbara K. Wheaton, 268 Elm Street, Concord, MA 01742, USA

Fasts and Feasts

by Theodore Zeldin

There have been four different passions behind feasts.

The first has been fear. The oldest feasts aimed at appeasing gods and ancestors, offering sacrifices of expensive foods to prevent the living from being punished for their misdoings; and often the priests, having eaten the food on behalf of the gods, got the credit if life continued, and the rain continued to fall. Kings and princes liked to use food to instil fear: royal feasting was a spectator sport with a message, a sport watched by hungry subjects, who trembled in awe observing the pleasures that only the powerful could enjoy. Feasts of fear include all those where rules of diet are enforced, where people eat what they must, rather than what they want. These are instances of food being used as a way of preserving order, ensuring obedience.

The second passion behind feasts has been rebellion. In the last century, banquets were a favourite way of starting, or preparing for revolution: food and drink stimulated fiery oratory. Carnival feasts were rebellions too, customary restrictions were suspended, poor people ate for a few days like kings and like those who oppressed them, but only temporarily, for a carnival is only a game, after which everyone goes back to his habitual grovel. The barbecues of Texas combine these traditions; politicians back-slap their electors and call them by their first names, in search of votes, forming neo-feudal armies to seize power.

A third kind of feast aims at happiness, the passion which has become the religion of our times. The consumer society is a permanent feast. The restaurant, invented during the French Revolution, allows anybody to have a feast, at any time, and all they need is a little money. The restaurant feast is not a feast by a whole society, but by a small group, a family, a couple, an individual. It is a modern idea that one lonely person can have a feast all by himself.

But the most modern feast of all is the one inspired by the passion for novelty. Feasts are normally rituals. But cooks now want to cook as no one has ever cooked before, mixing ingredients that have never met. This corresponds to the the ideal of creativity and originality, which rivals happiness as the dream of our times, and, in my view, is less elusive.

There have also been four different kinds of fast. In the beginning, people fasted above all to prove that they belonged to the same religion, that they shared the same beliefs and loyalties. Fasting is still a way of asserting one's identity, of agreeing to conform.

Then there is the fasting which expresses the opposite thought, uncertainty. How often should one eat? What should one eat? Three meals a day became one of the methods for strengthening family life, ensuring that children imbibed their parent's wisdom. The anorexics rebelled against that, and the fast food eaters, and the permanent nibblers, all of whom broke the rules. Dentists threatened that your teeth would fall out if you did not fast from sweets. The gaps between meals are mini-fasts: nobody is certain any more how long they should last.

To fast for spiritual or aesthetic reasons is a way of cleansing oneself, of using abstinence to obtain a feeling that one is more fully alive. The slimmers of today are the heirs of the hermits of ancient times, sacrificing pleasure for the sake of truth and beauty.

The worst kind of fasting is from lack of imagination. Every menu is a choice, implying rejection of possible alternatives. Humans eat only a very small proportion of edible foods; they have often starved rather than change their habits, rather than try something new. Rats will eat anything that does not poison them; tapeworms are content to sit at the same intestinal table, meekly accepting whatever meals their hosts offer. Humans are a little more imaginative, but not all that much. They are only just beginning to understand fully what it means to fast.

Feast and fast are an inseparable couple, who cannot do without one another. But I am glad that our Symposia have always been, above all else, feasts.

Traditional Foodways, Fast and Feast

by Astri Riddervold

The basic element in every culture, at any place on earth, at any time in history, is that man must eat. A certain amount of food is needed regularly. When, how and what people eat differ with time and place. To study the food and foodways of a certain society, the production of raw materials, preparation of the meal, the eating habits of everyday and feast, reveals basic factors in the culture of the society. Values, symbols, norms and rules are included in man's activity when food is produced and consumed. Studying the food culture is a good starting point for understanding a culture as a whole.

The differences are extreme, even today. In Africa, Kalahari women still use almost the whole day in collecting plants, roots, worms and small animals to be eaten in addition to what the men bring back from their hunt, – while in the nearest big town one can pick from the shelves in the supermarket in a short time all food that is needed for days and weeks in tins and packages, prepared, conserved and transferred in such a way that only the printed label reveals which were the raw materials.

However, when we speak about the traditional food of a society, in spite of the differences, they all seem to have something in common; the factors influencing man's activity when food for fast and feast is produced and consumed are more or less general.

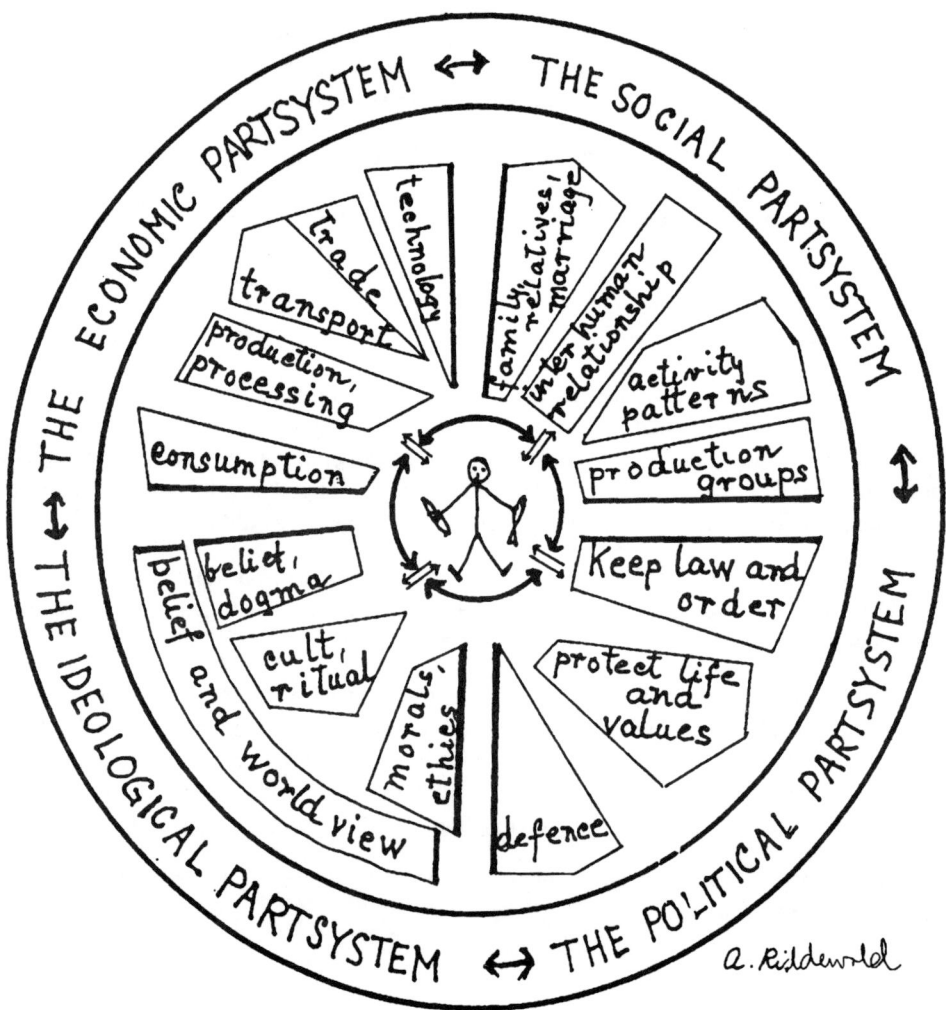

This is a model where significant variables influencing man's activity are listed. If a holistic perspective is wanted, they must all be taken into consideration. Their importance, however, differ with time and place. Every culture is unique. Its use is explained on the next page.

Culture will here be given a definition according to the Norwegian professor of anthropology A. M. Klausen saying:

> Culture is the total way of life of a human society.

And a little more detailed:

> Culture is the ideas, values, rules and norms that a member of a society inherits from the former generation and tries to pass on – often a little altered – to the next. In accordance with this definition food culture will be the part of the total way of life of a society which includes food, its production, preparation and consumption.

The activity of man to cover the primary needs is ruled by an interaction of several factors; the most important are listed in the model which has been given the shape of a circle to visualise an entirety. The factors are given as bricks in a puzzle, placed under a headline – a part-system where they are likely to belong; the arrows indicate the interaction on different levels.

Use of the Model

We start with the beliefs and world views of the individual. Most religions include rules about food and eating, which influence the traditional culture.

We move to the economic/ecological part-system: we must know where on the earth we are and what are the conditions for the exploitation of nature. The standard of technology is important, also such things as cooking places and pots. Other factors influencing consumption by the population are who owns the land and who uses it, and in which way the production is divided by society, trade and communications.

Studying the social aspects often gives a deeper understanding. Here it is possible to reveal the silent side of culture, the pride and prejudice, the symbols and values.

The political system and its ideology, which may differ from the ideology of the individuals, also influence man's activity and choice as regards food. Here we will only mention subsidies of all kinds, restrictions on imports and exports, etc.

When we have wandered round the circle, we will have learned a lot. Then we can start on a new round and go deeper into the question.

I will give a simple example which gave me an answer to the question of status and frequency of eating pork in the traditional food culture of Hungary.

Sheep and goats were originally the favourite animals kept by the farmers. During the long occupation by the Turks, who were Muslims and not allowed to eat pork, the Hungarian farmers changed to pigs in order not to have to deliver their production to feed the occupying forces. They conserved fruit as alcoholic drinks, perhaps for the same reason.

This explanation includes the ideological part-system and the economic and political aspects. If the social part-system were included, a deeper and better explanation might be given in the first round. before we start on the second.

To be able to go deeper into the understanding of food culture, models presented by two German scientists can be of great help: a structuralistic model concerning the economic part-system by Guenter Wiegelman, and one concerning the social part-system by Ulrich Tolksdorf. The first is published in *Ethnologia Scandinavica*, 1971, the second in *Kieler Blätter zur Folkskunde*, 1972.

In describing man's activity, we often choose to give priority to one or two of the part-systems. When dealing with daily food, the economic/ecological part is most important. The social aspect of the meal, however, often gives a deeper understanding, in particular regarding the feast. So when one chooses to focus on one or two aspects, it is of importance to be aware that all four play a smaller or greater part in the total picture.

Understanding Norwegian conditions

"History without geography is nonsense", to quote a Norwegian professor. In pre-industrial times the way of life was based upon the exploitation of the natural resources of an area.

After the last great Ice Age when the inland ice gradually receded, it left behind what we know as the European black earth belt, formed from a soft rich rock, which stretches diagonally across England, through northern Europe, including Denmark and southern Sweden, and east to the Urals. The possibility of power lay in this flat, rich earth. We all know of one of the systems it created: feudalism and the living conditions that that generated. When the ice retreated from Norway, there was no soft rich rock for it to work on, but on the contrary a hard and poor rock which did not easily break down. The land it left behind was a mountain land with only small pockets of fertile earth along the coast and in the valleys. Only in a few inland areas are larger extents of arable land to be found. The Arctic Circle goes across the middle of the country and without the Gulf Stream, which brings warmer water from Mexico northwards along the Norwegian coast, the country would have had a similar climate to Greenland.

Norway's earth has never provided a basis for riches and power. Feudalism with its economic and social conditions never came to Norway in its traditional form.

Marginality

The country is marginal in the broadest sense of the word. Only in a few areas – if in any at all – has the earth as a resource given enough for man to base his existence only on agriculture. The exploitation of resources far from one's dwelling, in the mountains, the forests and the sea, has been a condition of life. But the exploitation of these resources gave the people products that others also wanted, and Norwegians have traded with others throughout history. The trading of fish for grain was a condition for permanent settlement in the northernmost part of the country where grain does not ripen.

Despite this trade, Norwegians were, and are, farmers by origin and the main part of the population were farmers longer than most other Europeans, but perhaps in a different way.

The country's complex pattern of resources resulted in a system where the men were away from the home for long periods and the women were responsible for running the farm and for administering the collective stores. The men nevertheless registered themselves as farmers in the national censuses, even though they were fishermen or sailors and away from the farm for more than half the year. It was the wife who was the farmer, and the entire family had its basis in the land, in a farm they owned or had the right of use to, but few of the male members worked on the farm throughout the year. They usually partook in the work in the hectic summer season when a year's supply of food necessary for people and animals, had to be produced, harvested, prepared and conserved until a new harvest was brought in. Animals which were to be used for food, were always slaughtered in the autumn to save fodder, and the meat was conserved in different ways. Fish was caught in large quantities usually in winter, in the spawning season. The catch was conserved and stored for a year.

Generally one can say that the Norwegian traditional year cycle was a three months' period of production and a nine months' period of consumption. The late Spring and Summer season was hectic, often warm, sunny and light, also through the night, whilst in the Autumn and Winter frost, snow and darkness prevailed. Then transport was difficult, unreliable, sometimes impossible for long periods.

Raw material resources

The diet in Norway had to be based on storage housekeeping both in the towns and in the country into the 19th century. The keeping of livestock was common, also in the towns which had public grazing land for the town dwellers' livestock.

Fish and meat were preserved by drying, salting, fermentation and smoking, or by a combination of two or more of these methods. Fresh meat or fish was thought to be unwholesome. Fresh fish was only eaten during the summer. Milk and dairy products such as cheese and butter, sour skimmed milk, buttermilk and whey were important elements in the diet, in particular in the mountain area. In addition to cow's milk, the products of goat, sheep and reindeer milk were also used in the diet. Grain was a minimum factor in the older Norwegian diet; it was called "the food" or God's loan. Barley and oats, which are best adapted to marginal climates, were the usual grain types. Finnish immigrants in eastern Norway cultivated rye in the ashes after burning forest areas. They also brought with them their traditional type of baking oven and their fermented rye bread which spread to the neighbouring areas. From 1742 to 1914 the country from Trøndelag and further north had a reasonably reliable supply of rye flour for the winter from the trade with Russia which was allowed in this period. In this trade, the Pomor Trade, fish from the summer fishing by Finmark was sold to the Russians, who in part paid with ready ground rye flour. It was in fact usual for the fishermen to be paid in rye flour, called "russeflour". A great many families in northern Norway had a member concerned in this trade. In this way the winter supply of baking flour was assured. In the whole area large baking ovens can be found where fermented bread was baked, and this bread was eaten for the first meal of the day.

In the 19th century, the potato was introduced into Norway. It became very popular, as both the soil and climate proved ideal for its cultivation all along the coast to within the Arctic Circle. It was used boiled as a vegetable but also in different types of thin rolled bread – potato cake and potato lefse. The staple cereals, oats and barley, often did not ripen before they were ruined by the frosts of autumn.

Norwegians usually had four meals a day. Oats and barley were used for porridge or gruel, often made with whey. Norwegian bread, the crisp, thinly rolled flatbread, was also made from oats and barley. It was usually baked only two or three times a year, as it can be stored for months. Every meal include either porridge, gruel or flatbread. After the introduction of the potato, it replaced cereals in the midday meal. Herring and cereals were eaten up to four times a day by most of the population, both rural and urban. Salt herring was always served at breakfast, and often at one or two of the other meals as well. Inland, herring was usually served only at breakfast, at other meals freshwater fish was used, either salted, dried or fermented. In summer slices of cured meat (salted and dried) was eaten instead of herring and fish, and the grain food was substituted by thick sour milk.

On the coast, salted, dried or slightly fermented saltwater fish was used, and before the beginning of the 20th century fresh fish was seldom eaten. Such fish was regarded, like meat, as unhealthy. The usual Sunday midday meal consisted of a soup made from salt meat, pearl barley, and locally grown vegetables such as turnip, peas and potatoes. Pieces of salt herring could be used instead of salt meat, and the soup was then called herring soup.

The unsolved problem in this diet has been how the Norwegians obtained enough vitamin C. Before the potato arrived on the scene, a type of turnip was usually grown, and in certain areas grey peas. However, there are no figures for the quantities.

Scholars have claimed both in Sweden and Norway that the great amounts of wild berries which grow in both countries from north to south, from coast to mountain, have not been used in the popular diet. Later research, however, has shown that this is not correct for the areas north of Trondheim. On the contrary, preserved, wild berries were a part of the daily diet. In addition the wild plant angelica (*Archangelica*) has been used both for people and animals, fresh and preserved, in often large amounts, over the entire country. Several of the cookery books from the 19th century contain recipes for stews etc. of sorrel (*Rumex acetosa*) and mountain sorrel (*Oxyria digyna*), which at the very least indicates that the plants have been used as food.

How and where the food was prepared

"The variety is not great, but the food is plentiful and good", a topographical narrator wrote about the diet in Nordland in 1824.

We can assume that the food was not plentiful everywhere, but that there was, especially in the coastal areas, a certain variation in the diet through the use of several types of fish, fat and lean, preserved in different ways such as dried, salted, smoked, fermented and cured, or in combinations of these.

The different dishes were prepared in pots over an open fire. Smoked herring and salted lamb ribs were also grilled on the embers. Frying pans were not common. The woman had little time to spare for preparing food, and cured salt fish was eaten straight from the barrel, whilst cured salt meat was dried and eaten uncooked with porridge, flatbread or sour milk. When the potato came into use, it had to be boiled. The salted fish and meat were then boiled in the same pot, with turnip and peas if available. This saved both fuel and work and the potato was salted by the fish or meat. In this way salt was not wasted, and that was important.

Drink

For daily use pure water was drunk or mixed with sour buttermilk or whey. As a warm drink the northern Norwegians boiled an extract of caraway, water and skimmed milk, or dried cranberry leaves and dried cloudberry stalks could be used as tea. Beer brewing has strong traditions in southern Norway, but not in the north. The excess barley which was needed was not found there. However, even in the south beer was not a daily drink. It was part of the big occasions, holidays and festivals.

Norway has no traditional wine culture. The sources tell about the Vikings drinking mead. However, beer was the traditional alcoholic drink until a Swedish noble woman, Ewa Ekeblad, in 1748 found out how to produce alcohol from potatoes. In the following century this knowledge passed across the border to Norway, which in the 19th century was in union with Sweden. This strong alcohol, produced from the starch in potatoes and given its special taste by the addition of different herbs, has beside the beer become the traditional Norwegian alcoholic drink, our Aqua Vitae.

So while the farmers in southern Europe produced their alcoholic drinks from grapes, the middle Europeans from apricots, plums and pears, the Scotch, Danes and Swedes from grain, the Norwegians learned to be masters with their potatoes.

The towns

From the Middle Ages Norway had a few small towns along the coast. The diet of town households showed the influence from Denmark and Germany, but at the same time seem to have had their basis in the popular diet. The town patricians, who were few and of continental origin, were dependent on the possibility of obtaining fresh and imported raw materials. During the winter this was uncertain, and the town households also had to base themselves on their own supplies. But the town patricians had cooks who had time to attend to food preparation, and the cookery books bear witness to many time-consuming dishes. However, the cooks of the town came mostly from the countryside, as did the great majority of the population in the towns in the 19th century. They brought with them their food traditions and adapted these to the town's marketing system and to the time and money they could use on food and its preparation.

Changes in the popular diet

In spite of regional and individual differences in daily food, the basic diet was very much the same all over the country with only minor changes until the middle of the last century. Then a dramatic increase in the growth of population, new knowledge about bacteria, health and food led to the start of food research in Europe as in Norway. The century also brought about great improvements in technology and economy.

The traditional Norwegian everyday diet, which easily could be compared with the strictest lenten fare further south in Europe, had new elements added to it while some of the old elements disappeared. However, as a whole, the basic elements prevailed until after the last world war in 1945. When the rationing of butter, sugar, milk, meat and coffee came to an end in the 1950s, when government heavily subsided economically these status foods, when the wages and general standard of living increased quickly, when food industry developed even quicker, when a flourishing economy in the 1960s and the women's liberation movement in the 1970s brought also the married women into paid work, when ordinary people can afford to travel, Norwegian daily food became internationalised. However, the traditional diet is still part of our food culture, now more or less reserved for feast instead of fast. Deep freezers, which will be found so to say in every family, have become our storehouse, to a large extent, both in the towns and in the countryside. Our housekeeping is still partly a storage housekeeping. The difference is that nowadays the traditional raw materials are mostly preserved by deep freezing, which saves time, money and nutritional value.

However, after this post war period with its increasing standard of living, with supermarkets and MacDonald's, the food scientists recommend that we, to some extent, stay with our traditional food. We are recommended to eat herring several times a week, more fish, less meat, to use fresh raw materials (or deep frozen), more potatoes and wholemeal bread, porridge and sour skimmed milk and traditional Norwegian vegetables such as carrots, turnip and cabbage. Some Norwegians never changed their food habits, some of those who did seem to be listening to the research results. At least sales statistics say so.

Three Whole Days to an End
The Norwegian Peasant Wedding Feast as a Social Mirror

by Bjørn Fjellheim

A central aspect of the feast is the bringing together of people to socialise and to share food and drink. Most often, there is an occasion or an excuse for the feast, which gives it some of its content.

In the traditional peasant wedding feasts, as they were held in Norway down to the turn of the last century, the wedding ceremony in the church was central. So were also the different rituals during the feast that expressed the bringing together of man and woman in matrimony. Apart from that, there were days and nights of eating and drinking, of music, dancing and playing, of storytelling and gossiping, of saluting with guns and even with dynamite, of horse racing and of the unavoidable fighting with fists or knives. In short, the wedding gave people an opportunity to celebrate for days, a break in the laborious and monotonous everyday life.

By reading and comparing a hundred or more written accounts of wedding feasts, I find the wedding as an excuse for good company as obvious. That was what people were looking forward to. But, the bringing together of people of different ages, gender and social status - often from different areas - gave the feast other more serious dimensions. Careful reading and interpretation enables one to uncover layer upon layer of meaning to the feast. There is for instance the following and confirmation of traditional ways, there is the expression of gender in masculinity and femininity, the giving of contents to concepts such as morality and honour. There are also numerous attempts to alter traditions and challenge the customary notion of how to live the good life. The wedding feast also gave opportunities to express and challenge central cultural values in more institutional or ceremonial forms, ridiculing them or turning them upside down, as a means of lightening the internal pressure of culture.

There is, however, one aspect of the feast more serious than the others: in many ways the structure of the feast reflects the structure of peasant society. A challenge to this structure would not be tolerated. It would be met with immediate sanctions. The participants of the feast as the participants of society were treated according to their place in the social hierarchy of the local community. The participants were compared to each other according to social dimensions such as young or old, man or woman, married or unmarried, wealthy or poor. These dimensions together constituted the power structure of peasant society. The feast functioned as a gigantic mirror held up, thus reflecting each member in proportion to the others. It was a reflection of equality or inequality, of "us" and "them". The wedding feast gave a rare opportunity to do this, as it was one of the few occasions where all or most of the members of the peasant community were gathered together for a period of time.

In the following, I shall give a short description of the wedding feast. It will be followed by a discussion of some elements of the feast where the expression of society in the feast is most obvious. At last, I will conclude with some remarks on the need for such an expression in peasant culture.

The wedding feast

The feast lasted from two to eight days and nights. The number of guests would vary from about fifty to over four hundred. The duration would vary according to local tradition, but the length and especially the size of the feast was mostly an expression of the wealth of the hosts, the parents of either the bride or the bridegroom. The wealthy peasant would hold a grand feast, especially if the marrying couple were to take over the farm. Some of these feasts were so spectacular that they would live on in oral tradition for decades. On the other hand, the poorer people had to suffice with shorter wedding feasts and fewer guests. The feast in itself was thus a reflection of the distribution of wealth in society.

As a rule, the feast lasted for three or four days. Each day had its own name. In the southernmost part of Norway, the first day was called The Wedding Day, the second The Porridge Day and the third The Leaving Day. On the first day, the wedding ceremony in the church was the central part. On the second day the main meal was the bridal porridge, a part of the ceremony celebrating the bride as a married woman, having spent her first night in the conjugal bed. On this day, she wore the dress bearing the symbols of a married woman for the first time. On the third day, the feast ended, and the guests left for home. This was the day of the gift-giving ceremony, where the guests gave gifts in the form of money to contribute both to the costs of the feast and to give the newly weds some initial capital. All these ceremonies were surrounded by eating and drinking and dancing through the night.

If the wedding feasts went on for more than three days, the rest of the days were more informal ones. The feast just went on until the guests were heavily intoxicated by excessive eating and drinking and lack of sleep. For this reason, there were attempts in many parts of Norway by local authorities to prevent these long feasts.

The host needed a lot of helping hands to manage the feast. They were appointed as servants of the wedding feast. These were honourable assignments. There was the woman in charge of the food, the cooks, the maidens who served the food, the male cupbearer who served beer and liquor, the musicians and the servants of the bride and the bridegroom. The most important servant, however, was the master of ceremonies. His tasks were many during the wedding feast, but first of all, he was to see to that it went on according to tradition. He was a professional and a honoured man in society.

I have mentioned that the sheer length and size of the wedding feast could express social inequality in peasant society. The next, and obvious question is: Who were invited to the feast and who were not?

The invitation of the guests

In the written accounts there seem to be clear rules as to who were to be invited. There is a common pattern showing regional variety. The guests were to be invited among kin, neighbours and friends.

The peasant society was in many respects a kinship society, they invited relatives of the bride and bridegroom as far out as to the second and even third cousins.

One was also obliged to invite household members of the host's neighbouring farms. This obligation went as far as to the limit of the *belag* one belonged to. The *belag* was a limited group or cluster of farms with mutual rights and obligations. The hosts could, but were not obliged to, invite members from the *belag* of the parents-in-law.

Several accounts stress the friends of the bride and bridegroom as a special group to be invited.

The decision of who to invite was mostly based on obligation. The hosts had, however, a set of rights towards their guests. It was expected that the married people brought with them gifts of food to be distributed and consumed at the wedding feast. This contribution of food was taken into account as means to an end.

The invitation of the guests was therefore based on institutional rights and obligations, and was thus a serious matter. It went on with great ceremony a week or more before the wedding, performed by no less than the appointed ceremonial master. He went round from farm to farm, bringing forth his errand in a standardised speech, often in verse. He was standing up and would not sit down until those invited had accepted the invitation. This could take a while, because they showed modesty by finding many excuses. This could develop into an oral tug of war that could go on for a long time. A story is told about a ceremonial master who used half a day on a farm before the invitation was accepted. And he had to wait for an acceptance. To leave without it would be the same as if they were not invited, which was a great shame both on the hosts and their future guests. After they had accepted, the ceremonial master was seated and treated to some food and a glass of liquor.

The invitation of relatives, neighbours and friends, was institutionalised and based on sets of rights and obligations. Who were supposed to be guests in a wedding was therefore commonly acknowledged in society. This seems to be an expression of an egalitarian society as the Norwegian peasant society is often called. But there were developments in Norway during the eighteenth and nineteenth centuries that threatened this institution, and in some parts of Norway broke it. A population growth led to pressure on land as a resource, leading to a growing group of landless crofters. They rented a small piece of land from the peasants. In the lowlands of eastern Norway and Trøndelag, the farms were large and the peasants wealthy. Here, the crofters were heavily exploited as workhands on the farms. A class society was emerging. As a result of this development, social ties between peasants and crofters were broken. There emerged two sets of *belag* in areas where there had only been one, that is one for the peasants and one for the crofters. The peasants did not want the poorer crofters to take part in their feasts.

In most parts of Norway, however, the peasants and the crofters were members of the same *belag*. Here we have to look closer to see if there were cases of exclusion from the wedding feasts. In the written accounts it seems that every grownup person took part. But an obvious question is: who stayed home to look after the children and the animals on the farm? Supposedly the servants, young unmarried men and women staying at the farms for some years as workhands. There were also groups of people loosely attached to the peasant households such as *innerst*, a kind of day labourer, and the occasional pauper being on relief on a farm.

We find these people on the fringe of the feast – not as guests, but as people who enjoyed some of the goods from the table and the cellar. I will give a few examples:

In many parts of Norway, there was a tradition of bringing the food gifts on the night before the wedding. This was done by the servants or others not invited. They were treated to some of the food and drink prepared for the feast, and afterwards there was dancing. In one account, there is no mention of food, but if it was a boy who came with the gift, he was supposed to be made intoxicated on liquor and beer. If it was a girl, she was allowed to see the wedding dress.

In some parts of Norway, they gave a party after the wedding feast on the leftovers for those not invited.

There is also the tradition of the spectators, people who were not invited, but who came to the farm during the feast. From Telemark it is told that it was a great shame to come uninvited. Only the witless and the young men looking for a fight did that. They wore one black and one white sock to announce their errand. In other districts they were expected, the hosts even put platforms outside the windows to allow the spectators to see all the good food. But to approach the house on the kitchen side was not allowed. It was the same as begging for food. But in most areas, the spectators were treated to some drink and even some food during the feast.

The discussion of who was to be invited and who not, has uncovered two aspects of the wedding feast in peasant society. First, the development of a class society was clearly reflected in the altering of the invitation rules, splitting the society in two clearly defined groups. Secondly, in the more egalitarian society, there were also low status groups not invited. Nevertheless, they were allowed to partake in some of the celebrations, enjoying some of the food. Now, I will turn from the wedding feast in society to the society in the feast and look upon how the proper guests were treated. I will do this by two examples, the seating at the table and the distribution of the food among the guests.

The seating at the table

Having arrived on the first day, the guests were treated with an informal meal before they left for church. After returning from the church, the first main meal was to be served. At this point of the feast, the master of ceremonies had his most difficult task, and as seen from the outside, a most ridiculous one. Although he solemnly declared the meal to be served, it was impossible for him to get the guests seated. The bride and the bridegroom with their parents and their servants already sat at the top end of the long table. But the guests were standing outside the house or just inside the door. Nobody wanted to be the first to be seated. If the master of ceremonies approached one, he or she would turn away or protest. If he pulled at the arm or the collar of some, they would make stubborn resistance. Some of them hid, others fled. There is a story of a man who hid under the barn. The master of ceremonies had to creep after him and pull him with force from his hiding place. There is another story of a man who took a step backwards each time the master of ceremonies approached him. He found this quite amusing and continued to approach the man until he had walked backwards about 500 meters. Then the guest gave up.

There were serious matters at stake. The first guests had to be hauled, pulled or even carried to the table. Gradually, the task got easier, and finally the guests were seated and the meal could take place. They had then recreated the power structure of the society in a microcosm. The first to be seated was the most honoured man or woman among the guests. The succession from him or her recreated the social structure of the society at the table. I will give some examples from the accounts:

> "Nobody would sit in the high seat. It was then the task of the master of ceremonies to fill that seat. He pulled the collar one of the men he thought was the best. If there were some whom he thought worthy of such an honoured seat, he chose them first. Uppermost on the inside of the table, he seated the second best men and so on downwards. Uppermost on the wall side of the table, he sat the best women. At the lower end of the table, that is by the bed, sat the middle class of the community. At the table out on the floor, called the little table, the poorer people of the community were seated."

I will give another example which goes even further in detail on how the people were seated in relation to each other.

> "The seating at the table followed a certain order of rank, and God have mercy on those who did not respect this arrangement. It was a great insult to the person who eventually was displaced from the seat that he had the right to. Uppermost sat those who had full farms. Then came those with farms of two thirds the size, then those of half size and at last those of the small farms and the crofters. Within each class of rank neighbour and kin relationships could play a part. Nevertheless, nobody could be so free as to go and take his seat. It was the task of the master of ceremonies to have each guest seated and on his proper seat, and it had to happen with much stalling and resistance. Nobody was supposed to come first in the row or far up at the table by his own free will. Nobody was to show that he knew his place."

This ritual seems to be of the most crucial importance, and it demanded a great knowledge of the status of each guest from the master of ceremonies. If he did something wrong, that is if he seated a person below his own rank at the table, both he and the hosts could get an enemy for life. But why did they have to go through this drama every time? It was obviously a confirmation of the social order, a reminder to each and all where their place was in society. But there also had to be changes, people married, inherited farms, grew older and died. The seats were there, but the people to fill them changed. Maybe the change in the social status of a person found its first and foremost cultural expression at the feast table.

The two examples describe how people were seated round one or several tables in a room. In most cases, however, the guests were too many to be seated in the same room at the same time. The solution to this was to use several rooms or to serve the guests in up to three groups. The second and third group had to wait for their turn to be served.

The distribution of food

The inequality of the guests was further demonstrated by what food they were served. Only a few accounts describe the uneven distribution of food at the wedding feasts. It seems to me more a question of lack of communication in the major parts of them than of exceptions from a rule. An example:

> "The best courses were placed on the long table (where the newly wed and the best guests were seated). Firstly of the farm's own supplies. Secondly of the food gifts from the best farms. It was common practice that the food gifts got the rank according to who they belonged to. It could sometimes happen that the gifts were not valued according to the people who had given them. In such cases they had to go up and down according to the judgement delivered by the women in charge of the food. They were the high court in all questions concerning the table."

The story is still told about a feast in the 1860s, where they had put the food gift of a crofter's wife at the table where she was seated. It was *kling*, thickly spread flatbread or *lefse*. It was highly appraised by the other guests at the table, as they found out that she had put sugar on it, which was unheard of among the poorer people. When the women in charge of the food found out, they took her *kling* from the table and put it on the long table. The story-teller concludes with the following remark: "I swear that this is the truth"

The masters of ceremonies acted as diplomats when they seated the guests. The women in charge of the food as judges when serving it. This was yet another demonstration of inequality among the guests. It also demonstrates the status a rich and large food gift gave to the woman who brought it.

When the first main meal on the evening of the first day was over, everybody knew their place at the table. And if they did not know their place in the community before they came to the wedding feast, they would for sure know it after they left.

From Everyday Diet to Feast Food: an example from the Hemsedal Country District in Norway

by Marit Ekne Ruud

Introduction

In this paper I will discuss some aspects of the everyday diet and feast food among peasants in Hemsedal, a country district in Norway, in an economic and ecological perspective. The material for this research is mostly inquiries on food and meals from the Norwegian Ethnological Research (Norsk Etnologisk Gransking), collected in the beginning of the 1950s. The greater part of the answers cover the youth and childhood of the respondents or their parents, i.e. from the last decades of the 19th century to about 1920. This period represents a fundamental change in the economic and social structure of the Norwegian rural society. I will in this presentation use quotations as illustrations, and the form "they" instead of "we" is often used related to the older days.

Hemsedal is a mountainous district in the northern part of Buskerud, in the southeast of Norway, bordering on Sogn and Fjordane to the west. 80% of this small country district attains an altitude of 900 meters or more. The most important economic activity has been farming, and as we can imagine, the resources were marginal exploited to an extreme degree. Barley has been the main product, and later on also potatoes. However, there was only a small part of the soil that was cultivated with grain and potatoes: in the mountain areas the resources were also based on cattle and dairy farming to a much greater extent than in the lower districts. This means cultivation of fodder. Beside the arable farming, the district of Hemsedal, just like other mountain areas in eastern Norway, had good conditions for grazing and the mountain summer dairying was, and still is, an important part of the farming system.

In spite of the thorough exploitation of the natural resources, no one could live from farming alone. In addition to hunting and fishing in the mountain rivers, activities that gave an extra income, people were mostly selling or exchanging different kinds of dairy products. In the first part of 19th century they went to Drammen, the nearest town, with their products and brought grain back. When the road over the mountain from Lærdal and Sogn was finished in 1844, they started trading with farmers and fishermen who came over the mountain from the Sogn district to sell fish and herring.

The everyday meal

The meal routines have to be seen in close connection to the working sessions of the farm, and in rural society the work during the day was dependent on the cycle of the year. The short Norwegian summer did not permit the agricultural tasks to be delayed. Work had to be done within very short limits of time. People started early in the morning often before sunrise, and finished late in the evening. The meals also had an important function of breaks and rest from the work. The meal had also an important social function, as it was during the meals that one could meet and socialise.

It was common to have four main meals a day, but during summer five or six meals were usual. In the following I will quote from the inquiry from Hemsedal:

"In summer they usually rose at four o'clock in the morning, or maybe earlier. The first meal was coffee and bread and butter. The first between-meal period lasted till 8 o'clock, then they had breakfast: in summer it was always *soll* – flatbread in sweet or sour milk, sometimes together with *spekeflesk* – dried and smoked leg of pork or lamb with flatbread. The next meal was at 11 o'clock – *dugurd* – the second morning meal. Porridge was always served for this meal. The porridge was based on water and barley (also called water-porridge). This was eaten together with skimmed milk and soft cheese. After a rest, they got a cup of coffee and a little bread before they started working. The next meal was at four o'clock in the afternoon, called *non* – the afternoon meal. The food was the same as for breakfast: *soll* and *spekeflesk* with flatbread. After a rest and a cup of coffee, they worked till eight or nine in the evening. For the last meal they also ate porridge and milk, the same food as in the second morning meal. In summer and also in other special working sessions during the year, it was of importance that the preparation of the meal took as little time as possible. The diet was therefore very regular. "Another quotation says: "During summer they didn't have time to make hot meals, because the women were needed in the fields. They had flatbread, *soll* and *spekemat*, porridge and milk the whole day long".

"In winter the first meal was at eight in the morning. The rest of the meals were about the same as in summer. They had two porridge meals in winter too, but they might spend more time preparing the *non* meal. They often had salt herring with flatbread, or fried pork, meatball made of blood, flour and potatoes or shaped meat with potatoes (this was eaten specially during the slaughtering period), or porridge soup."

In these quotations we can see the differences between the summer and winter seasons, and also a typical everyday diet from the Hemsedal district. I will comment briefly on some of the dishes that are typical for a mountain district like this one. The flatbread was eaten for almost every meal, and it was basically made from barley and water. In Hemsedal they also had another kind of everyday bread: a small, thick potato-cake. I quote: "The potato-cake was used to replace or save the other bread made of rye, so they ate a lot of potato-cakes." We can in this example see a connection between the marginality of grain and the use of potatoes in the bread. The rye was bought or exchanged for other goods, and was not cultivated in Hemsedal. I quote: "In my childhood we had something called rye-cake, that was oven-baked bread. We had ovens from 1900 or a little earlier, but bread was not eaten everyday until 1920. The coach stages here in Hemsedal, however, got ovens in the 1860s and baked 20 breads at a time".

The potato-cake was mostly eaten in the morning and together with coffee during the day, with butter and all sorts of cheeses. The butter was however seen as a luxury, and the butter was often replaced by pork lard after the slaughtering in autumn.

The diet of the *non*-meal alternated between salted herring and dried or smoked meat. Fresh meat was eaten only in autumn during the slaughtering. Even though the rivers and lakes in Hamsedal were rich in fish, there was hardly any fish in the diet at all. Most of the fish were fermented, mostly for trading, and only to a certain extent eaten as daily food together with potato during the year. However, sometimes in the middle of summer people went fishing and they had fish for breakfast or *non* together with flatbread. Salted herring and stockfish were the only fish from the sea used in the diet. To get fresh seafish was impossible because of the distances. The following quotation gives a picture of the situation:

"The sea fish came from the Sogn district until the railway from Bergen was finished. The peasants went over the mountains to Lærdal and bought fish, or the peasants and traders from Lærdal came to us with fish and other goods. They mostly sold salted herring and some times porkets. The trading was bartering: we had skins and fur, dried porklegs, old cheese and butter. Fresh sea fish was impossible to get, and they had only salted herring and stockfish for sale. The salted herring with boiled potatoes was eaten quite often, especially during wintertime. The stockfish was lye-treated as *lutefisk* and only used for Christmas and other feasts. In my youth we started to buy fish from Bergen: we ordered a case of fresh herring. We had to share with the neighbours, one case was too much for a single household. To keep the herring fresh, we put the case in the snow. The herring was eaten boiled, with potatoes."

As mentioned above the porridge was eaten at least twice a day during the year. I quote: "Plain porridge (water-porridge) was one of the main dishes in the diet in older days and still is to a certain extent. The older people have eaten porridge and milk twice a day every year during their whole life. They used the best flour for the porridge, and the other for flatbread. On weekdays they used only water. When the water started boiling, they mixed the flour while stirring. The porridge should become hard and thick." Also they tell that in some places the porridge was boiled only once a day. They ate reheated or cold porridge in the evenings. This was especially done in summer to save the women's time.

The everyday meal was consumed in a simple way. There was little or no use of plates. The flatbread was served as a plate with the herring or the dried meat upon it. Some had their own private knives for cutting the food, and they mostly used the fingers. Everyone in the household had a spoon for him or herself. The fork was not in use until the years around 1900.

The household met at the table to share the food, but there was not always plenty to share. The housewife often had to portion out the fish and meat and sometimes also the butter to each member of the household. The cheese and milk, and also the flatbread, were not handed out in portions, there was enough for everyone. The porridge was eaten directly from the bowl on the middle of the table. Everyone put the spoon in the same bowl, and then in a cup of milk before it reached the mouth. This custom survived till around 1900. Seen from an hygienic point of view, the porridge bowl must have been a source for spreading of diseases. However, the bowl placed in the middle of the table must be regarded as a practical custom, and also as a symbolic one: the symbol of fellowship.

The status of the different foods

In spite of some variety in the food and the meals, the diet was regular and monotonous. Some of the food was served for almost every meal, e.g. flatbread. The way of cooking and the products of the farm gave stability in the food structure. The variety was due to the change of products during the different seasons, but also to the different values that the food represented.

The everyday meals were based on simple and plain food, and this reflects the economic and ecological foundation of this mountain district. By studying the food that was served during the week and during the different seasons, we can see how people attached varying importance to the dishes. This can be seen, e.g. in the cases where the same dishes made of other and often better ingredients served for special occasions, in what situations the food was eaten and also and finally in the frequency of eating the food. I shall give some examples.

As we have seen, people had porridge made of water and barley at least twice a day for the everyday meal. On Sundays there was a difference: The porridge was based on milk instead of water. If we had been invited to a feast or a celebration we would still have been served porridge, but on such occasions it would be based on fat sour cream *(rømmegrøt)* or rice and milk *(risgrøt)*. Sour cream and rice were both luxury products: the sour cream was a product of the farm, and the rice was bought or bartered.

Butter was to a certain extent used in the everyday diet. Hemsedal was a dairy farming district, but in spite of this, butter was regarded as a luxury product and was used mainly for festive occasions. In the everyday diet it was replaced by lard in the autumn. The butter was also an important commodity produced for sale. I quote: "Most of the peasants here in Hemsedal had cattle, and we thus had enough butter for the whole year. But the butter was a good trading product and easy to sell, so we were careful with butter in the everyday diet. The summer butter was the most attractive butter for sale. But we had always some of it left for the haymakers later in summer." From this quotation we see that butter had a status, both in an economic and in a symbolic sense. The haymakers were always treated well and the food they were served when the hay harvest was finished was the very best.

Beside the rye-bread and the potato-cake used in the everyday diet, people had something called *rømmebrød* – cream bread. This was a flat bread or cake typical for the mountain districts, used as coffee-bread. In the following quotation we can see how this bread was based on different ingredients, depending on its use." The cream-bread had different qualities. In the everyday bread they used pork lard, and it was eaten mainly in summertime, with coffee. For special occasions as feasts they used fat cream. The cream bread was always served at festivities."

Lefse – a thin pancake from rolled dough, served buttered and folded – is another example. *Lefse* was made of flour, water and fat and was also most often served at festivities. For the workdays, however, they mixed the flour with potatoes.

The economic aspect can be seen through these examples, were the same food had different structure everyday and in feasts. Both the *lefse* and the *rømmebrød* were first of all food served at feasts, but sometimes they also served as everyday food. In that case the cream and butter were replaced with something of less luxury.

One of the most important work sessions during the year was haymaking, especially in this cattle area, and the farm was dependent on extra employees, haymakers, to get the hay made in time. Porridge was always served at festivities marking the end of the hay harvest. This porridge was basically made of cream, among the best and the most exclusive goods the farm could offer. We can see that the work was appreciated by serving feast dishes, and the porridge was therefore given a symbolic value. A clever haymaker was an important person and had to be taken well care of. Another aspect of importance is the role of the housewife: to serve the best porridge to the haymakers gave status. The haying porridge was an important and institutionalised custom in several districts in Norway, not only in Hemsedal, up to our time.

An alternation between the working days and the day of rest can be seen in the Sunday food. "On Sundays there was always meat soup boiled with potatoes or meatballs for dinner *(non)*. Sometimes we had dessert, often made of milk or cream." On Sundays it was important to eat something different and better than on the other days, to mark the difference between working days and Sundays. In the typical fishery districts they often had meat for Sunday dinners. The opposite was the case in the other districts. In Hemsedal they seldom had fish for dinner (except for herring), but every now and then they had fermented trout or *lutefisk* for Sunday food. An important aspect is also that on Sundays the housewife had more time to spend on preparing the food than the other days. Somehow, the time spent on cooking was often dependent on the visit to the church.

The feast food

The main difference between the everyday diet and the feast meal is first of all the quantity and richness of the food. There was a lot of food at the table, plenty for everyone. As we have seen, the food was also made of the luxury goods from the farm and with a lot of fat, such as butter and cream products. The daily diet was often only with a minimum of fat. A third aspect is the status of the food that was seldom served otherwise, it was hard to get or very expensive.

The wedding celebration was the most important and comprehensive feast in the old rural society. The feast lasted for three or some times four days (that custom ended in the years 1870-90), and we can imagine that they spend a lot of time preparing the food for 60-70 guests or more. The wedding-feast took place at the farm of the groom. However, in this society of self-preservation, there was not room for large feasts without help from the neighbours. The resources of the farm were based on one year's consumption for the household. I will focus on the food and meals, and the importance of neighbour-help on these occasions. In the old peasant society neighbouring farms were grouped in small units called *belag*. The farms in the specific units had obligations to help each other on certain occasions: e.g. in weddings, funerals and roofing. It was seen as a contribution to everyone.

In a wedding-feast the neighbour-help consisted first of all of the food gift brought in a special basket. I quote: "The gift basket for the wedding-feast consisted of *lefse* and *rømmebrød* put in decorated baskets. The quantity depended on the wealth of the neighbour-farm. They also brought beakers with porridge made of rice and sometimes *rømmegrøt* – cream porridge. This custom ended in 1890s." In other districts in eastern Norway they brought cream for cooking the porridge to the wedding-farm. The wedding celebration took place in June, between the seasonal work sessions. Most of the cattle were at the summer farm, and cream from the cows at the main farms had to be collected from the neighbours.

"During the wedding they had several meals. For the first meal they got coffee and *rømmebrød*, *lefse*, all kind of cheeses, butter etc. They also had beer and liquor (that was served the whole day). At my parents' wedding they did not serve liquor, the first wedding in Hemsedal without. This was in 1898. It was because of religious reasons. After the church wedding, the main meal consisted of boiled meat and potatoes, meat soup, porridge made of rice or cream, *lefse* with butter, some times fresh trout or fermented trout. Beer from the farm was served from a beer-bowl, the bowl was passed round the table and everyone took a mouthful from the same bowl. They drank a lot." The other meals were similar to these.

The feasts were also very important for the status of the farms and for the housewife. Beside the best food that was served, the food was also decorated such as the butter and the cheeses, and the baskets and the beer-bowl were painted. They used decorated plates and not a common bowl for the porridge, and the fork was first introduced at the feasts before it became an everyday custom. In some places the gift-basket was returned to the neighbour-farm with some of the feast food, and it was of a great importance that this food was proper.

The custom of the food gifts in special baskets ended in the beginning of 1900. Because of the economic change in the society, the peasants were no longer dependent on help from each other. However, the food gift custom was so ritualised that we even today still bring food gifts for special occasions, often a cake. Today it is not for an economic reason but more as a practical help to get everything settled in time. Another important aspect is that we now give the food as a gift, and are not expecting something in return.

In this paper I have presented some aspects on everyday food and feast food, discussing the different form and use of the food. My empirical study has been a Norwegian mountain district called Hemsedal, a district that can be seen as a typical Norwegian mountain peasant area. As we have seen, the diet has been very regular and is closely related to the ecological and economic foundations in this area.

Literature

Flaten, Hans, 1920: *Hemsedal 1814-1914*. Hemsedal.
Grøttland, Kristine Lind, 1962: *Daglig brod og daglig dont*. Universitetsforlaget, Oslo.
Nordstrøm, Ingrid, 1988: *Till bords*. Carlssons Bokforlag, Stockholm.

Inquiries nr. 24 (Food and Meals) and 37 (Feast Food) from The Norwegian Ethnological Research (Norsk Etnologisk Gransking).

The Way the Contemporary Western Assyrians take Food in the Middle East during Fasts and Church Holidays

by Michael Abdalla

In this study I shall concentrate only on the group of Western Assyrians, i.e. those living in the early Christian era within the boundaries of the then Byzantine Empire; the people inadequately called 'Jacobites' in European literature [1]. These people retained their national identity to a larger extent than did other Assyrians. From the time of the Fourth General Council in Chalcedon (AD 451) they have been a separate Christian community. At present they number about one million; and there are nearly two million more living as emigrants in Europe, North and South America and Australia.

Over the centuries, specific fast and holiday rites were developed by these Assyrians, enriched by different forms and folk beliefs, in which even today one can find some elements of a pagan character. I know this group of Assyrians best for I am descended from it myself and lived in such an environment for 19 years - at first in the village of Tel Alo and then in the town of Qamishli, both in north-eastern Syria, by the Turkish frontier. The period of my youth stuck in my memory as a period full of deep spiritual experiences, the like of which could not be felt in Europe; and the atmosphere of those days cannot be reconstructed in any way.

Polish literature dealing with the Christians of the Middle East is surprisingly scant, and publications in other languages are rather difficult of access. However, this does not prevent me from discussing the subject of fast-periods and holidays among Assyrians, since I know about it from personal experience. Information about the dates of the fast periods and holidays, as well as their origin, comes from my personal library on general religious matters (works written mainly by 'Syrian' priests in Arabic and Assyrian). My descriptions of the folk customs are based on personal memories from my youth; but with some blanks, caused by the fact that for many years I could not visit my native territory to refresh my memory.

The manner in which Assyrian Christendom treats the question of fasting is of great interest. The authors comment on the principles of fasting extensively and in minute detail, quoting the opinions of the Fathers of the Church on it, giving examples of extremely strong will-power shown in the struggle against meeting basic physiological needs by eating. They warn of the severe punishment which God may mete out towards those who neglect this duty. In their opinion, fasting has an important position in the whole process of worship and in achieving victory over the forces of evil. The early history of the Eastern Churches abounds with examples of this. The heroism of St. Simeon the Stylite (c. 389-459) is well known not only to the Christians of the East. In the first ten years of his ascetic life (aged 16-26), he ate only once a week, while other monks interrupted their fast every second day. He then spent the forty days of Lent in a walled up cell not touching the ten loaves of bread and the jug of water that were there. St. Simeon repeated this awe-inspiring experience for twenty-eight consecutive years. He spent the next thirty years on a pillar which he kept raising until it reached the height of approximately fifteen metres [2]. In the extremely rich literary output of the 13th-century Assyrian philosopher, Bar Ebraya, we find whole chapters, supported by concrete examples, which treat fasting as 'mountaineering towards perfection', a way of attaining a spiritual state which brings man closer to angels [3].

The antiquity of fasting can be proved by the fact that as early as the 5th century AD the following personal names can be found: 'Ṣoma', 'Ṣouma', 'Ṣoume'. There were also surnames: 'Barṣoma', 'Barṣouma' and 'Barṣoume'. These mean 'fast' and 'son of fast' [4]. Even today such names are not rare among Assyrians [5]. It can be assumed that they had their origin in the early Christian era, when very strong ascetic movements appeared in Mesopotamia, which treated fasting as a means of bodily mortification and strengthening of the spirit. The adoption of Christianity by Assyrians meant a break with everything that was pagan.

In the manuals of ecclesiastical writers, questions about fasts occupy significantly more space than holidays. The fast, viewed as a period devoted to preparation for receiving sacraments in a worthy manner and for participating in holy services in spiritual and moral purity, and the grace of God coming from it, are seen to have significance as a factor integrating the nation [6]. Christ, the Holy Mother and the Holy Spirit should be honoured and tribute paid to them in the form of fasts; whereas holidays represent in an outstanding way that moderation which renders tolerable the restrictions imposed on themselves by the fasters, restrictions which are not only gastronomical ones. At least, that is how the youngest part of society treats them.

Fasting tradition is handed down from one generation to another, from grandfather to grandson. The multi-generation

Assyrian families cultivate it in a sacred fashion, and with all its consequences [7]. Church teaching reminds one of the commandment to fast; and fasting is also recommended as a means of doing penance. Fasting is also a subject taught in some Assyrian private schools, as well as in 'Sunday schools' adjacent to a church. '*Hu Aloho qron l-sawmo*' (The God calls upon me to fast) is the title of lesson 22 in a textbook for the fifth standard of Assyrian primary school [8], which was the textbook I learned from personally in my native town Qamishli in 1963 (see photo). Since I regard this text as an interesting one from the pedagogical point of view, I present a summary translation:

... A king who was out hunting met a farmer, advanced in years, who had been ploughing the field since dawn and invited him to have breakfast with him. But the old man answered: "I am sorry my Lord, I had been invited to a finer breakfast by a greater Lord than you. God himself called on me to fast!"

The embarrassed king looked at the old man softly and said, "Are you fasting even on such a long and sweltering day?"

"I am fasting today, because I am afraid that the next day will be even longer and more sweltering," the farmer answered.

"Eat today and start your fasting tomorrow," the king advised.

On hearing it the old man asked, "Can you guarantee me that I shall live tomorrow?"

"I cannot guarantee the next hour of living even for myself," the king answered.

A List of Fast-Periods, their Genesis and Characterisation

For the Assyrians who belong to the West-Syrian Orthodox Church of Antioch, five fast periods have been obligatory for centuries. The duration of these has not been changed much during these centuries. While some periods - usually the continuous ones - were shortened, adapting them to new conditions of living, others were automatically prolonged. The Fathers of the Church justify their decisions on the basis that fasting was established by Christ and that the Church took on the responsibility for arranging fasts in accordance with needs and possibilities. Nowadays, there are about 140 fasting days in a year (see table).

The first Patriarch to lessen the severity of fasting in this century was Ignatios Elias III (†1932). Change was dictated by the compulsory migration of thousands of Western Assyrians, as a result of persecution in Turkey in the years of 1914-18. The conditions in the new places of settlement (Syria, Lebanon, North and South America) were not conducive to observance of the old fasting customs. During the synod in Jerusalem in February 1927, on an appeal from the above-mentioned Patriarch, a delegation from the USA, with the participation of lay persons, presented a 17-item programme of reforms in order to discuss the current situation of the Church. The programme, among other things, talked about the need to shorten the fast-periods for immigrants in that country and to limit the prohibition on contracting marriages to the Holy Week and the Nineveh Fast only [9]. In fact, the Patriarch consented, in 1930 for the first time, that all the believers in this Church could eat fish [10] and that those living in the USA should fast only in the first and last weeks of Lent, observing the duty of fasting on every Wednesday and Friday in the intervening five weeks [11].

Other reforms were introduced by the next Patriarch, Ignatios Afrem I Barsom (†1957). In response to requests from the Eastern Christian Sect in India, he applied similar principles for observing Lent to them. The reform proclaimed by this Patriarch was the most radical so far. In his Bulla, dated 7 December 1946, we can read, among other things, about the reduction of Advent from 25 days to 10 (from 15 to 25 December in the morning); of the Assumption of the Holy Mother Fast from 15 days to 5 (from 10 to 15 August in the morning)[12]; of the Apostles' Fast from 10 days to 3 (from 26 to 29 June in the morning). The most recent simplification was made by Patriarch Ignatios Ya'kub III (†1980), who extended the new principles of Lent, observed so far in the USA and India to all believers of the Church. Nevertheless, this is not tantamount to a gradual or constant reduction of fasting. In fact it should be pointed out that almost all Assyrians living in Turkey, as well as some of those living in Syria, fast for the whole 48 days before Easter, though some of them quite willingly take advantage of the dispensation, dated 6 February 1966, which allows, among other things, the organisation of feasts, baptisms and wedding receptions in this period.

Apart from the above-mentioned periods, it is obligatory to fast from midnight for those who want to receive Holy Communion on that day [13].

Details of Important Fasting Periods

Now follow comments on the Wednesday and Friday fasts and on three others:

Wednesdays and Fridays - *Arb'o wa-'rubto*

Fasts on Wednesdays and Fridays, almost every week, were most probably established by the Apostles themselves, echoing the Jewish tradition of fasting on Tuesdays and Thursdays (Luke 18:12). The choice of those two particular days by the first Christians was probably not caused by an intention to break with the old tradition of Christian Jews, but by the fact that, according to the teaching of the Church, Jesus was sentenced to death on Wednesday and crucified on Friday [14].

As for most fast days, fasting on these two days meant day-long total abstinence (until the time called even today *tša' šo'in* - 'nine hours', - either until 9 p.m. or nine hours after dawn).

The number of fasting Wednesdays and Fridays is not the same every year, and at present equals 64-74 days. This number does not include Wednesdays and Fridays which fall in the constant long fasting periods, nor the whole seven weeks from Easter until Pentecost, during which fasting on Wednesdays and Fridays is not binding. (Jesus told them: "Can you persuade wedding guests to fast, as long as the groom is with them? But the time will come when the groom will be taken away from them, and then they will fast on those days." Luke 5:34-5) [15]. Fasting on those two days is also suspended if a church holiday is celebrated on them.

Niniveh Fast - *Ṣawmo d-Ninwe*

The Niniveh Fast lasts for three days and begins on Monday of the third week before Lent [16]. It commemorates the Assyrian capital, which the prophet Jonathan was to reach at God's command, though against his own will, to warn the inhabitants of that ancient metropolis (in about 862 BC) about the approaching wrath of Heaven. This event, because of its symbolic meaning, became commemorated in Christianity (Matthew 12:39-41, 16:4, Luke 11:29-30), and especially in the Eastern Churches. Ecclesiastical authorities inform us that St Efrem the Assyrian (†373) devoted seven homilies to the Niniveh Fast[17]; that it originally lasted for six days; and that it used to be proclaimed either every thirty years or in situations which called, not for arms (no longer recognised), but for spiritual forces to overcome some crisis. In the national memory, hazy accounts survive of three early medieval events, which thanks to the proclamation and observance of a Niniveh Fast came to a happy end:

- The inhabitants of the city of Tekrit (in present central Iraq) fasted for three days in order to request God not to let the Arabian conquerors ill-treat them.

- In the 6th century a pestilence called šar' ut afflicted Mesopotamia. The symptoms were three black spots on the palm of the hand; and one could die immediately, just after looking at them. A three day fast diminished the proportions of the catastrophe.

- Some young Assyrian girls from the city of Al-Hira (in present day Iraq) took an Arabian commander's fancy. He desired to have them for himself. Aware of the fact that a refusal to the Muslim meant revenge and cruelty, the Bishop hid the girls in the city temple. After three days of strict fasting, they were surprised at the news that the Muslim libertine had died suddenly, which meant that they were saved.

Thus, whenever the Assyrian Christians faced danger, they did not resort to active self-defence or violence, but fasted, committing their fate to the hands of God. Is it possible that the continued observance of the Niniveh Fast at present is some kind of proof that such danger is not over yet?

A characteristic contemporary version of the Niniveh Fast is a two-and-a-half day abstinence, adopted by some Assyrian Christians for such worthy aspirations as the return of a relative from the army; the recovery of a sick person; passing an important examination; meeting a life companion, etc. This particular struggle with one's own weakness is usually terminated by a ceremonial collective feast, taking place in church with the participation of others, not only those who have fasted. Some anonymous worshippers prepare characteristic dishes for the feast which are not normally eaten in other seasons of the year. They bring fruit, nuts and other delicacies.

The most popular dish which always accompanies the feast of the Niniveh fast is called *pohine* or *qawite*. There are always seven ingredients: squash or sunflower seeds (*sgad l-šemšo*) or seeds of pumpkin-like plants; wheat grain (*hete*); barley grain (*s'ore*); maize (*dahno ša'uto*), gram seeds (*hemṣe*); grape or date syrup (*debes*, *dybys*) and salt. The dry ingredients are roasted, each separately, and then crumbled and mixed together. Next, an ample amount of hot, diluted syrup is poured over them. The pulp thus obtained is again mixed thoroughly and small balls are formed of it. The food prepared in this way is carried to church and eaten by everyone after the service.

A rarer dish called *zarda* is also sometimes eaten: thick milk soup with rice and sugar, seasoned with nutmeg and decorated with powdered cinnamon. It is eaten on the third day of fasting, after sunset.

The Forty-Day Fast - Ṣawmo arb'inoyo

This is the longest continuous fasting period and probably the only one (not taking into consideration the latest dispensation, of which most Assyrians in the Middle East have anyway not taken advantage) which has not been reduced for centuries. It has been known since the 3rd century, and is retained in honour of the first person of the Holy Trinity, God the Father. Long ago St Efrem the Assyrian encouraged people to observe it in one of his songs, sung even today on every day of this fasting period except Saturdays and Sundays during afternoon services. Here are the lines of the fragment which is of interest to us:

(Assyrian text)
Ṣum ṣawmo darb'in yawmin!
Whab lahmoh layno dkafin!
Wṣalo byawmo šba' zabnin!
Aḫ dileft men Bar Išay.

(English translation)
Fast during forty-day fasting period!
And give your bread to those who starve!
And pray seven times a day!
As you have learnt from Bar Išay. [18]

The Forty-day Fast is the first, longer part of Lent. Formerly it was observed separately and began just after the day commemorating the baptism of Christ, i.e. on 7 January. In this way, believers sought to imitate Christ, in accordance with the evangelists. Those who fasted did not eat any food containing meat, even in vestigial quantities, and, in addition to that, observed strict fasting from midnight until sunset except on Saturdays and Sundays. Before the fasters resumed eating, they used to gather in church, where they would read from the Gospels and participate in the mystery of the Eucharist.

The second part of Lent began a week before Easter, called *šobu'o d-ḥašo* (week of mortification). From Monday of that week, strict fasting was observed every day, and was ended in the evening by eating only bread and salt [19]. From Friday night, the time of Christ's crucifixion, until midnight between Saturday and Sunday, total abstinence was obligatory. I have no data about when these two fasts were joined together to constitute the *ṣawmo rabo* (big fast), which immediately precedes Easter. Easter is called *'ido rabo* (big holiday).

Nowadays Lent begins seven weeks before Easter. It is a movable fast, lasting 48 days. It is customary for the Patriarch to make an appeal to the worshippers, on the day preceding Lent; this is read after Sunday Mass in all churches and printed in the central ecclesiastical organ [20]. Its main emphasis is on the need to combine fasting with prayers and charity; for these three elements, like the Holy Trinity, constitute three complementary values.

Lent is preceded by a mini-festivity. Village girls wearing traditional dresses, dress a doll (*kalo*) and carry it from one holding to another dancing and singing a special folk song in order to gather *burgul*, eggs, milk fat (*mešho*), salt and kitchen utensils. Then they go to a ploughed field, where they cook a meal over an open fire. They bury part of this in the ground and take the rest of it to the village to offer to the inhabitants. This colourful custom, probably of some pagan origin [21], sometimes causes quarrels. Boys jealously watching the girls' display often dig out the hidden food, and the girls of course object to this [22].

An important concurrent of Lent are the promises, made publicly by children, that they will not use vulgar words, swear recklessly by God, the Cross, Jesus, the Holy Mother or saints. The children usually do it in pairs, with friends of the same sex, obliging themselves to give each other a hen's egg for every mistake or conscious departure from the terms of the oath, on the first day of Easter.

In the middle of Lent, wheat dough or leaven, in which a coin is hidden, is made. This is formed into the shape of stars, one for each person in the family. After being baked, the star-shaped pieces of bread, called *rozune*, are served for supper. The finder of the coin is regarded a 'lucky person'. This bread is sometimes baked the previous night and carried onto the terrace roof, so that "the stars could see it" during the night. Some rolls are baked the following day in the morning to be taken to church and eaten after the service by those fasting.

In Holy Week, sugar and all sweet dishes are eliminated from the menu. After the service, on Good Friday, called *dazqifuto* (crucifixion), those who are leaving the church are offered a bitter drink, prepared from the diluted juice of aloes [23]. This drink is also taken home for the remaining members of the family, and the walls of the house are sprinkled with what is left of it, to bring good luck. "The one who chews chewing gum on Good Friday, chews the meat of his forefathers" - that is the warning said to children by their parents.

The Fasting-Period of the Apostles - Ṣawmo dašliḥe

The Apostles' Fast is considered the oldest fast, for it was begun and established by the Apostles themselves. Its name may suggest that it is observed in honour of the Apostles. However, this is not so; for, according to the Church, they are included among mortals. This fast is observed in honour of the third person of the Holy Trinity, the Holy Spirit, whose power enabled the Apostles to preach the news of redemption. It used to be a movable fast for, as Bar Ebraya wrote in the 13th century, it began on the first Monday following Pentecost and always lasted until 29 June, i.e. until the holiday of Apostles Peter and Paul (celebrated by the Church even today). Nowadays it is a fixed three-day fast.

Basic Fast Meals

Long fasts and their characteristic menu, which forbids the use of any products or additives of animal origin or their derivatives (i.e. meat and its products, dairy products, poultry, eggs and animal fat) forced families to gather a proper supply of vegetarian food. The basic fast food includes meals made of pulse crops: broad beans (*baqylle*) and gram (*Cicer arietinum*, chickpea, *ḥemṣe*) - either boiled or in the form of a purée dressed with oil and lemon juice and mixed together with sesame pulp called *tahine*. Boiled beans (*qusso*) and lentils (*ṭlawḥe*) are also popular, mainly in the form of soup.

Lentils especially enjoy great approval. For centuries they have been the main, fixed and legendary dish, prepared every fasting day, whatever the season of the year. Before beginning work in the fields - ploughing, harvest - even before dawn, Assyrian farmers had to eat their fill of hot lentil soup, in which pieces of bread were often dipped. This dish is not only very tasty, but it is also of unusually high nutritional value [24].

The larder should also contain potatoes, which are eaten in different forms, e.g. fried, mashed, stuffed or roasted. There are usually enough dates (*tamre*), to be eaten both raw and fried in oil, and date syrup, which is delicious with sesame pulp and bread (*lahmo*) and is a favourite children's dainty. Onions are also widely used, often stuffed, also garlic, and on some occasions halwa too. All these products are bought in such quantity that there should be enough of them for the whole period of a given fast.

Provisions traditionally made in summer supplement the fasting fare. These include grape products (*enwe*); raisins (*absoto*); syrup; *halile* (grape syrup mixed with semolina and heated until it becomes thick and then dried in the sun and cut like bars); *bastiqe* (grape syrup mixed with wheat flour and heated until it becomes thick and dried in slices); and *oqude* (*bastiqe* with nuts). Among corn products we should name *ryštan*, (a kind of macaroni), which tastes nice after being parched with a little oil. There are also pickled products: carrots, cauliflower, cucumbers, not quite ripe tomatoes, cabbage, peppers, radishes, beetroot, French beans and others. Tomato purée and dried vegetables are commonly used: peppermint, parsley, okra, eggplant (which is also eaten raw in large quantities, fried in slices, stewed, roasted and preserved in oil), spinach and others.

This list is enriched by wild plants, gathered by rivers and in fields, such as sorrel; vegetable purslane; Armenian marsh mallow (*Althæa armeniaca*, *toleke*, *lahmo d-sefre*); thyme; endive; and chicory, all of which after proper preparation can be separate dishes.

The only fat added to fast food is vegetable oil, obtained from the seeds of sesame and sunflower, cotton and olives.

Folk knowledge accumulated over the centuries about the features of given vegetable products and their cooking, as well as the experience of housewives in planning and diversifying the dishes, not only lessens the potential negative effects of the lack of animal products in the diet, but makes the fasting menu rich, attractive and truly healthy. For almost one third of the year Assyrians are absolute and real vegetarians [25].

Every day of the fasting period, except Saturdays and Sundays, some of the people fasting do not eat anything at all from the moment they wake up until noon, drinking not even a drop of water nor smoking cigarettes. They have the first meal after a short church service, which takes place, as an addition to the usual services, at about 11 a.m. By tradition there is a host, cut to pieces (instead of Holy Communion which those fasting used to receive every day during the fast) inside the temple, by the door; outside the temple on a table there are pieces of fresh bread. Every person leaving the temple takes one piece of the host, making the sign of the cross, and one piece of bread, usually thanking an absent donor for it and wishing him fulfilment of his request to God. Boys and girls also take part in the fasts quite voluntarily, like the adults.

Holiday Cooking

The West-Syrian Orthodox Church of Antioch, to which a number of Assyrians belong, celebrates many holidays. Some of them are called 'moronoye', ('Lord's'), while others are connected with the Holy Mother. Each of them has its own individual liturgy and characteristic melodies, often to the same words. The most solemn of them are: "*Ido d-mawlodo d-moran babsar*" ("The holiday of our Lord being born in flesh and blood"), also called *Ido z' uro* (small holiday) as well as *Ido daqiomto foruqoyto* (the holiday of the Redeemer's resurrection), commonly called *Ido rabo* (big holiday).

Holidays are looked forward to because of the relatively long duration of the fasting periods which precede them, and because of their particular historical and spiritual dignity.

Christmas Eve in the form celebrated solemnly by Catholics, is unknown to this group of Assyrians. On Christmas Eve, small groups of children, who symbolize the shepherds, ask about the place of Christ's birth. They walk from house to house receiving traditional treats, such as raisins, nuts and roasted gram. On the first day of Christmas, meat dishes are eaten. The most important of these is *marga* - lamb stewed with onions and black pepper. Men troop along from house to house, wishing their table companions all the best. Then they are treated to a few pieces of *marga*, to the best kind of sweets, to chocolates with liqueur inside, and sometimes to a glass of home-made grape wine or even a sip of strong arrack [26].

The ecclesiastical year begins on the last Sunday of October, if it falls on the 30th or 31st day of the month, or the first Sunday of November. All the Sundays, both the one immediately preceding Lent, called 'Sunday of Galilee

Kana' and the next six ones are known as 'Sundays of Miracles'. On the Sunday preceding Easter, called 'Sunday of Hosanna' (Catholics call it 'Palm Sunday') small loaves of bread of fermented wheat grits are baked in the shape of a cross. Their surface is glazed with sesame oil and turmeric. There is a popular saying connected with this holiday: "You will not truly participate in the celebration of Sunday of Osanna, if you do not chew the gum dyed [yellow] with turmeric or saffron." On that day alone there is a solemn procession outside church.

Easter is celebrated quite differently. The meals are begun with eating blessed eggs[27] which are lightly dyed by being boiled with onion skins[28].

Children pay their 'debts' with eggs for not keeping their promises, described earlier, and play in squares, knocking a 'pole' of one egg against a 'pole' of another. The loser is the one whose egg gets broken. That is why parents often test the hardness of the egg by "knocking the shell of an egg against their teeth"[29]. Next, dairy products are served, mainly milk soup with rice and sugar, called *dašešto*. On the second day of Easter, the menu is enriched by *burgul* and yogurt. These dishes are eaten commonly in memory of the dead. The whole ceremony takes place in a cemetery, where all the villagers spend the afternoon by the graves of their nearest. This custom is called *tnahto*.

Some regard eating meat for the first two or three days of Easter as a sin. Most probably it has some preventive meaning. Meat dishes can cause some disturbances in the digestive process of the alimentary canal, which has been digesting a different kind of food for seven weeks. An essential element of a holiday bill of fare consists of cakes called *kilicha*, especially liked by children. They are made from wheat flour, fat, cinnamon and nutmeg; they are of different shapes, geometric or vegetable patterns, and are cut out with scissors, knives and various moulds.

The New Year festivity is the most 'open' and the one at which the richest range of delicacies is provided. It is usually spent at home in the company of all members of the family, sometimes supplemented by other relatives and friends. The family provides itself with all available foodstuffs, for a "different taste must fall on each tooth." Two great attractions of the New Year table are water-melons and tomatoes, which are normally not seen in this season of the year. Some farmers store not quite ripe fruit, picked in summer, in chaff where it ripens slowly, attaining edible quality after three to four months, i.e. at the time of the New Year. At no other time of the year could I see such well-stocked shops or sense such a joyful atmosphere. After sunset various kinds of fruit, nuts, dry grape products and alcoholic drinks appear on the tables. Everybody, each sitting with a burning candle in front of him, enjoys the food and sings songs, usually of religious content. Exactly at midnight, after the company have expressed good wishes to one another, beginning with the oldest person, the main New Year dish is served - hen or duck stuffed with rice.

This study of fast-day and holiday cooking among the Assyrians of the West-Syrian Orthodox Church of Antioch is certainly not exhaustive. I have no basis for establishing that members of the group who live in Syrian cities, as well as in the villages and towns of Iraq and other countries in the Middle East, take food in the same way. Even if they observe canonical fasting periods, they may have, indeed surely do have, their own specific cuisines, influenced by the environment and current circumstances. Nevertheless, I think that the possible differences in this domain may be more visible between Assyrian village and town inhabitants, within the same country, than between Assyrian village inhabitants in neighbouring countries in the Middle East. My personal observations and my conversations with representatives of Eastern Assyrians have convinced me that despite one thousand five hundred years of isolation, the fast-day and holiday cooking of these two main groups of Christian Assyrians still show many common features. It would also be worth analysing the extent to which the ritual cooking tradition has been retained by those Assyrians who have been in union with Rome since the 16th century, adopting the names 'Chaldeans' and 'Syrian Catholics'.

	Name of Fast	Fasting Period in the 13th C.	Number of days	Fasting Period in 1930	Number of days	Fasting Period Nowadays	Number of days
1	Wednesdays and Fridays	All of them except: holidays, 7 weeks after Easter and those falling in other fasting periods	about 47-60	All of them except: holidays, 7 weeks after Easter and those falling in other fasting periods	about 58	All of them except: holidays, 7 weeks after Easter and those falling in other fasting periods	about 64-74
2	Niniveh Fast	From the third week preceding Lent	3	From the third week preceding Lent	3	From the third week preceding Lent	3
3	Lent	From the seventh week preceding Easter	48	From the seventh week preceding Easter	48	From the seventh week preceding Easter	48
4	Fast of the Apostles	From the first Monday following Pentecost till 29 June	about 3-34	From 19 to 29 June	10	From 26 to 29 June	3
5	Fast of the Assumption of the Mother of God	From 1 to 15 August	15	From 1 to 15 August	15	From 10 to 15 August	5
6	Advent	From 15 November or 1 December to 25 December	25-40	From 1 to 25 December	25	From 10 to 25 December	15
Total			about 141-200		about 159		about 133-43

Notes

1. St Jacob Baradeus (6th century) did not establish a new church, but rescued the existing national church from terrible Byzantine persecution.

2. Around the St Simeon column a huge octagonal cathedral was built covering an area of 9000 square metres. It had a grandiose dome and was in the centre of four sacral objects in the form of a cross. Ruins of that formerly vast cathedral, destroyed by the Arabs in the seventh century, can be found today not far from Aleppo in Syria. A Holy Mass is said there once a year on the anchorite's day.

3. Bar Ebraya (Mar Gregorios Barhebraeus, Catholicos of the East 1226-86), *Al-Iṭiqon* (Ethicon) (Qamishli, Syria 1967), 146.

4. In the 5th century two divines, both called Barsouma, are of great importance in the history of the church. The first of them was a Monophysite monk who participated in the Third General Council in Ephesus (431) and propagated Monophysitism in west Syria. The other, whose dates were about 415-92, was educated in Syrian Edessa, and then became the co-founder of the High School of Theology in Nisibis (457). The statutes of this school came to be regarded as a model set of rules for a Christian high school and have remained so until present

times. See J.M.Szymusiak and M.Starowiejski, *Słownik wczesnochrześcijańskiego piśmiennictwa* (Dictionary of Early Christian Literature), (Poznan 1971), 86. Detailed information concerning high schools of theology in Edessa and Nisibis is contained in the monograph by N. W. Pigulewska, *Kultura Syryjska we wczesnym średniowieczu* (Syrian Culture in the Early Middle Ages), (Warsaw 1989), 42-115. This extremely interesting book was translated into Arabic from Russian, in which it had been written originally, and edited in Syria in 1990 under the proper title: *Taqafat As-syrian Fil-Qurun Al-Wusta* (Assyrian Culture in the Early Middle Ages).

5. Among Muslims of the Middle East, the name '*Id*' occurs; it means holiday.

6. While living for many years next to Muslims and observing their behaviour during their only fast in the year (Ramadan), I had the impression that most of them treated this question quite differently from the Christians. Their fasting consisted in neither eating nor drinking anything from sunrise to sunset every day of the month of Ramadan. Outside this time of the day, they eat hearty and cloying meals of unrestricted content, whose amount usually exceeded the amount of food really needed by the human body. During the hours of fast, Muslims are apt to find it unacceptable that anybody should eat in their presence. So provident owners of restaurants and cafes draw dark curtains over the front windows, so that passers-by will not see those eating inside. There are sometimes cases of punishing a dissenter who, forgetting about these restrictions, automatically lights a cigarette in the street. Another external indication of Ramadan fasting is a significant, though groundless, decrease in productivity of all kinds of goods. Some of those fasting will even ask a Christian to draw water from the well for them. It is also a Christian who attends to the gun which sounds at the moment when a light is lit over the minaret of the mosque to indicate that the sun has just risen or set; this is the signal to stop or begin eating.

Among Assyrian Christians the atmosphere of fasting induces a spirit of reflection and a constructive attitude towards everything happening around them. The fast in the Assyrian manner makes a man humble, quiet, sensitive to the pain of others and of outstanding self-control. The subjugation of bad habits, moderation, the fight against infatuations and sins, and spiritual exculpation are most probably the main signs of Assyrian fasting. "One who is fasting should not hurry to use his tongue, hands or legs to do any harm to anybody." So preached the 13th century Assyrian philosopher, Bar Ebraya.

In an Assyrian village in the Tur Abdin region (central-southern Turkey) in the sixties, there was a paradoxical event which lives in the memories of the inhabitants of the whole countryside, and which proves the deep-rooted fasting traditions of the Assyrians. A man was preparing home-made ammunition; he was wrapping lead in a piece of cloth, greasing it with butter and putting it into his mouth to wet it with his saliva. He was doing it automatically, not remembering the rigours of the fast. His wife saw it and spoke to him about it. When he realised what he had done, he regretted it very much. He began to cry, to beat his breast and begged God to forgive him. Seeing this lamentable reaction, his wife reminded him that he had not shown as much repentance after he had shot dead two sheep thieves, as he did now after this, after all, unimportant sin, for which he could in any case atone. In fact it can be atoned for, though, as far as I can remember, if one ate even one "holiday" dish during any fasting period (even on the last day) it invalidated the whole fast. Quite often, during confession, the priest imposed an obligation of a repeated fast on a fast-breaker; this meant that the whole period of fasting was doubled.

7. Even intimate marital intercourse, wedding receptions, parties connected with baptism and birthday are suspended.

8. Qarabasi, A. N., *Herge d-quryono l-sedro hmišoyo* (Primer for the Fifth Standard) (Qamishli, Syria 1963), 22-23.

9. Chukkey, M. F. (ed.) *Na'um Faiq-dikra watahlid...* (A Biography and Anthology of the Work of Na'um Faiq) (Damascus 1936), 367-69.

10. "But the best fish is in dreams." This is interpreted as presaging good luck and abundance.

11. Bar Ebraya, above, 152. Issac Saka, Metropolitan, *As-syrian-Iman wahadara* (The Assyrians - Faith and Civilisation), V (Damascus 1986), 294.

12. An Italian Carmelite monk, while travelling through Mesopotamia in 1656, noted that when parents wanted their son to become a monk in the future, they prepared him in the following way. From his earliest years he did not eat meat or meat products, and did not drink alcohol. If the boy "devoted to God" broke this canon even once, he lost his parents' trust which meant that he stopped being a candidate for service to God. That Carmelite monk who wrote with admiration about the fasts of Christians in Mesopotamia (naming almost all of them except the Niniveh fasting period), stated that the most arduous was the 15-day fast preceding the Assumption of the Mother

of God, which falls on sweltering summer days. He also stressed one more observation: the Christians he met in Mesopotamia did not fast on Saturdays - they ate meat on that day! See *Il Viaggio all' Indie Orientali del Padre F. Vincenzo Maria di S. Caterina de Siena*, (Venezia 1683). This book was translated into Arabic by Butros Haddad who published a fragment of it in *Journal of the Syriac Academy*, I, (Baghdad 1975),179-203. I drew the above information from this (p 188). It is worth adding that the torrid heat of the August days of this fasting can be alleviated by eating water-melons, greatly praised by that Carmelite monk, who admitted; "Never have I seen in my life water-melons similar to those of Mosul; the diameter of some of them is more than one ell long." According to my recollections, there were water-melons of that size in Assyrian villages in Syria in the 1950s and 60s.

The cult of the Holy Virgin is widespread among Polish Catholics. Some foreign and native observers express their opinion, even in mass media, that this cult is the most apparent manifestation of Christianity in this country. Nevertheless there is no fast day in the Polish Catholic calendar devoted to the Holy Virgin. In general, if we assume the measure of fasting as a criterion of devotion, the Churches of the East would take precedence.

13. During my stay in Sweden in 1990 I met a few Assyrian women, in their sixties, who were celebrating a 13 day Fast of the Cross (from 1st to 14th September in the morning; the latter is an important holiday - the Holiday of the Cross). This fast does not exist in the Church calendar and its additional observance, especially by elderly people, is a way of expressing their increasing nearness to God.

14. Saka, above, 302.

15. Biblia tysiąclecia (The Bible of the Millenium), 3rd ed., (Poznan-Warsaw 1980), 1187.

16. In 1990 the Niniveh Fast fell on 5-7 February. Church services in that period could not be connected with the Holy Mass.

This fasting period is known and observed also by other societies of Christians of the Middle East.

Eastern Assyrians call it *ba' uta d-Ninwe* (begging of Niniveh), and in some old documents it also occurs under the name *ṣoma dabṭulaṭe* (Fast of the Virgins). They observe it especially strictly, because, they explain, they live closer to their capital, Niniveh, destroyed in 612 BC. Since the earliest era of Christianity, the Niniveh Fast has lasted for three days, a duration which, according to them, was connected with the Holy Trinity. At Tel Kef (now in Iraq) the fast is accompanied by some superstitions, such as not taking a bath (for fear of "vibration of the head") and not combing ones hair (to avoid headaches). Only on Friday morning, called 'Friday of the Gullet', after the first cock-crow do the people begin eating. It is a favourable portent if among the dishes served are *kubba* (wheat and meat balls) and *aprahe* (stuffed vine leaves). If these have remained ready throughout the three-day fast, they must have been prepared on Sunday. Eating these dishes will surely "prevent a headache and will cure chronic migraine".

With the aim of increasing the number of those fasting, a story is repeated in Tel Kef about a certain mare from Niniveh which was the only animal that did not want to obey God. It escaped secretly with its colt to the other side of the River Tigris in order to feed the colt with its milk. God punished the mare by changing it into a mule. See Kheri Qawmiye, *Qala Suryaya* (The Assyrian Voice) (Baghdad 1980-81), 64-9.

The Niniveh fasting period was introduced to the calendar of the Coptic Church, under the name 'Jonathan's Fast', in the 6th century by the Patriarch of Alexandria, of Assyrian origin, Anba Aprem Ben Zar'a. See Yuhanon Dolaban, 'Ṣawm Naynawa' (The Niniveh Fast), *Al-Ḥikma*, 4, 1 (Jerusalem 1930), 62-4, cited in Saka, above, 303-6.

Zakka I Iwas, the present Patriarch of the Church, claims, however, that the above-mentioned Anba reigned as Patriarch of Alexandria in 968. See his article: '*Lamḥat min tariḥ An-nabi Yunan wa-ṣawm Naynawa*' (Outline of the history of the Prophet Jonathan and the Niniveh fasting period), *The Patriarchal Journal*, 19, 2 (Damascus, 1981), 66-72. If this date is not wrong, the Coptic Church would have had the opportunity to observe Jonathan's Fast only since the 10th century.

It is worth mentioning the circumstance that led to this. It happened that Anba, in a way a stranger to the Copts, showed his solidarity with them by keeping the fast called 'Hercules' Friday'. Enchanted by this gesture, the Copts responded by observing the Niniveh Fast, and this subsequently became obligatory for them.

The Armenians, however, observe it as 'St Sarkis Fast' in accordance with the old six day (in other words, West Syrian) primary version.

Patriarch Zakka I Iwas, mentioned above, quoting sources from the 6th century, wrote that the Niniveh Fast was so called because the first groups to observe it lived near old Niniveh. See Zakka I Iwas, above, 71.

17. Dolabani, above; Zakka I Iwas, above.

18. Bar Isay, that is to say biblical David.

19. Those times cannot have been so long ago, since - as I recall quite well - my grandfather, who died in 1964, behaved similarly.

20. During Lent, the Holy Mass is conducted very rarely, even in monasteries, where it is usually conducted every day in other seasons of the year. The only exceptions are the 24th day of Lent, called *falgo d-sawmo* (which means half of Lent, even though the number of fasting days is uneven), which falls always on a Wednesday, and Thursday and Saturday (in the afternoon) in Holy Week. Apart from that, the Holy Mass is conducted on any day of Lent if a church holiday, for instance that of the Annunciation, falls on it, even if it be Good Friday.

21. To explain the genesis and intention of this folk custom would require a long commentary.

22. Among the eastern Assyrians a custom proving their scrupulous preparation for Lent has been preserved. In the morning of the first day of the seven week Lent, village women go to the river taking kitchen utensils and the ash from their stoves with them. They wash the utensils carefully with the ash "to remove possible remains of the animal fat that could be left after cooking festive dishes in them". There is a popular saying connected with this folkloristic scene: "*soma l-tar:a wate, w qetma l-qusaryate*" (Fast reached the door and ash reached the utensils).

23. With Eastern Assyrians, on Good Friday wheat bread is fried in sesame oil and then sweetened with grape syrup and eaten while still warm.

24. My grandfather always used to encourage me to eat lentils as often as possible, claiming that they make the body as strong as the iron which they contain. The strange thing is that at the time none of the village people had the slightest idea about the chemical composition of food: they thought that the only function served by eating was to fill the stomach. Now it has turned out that my grandfather's statement is true. Scientific research has proved that lentils are indeed rich in iron (approximately 8 mg. per 100 g.). That is why lentils are used, even in clinics, to cure anemia; they cause a rapid increase in the amount of haemoglobin in the blood. They are also rich in lysine, an amino acid deficient in wheat. For many more details of the nutritional value of lentils, see: J. W. Cowan, M. Esphahani, J. P. Salji, A. Nahapetian, 'Nutritive Value of Middle Eastern Foodstuffs, III - Physiological Availability of Iron in Selected Foods Common in the Middle East', *J. Sci. Fd. Agric.*, VIII, 6 (1967), 227-31; J. Jamalian & P. L. Pellete, 'Nutritive Value of Middle Eastern Foodstuffs, IV -Amino Acids Composition', *J. Sci. Fd. Agric.*, IX, 7 (1968), 378-82.

25. Strict fasting is not obligatory for everyone. The Church gives a dispensation from it to: pregnant mothers; feeding mothers; the old and the sick; and others if there is good reason. As long ago as the 13th century, Bar Ebraya wrote: "It is forbidden to drink wine in Lent. Wine can be given only to women who have delivered a baby, even if it is Holy Saturday." See *Nomocanon*, (Bar Hebraeus Verlag, Netherlands 1986), 33-4.

26. On Christmas Day, which I celebrated for the last time in the village in 1958, there was an unpleasant incident. One of the men, after walking from one family to another with good wishes, picked up a gun and wanted to shoot his wife. Fortunately the magazine turned out to be empty. The behaviour of this man was explained by the fact that one of the hostesses must have regaled him with arrack in which she had deliberately dissolved some secretion from the ear, which evokes aggression.

27. Among Assyrians eggs are a symbol of Christ's Resurrection. For "like a nestling, which leaves the shell unaided, the living Christ left his tomb." There is also a superstition which says: "If the cracking of an egg, being baked in hot cinders, does not spring a surprise on you, you will find a fortune." In some Assyrian circles, an incredible and naive story is repeated, by way of explaining the connection between Christ's Resurrection and colourful eggs. It says that, along the Way of the Cross by which Christ was led to Golgotha, there were crowds of Jewish women holding their children at their breast. Each of them was carrying an egg to throw at Christ. But whenever they took the eggs into their hands to throw them, they became coloured. Then the children, fascinated by the coloured eggs, reached out for them and made it impossible for the women to throw them at Christ.

28. A well-known Polish nutritionist, Irena Gumowska, writes: "Dyed eggs are older than Easter. They were found, for instance, on the territory of the former Assyrian state, i.e. they are about 5,000 years old." See I. Gumowska,

Cztery pory roku w gospodarstwie domowym (Four Seasons of the Year in the Household), (Warsaw 1967), 112.

29. This naive children's game may sometimes turn into a conflict with the participation of the elders. Qoriaqos Hanna, the author of an interesting study: *Qariat Tellesqof bayna al-maḍi walḥader* (Tellesqof Village - Yesterday and Today), writes that in 1932 a two day 'egg war' took place in the village with the use of sticks. It was caused by an argument between two boys, each from a different district. One of them accused the other of using a non-hen's egg in the game, arguing that it showed atypical hardness of the shell. See *Min turaṯina aš-ša'bi fi qura Naynawa* (From our Folklore in the Neighbourhood of Mosul) (ed. Society of those Speaking Assyrian in Iraq 1981), 232-33.

The Festival of Christmas

by Joan P. Alcock

The festival of Christmas is celebrated at the darkest and most dismal part of the year, yet at a time when hope revives. Christmas follows immediately the winter Solstice. The shortest day has passed, the sun regains strength and the cycle of life can begin again. Although this paper concentrates on Christmas, the festive day is part of the Twelve Day festival which includes New Year's Day and Twelfth Night. In fact this isolation of Christmas Day with the inclusion of Christmas Eve and Boxing Day is a comparatively recent innovation. Modern custom, however, is tending to revert to the older custom. The holiday period now seems to run from Christmas Eve until January 2nd; indeed if Christmas Day and New Year's Day fall at weekends, the period can easily embrace twelve days even if not the traditional Twelve Days.

This paper will concentrate on the British season of Christmas with occasional excursions to Europe and America where different customs prevail. Everywhere, however, there is a similarity of purpose. It is a time of celebration, of feasting, merriment and jollity with overindulgence viewed tolerantly. This in itself is a reminder that during the winter months food might be limited in both quantity and quality but, in the festive period, at least, it would be increased in quantity so that body and spirit would be revitalised to face the bleak period of January and early February when the life spirit was at its lowest.

Origins

The Christian festival had its origin in the pagan festivities for the passing of the winter Solstice. In the Iron Age great bonfires were lit to drive away the demons of darkness but the date of December 25th, decreed as that of the Saviour's birth, was an arbitrary date chosen by Pope Julius I (AD 337 - 53) who bore in mind a tradition recorded by St. Chrysostom. This was a shrewd move for it embraced the sun's rebirth at the winter Solstice and the rituals attached to the *Dies Natalis Invicti Solis* (the Birthday of the Unconquered Sun) and of Mithras, God of Light, worshipped by soldiers and traders and associated with the Phrygian God, Attis. The Roman World already had a great festival at that time of year, the Saturnalia sacred to the god, Saturn, and his wife, Ops, two of the oldest deities in the Roman calendar. It was Saturn who ruled as King during the Golden Age but he devoured his sons at birth so that he would not leave a male heir when he was deposed from his position by Jupiter.

This grotesque act inspired a kind of debauchery and licence on the Saturnalia, the 19th December. When Caesar reformed the calendar the festival was transferred to the 17th and this was confirmed by Augustus who ordered the 19th to be sacred to Ops. Soon usage made it a double festival, two days for the Saturnalia and two days for the Opalia. Later, Caligula ordered the 21st to be devoted to youth festivities so that revelry stretched to a week. Its great popularity was that once in the year distinctions of rank were set aside. Slaves were made the equal of their masters, who often exchanged clothes with them. (This tradition was continued in the Mummers' plays and was recorded as a custom in the East End of London before and during the Second World War. One might also note the custom in certain British regiments where the commanding officer serves the youngest private his Christmas Day dinner.) Gifts were exchanged, in particular lanterns and oil lamps, for light was considered essential to combat darkness. Saturnalia was followed by the festival of Kalends celebrating the turn of the year. This, lasting for three days, included a further exchange of gifts and the decking of houses with branches of trees and wreathes especially evergreens, symbol of fertility.

Early Christian Tradition

This was the Latin festival. From the Teutonic and Norse areas came the festival of Yule equally associated with light, greenery, feasting and the exchange of gifts. At this time the Wild Hunt was abroad and Odin, Thor and Frey were worshipped. Mistletoe was cut, a plant whose name in Celtic meant all-healing, associated with fertility and with protection against ill-luck. The main feature of the festival was the lighting of bonfires to represent the new life of the sun which begins to reinvigorate itself on the 21st December. The Christian Church, adaptable in its wisdom, combined these festivals, Pagan, Norse, Teuton, into a commemoration which extended from Advent to Candlemas weaving into it ritual, ceremony and legend.

This blend of Christian and Pagan symbolism could be adapted to suit Christian and Pagan tastes although inevitably the Church tried to stamp out unbridled licence to give "Christ's Mass" its spiritual significance. The whole festival of Twelve Days was acknowledged by the Council of Trent in AD 567. Roman customs continued so that the

Saturnalian custom of servants dominating masters continued in the creating of a 'Boy Bishop' in some Cathedrals, who acted as the Lord Bishop until Holy Innocents Day (December 28th), and the good natured feasting degenerated into riotous assembly in the Feast of Fools.

In AD 601 Pope Gregory the Great had instructed St. Augustine to deck Christian Churches with greenery as had been the pagan temples and to solemnise the Christian feasting so that praise of God came before praise of pagan gods. The festival of light continued to be celebrated in Scandinavia on St. Lucia's Day. On December 13, the day of their winter Solstice, the Lucia Queen appears in Swedish villages wearing a crown of lit candles and bearing trays of food and drink to ensure goodwill and plenty. Her white dress, crossed with a red sash, symbolises light and fire.

Symbolism ran through the festival season. Holly was the symbol of the Crown of Thorns, ivy protected from evil. One was the masculine principle, the other the feminine, both enshrined forever in the carol. Sterile holly (with no berries) was unlucky so it had to be wrapped round with ivy. Mistletoe was not accepted in the church for it was associated with Druidism and though it was all-healing its representation was ambiguous. In Norse legend it had killed Baldur, the god of light. Carols at first were something abandoned and sinful but by the 14th century they had become respectable. The oldest carols, as words sung to tunes, date from the 15th century. Their origins lie in the songs which emerged from the Mystery plays, from folk tunes and ballads. They were essentially songs of the people and as such retained simple lyrical tunes.

Tudor Festivities

In the Middle Ages Christmas was associated with feasting and good cheer. Lords, Princes and Kings were expected to provide their followers with food and wine over the Twelve Days. The Reformation did little to curb this tradition of hospitality. The Petre family at Ingatestone Hall (Essex) celebrated all the twelve days when family, friends and retainers would be expected. On Christmas Day, 1552, the table groaned with six boiled and six roast pieces of beef, a loin and breast of pork, a neck of mutton, a goose, four rabbits, and eight warden pies (pears baked with saffron). For supper five joints of mutton, a rack of pork, two rabbits and a venison pasty were served. As Christmas Day fell on a Friday in that year there was a dispensation from fasting. It was on New Year's Day, also a Friday, that the family theoretically fasted on fish - plaice, whiting, mudfish, ling, cod, salmon, and eggs and cheese. But the great day was Twelfth Night when 200 people dined on beef, pork, veal, suckling pig, mutton and venison pasties, geese, partridge, capons, woodcock, teal and larks. Even if the family were not present at the Hall the tradition of hospitality did not fail. On the Sunday before Christmas Day about twenty servants and twelve local visitors consumed three pieces of boiled and one roasted piece of beef, a neat's tongue, a baked leg of mutton, two rabbits and a partridge - all good solid food washed down with beer brewed in the household.

The Puritan Influence and the Decline of Christmas

The advance of Puritanism resulted in an increasing denunciation of the lewdness and debauchery which was disfiguring the Christian festival. The carol in particular was condemned for promoting these traits. Scottish Presbyterians allied with English Puritans to suppress the festival. In 1644 Christmas Day was decreed to be a fast day and in 1647 the Puritan Parliament abolished Christmas Day together with other festivals. In 1652 Parliament sat on Christmas Day and four years later a tract by Hezekiah Woodward referred to Christmas Day as "The Old Heathen Fasting Day, in honour to Satan, their Idol-God". In England Christmas Day was celebrated furtively; in Presbyterian Scotland, the strict Calvinistic attitude appeared to suppress its significance replacing it by more secular New Year celebrations.

Christmas Revived

Although the Parliamentary order abolishing Christmas Day was replaced, together with other legislation, when Charles II returned, much of the festive spirit had gone. There seemed to be little desire to keep Christmas customs in the 18th century - an age of enlightenment and rational thinking. These remained the preserve of the lower classes and in the next century they had to be hunted out by antiquarians. Carols were preserved in folk song and the texts in broadsheets but by the 19th century they seemed to have been on the verge of extinction. Yet in that century came a remarkable revival of the old carols and the composing of new carols and hymns generating an enthusiasm which continues today. Nor did the revival stop at carols; old customs were sought out, traditional festivities generated, a whole new folklore was established. This revival was due mainly to two influences. The first was the enthusiastic promotion of Christmas by authors such as Charles Dickens and Washington Irving. The second was the longing on the part of Victorian middle class society for an idealised past which would unite the family in sentiment and in charitable thoughts towards those who were less fortunate in acquiring the material things of life.

Charles Dickens's Influence

Dickens is always credited with reviving the spirit of Christmas. His essay, 'A Christmas Dinner' in *Sketches by Boz* (1836) begins, "Christmas Tide; A man must be a misanthrope indeed in whose breast something like a jovial feeling is not aroused - in whose mind some pleasant associations are not awakened - by the recurrence of Christmas." The centre of activities was the family. "A Christmas family party! We know nothing in nature more delightful." Hence the emphasis is on Christmas Day, but in *Pickwick Papers*, written in the same year, the main festivities take place "according to annual custom, on Christmas Eve, observed by Old Wardle's family from time immemorial". These customs do include kissing under the mistletoe, playing snapdragon, and Blind Man's Buff, drinking a "mighty bowl of Wassail" and telling ghost stories. But on Christmas Day the main event is Mr. Pickwick's disastrous fall through the ice. Food and festivities play a lesser part and the main Christmas meal is dismissed by the terse phrase "after a substantial lunch". In *A Christmas Carol* (1843) (carol here having its old meaning of tale or ballad) the festivities at Old Fezziwig's also take place on Christmas Eve and include forfeits and dances accompanied by cake, cold roasts, a "piece of cold boiled", mince pies and plenty of beer. This however, had happened when Scrooge was a youth and would be part of middle class celebrations. The Cratchits had their dinner on Christmas Day when Bob had his holiday. This was a substantial meal of goose with sage and onion stuffing eked out with apple sauce and mashed potatoes followed by pudding, apples, oranges and a shovel full of hot chestnuts.

Across the Atlantic Washington Irving promoted the Christmas Spirit and it was the American State of Alabama which in 1836 was the first state to make Christmas Day an official legal holiday. Other states followed until finally Oklahoma succumbed as the last state in 1890.

In European countries Christmas, and in particular, January 6th, had been kept as a religious festival having different traditions some of which were to find their way to Britain.

The success in Britain of *A Christmas Carol* and of the other Christmas descriptions in Dickensland was soon apparent. Dickens had helped to create the myth of a traditional Christmas. In this he was aided by other writers such as Scott who promoted the romantic element, summed up in *Marmion*.

> "England was merry England, when
> Old Christmas brought his sport again
> 'Twas Christmas broached the mightiest ale
> 'Twas Christmas told the merriest tale"

The Victorian Revival

Above all, however, it was the Victorian middle class whose social conscience harnessed to undoubted philanthropic intention gave Christmas its association with charitable endeavours spurred on by moral purpose. The emphasis on family enabled Christmas to become an emotional occasion, when, after morning service, the family would gather round the table (a place being found for the elderly aunt or a batchelor uncle) to partake of a meal which was meant to promote goodwill and friendship. This gathering was helped by the expansion of the railways. Journey times were shortened. The stagecoach journey from London to Manchester had taken two days. By 1861 the train journey was 5 1/2 hours. The worship of family spread beyond the immediate home to the workhouse, the orphanage and the prison. A moral crusade promoted the ideal of an institutionalised family which must not be deprived of Christmas. Charity and goodwill were therefore fostered. This led to such events as were reported in *The Daily Telegraph* for December 27th 1886. A Christmas dinner was given for 500 young people employed in Pantomime and deserving children in the neighbourhood of a mission in a poor locality. The allowance for each child was 1/2 lb roast beef, 3/4 lb baked potatoes, 1/2 lb of plum pudding, a mince pie, a roll, two oranges and half a pint of tea or coffee. Anything not consumed was packed in paper for them to take home. The children cheered when they smelt the beef, cheered when the pudding came and cheered when they could eat no more. Such scenes became commonplace to gladden the heart of the Victorian middle class.

The ideal of a family Christmas was also helped by Prince Albert who promoted Christmas festivities at Windsor and who has been credited with introducing the German custom of the Christmas tree decorated with candles, tinsel and ornaments. The 1848 *Illustrated London News* drawing of the Queen, the Prince and the Royal Family at Windsor gathered round the Christmas tree solidified the image. German merchants who had settled in Manchester brought the same custom with them while Germans who settled in Pennsylvania are said to have introduced the custom to the United States.

The festival soon centred on Christmas Day and Boxing Day, rather than the Twelve Days, and, these were made official holidays, rather than being dependent on the whim of the employer, as Scrooge had done when he grudgingly allowed Bob Cratchit to have Christmas Day off. The 1833 factory Act made Christmas Day a holiday for children under twelve but the rest of the family had to work. Eventually Boxing Day was created a public holiday in 1870 and the two day holiday period made an extended visit to the family worthwhile. One explanation for the name Boxing Day is that it is associated with the almsboxes which were opened for the relief of the poor on St. Stephen's Day. Another is that it came from the earthenware boxes used by apprentices to collect monetary gifts. It is another reminder of the charity expected to be given to the poor at this time especially when it took the form of clothing or feeding the hungry.

The Twentieth Century

It has only been in this century that the full celebration of Christmas could become normal practice for the majority of people. Before the Second World War Christmas gifts for many people were still an apple and an orange and a bigger piece of meat on Christmas Day. The spiritual significance might be there, never more so than in 1914 when the longing for peace created the Christmas Truce in the trenches of Flanders. During the truce, which lasted over the Christmas season, British and German troops sang carols, often alternating with one another. On one sector of the front the London Rifle Brigade, having heard the Germans singing *Stille Nacht*, commenced *The First Nowell*. A German rendering of *O Tannenbaum* led to a combined effort of an English *O Come all ye Faithful* and a Latin *Adeste Fidelis*.

In the Second World War the stress of the bombing, the strain of parting, the longing for home led to an intensification of sentimental feeling which even the imposition of rationing could not repress. Tinned plum pudding, mock marzipan and mock goose replaced traditional fare. Advertisements recommended lemon sauce made with lemon essence and a sharp sauce for stewed mutton made with dried egg, mustard, flour, sugar, vinegar and mayonnaise. The Ministry of Food provided recipes for Christmas cakes made with dried egg, grated carrot and potatoes. Hospitality was on as generous a scale as possible especially to those who were bombed out in the Christmas raids of 1940 or to members of the forces - Dutch, American, French - in fact all the allied forces stationed in Britain.

It was however the period after the war, the 1950s, which began the present Christmas Season. This was the Age of Affluence when more people earned more money than at any time previously. Increasing wealth combined with a nostalgia for things past and assiduous promotion by commercial interests created a festive season in which indulgence towards others and towards oneself was expected. Gradually, the Christmas season has been extended until it now seems to begin immediately after the summer holidays have ended.

Radio broadcasting had attempted to create a family atmosphere with a gathering round the fire at 3pm to hear the Royal Speech. This modern ritual had begun in 1932 when King George V was persuaded by Sir John Reith, Director General of the BBC, to address his people. Soon the family atmosphere was extended to the family of the Empire. Now the gathering is round the television when the Queen addresses the family of the Commonwealth, but TV has created its own pattern of Christmas with assiduous promotion of goodwill, comedy shows and films. Both radio and television can be used to promote that spirit of charity of which the Victorians so approved. A radio appeal for empty accommodation by Crisis at Christmas can result in warehouses being offered to house and feed the homeless. The promotion in 1984 of a hit record resulted in Band Aid's great success, *And Do They Know It's Christmas* with its royalties providing aid to Third World countries.

Christmas Traditions

Christmas traditions, in spite of modern sophisticated patterns, have continued. Christmas trees with the Christchild becoming a fairy doll decorate most homes. Artificial ones are held to be preferable to real ones, which cause problems by shedding their leaves. The Victorians put gilded nuts, sweets and fruit on the tree where they remained until it was dismantled on Twelfth Night. These sweets have a commercial equivalent in glass ornaments. The first communal Christmas tree appears to have been one set up on Mount Wilson at Pasadena in California in 1909. Each year from 1946 the people of Oslo have presented a tree to the citizens of London to be set up in Trafalgar Square as a reminder of the help given to Norway by Britain during the Second World War.

Paper decorations, first used in the 19th century when mechanical cutting of paper became common, continue to be popular. The Christmas card is an English institution linked with the Victorian revival. The first one appeared in 1843 when Henry Cole, first Director of the Victoria and Albert Museum, suggested that John Horsley might design a Christmas card. A thousand copies were printed, which, perhaps inevitably, showed a happy family sitting down to a Christmas feast. The introduction of the penny post allowed people to send cards cheaply and their number was increased when unsealed envelopes could be posted at a cheaper rate, a custom which lasted until the 1970s. New

Year cards were more popular on the continent especially in Central Europe where one design featured the Christchild carrying the cross and the words *"Ein gut selig Jahr"*.

The Christmas cracker derives from France. Thomas Smith, a Norwich man, adapted a French idea of putting bonbons into a paper roll with a twist at each end. Standing in front of his roaring fire he heard the yule log crackle and decided that a crack could be added to the paper. Pulminate of silver was put on to the two ends of a strip of paper which were sandpapered. This would produce a spark to give the bang when pulled apart. Sweets and love mottoes were the first objects to be included; later trinkets and paper hats were included together with excruciating but inoffensive jokes. These have hardly altered since the 1870s. "What does a duck get for Christmas?" "Quackers". "How far can you go into a wood?" "Halfway, because then you are coming out". Crackers are most popular in Britain and few are sold elsewhere. Sales are also strictly seasonal but they are rising. In 1987 52 million crackers were produced in 100 different lines costing from £2 to over £75 a box.

Revived Traditions

Some traditions have died out. December 28th is Holy Innocents' Day or Childermas, the day associated with Herod's Slaughter of the Innocents and the unluckiest day of the year. On that day church bells rang a muffled peal but this has now ceased. The mummers' plays, where the hero (usually St. George) is slain and miraculously brought back to life by the Doctor accompanied by a motley collection of characters - the Turkish Knight, the King of Egypt, the Dragon - are now rarely performed. But in other parts of Europe - Austria, Poland and Germany - masked and grotesque figures parade through the streets.

A new lease of life has been given to the Christmas Crib. This custom is attributed to St. Francis. *The Life of St. Francis* by St. Bonaventura tells the story that in 1224 Francis "was minded at Greccio to celebrate the memory of the birth of the child Jesus with all the added solemnity that he might for the kindling of devotion. That this might not seem an innovation he sought and obtained licence from the Supreme Pontiff and then made ready a manger and bade hay together with an ox and ass to be brought within the place". There were references to a crib in Rome as early as the 4th century but it was St. Francis who popularised the custom. It was associated with Catholic countries especially Naples and Sicily where the most elaborate scenes, extending well beyond a humble crib, were created. The Protestant world adopted them enthusiastically in the 1980s so that in churches, schools and city centres the crib, with attendant Joseph, Mary and the animals, became part of the Christmas tradition. In Germany figures of three kings are added to the crib on 6th January, the feast of Epiphany or *Dreikönigstag* (Three King's Day).

If the crib is Catholic in origin then so is Midnight Mass on Christmas Eve. This has only been in general use since the Second World War but has now become traditional in some Protestant churches. The Methodist Church prefers to hold a Watchnight Service on New Year's Eve. Recently the Moravian Christingle service has become popular. At Ockbrock in Derbyshire a group of Moravian brethren arrived to found a community dedicated to the simple life. Nearly fifty years later a girls' school was founded by the community which continues to flourish. Each Christmas the girls process into the severe, simple chapel, each holding an orange (the world), wrapped round with a red ribbon (the blood of Christ), and into which a lit candle is placed (the light of the world). As a contrast one of the largest of the Christingle services now takes place in Norwich Cathedral.

Candles have always been part of the Christmas celebrations. Candles lit within the house guide the Christchild by their gleam to bless the household. At St. John's College, Cambridge a huge candle was said to have burned throughout all the twelve days. Christmas candles are sold with twenty four hours marked on them, one for each hour of Christmas Eve.

The most popular Christmas Service is probably that of the Nine Lessons and Carols. Yet this seemingly age-old service has a modern origin for it was only in this century that Bishop Benson devised the service for Truro Cathedral and as late as 1918 that it was first heard in King's College Chapel, Cambridge. Since its first broadcast in 1930 it has come to epitomise the true spirit of Christmas. And perhaps that real spirit is needed more today. There is now almost a feeling of being entrapped in the house at Christmas on an extended holiday, with transport services closed down and few shops open so that there is a distinct lack of that family feeling so deeply felt by Victorians. As each Christmas draws to a close there is a feeling of relief, "Thank goodness that's over again for another year".

And yet, each year, as Christmas draws closer, in spite of the increasing commercialisation, the relentless advertising - only another 30 days to Christmas - the tawdry decorations, the bad taste of the illuminated plastic Christmas crib, there still arise feelings of nostalgia for Christmas long ago. The cake, mincepies and puddings are made or bought, the tree and house are decorated, friends and relatives invited, or the hotel booked as an escape route to avoid having relations in the house. And then, on Christmas Eve, as that thin, treble choirboy's voice rising to the vaulting of King's

College Chapel begins, *Once in Royal David's City*, a feeling of expectation grows. Christmas has come once again.

Father Christmas, Santa Claus

Christmas is associated with giving and the greatest giver of all is Father Christmas or in his other guise, Santa Claus. The word guise is appropriate, for the present day figure is a culmination of one of the guizers or mummers, who went round at Christmas to perform plays designed to extort money from the spectators. In the Limpley Stoke (Wiltshire) play he carries a large knobbly stick with which he clears a space for the players and also protects the purse. He opens the play.

> "Here comes I poor old Father Christmas
> Come welcome or welcome not
> I hope poor Father Christmas
> Will never be forgot
> Christmas comes but once a year
> And when it comes he brings good cheer
> Such as roast beef, plum pudding, mince pies
> Who likes it better than Old Dad and I"

But his origin is older. The mummers' plays are the tattered memories of primitive rituals commemorating the conflict between darkness and light and marking the death of the old year and the rebirth of the New, probably also connected with renewing the fertility of the earth. In Norse legend the gift-bringer was Odin, who rode the midnight skies, bearer of gifts of wisdom and healing. This was the older sinister part of Christmas.

The Victorian middle class linked Father Christmas to the continental tradition of St. Nicholas, Bishop of Myra in Asia Minor in the 4th century, patron saint of sailors because he quelled storms, and of maidens because he brought gifts of gold as dowries for the daughters of a poor man. He brought three boys to life who had been murdered by an innkeeper. The restoration of their bodies, preserved in vinegar, was no problem to the Saint. On St. Nicholas Day (December 6th) in Holland and Germany children put out clogs filled with hay or carrots for the Saint's horse. In return he left sweetmeats for good children and birchrods as a warning to bad ones. In Germany they were left a stocking full of cinders.

As a seafarer, in Holland he came from the sea, accompanied by Black Peter, a figure derived from the Spanish occupation of the Netherlands in the 16th century. As Santa Klaus he was taken to the New World by the Dutch Settlers of New Amsterdam (New York). He became immortalised in 1809 by Washington Irving in his *History of New York* and was fixed in tradition by a poem published in a local paper, the *Troy Sentinel*, in 1823. Clement Clark Moore's poem, *'Twas the Night before Christmas* ensured that the reindeer Dasher, Dancer, Prancer, Vixen, Cornet, Cupid, Donner and Blitzen were the constant companions of Santa Claus. They were joined by Rudolph the red-nosed reindeer in the 1970s, who saved the situation when Santa's sleigh broke down. Santa Claus' method of arrival was also fixed.

> "And then in a twinkling I heard on the roof
> The prancing and pawing of each little hoof,
> As I drew in my head and was turning around,
> Down the chimney St. Nicholas came with a bound."

There was no mention of how he looked except that "he was dressed all in fur from his head to his foot" with a bundle of toys on his back. But his appearance was clinched by Thomas Nast's drawing in 1863 in *Harper's Weekly* as a jolly, pot-bellied, white-bearded figure in trousers, jumper and matching long cap all trimmed in fur.

In Britain the robed, hooded figure became the traditional Father Christmas, a combination of pagan mummer and Christian Saint. No connection with December 6th survived. Instead a mythical bringer of gifts emerged in the late 19th century. A Santa Claus Fund distributed gifts to the poor. Even so, there was often a great gap between a child's expectation and the gift which a parent could afford. The ritual of the glass of sherry or wine and the mince pie left for Father Christmas was part of the ritual of exchange of gifts. The hanging of the stocking and the letters written to him were part of the folklore of childhood. He was everywhere. He visited children at Christmas parties as well as the troops on the battlefield; he climbed onto ships at sea and descended in a helicopter to lighthouses. Television exploited his advertising power and the post office set up a special department to cope with the thousands of letters addressed to him at the North Pole. Eventually North Pole (Colorado) and Santa Claus (Indiana) took upon themselves to answer letters sent to them by children whose faith in the gift bringer remained undiminished.

In Scandinavia and Central Europe, Christmas Eve is more important than Christmas Day especially in Germany where on *der heilige Abend* it is *das Christkind* who brings the presents. The Christmas tree is decorated with apples and gilded nuts. Presents placed on a little table include *der bunte Teller*, a dish laden with apples, nuts and raisins, and biscuits baked especially for this day. Apples are for the Tree of Knowledge in Paradise, nuts and raisins are for the mysteries of life and the sweetness of life enclosed within its difficulties. Scandinavia also has special biscuits given as gifts - *pebernodder* in Denmark, *pepparkakor* in Sweden. These recall the gingerbread St. Nicholaus biscuits prepared in Holland for the Saint's Day, and the gingerbread made in Poland from a dough left for four weeks before baking. In Sweden a bowl of rice-porridge is left for a small gnome called *Julenisse* who comes to deliver presents. Spanish and Italian children have to wait for their presents until Twelfth Night. The Three Kings riding on camels (or in the Madrid procession in a motorcade) bring traditional gifts which include marzipan animals to the former but gifts in Italy are delivered by the witch *la Befana*. Each country has developed the art of gift-bringing to suit its own tastes.

Food

In all Christmas activities food, as is only to be expected, plays a most important part. In the middle of winter, when the days were at their shortest and an icy wind blew, food and drink would be hoarded for the festive season. The culmination of the festivities was Twelfth Night in the Middle Ages but the whole of the Twelve Days would be part of one large feast when gold, frankincense and myrrh were offered by the Sovereign on behalf of his people. Later Christmas Eve and then Christmas Day became the central part of the Feasting.

As food became more plentiful there was less need to store it but certain dishes became associated with Christmas, sometimes because they had a symbolic meaning, sometimes because they were too expensive to be eaten all the time. Tradition also plays a large part in when certain foods are eaten. There is a feeling of satisfaction and well-being on the part of the provider of such a feast and an expectation on the part of those who are to receive the fruits of what is often provided with lengthy preparation and hard work. All such feelings may come together particularly at Christmastide.

Meat and Poultry

Although in the Medieval period a certain number of cattle and sheep were culled during the winter the bulk remained for breeding purposes in the spring. Amongst these, however, some of the choicest animals were left for slaughtering before Christmas. If fresh meat was not obtainable, dried or salted meat would suffice but obviously fresh meat was preferred. Pork was especially important especially as all parts of the pig could be used. Suckling pig provided a tasty meal but wild boar, available until the 15th century, was appreciated as it was richer in flavour than domestic pork. It could be the basis of brawn served with vinegar or a syrup of wine and honey. To get the best meat from a young wild pig, he should be shut up in a sty before December, with the straw changed three times a day, and fed on acorns and fresh sweet milk. By Christmas he should be satisfactorily fat and provide tender wholesome flesh.

Chaucer drew attention to the importance of the boar at Christmas

> "Janus sits by the fire with double beard,
> And drinketh of his bugle horn the wine;
> Before him stands the brawn of tusked swine
> And "Nowel" cryeth every lusty man"

The Boar's Head

The boar's head formed part of ceremonial tradition. It was carried into medieval halls especially those of the Inns of Court and the Royal Court. The most famous ceremony to survive is that held at The Queens College, Oxford, which is reputed to have first taken place in the 14th century. The date has been changed from Christmas Day to the Saturday evening round about the 15th December and the ceremony is followed by a Gaudy at which up to 150 past and present members of the college sit down to dine but not on Boar's Head. The origins of the original ceremony are obscure but they seem to go back to the 14th century. An old story associated with it recalls that a student was walking in Shotover Forest when he was charged by a wild boar. Fortunately he was studying a volume of Aristotle so crying, "swallow that if you can", he thrust it into the jaws of the beast thus, as the story concludes, "choking the savage with the sage". The boar's head was brought back in triumph with the book still between the jaws. A more likely origin is that the large number of Northcountrymen who came to the college, found the distance too far to go home for the short Christmas break. They therefore devised this ceremony, but they were not alone in having this festive dish for it was popular in halls, colleges, schools, the Inns of Court and the Royal Court. The head, usually shaped out of brawn, was decorated with mustard or honey and had an orange, apple or lemon stuffed in the mouth. Carried on a gold or silver dish, garnished with fruit and herbs, the boar's head was borne in triumph into the hall. This recalls the presentation of the champion's portion to the greatest warriors during the Celtic period.

The procession was one heralded by trumpets and accompanied by a choir, who sang a carol particularly associated with the dish. The version still sung at The Queen's College begins:-

> "The Boar's Head in hand bear I
> Bedecked with bays and rosemary,
> And I pray you, my masters, be merry
>
> Quot estis in convivio.
> Caput apri defero
> Reddens laudes Domino"
>
> (The boar's head I bring, giving praises to God)

This is a late version of one known to have been published in Wynkin de Worde's *Christmasse Carolles* of 1521 but an earlier version may date from the 14th century.

The orange or apple was usually presented to the chief chorister while sprigs of rosemary, for remembrance, were presented to the chief guests. Pork sausages served with turkey are a reminder of the popularity of the boar. Recently wild boar have been reintroduced into Britain to be farmed for their flesh. Pork continued to be a Christmas dish. The dinner prepared by Mrs. Joe Gargery in *Great Expectations* (1861) consisted of a leg of pickled pork and greens and a pair of roast stuffed fowls. A handsome mincepie had been made the previous morning and the pudding was already on the boil. After the meal had been eaten the Gargerys and their guests, Mr. Wopsle, Mr. and Mrs. Hubble and uncle Pumblechook were to partake of a handsome pork pie presented by the latter. It was only the arrival of the soldiers searching for escaped convicts which prevented the company from discovering that the pie had already been purloined by Pip for the convict, Magwitch.

In Sweden a popular Christmas dish is ham baked with a crust of mustard and breadcrumbs. The water in which the ham has been cooked is kept so that everyone can dip a piece of rye bread into it to eat soaking wet. This dipping is a time-honoured Swedish ritual to show that nothing needs to be wasted. Norwegians serve *ribbe*, huge chops of pork roasted in the oven and accompanied by sauerkraut flavoured with caraway seeds.

Fish

Fish has never been popular in Britain for Christmas but in Central Europe carp is a traditional dish on Christmas Eve. In Poland a wafer is divided amongst everyone before the meal in order to indicate equal shares in the good things. Even the animals may receive a piece and a little is laid on the plate set at the table for the dead. A little of each course will also be placed on the plate. Some households prefer that the extra place is laid for the Christchild, while in South Germany it is left for the Virgin Mary offering her the hospitality which was denied to her during her lifetime in Bethlehem. A Polish meal may begin with with borsch or mushroom soup. This is followed by boiled or stuffed, baked carp served with horseradish sauce accompanied by peas and cabbage. Dried fruit compot of prunes and figs follows. Christmas Eve dinner in Sweden may consist of a variety of meats, brawn and sausage accompanied by browned cabbage boiled and pounded to a mush then mixed with butter and thick cream. This is followed by *Lutfisk* with mushroom sauce followed by rice-porridge, cake and biscuits. A bowl of porridge may be put outside for the Christmas elf. A buffet of meats and fish, which may contain dried carp, may be put out for the whole twelve days. This is because the Christmas spirit must not be allowed to leave the house so every visitor must be fed and given a drink.

Poultry

In England the most popular dish for Christmas by the 19th century was the turkey. This bird, indigenous to the New World, is said to have been introduced into Britain by William Strickland to whom Queen Elizabeth granted the right to have a turkey as an heraldic crest. But it is also said to have been brought from Mexico to the Spanish Netherlands in the early 16th century and from there it came into England. During the 16th and 17th centuries however, goose and capons were more acceptable as were peacock and swan though these were dishes more suited to a rich man's table. They could be skinned before roasting, then the plumage was replaced so that the birds could be carried to table in full splendour. Another method of serving was to cover the birds with thin leaves of silver or gold. The correct name for carving a peacock was to despoil it and perhaps this was often regretfully done as the bird must have presented a gorgeous sight.

Huge flocks of geese and turkeys were driven to market before Christmas from their rearing places in Norfolk, Suffolk and Lincolnshire. They were walked over hot tar first, or more kindly perhaps, fitted with little leather shoes. Turkey became more popular in the 19th century because it was a big bird easily reaching 30lbs. It had to be taken to the baker's ovens for baking on Christmas Day, a practice which did not die out until after the Second World War. Gradually the large birds became less popular, 20lb, then 16lb. At the present time a weight of six pounds is very popular, but turkey roll, turkey breast or turkey leg are also popular as providing a great deal of meat, which can be cooked in a small oven. It is also no longer necessary to save up in a Turkey Christmas club in order to buy the bird. The trend towards smaller birds has resulted in 1990 in the competition to breed the world's heaviest turkey being scrapped by the British Turkey Federation. In 1989 the winner weighed 86lb and was sold at a charity auction for £4,400. Animal Rights Organisations who have always complained that breeding heavy birds was cruel, for they were unable to walk and sometimes their legs broke, welcomed the news.

Poultry was often jointed to be made into pies. A Yorkshire Christmas pie consisted of a fowl, placed within a pigeon, placed within a partridge, placed within a goose, placed within a turkey. This solid 'bird' would be put in a large dish surrounded by jointed pieces of hare and wild fowl, covered with a pastry top and basted well. Such a dish, without the pastry, has been revived for modern tastes. The Pure Meat Company of Moreton Hampstead in Dorset offered at Christmas 1989 a five bird roast: a pigeon, inside a pheasant, placed within a chicken, set within a turkey all wrapped round by a goose. In the centre was spiced pork stuffing. All the birds were boned to aid carving. It was estimated that this would serve fifteen to twenty people. The cost, £97.50, included delivery. If that bird is too big the Company has a three bird roast: a duck wrapped round a chicken enclosing a pigeon and with the spare places filled with sage and apple stuffing. In 1990 this retailed at £34.50. In that year the Company also started to sell what they described as Wild Blue (a cross between wild boar and domestic pig) which was stuffed with apple, sage and cider stuffing. It was reported to be full of flavour and to have a particularly fine crackling.

Other households have made do with less. Goose was cheaper in the 19th century as it was tougher than turkey. The Cratchit household ate goose stuffed with sage and onion eked out by apple sauce and mashed potatoes. Scrooge was raising the standard of their dinner by sending them a turkey on Christmas Day. Rabbit, pigeon and even blackbird pie was popular, the latter a sad sight, perhaps with the feet protruding through the pastry. Goose has become popular again in the 1980s. It has always been popular in Denmark where it is eaten stuffed with apples and prunes accompanied by red cabbage, caramelised potatoes and lingonberry sauce. Chicken once regarded as a Sunday or Christmas treat is now so common that apologetic admission of it is made for Christmas Day dinner.

More traditional methods of rearing poultry have given place to modern production ways of creating smaller birds. They may be more tender but seem to lack taste. They are sold whole or jointed and at all times of the year which means that poultry has lost its festive appeal. This has given the butcher a chance to promote sirloin or pork to a festive role. Peppered sirloin provides variety and different types of stuffing can be added to pork.

At the Fezziwig's party on Christmas Eve Scrooge and his fellow apprentices ate great pieces of cold boiled with cake and mince pies washed down with beer. Beef had always been popular because it could be cooked in large joints. It was popular throughout the year not only on Christmas Day so that it was more a food for celebratory occasions than associated especially with Christmas.

In the trenches in 1915 the troops ate corned beef. In the heart of India and Australia barbecued steak is often eaten. The strangest Christmas meal of all was perhaps that provided at Voisin's restaurant during the siege of Paris in 1870. The menu consisted of consommé of elephant, braised kangaroo, truffled antelope pâté, *chat flanqué de rats*. Sliced spaniel, camel's kidneys and elephant's trunk were served at New Year. The starving Parisians were eating their pets and the zoo.

Mince Pies

One survival of the Middle Ages' love of mixing meat with sweet fruits is the mince pie. The modern mince pie is derived from mutton pie or shred pie so-called from the shredded fat which provided a great deal of nourishment during cold winters. Meat (sometimes fish) and poultry together with fat and dried fruit were packed into a pastry case. The fruit, added as a preservative, may also have disguised a tainted taste.

Mince pies seem to have become traditional to Christmas by the end of the 16th century although their mixture of mutton, fruit, spices and eggs was merely one of several pies containing meat, game, offal, sometimes minced together. (Mutton and apricot pie is another survival.) The meat and suet were in equal quantities and the fruit could be soaked in brandy or sack for several months to enhance the flavour and preserving qualities. This also allowed pies to be made well in advance of the Christmas season. Originally the pies were of an oval shape called coffins but Catholic tradition associated their shape with that of the manger and shaped pastry was placed on the top to indicate the infant Jesus so that by the end of the 16th century they had taken on more than Robert Herrick's culinary meaning:

> "Drink now the strong beere
> Cut the whole loafe here
> For while the meat is a-shredding;
> For the rare mince pie
> And the plums stand by
> To fill the paste that's a-kneading."

The *Gentleman's Magazine* for 1787 commented that mince pies originated in the presentation of gifts, gold, frankincense and myrrh on the birth of Jesus, an event commemorated by cradle shaped cakes filled with fruit and meat. The Puritans regarded the symbolic forms of this pie as being idolatrous so that it was forbidden to make them during the Commonwealth. When the spirit of Christmas returned the making of mince pies was resumed but a round shape now seemed more convenient. Some superstitions still remained. To refuse one was to bring bad luck while to eat one on every day of the Twelve Days was to bring good luck for the twelve months of the year. A wish should be made when taking a bite from the first mince pie. Pepys records that on the 6th January 1661-62 the guests at Sir William Penny's celebration 'had besides a good chine of beef and other good cheer, eighteen mince pies in a dish, the number of years that he hath been married'.

Meat continued to be added to mince pies but it need not be mutton. Eliza Acton's *Modern Cookery for Private Families* (1845) gives a recipe for mincemeat containing oxtongue although "the inside of a tender and well-roasted sirloin will answer quite as well as the tongue". Shredded suet was also included (1 lb of tongue to 2 lb of beef kidney suet). Mrs. Beeton's recipe contains minced lean beef. Gradually the meat was left out but the shredded suet has remained as part of the traditional taste of mincemeat. Even mock mince pies in the recipes of the Second World War required suet although the fruit was reduced to apples and currants (2 lb apple minced with 1 1/2 lb currants and 1 lb suet). The pastry is usually short pastry although the Victorians often used puff pastry.

Traditionally, mincemeat should contain firm, hard apples, mixed dried fruit (currants, raisins, sultanas, candied peel), shredded beef suet, sugar, spices and alcohol (brandy, sherry). Chopped almonds may be added together with lemon and or orange juice. Eliza Acton added two lemons "boiled quite tender and chopped up entirely with the exception of the pips". The mixture requires at least two weeks to mature. A vegetarian mincemeat has been prepared leaving out the suet, and a modern variation is to use a meringue topping instead of the pastry lid. Mincemeat has now ceased to be entirely associated with Christmas. It is often served as part of apple pie or in a mincemeat roly-poly.

Christmas Pudding

The origin of the Christmas pudding lies in one of the earliest foods devised by man. This was pottage, a thick soup consisting of oats or pulses boiled until firm with the addition of scraps of meat or fish and flavoured with herbs. There was no end to the variety of ingredients which could be added. Breadcrumbs gave an additional thickener, egg yolks could be used as a binding agent and fruits and spices would give variety. The dish continued as a filling dish to be eaten at the beginning of meals and as a meat or suet pudding. However in the Tudor period dried plums or prunes were added to it which provided a mixture so popular that it became known as plum pottage or plum pudding. The oats were gradually replaced by bread which acted as the thickener. Robert May in *The Accomplisht Cook* (1660) mentions plum pudding and William Rabisha in *The Whole Body of Cookery Dissected* (1673) refers to it as being a special Christmas dish. An oatmeal hasty pudding continued to be made as an instant hot meal by adding oatmeal to boiling water and serving it with butter, sugar or treacle.

It was not linked solely to Christmas as it was eaten on other occasions especially at Harvest Homes when a harvest "safely gathered in" could be celebrated. The name of the pudding was still plum pudding. Hannah Glasse in 1747 had given a recipe for Christmas plum porridge but, Eliza Acton in 1845 was still referring to plum pudding which she said should be sent "quickly to table with Devonshire Cream or melted apricot marmalade for sauce". The meat content was now "half a pound of the nicest beef-kidney suet" and the fruit was raisins and currants. She baked her pudding in a moderate oven but by 1861 Isabella Beeton was boiling her Christmas plum-puddings in elaborate moulds. She reported that it was "seasonable on the 25th December and on various festive occasions till March". Her pudding for adults included brandy. Her "plain Christmas pudding for children" was moistened with milk and included flour and all-spice as well as suet and breadcrumbs. A lot of hard work went into making these puddings because the fruit had to be stoned, washed and dried and picked clean of grit, the suet scraped from the kidneys, cut and shredded and the lemons grated. The pudding could be boiled in a basin or mould or placed in a cloth made watertight by wetting and buttering it and thickly dredging it with flour. The pudding was then drawn up into a bundle and boiled in a huge copper. The cloths had often served for the family wash producing a smell vividly recalled in *A Christmas Carol*.

"Helloa! A great deal of steam! The pudding was out of the copper. A smell like washing day! That was the cloth. A smell like an eating house and a pastry cook's next door to each other, with a laundress's next door to that! That was the pudding! In half-a-minute Mrs. Cratchit entered - flushed but smiling proudly - with the pudding like a speckled cannon-ball, so hard and firm, blazing in half of half-a-quartern of ignited brandy and bedight with Christmas holly stuck on the top."

The rapture with which the pudding was greeted - Bob Cratchit said that "he regarded it as the greatest success achieved by Mrs. Cratchit since their marriage" - was in contrast to Scrooge's own view that "every idiot who goes about with "Merry Christmas" on his lips should be boiled with his own pudding, and buried with a stick of holly through his heart".

The round pudding has been revived during the 1980s. The National Trust and Fortnum and Mason's have sold round Christmas puddings, and a round china mould which splits into two halves is on sale. Most people however steam the pudding in a basin or buy it ready-made in a foil container. Mrs. Beeton recommended boiling the pudding for six to eight hours and two on the day. An elderly cook who lay on her death bed having served the family loyally for fifty years, was implored by the elderly Earl to reveal the secret of her splendid Christmas puddings. She raised her head slowly. "Boil for a week, my Lord", she said - and expired.

Christmas puddings are traditionally made with thirteen ingredients for Christ and the twelve apostles. But there is variety in what could make up the thirteen. One list might be flour, breadcrumbs, spices, suet, eggs, fruit, apples, almonds, candied peel, brandy, sugar, juices of lemon or orange and treacle, but others might count the dried fruit as three (raisins, currants, sultanas) and leave out the eggs but add carrot. The permutations are endless and peculiar to individual families.

Traditionally puddings should be made on the Sunday nearest to St. Andrew's Day (November 30), the 25th after Trinity known as Stir Up Sunday after the Collect (prayer) for the day, "Stir up, we beseech thee, O Lord, the wills of thy faithful people; that they, plenteously bringing forth the fruit of good works, may be of thee plenteously rewarded". Mrs. Beeton recommends making them "a few days before they are required for table". Pip, however, in *Great Expectations* stirred the pudding on Christmas Eve "with a copper stick from seven to eight by the Dutch clock". In more organised households every member of the family should have had a turn at stirring all in an anti-clockwise direction or east to west in honour of the Three Kings, with a wooden spoon which represented the manger. On a ship or in a regiment the first stir is made by the Senior Officer. Some households allowed three stirs to each person, who made three wishes, three being a symbolic number. Large families made thirteen puddings but the thirteenth was given to a tramp or left to moulder as a memento of the apostle, Judas. It might however be difficult to make such a pudding moulder unless it was left unsteamed, for puddings can be kept from one year to the next and often improve with age.

The brandy poured over and lit to form a halo of flames represents Christ's passion. The sprig of holly stuck on top represents the Crown of Thorns and is a protection against evil. James Joyce saw the pudding as a nationalist symbol. The Daedalus family (*Portrait of the Artist as a Young Man*) brought in the pudding, studded with peeled almonds and sprigs of holly with a bluish flame alight around it and a little green flag flying from the top.

Silver charms were originally added by the Victorians. They might be handed down through the family and new ones have been on sale in recent years. The silver sixpences and threepenny pieces of pre-1971 decimal coinage were popular although they could be regarded as a great hazard for they were easily swallowed. Paddington Bear seems to have suffered the fate of many children, being turned upside down and thumped when it was feared he might have swallowed a silver sixpence. (Michael Bond, *More About Paddington*). The threepenny piece meant wealth, a ring indicated marriage within twelve months, a thimble indicated spinsterhood and a button ordained a bachelor. In the Victorian gold fields in the nineteenth century the demolishing of the pudding was carried out with great alacrity because gold nuggets replaced, or were added to, the silver charms.

Plum pudding or Christmas pudding belongs entirely to Britain although the desire for it is carried to other parts of the world by expatriates. It can be eaten at any time of the year although it never tastes the same as when eaten at Christmas Day even in the heat of an Australian summer. It can be accompanied by white sauce, lemon sauce or hard brandy sauce or butter. It was not a traditional Christmas food but as it was served to celebrate the birth of a baby it is easy to see how it became associated with Christmas. Any pudding left over can be finished on Boxing Day possibly by heating pieces under the grill, topped with butter and sugar so that a bubbling sauce forms. It can be eaten cold for breakfast or tea accompanied by cheese. Until the period after the Second World War the traditional accompaniment to the pudding was Guard Sauce, a hard brandy butter sauce, spiked with bitter almonds. A recipe in a 1945 cookery book gives 2 oz of butter, 1 oz castor sugar, 16 bitter almonds and half a wine glass of brandy.

Vegetarian Christmas puddings, without the suet or with margarine substituted for suet are now a popular selling line. Something akin to a vegetarian plum pudding had to be devised during the Second World War, when the mixture consisted of grated carrots, apples, a little fruit and breadcrumbs. Gravy browning gave a dash of colour, and milk took the place of spirits. The liquid added is a matter of taste - rum, sherry, brandy can be added while some people remain devoted to Guinness or stout. One of the strangest puddings was that served at St. Bartholomew's Hospital during the War when the recipe asked for three bottles of lemon Kia-ora and three bottles of orange Kia-ora. A French recipe served in 1960 added half a pint of rum and a bottle of stout. The recipe also asked for 18oz suet which produced a very heavy pudding.

For those who dislike Christmas pudding or find it too heavy, recipes for an icecream pudding have been devised and these are also on sale. Other people may feel sympathy with Alice in *Through the Looking Glass* when they have to face Christmas pudding yet again. Alice was introduced to a large plum pudding by the Red Queen, "Pudding - Alice", "Alice - Pudding", who then ordered its removal. Somewhat annoyed Alice ordered the waiter to bring back the pudding and cut a slice to offer it to the Queen "What impertinence", said the pudding, "I wonder how you'd like it if I were to cut a slice out of you, you creature", Alice was so startled that she could only gasp. "Make a remark", said the Red Queen, "it's ridiculous to leave all the conversation to the pudding".

On the literary side the pudding features in one of the most famous of all poems relating to Christmas of which people can quote only the first line, 'It is Christmas Day in the Workhouse'. In the second verse we are told that the guardians and their ladies:

> 'Have come in their furs and wrappers,
> To watch their charges feast.
> To smile and be condescending,
> Put pudding on pauper plates,
> To be hosts at the workhouse banquet
> They've paid for with their rates.'

Surprisingly plum pudding does not appear frequently in nursery rhymes although plum cake does (the lion and the unicorn were given it 'to drum them out of town' and Jack -a- Dandy loved it). James Orchard Halliwell in his *Nursery Rhymes of England* (1842) presents the following riddle:

> Flour of England, Fruit of Spain,
> Met together in a sea of rain.
> Put me in a bag tied round with string
> If you'll tell me this riddle, I'll give you a ring.

To which the answer is 'Plum pudding'.

In David Copperfield (1850) Mrs. Micawber draws attention to one of the most well-known nursery rhymes when she says, 'I know less about his life than I do of the Man in the Moon connected with whose mouth the thoughtless children repeat an idle tale respecting cold plum porridge, The Man in the Moon 'who came down too soon and asked the way to Norwich' was known from the 17th century. It is extremely unlikely that he burnt his mouth with cold plum porridge, which appears to be a latter addition. Another version, however, known as early as 1784, says that he burnt his mouth with supping hot pease pottage. This makes more sense and seems to indicate that pease pottage (medieval) can become confused with plum pottage (16th-17th century) and plum porridge (vis Mrs. Micawber) evolving into plum pudding.

Perhaps the pudding has never been so appreciated as in the trenches, in 1914, during the first Christmas of the First World War. Plum pudding or plum duff made a welcome addition to a monotonous diet of corned beef (bully beef), Maconochie's stew (meat, potatoes and beans), biscuits and tinned jam. Food parcels were sent from England or packed into the kit of soldiers returning from leave. Lady Rawlinson, wife of Lieutenant General Sir Henry Rawlinson, Commander of the IV Corps, gave a Christmas card and a pudding to every man of her husband's Corps, which included men of the Royal Scots, the Scots Guards, the Gordon Highlanders and the Wiltshire, Devonshire and Bedfordshire Regiments. Few Christmas dinners on the Western Front were without plum pudding, some set alight with legally obtained or scrounged brandy. The Honourable Artillery Company, as reported in the *Evening News*, 4th January 1915, followed Christmas pudding, flamed with brandy, with a savoury of bread and butter covered with bloater paste or paté de foie gras, depending on taste. Some Christmas puddings were even exchanged for sausages, sauerkraut, and chocolate with German troops during that extraordinary 1914 Christmas truce. Meanwhile, in Sandringham, as reported in the *Daily Sketch*, their Sovereign, King George V, and the Royal Family were dining in traditional fashion on turkey, goose, a baron of beef, venison from Sandringham Park, cygnet from the Thames, boar's head, and a flamed plum pudding, which was served by the King.

Christmas Cakes

Every country seems to have some form of biscuit or cake which is made only during the festive season. In England it is a Christmas cake, a round or square, dense, rich cake full of fruit, covered with marzipan and coated with icing. In the north it is eaten with cheese and or slices of apple which alleviate the cloying taste. Christmas cake is a rich variation of plum cake, a fruit cake which had become popular during the seventeen century, having huge amounts of dried fruit in it. The popularity of prunes (dried plums) eventually gave place to other dried fruit but the name continued to be attached to plum cake. At first ale yeast was used to make the cakes rise as the mixture was placed merely in a mound in the oven. By the end of the 17th century a tin hoop had been invented to hold the cake in shape and this was particularly useful in the next century when eggs became the raising agent. *A New System Of Domestic Cooker* "by a lady" (Mrs. Rundall) (1811) recommends twelve eggs and half a pint of good yeast to make the cake rise. (The eggs however would be very small ones so that a modern equivalent would be three or four good sized ones.)

In England a tradition seems to have developed of giving small plum cakes to each member of the family on Christmas Eve. These might contain caraway seeds but these were dropped from the recipe in the 18th century. Plum cakes could be also presented to Royal personages. The records of Guildford show that a large plum cake was presented to the Duke of York, later James II, when he visited the town in 1674. That tradition was revived in 1957 when Queen Elizabeth II and the Duke of Edinburgh visited the city. In England and France a large cake was baked before or at Epiphany to commemorate the Three Magi. This was the King's Cake and into it was dropped a bean and a pea. When the cake was divided into slices whoever had the bean became king and the person with the pea became queen be they man or woman. In Denmark a somewhat similar custom holds when the traditional Christmas Eve dinner begins with a rice pudding flavoured with vanilla and sherry, mixed with cream and served cold covered with cherry sauce or cherry heering. Into the pudding has been placed one almond. Whoever has it wins a prize. In England a large cake, possibly a gingerbread, was traditionally cut on Twelfth Night. That custom which is said to have been known in the 14th century has now died out and it is the fruit cake which is now associated with Christmas but in Spain epiphany cakes are sold before the traditional procession of the Three Kings on 6th January. *Roscones de reyes*, large bun rings decorated with chopped nuts, glacé cherries and angelica, are baked, each containing a *sorpresa* of a ceramic or plastic trinket. These trinkets were originally of gold and silver and the buns are traditional fare on the morning of Twelfth Night. One place in Britain does keep the tradition still. The Baddeley Cake is still cut on Twelfth Night at the Theatre Royal, Drury Lane. Robert Baddeley, an actor who had originally been a pastry cook, left £100 in his will in 1794 to be invested in 3% funds so that the interest could be used to buy ingredients for a cake to be baked and divided amongst actors who would be playing in the theatre at Christmas time, "so their merrimaking should prevail." The celebrated Lilian Baylis inaugurated a similar custom in the 1920s at the Old Vic Theatre which she ran as her private domain. When the ballet and the opera divided for the Shakespearian and other drama productions, the cake was cut on alternate years at the Old Vic and Sadlers' Wells Theatres. Because of changes in ownership the custom has fallen into abeyance.

Another type of fruit cake is the Scottish Black Bun, a very rich, dense, spicy fruit cake mixed with whisky and wrapped round with an enriched bread paste. This also contained caraway seed. It is eaten not at Christmas but at Hogmanay. A Danish Christmas cake is a much lighter version than the English one for it uses fresh pineapple amongst its ingredients to make a very moist cake. Another alternative is a 'white' Christmas cake made with candied fruits including pineapple, cherries and angelica.

Stollen (Weihnachtstollen)

In Central Europe a rich yeast fruit bread is said to have been baked as early as the 14th century in an oval shape, covered with icing sugar, to represent the babe wrapped in swaddling clothes. In 1329 Bishop Henry of Nuremburg granted the Bakers' Guild in that city new privileges on condition that the bakers provided him and his successors with two "*Stollen* each, made out of half a bushel of wheat" every Christmas. Another tradition says that the *Stollen* is of Saxon origin and that its oval shape represents the crib of Jesus. In Saxony it is known that in 1672 the Brotherhood of the Bakers' journeymen petitioned the Elector of Saxony to grant them the privilege of an annual procession at Christmas. This was agreed on condition that three *Stollen*, each three yards long, should be carried annually by six journeymen to the castle to be presented to the Elector. This took place until 1827 when the Brotherhood was dissolved. The Bakers' Guild then continued the custom until 1915. There are several varieties of *Stollen*. Polish *Stollen* has marzipan in the middle of it. Dresden *Stollen* contains rum. Viennese *Stollen*, as made to the recipe of the Imperial Master Baker, was sprinkled with icing sugar. Traditionally it is of elliptical shape six inches long and about four inches wide pinned down in the centre to form two thick lips. One part is brushed with melted butter then one lip is folded over the other. *Stollen* has now become popular in England being both imported and made by local bakers.

Other Breads and Gingerbreads

A much lighter form of bread is the Italian *panettone*, a raised fruit bread glazed with sugar, eggs and dotted with almonds. Another version flavoured with rum has candied fruits and raisins. The Danish spiced fruit loaf, *Julekage*, is heavier and more like a *Stollen*. The Hungarian *beigli* is a bread-cake with a rich poppy-seed or walnut filling. In Switzerland, a yeast dough provides a version of a Twelfth Night cake. A rounded shape is surrounded by five or six smaller balls, one of which contains a small china figure.. and the finder becomes king. The top of the cake is sprinkled with nibbed almonds and sugar. In France *galette* is served on January 6th. This puff pastry with a ground almond and egg filling has hidden in it a small 'favour' or lucky charm. In 1989, the Bicentenary year of the Revolution, these took the form of small figures dressed in revolutionary dress. Whoever finds the charm wears a golden crown; in the shops a crown is sold with every galette. The Christmas bread plait (*vanochka*) made in Czechoslovakia consists of plaits of four, three and two strands placed one on top of each other. The Swedes bake a *Julhög* or yule pile. This can be a mixture of different breads - rye, wheat, saffron buns topped by a heart shaped biscuit and an apple. Older people may bake a showbread, a huge, round loaf glazed and decorated with dough figures. This was displayed during the twelve days, then crumbled to spread over the land thus ensuring its fertility. Sweden also prepares brandy-flavoured ribbons of dough fried in boiling fat. In France, *pain d'épice* is a tradition as is *bûche de Noël* adapted by Britain as chocolate log or Yule log, a Swiss roll filled with coffee or chocolate buttercream and covered with chocolate fondant icing. A Father Christmas, a robin or a seasonal greeting created from marzipan may be placed on the top.

Various types of gingerbread and honey-cakes are baked throughout Europe. St. Nicholas gingerbread biscuits are presented to good children in Holland on 6th December. Dutch housewives also bake *kerstkransjes*, biscuits with holes in them so that they can be threaded with ribbons and hung on the Christmas tree. Danish housewives bake gingerbread men on Christmas Eve, while Swedish homes have spiced biscuits: *brune kager* and *jodekager*.

In Central Europe a large variety of ginger and spiced cakes are baked. These are a mixture of honey, wheat and rye flours and spices(cinnamon, cardamon, nutmeg, ginger, cloves), cut into various shapes and decorated with Christmas motifs - *Lebkuchen*, *Pfefferkuchen*, *Honigkuchen* and *Aniskuchen*. These types of cakes are also the main ingredients of the fantastic gingerbread houses (*Lebkuchen Häuschen*) which, once devised entirely at home or in the baker's shop, are now provided in do-it-yourself kits.

An old tradition associated with cakes, biscuits and bread baked on Christmas Eve or Christmas Day is that they would never go mouldy. They could be left until they dried then ground up and mixed with water to alleviate sickness.

Marzipan

Although marzipan figures are often associated with Christmas the name comes from the Arab word *mauthaban*, a small box made of wood shavings in which small silver coins were kept. In the 13th century these boxes were used as containers for sweetmeats of almond and rosewater. In time the name was transferred to these sweetmeats. As a food the name may be older originating in North Mesopotamia. The product was known in Europe in the 15th century; in France it was *marce pain*, in Germany, Marzipan. In Italy it was used to make figures of men and animals often having an allegorical meaning. The idea came into England where the figures were known as 'subtleties'. In the Tudor period these had fallen out of favour but a very popular table decoration was a centrepiece called a marchpane, often formed into a hoop and decorated with sugar and rosewater and gilded with gold leaf. A marchpane was thus an object to be employed and eaten in its own right. Not until the 18th century did it become the traditional layer on top of a plum cake providing a base for a sugar icing. Formerly icing had been placed directly on to the cake itself before baking in the oven.

The tradition of a marchpane seems to have continued elsewhere. In Holland, the Christmas wreath (*kerstkrans*) is made. The almond paste is rolled into a rope and covered with puff pastry. This is then formed into a ring with cherries placed in a deep cut. The ring is brushed with apricot purée and water icing and may be decorated with candied fruits.

Its final decoration is a candle and a five pointed star.

The Germans continue the tradition of brightly tinted marzipan moulded into the shape of fruits and figures, which are often used as Christmas tree decorations. Prince Albert seems to have brought this tradition with him from Germany. A description in the *Illustrated London News* in 1848 of the Christmas tree at Windsor says, "Pendant from the branches are elegant trays, baskets, bonbonniéres and other receptacles for sweetmeats... fancy cakes, gilt gingerbread and eggs filled with sweetmeats are also suspended by variously coloured ribbons from the branches."

Marzipan figures – *figuritas de mazapán* – are also made in Spain. Toledo specialises in Christmas eels. Coils of burnt almond paste with eyes of glacé cherries or pieces of angelica lie curled in round boxes with crystallised fruit filling the spaces between the coils.

Christmas Drinks

Wassailing

Christmas is synonymous with good cheer and plenty to drink. Sales from supermarkets, wine merchants and off-licences boom in the week before Christmas, but few people now make a traditional Wassailing drink. The term: Was Hal, Waes Heil (Good Health or Be Healthy) is an Anglo Saxon one which was linked with the empty begging bowl and the expectation that it would be filled at Christmas. The usual drink was 'lambswool' which was - and is, for the drink has been revived in the West Country - a mixture of hot ale, spices, sugar, breadcrumbs and roasted apples into which beaten eggs and cream can be stirred. In the Shetlands a similar drink called Whipcoll consists of egg yolks beaten with sugar, cream and brandy. However this is more like the pick-me-up which is drunk by older people as a tonic. It was the addition of the ale, spices and apples which gave the distinctive flavour to the wassail-bowl. The American egg nog, at first made with spiced wine and creamy milk, then with the addition of spirits and beaten eggs (12 eggs to one pint of brandy, a quart of cream with spices and sugar), may be something similar. The eggs however, may be split so that yolks and beaten-up whites are added separately.

In the Dingley Dell Christmas festivities at Mr. Wardle's house in Pickwick Papers the company drank "from a mighty bowl of Wassail, something smaller than an ordinary wash house copper, in which the hot apples were hissing and bubbling with a rich look and a jolly sound that was perfectly irresistible." The silver gilt bowl owned by Jesus College, Oxford, and reputed to be a wassail bowl, is actually a punch bowl given to the college by Sir Watkin Williams Wynne in 1726. It is not used at Christmas but on St. David's Day each year for the imbibing of the 'College Swig' by members of the Graduate Common Room.

A wassail bowl was carried through a town or district at Christmas for the singing of a song. Each area had its own words. Wassailers from Harrington (Worcestershire) sang:

> "Wassail, wassail through the town,
> If you've got apples throw them down
> Up with the stocking and down with the shoe
> If you've got no apples money will do".

From these songs eventually derived the Wassail carol. Again there are several varieties of which the best known is the one from Yorkshire:

> "Here we come a-wassailing
> Amongst the leaves so green
> Here we come a-wassailing
> So fair to be seen
> Love and Joy come to you
> And to you your wassail too
> And Gold bless you and send you
> A happy New Year
> God send you a happy New Year"

The accent in the carol is good wishes to the recipient but there is also a demand element. One verse orders a table to be brought out and spread with a cloth. In Somerset, as is only to be expected, "a drop or two of cider won't do any harm". Elsewhere bread, beef, ale or beer are requested. The Yorkshire carol says, "Bring us out a mouldy cheese and some of your Christmas loaf". At Grampound in Cornwall a piece of silver was demanded "in token of your love".

As an alternative the full bowl might be taken round and householders requested to drink from it, or it could be presented empty to be filled with what the household would give so that a heady mixture might be the result.

The reference in the Worcestershire song of throwing down the apples refers to the West Country custom of wassailing the apple trees. This took place during the Twelve Days, either on New Year's Eve or on Twelfth Night. Some areas have kept up this custom, in particular the cider-apple growing areas in Somerset and Devon. At Carhampton in Somerset the custom is observed on the 17th January, the eve of the Twelfth Night before the calender was changed. The police are warned what will happen as the ceremony takes place after dark. A cake soaked in cider is put at the foot of the chosen tree. Cider is poured round the tree or the branches pulled down and then dipped in a pail of wassail. Cake may be tossed into the branches. Toasts are made to the tree, horns are blown and shotguns fired. This form of merrymaking comes from the oldest of origins, that of driving away evil spirits and waking the spirit of the tree into life for a new year. Trees are living entities and need to be treated with respect. It is possible that the wassailing customs replaced a human sacrifice.

Other trees could also be wassailed as indicated by Robert Herrick:

> "Wassail the trees that they may bear
> You many a plum and many a pear
> For more or less fruits will they bring,
> As you do give them wassailing."

The ceremony or a variant of it is probably older than the Anglo Saxon period. The presentation of food and drink to the tree recalls the presents given to inanimate objects by the Celts, a practice which was condemned by the early Fathers of the Church but which survives in such customs as tying rags to bushes to request a favour and depositing coins in water.

Punch

A drink which has become associated with Christmas but which has its origins in a far warmer climate is Punch. The name is said to derive from the Hindu word, panch, a reference to the five ingredients - wine or spirits, spices, sugar, lemon juice and hot water. Christmas is the excuse to stir together the most lethal mixtures but the best punch is created from a harmonious proportion of ingredients. In Scandinavia *glögg* can be a mixture of red and white wine, bitters, spices (especially cloves and cardamom), and acquavit; at the last moment almonds are stirred in.

After Mr. Pickwick's disaster on the ice, a bowl of punch was produced and a great carousal was held in honour of his safe escape. Magdalen College, Oxford, owns a Founders' Cup which was filled with hot punch after the Christmas service. The President drank first then passed it round for the Fellows' participation. At one time the supper on Christmas Eve began with a first course of frumenty. This dish of hulled corn boiled in milk seems originally to have been regarded as a fasting dish. Later yolks of eggs, mace and dried plums were added making it into a liquid version of plum pudding.

Snapdragon

Although not a drink this game of snapdragon includes brandy poured over a shallow dish filled with dried raisins. This is ignited and then each person had to snatch a raisin without being burned. Lights were extinguished so that blue flames could be seen at their best.

Mulled Ale

Mulled ale or mulled wine heated with spices, especially cinnamon and cloves, is very popular. The liquid may be heated in a saucepan but the more adventurous can heat a poker to red heat then thrust it into the liquid so that it writhes and sizzles.

Vegetarian Christmas

Most Christmas fare relies on animal products - the suet in mincemeat and Christmas pudding, gelatin in jellies and mousses and the traditional dinner of poultry with sausage-meat stuffing. An increasing dislike or wariness of eating meat has resulted in the popularity of providing vegetarian or vegan meals at Christmas. Traditional Christmas foods are therefore replaced or adapted in order to provide festive menus. The Vegetarian Society and the Vegan Magazine have offered suggestions of a savoury nut or chestnut roast as the centrepiece for a Christmas meal preceded by avocado and tofu paté. Mushroom and stilton or vegetable pie baked in wholemeal pastry replaces the traditional meat pie. Vegetarian mincemeat made without suet is used in mincepies and fruit salad or sorbet replaces the traditional pudding.

Icecreams made from soya milk and tofu, flavoured with natural ingredients, are provided by Berrydale Ices. As these are lactose-free they are suitable for anyone who has an allergy towards milk products or wants an easily digestible, low cholesterol diet. Christmas eating may be said to have moved into a healthy eating stage, and indeed, whether it be a vegetarian or meat-eating Christmas let Goodwill prevail so that "A Merry Christmas and a Happy New Year" continue to be the traditional greeting for the next 2000 years.

Since writing this paper I have been in communication with the Archivist of St. John's College, Cambridge, who has thrown a different light, in a manner of speaking, on the oft-repeated story of the St. John's College candle, which is said to have burned during Christmas. The Archivist informs me that it was a brazier which was left burning in the hall during Christmas time from about the 16th Century until c.1865, when gas was installed. After that it became customary to leave a few gas jets burning in the hall until midnight from St. John's day (27th December) until Twelfth Night. This custom ended in the 1890s.

Recipes

Mrs. Rundell - 1811

Plum Cakes.

Mix thoroughly a quarter of a peck of fine flour, well dried, with a pound of dry and sifted loaf-sugar, three pounds of currants washed and very dry, half a pound of raisins stoned and chopped, a quarter of an ounce of mace and cloves, twenty Jamaica peppers, a grated nutmeg, the peel of a lemon cut as fine as possible, and half a pound of almonds blanched and beaten with orange-flower water. Melt two pounds of butter in a pint and a quarter of cream, but not hot; put to it a pint of sweet wine, a glass of brandy, the whites and yolks of twelve eggs beaten apart, and half a pint of good yeast. Strain this liquid by degrees into the dry ingredients, beating them together a full hour, then butter the hoop, or pan, and bake it. As you put the batter into the hoop, or pan, throw in plenty of citron, lemon, and orange-candy.

If you ice the cake, take half a pound of double-refined sugar sifted, and put a little with the white of an egg, beat it well, and by degrees pour in the remainder. It must be whisked near an hour, with the addition of a little orange-flower water, but mind not to put much. When the cake is done, pour the iceing over, and return it to the oven for fifteen minutes; but if the oven be warm, keep it near the mouth, and the door open, lest the colour be spoiled.

Another.—Flour dried, and currants washed and picked, four pounds; sugar pounded and sifted, one pound and a half; six orange, lemon, and citron peels, cut in slices; mix these.

Beat ten eggs, yolks and whites separately; then melt a pound and a half of butter in a pint of cream; when lukewarm, put it to half a pint of ale-yeast, near half a pint of sweet wine, and the eggs; then strain the liquid to the dry ingredients, beat them well, and add of cloves, mace, cinnamon, and nutmeg, half an ounce each. Butter the pan, and put it into a quick oven. Three hours will bake it.

Very good common Plum Cakes.

Mix five ounces of butter in three pounds of dry flour, and five ounces of fine Lisbon sugar; add six ounces of currants, washed and dried, and some pimento, finely powdered. Put three spoonfuls of yeast into a Winchester pint of new milk warmed, and mix into a light dough with the above. Make it into twelve cakes, and bake on a floured tin half an hour.

Little Plum Cakes to keep long.

Dry one pound of flour, and mix with six ounces of finely-pounded sugar; beat six ounces of butter to a cream, and add to three eggs, well beaten, half a pound of currants washed, and nicely dried, and the flour and sugar; beat all for some time, then dredge flour on tin plates, and drop the batter on them the size of a walnut. If properly mixed, it will be a stiff paste. Bake in a brisk oven.

Eliza Acton - 1845

MINCEMEAT.

(Author's Receipt.)

To one pound of an unsalted ox-tongue, boiled tender and cut free from the rind, add two pounds of fine stoned raisins, two of beef kidney-suet, two pounds and a half of currants well cleaned and dried, two of good apples, two and a half of fine Lisbon sugar, from half to a whole pound of candied peel according to the taste, the grated rinds of two large lemons, and two more boiled quite tender, and chopped up entirely, with the exception of the pips, two small nutmegs, half an ounce of salt, a large teaspoonful of pounded mace, rather more of ginger in powder, half a pint of brandy, and as much good sherry or Madeira. Mince these ingredients separately, and mix the others all *well* before the brandy and the wine are added; press the whole into a jar or jars, and keep it closely covered. It should be stored for a few days before it is used, and will remain good for many weeks. Some persons like a slight flavouring of cloves in addition to the other spices; others add the juice of two or three lemons, and a larger quantity of brandy. The inside of a tender and well-roasted sirloin of beef will answer quite as well as the tongue.

Of a fresh-boiled ox-tongue, or inside of roasted sirloin, 1 lb.; stoned raisins and minced apples, each 2 lbs.; currants and fine Lisbon sugar, each 2½ lbs.; candied orange, lemon or citron rind, 8 to 16 oz.; boiled lemons, 2 large; rinds of two others, grated; salt, ½ oz.; nutmegs, 2 small; pounded mace, 1 large teaspoonful, and rather more of ginger; good sherry or Madeira, ½ pint; brandy, ½ pint.

Obs.—The lemons will be sufficiently boiled in from one hour to one and a quarter.

SUPERLATIVE MINCEMEAT.

Take four large lemons, with their weight of golden pippins pared and cored, of jar-raisins, currants, candied citron and orange-rind, and the finest suet, and a fourth part more of pounded sugar. Boil the lemons tender, chop them small, but be careful first to extract all the pips; add them to the other ingredients, after all have been prepared with great nicety, and mix the whole *well* with from three to four glasses of good brandy. Apportion salt and spice by the preceding receipt. We think that the weight of one lemon, in meat, improves this mixture; or, in lieu of it, a small quantity of crushed macaroons added just before it is baked.

MINCE PIES. (ENTREMETS.)

Butter some tin pattypans well, and line them evenly with fine puff paste rolled thin; fill them with mincemeat, moisten the edges of the covers, which should be nearly a quarter of an inch thick, close the pies carefully, trim off the superfluous paste, make a small aperture in the centre of the crust with a fork or the point of a knife, ice the pies or not, at pleasure, and bake them half an hour in a well-heated but not fierce oven: lay a paper over them when they are partially done, should they appear likely to take too much colour.

½ hour.

MINCE PIES ROYAL. (ENTREMETS.)

Add to half a pound of good mincemeat an ounce and a half of pounded sugar, the grated rind and the strained juice of a large lemon, one ounce of clarified butter, and the yolks of four eggs; beat these well together, and half fill, or rather more, with the mixture, some pattypans lined with fine paste; put them into a moderate oven, and when the insides are just set, ice them thickly with the whites of the eggs beaten to snow, and mixed quickly at the moment with four heaped tablespoonsful of pounded sugar; set them immediately into the oven again, and bake them slowly of a fine light brown.

Mincemeat, ½ lb.; sugar, 1½ oz.; rind and juice, 1 large lemon; butter, 1 oz.; yolks, 4 eggs. Icing: whites, 4 eggs; sugar, 4 tablespoonsful.

Isabelle Beeton - 1861

CHRISTMAS PLUM-PUDDING.
(*Very Good.*)

1328. INGREDIENTS.—1½ lb. of raisins, ½ lb. of currants, ½ lb. of mixed peel, ¾ lb. of bread crumbs, ¾ lb. of suet, 8 eggs, 1 wineglassful of brandy.

Mode.—Stone and cut the raisins in halves, but do not chop them; wash, pick, and dry the currants, and mince the suet finely; cut the candied peel into thin slices, and grate down the bread into fine crumbs. When all these dry ingredients are prepared, mix them well together; then moisten the mixture with the eggs, which should be well beaten, and the brandy; stir well, that everything may be very thoroughly blended, and *press* the pudding into a buttered mould; tie it down tightly with a floured cloth, and boil for 5 or 6 hours. It may be boiled in a cloth without a mould, and will require the same time allowed for cooking. As Christmas puddings are usually made a few days before they are required for table, when the pudding is taken out of the pot, hang it up immediately, and put a plate or saucer underneath to catch the water that may drain from it. The day it is to be eaten, plunge it into boiling water, and keep it boiling for at least 2 hours; then turn it out of the mould, and serve with brandy-sauce. On Christmas-day a sprig of holly is usually placed in the middle of the pudding, and about a wineglassful of brandy poured round it, which, at the moment of serving, is lighted, and the pudding thus brought to table encircled in flame.

CHRISTMAS PLUM-PUDDING IN MOULD

Time.—5 or 6 hours the first time of boiling; 2 hours the day it is to be served.
Average cost, 4s.
Sufficient for a quart mould for 7 or 8 persons.
Seasonable on the 25th of December, and on various festive occasions till March.

A PLAIN CHRISTMAS PUDDING FOR CHILDREN.

1327. INGREDIENTS.—1 lb. of flour, 1 lb. of bread crumbs, ¾ lb. of stoned raisins, ¾ lb. of currants, ¾ lb. of suet, 3 or 4 eggs, milk, 2 oz. of candied peel, 1 teaspoonful of powdered allspice, ½ saltspoonful of salt.

Mode.—Let the suet be finely chopped, the raisins stoned, and the currants well washed, picked, and dried. Mix these with the other dry ingredients, and stir all well together; beat and strain the eggs to the pudding, stir these in, and add just sufficient milk to make it mix properly. Tie it up in a well-floured cloth, put it into boiling water, and boil for at least 5 hours. Serve with a sprig of holly placed in the middle of the pudding, and a little pounded sugar sprinkled over it.

Time.—5 hours. *Average cost*, 1s. 9d.
Sufficient for 9 or 10 children. *Seasonable* at Christmas.

50 years ago...

The Daily Telegraph

November 19, 1938

CHRISTMAS PUDDINGS: RECIPES FROM THE PALACE AND No 10

By Marianne Mayfayre

PREPARATIONS for Christmas pudding making have begun, in the throes of brilliant State entertaining and vital political talks, at the two greatest homes in the land, those of the King and of the Prime Minister.

The King and Queen will keep Christmas with their relatives at Sandringham. The Royal Family tradition of having Christmas puddings that have been made in the Royal kitchens will be observed. Once more the Buckingham Palace kitchens are making ready for the great family festival, under the direction of the King's chef M René Roussin.

There may be a Christmas family party again at Chequers. Tradition will hold sway, except in the choice of the Christmas pudding. Mrs Chamberlain likes to adventure in quest of new recipes, so that there will be the spice of novelty at the Prime Minister's festive table.

The recipe used by the King who taught the English to eat Christmas pudding — Hanoverian George I — will be the basis of the pudding served at the royal table at Sandringham this year, with modern touches to give a lighter texture and richer colour, such as the addition of ground almonds and use of beer.

This is how the Palace puddings will be made:

To each 1¼lb finely shredded suet will be added 1lb breadcrumbs, ¾lb sifted flour, ¾lb ground almonds, 1lb each demerara sugar, stoned raisins, currants and sultanas, 4oz each thinly sliced candied citron, lemon and orange peel, 1 teaspoonful mixed spice, scraping of nutmeg, pinch of salt, 1lb eggs weighed in their shells, ¼ bottle sherry, 1 wine-glass brandy, ¼ pint beer or more if more moisture is needed.

Ingredients will be mixed in the usual way and allowed to stand 12 hours in a cool place to absorb the liquid, then basins are filled and puddings boiled eight hours.

Mrs Chamberlain will be interested in her family's verdict on the recipe she has selected this year for her Christmas puddings. She has never tried it before. Interesting points are the introduction of an orange and use of ginger.

Her cook, Mrs Farrell, will take 2lb each of chopped suet and breadcrumbs, 1lb each of flour, chopped apples, raisins, sultanas and currants, ½lb each of candied peel and chopped almonds, 1lb demerara sugar, the juice and grated rind of one lemon, one orange, 1oz mixed spice, six eggs, ½ pint rum or brandy, 1½ pints of stout, ½oz salt and 2oz ginger.

All ingredients will be mixed thoroughly, left 24 hours and boiled or steamed eight hours, then left to cool. Pudding cloths will then be replaced by fresh ones. When required, each pudding will be steamed another two hours.

Great Grandmother's Christmas Pudding

8 oz/225 g SR flour
4 oz/125 g breadcrumbs
12 oz/350 g chopped suet
8 oz/225 g raisins
8 oz/225 g sultanas
8 oz/225 g currants
4 oz/125 g mixed peel
2 oz/50 g glacé cherries
2 oz/50 g ground almonds
8 oz/225 g demerara sugar
8 oz/225 g chopped hard apple (optional)
2 tbs marmalade
1 tps mixed spice
grated rind and juice of 1 lemon and 1 orange
4 eggs beaten in rum and/or brandy.

Mix all together. Add more spirits to moisten if required.
Steam 8 hours and 2 hours on the day.

Bibliography

Eliza Acton, *Modern Cookery in all its branches*, 1845.
Mary Baker, *Christmas Customs and Folklore*, 1968.
James H. Barnett, *The American Christmas*, 1954.
Isabella Beeton, *The Book of Household Management*, 1861.
Maggie Black, 'The Englishman's Plum Pudding', *History Today*, Dec, 1981.
John H. Bouquet, *Christmas to Candlemas*, 1931.
Margaret Brentnall, *Old Customs and Ceremonies of London*, 1975.
E. K. Chelmers, *The English Folk Play*, 1933.
T. G. Crippen, *Christmas and Christian Lore*, 1923.
Evelyn Dix and Jean Smith, *A Victorian Christmas*, 1989.
Kay Fairfax, *Homemade Christmas*, 1987.
Felicity Gilmour, 'A Mummers' Play from Limpley Stoke', *Wiltshire Archaeological Magazine* (83), 1990.
J. M. Golby and A. W. Purdue, *The Making of the Modern Christmas*, 1986
Miles and John Hadfield, *The Twelve Days of Christmas*, 1961.
Molly Harrison, *The Story of Christmas*, 1951.
E. Hull, *Folklore of the British Isles*, 1928.
Christina Hole, *Christmas and its Customs*, 1957.
Christina Hole, *A Dictionary of English Folk Customs*, 1978.
E. O. James, *Seasonal Feasts and Festivals*, 1961.
A Lady (Mrs. Rundell), *A New System of Domestic Cookery*, 1811.
C. A. Miles, *Christmas in Ritual and Tradition*, 1912.
K. Palmer, *The Folklore of Somerset*, 1976.
J. A. R. Pimlott, *The Englishman's Christmas*, 1978.
R. L. Tongue, *Somerset Folklore*, 1965.
W. Sansom, *Christmas*, 1968.
G. Weightman and S. Humphries, *Christmas Past*, 1987.
L. Whistler, *The English Festivals*, 1947.
R. Whitlock, *The Folklore of Devon*, 1977.

Emma's Wedding Feast
- A Glance at Flaubert's Madame Bovary

by Rose Arnold

Emma's wedding is a very famous literary feast. I have chosen to talk about it because it is so well known, and because it is so attractive – most of us, I think, would like to go out of here into Old Rouault's barn and see such opulence spread before us. Eating, of course, carries enormous weights of social and psychological significance. It is a behaviour with a symbolic as well as a biological function, which "replaces, epitomises or signals other behaviours".[1]

Flaubert's proud boast was that there was not a detail of imagery or description which was not essential to, and integrated in, his art. Now in this novel, which is the story of a marriage, he devotes just seventeen words to the religious and civil wedding ceremonies. Then follow several pages about the wedding breakfast, including more than a hundred words on the wedding-cake – strictly speaking, the *pièce montée*. Clearly, something more important than lip-licking evocation is happening in these pages.

I hope to analyse, a little, the significance of the foods on the table, and the way in which Flaubert presents them to us. First, to set the scene.

Charles Bovary, a young widower with an dreary first experience of marriage is now marrying Emma, the charming, sensual daughter of a Norman peasant. Old Rouault is affluent, because the land is bounteous. He keeps peacocks among his other poultry, and with the same sort of opulence has had his daughter educated into ladylike behaviour and notions which disqualify her for life on the farm. The wedding feast he lays on for her is very different from her romantic desire for marriage "at midnight, by the light of torches" (she has been reading Walter Scott). She is marrying to escape from the coarseness and monotony of life on the farm – Flaubert, to illustrate this, has a beautiful vignette of Emma, crossing the fields from the *mairie* to the farm, behind the ribbon-bedecked fiddler who leads the procession, stopping to remove fastidiously (with gloved hands) the thistles which have snagged in her train. Charles longs for the calm, stability, plenty and tradition which the farm, especially the farm kitchen, has come to represent to him during his courtship of her. She marries him for a dining-room and finger-bowls; he wants the robust simplicity of peasant life: the marriage is, of course, doomed.

Her father, and the custom of the region and her class, dictate the gargantuan feast Flaubert describes in such detail. If Emma's vision, all sensibility and ambience, is drawn from Scott, her father's is the immemorial peasant hankering for the Land of Cockaigne: both ignore the psychic significance of the wedding to the two individuals concerned, since both are in their different ways materialistic. But Emma's ideal – strong on style – lacks substance, whereas the table at the centre of the celebrations, with its lovingly detailed plenty, can stand as a symbol of the centrality of the table, and of the sustenance it bears, to family life. The feast extends the warmth of the summer kitchen, the promise of all that was missing from Bovary's first marriage.

Flaubert's portrayal of the wedding breakfast is in an old tradition of depicting peasant feasts which goes back at least to Breughel, a tradition with bucolic and arcadian versions to suit contemporary fashions, which concentrates upon the amplitude of the provision and the festivity of the guests. Some of you may be familiar with the Breton peasant wedding of 1913 described by Pierre Jakez Hélias in *Le Cheval d'Orgueil (The Pride Horse)*, which has been made into a film:

> "It was a poor people's wedding. There were scarcely more than a hundred and twenty guests ... for two entire days of feasting ... according to custom, the caterer invited the family for the third day, to eat up the leftovers." [2]

Flaubert dismisses in a sentence the civil and religious marriage ceremonies, without any comment or description. Instead, he concentrates upon the procession which troops across the fields in the wake of the fiddler, giving us a comic picture of working-men crammed into grossly uncomfortable, ill-fitting new clothes and young girls terrified of their finery. Charles has been attracted by the solidity and integrity of peasant values, which the *basse-cour* and kitchen at Les Bertaux seem to symbolise:

> "He loved the barn and the stables ... he loved Miss Emma's little clogs on the washed flagstones in the kitchen ..."

But perhaps this life has attractions only for those who observe it from outside. Just as Emma aspires to middle-class status, so the guests at the wedding, and the feast itself, are affected by a desire to ape the world of fashion. The few men who attend wearing the old, dignified *blouses de cérémonie* are relegated to the foot of the table, and there are no women wearing the Cauchoise headdress in which Emma's mother was married a generation earlier.

The part of the feast not ordered from Yvetot demonstrates the simple opulence provided from the farm, and Flaubert lists it with a certain ceremoniousness which the reader feels such a catalogue deserves. The food, then, is simple and ample. Care has been taken to vary the method of preparation of the meat, as well as with its presentation.

The sucking-pig centrepiece is interesting. To kill an animal so young denotes the kind of extravagance appropriate to such a feast, sacrificing as it does enormous potential quantity of meat for delicate quality. This human habit of using culinary extravagance as a mark of extraordinary rejoicing is precisely that used by Lévi-Strauss when he makes his contrast between roast and boiled meat – boiled meat, giving the *bouillon* as well as the *bouilli*, is more economical but, at least according to Lévi-Strauss, dull. Flaubert must have had the same attitude as Lévi-Strauss, for elsewhere in the novel he uses the steam rising from a *bouilli* as a crucial simile for Emma's boredom and the dullness of her life.

I will confess at this point that I have a problem with roast sucking-pigs: they do seem to me to be horribly like roast babies, and I find my gorge rising at the idea of connecting them with a wedding (with its sub-text of subsequent christenings). Grimod de la Reynière, however, was clearly of a different opinion. This is from the *Manuel des Amphitryons* (1808), immediately following the passage which describes regaling two ladies with the two halves of a roast hare's brain:

> "… this pretty little animal makes all the pretty ladies swoon with pleasure as soon as it appears in the midst of them at a feast." [3]

This sumptuous and extravagant centre-piece is surrounded by *andouilles à l'oseille*: evidently specialities of the region, but one whose recipe I have been unable to trace – I am hopeful that somebody here may be able to enlighten us?… Otherwise, we may note the way in which Flaubert emphasises the plenty of the feast: the cream is yellow and solid, in great bowls; every dish, apart from the piglet, is supplied in multiples of 3 or 4; the cider is attempting to escape from the bottles; the wine glasses are full to the brim. There is pork, beef, lamb and chicken, and, as befits a feast of such heroic importance, no space even to mention the vegetables which may be presumed to adorn the dishes – and which are anyway insignificant beside all that meat.

The tradition in which Flaubert created this feast reaches back, as we see in other novels of his, into ancient times. Elsewhere he recreated with relish the strange feasts and festivities of Carthage and Jerusalem, or the lavish spreads laid on in mediæval castles. In fact he delighted in food, as a Norman should. We find him boasting, in a joking list of his personal qualities:

> "One day for a bet I ate XV sirloins," (he wrote the figure as XV – again we see his association of feasting with the past), "and I can still drink a bottle of brandy without any problem." [4]

And there is in the splendour of this lie an archaic, Rabelasian pleasure in quantity as well as quality which is delightful – Flaubert as the infant Gargantua. It is apparent in all sorts of glimpses in the novel that Flaubert's sympathy lies with the social generosity implicit in the provision of ample, simple foods.

- Which brings us to the part of the wedding feast which is very far from simple: the *pièce montée*, which I do find myself still thinking of as the wedding-cake, since it serves that same central purpose on the table. The *pièce montée*, like the appearance of the guests, is another example of comic bourgeoisification at the wedding. A gratuitous offering from an Yvetot *pâtissier* just setting up in business there, it is a tour de force whose bad taste is evident, although to the unsophisticated wedding-guests it is an object of wonder and admiration which "made them cry out". Its comic value repays a little exploration.

First, its provenance. The *pâtissier* has set up business in Yvetot, the local market-town. Yvetot held an important place in Flaubert's private mythology. It was to him the epitome of the small, backward, introverted market-town, light-years behind Rouen, its neighbour, which in itself of course was dreadfully provincial by comparison with Paris. It is worth remembering, too, that in his dictum on the equal presentability of all things as suitable raw material for the novelist, "Yvetot equals Constantinople", Flaubert picked the Norman town as the epitome of mediocrity; the same sort of jibe occurs in *Idées reçues*, his lifelong collection of clichés and misinformation, which includes "See Yvetot and die – See also Naples". Thus the wondrous thing – as they see it – comes from a mediocre source perceived by the wedding-guests as a place of sophistication.

The bottom layer of the cake is Palladian: classical forms against a Wedgewood blue background. Its central tier is

Gothic. Its summit is Pastoral. The colours used on the cake are splendid in their crudity: blue, gold, green, white, orange, brown and (probably) red. There is a general glueiness about its appearance, since it includes angelica, raisins, jam and chocolate. Not all of it is actually edible, since the bottom layer is cardboard and plaster. What there is to eat under the decoration is *gâteau de Savoie*, not, of course, the delicacy of that region, but "a very soft, rich, sticky sponge, reminiscent of lemon curd".[5]

Then there is the symbolism so carefully built into the piece by its architect: a temple with columns and statuettes, a Cupid on a swing. There is here a dim memory of the very different pastoral idylls of Fragonard and Boucher, vulgarised to 'Yvetot' level, but still, a just reminder that weddings are religious ceremonies performed in temples, and that their raison d'être is love.

There is also, of course, a great deal of alcohol at the feast, ranging from the wine, *cidre doux* and eau-de-vie on the table, to the *grogs au kirsch* consumed in the small hours by M. Bovary père. There are no details of conversation beyond a comment on Charles' awkwardness and slowness of wit, and the behaviour of the guests merely outlines a pattern which may be imagined by the reader, ending in the drunken departure of the majority of the guests. And Emma herself? Since she took the prickles out of her dress, she hasn't even been mentioned.

This descriptive passage, as I suggested at the outset, carries far more weight than just its "foodie" value – delightful though that is. The jarring note which is introduced by the wedding cake – its stark contrast with the good food provided by the farm – exemplifies the picture painted in the novel of a society in the process of change: change which Flaubert deplored. Emma's inability to participate in the feast is symptomatic of her dissatisfaction, a dissatisfaction which manifests itself in what amounts to anorexic behaviour. Food, meals, gifts of food, imagery of growth and devouring permeate the whole novel, yet we never see Emma eat – she is always playing with nutshells on the tablecloth, or making compressing breadcrumbs into little cannon-balls. Only once does she stuff her mouth and eat heartily, and that of course is when she takes the arsenic which kills her. To Flaubert, to be able to eat heartily, to feast, to provide, to share, is to be able to live life fully: failure to enjoy the feast is failure to affirm life itself.

Notes

1. Roland Barthes.
2. *Le Cheval d'orgueil* p.41 – P. J. Hélias – Plon, 1975.
3. *Manuel des Amphitryons* p.24 – G. de la Reynière – (1808) – Eds. A. M. Métailié, 1983.
4. Flaubert – Correspondence – Letter to Feydeau dated 21.8.59.
5. *The Constance Spry Cookery Book* – Dent, 1956 / CBC 1967.

From *Madame Bovary*, by Gustave Flaubert (1859), Part 1, ch. 4:

C'était sous le hangar de la charretterie que la table était dressée. Il y avait dessus quatre aloyaux, six fricassées de poulets, du veau à la casserole, trois gigots et, au milieu, un joli cochon de lait rôti, flanqué de quatre andouilles à l'oseille. Aux angles se dressait l'eau de vie dans des carafes. Le cidre doux en bouteilles poussait sa mousse épaisse autour des bouchons, et tous les verres, d'avance, avaient été remplis de vin jusqu'au bord. De grands plats de crème jaune, qui flottaient d'eux-mêmes au moindre choc de la table, présentaient, dessinés sur leurs surface unie, les chiffres des nouveaux époux en arabesques de nonpareille. On avait été chercher un pâtissier à Yvetot, pour les tourtes et les nougats. Comme il débutait dans le pays, il avait soigné les choses; et il apporta, lui-même, au dessert, une pièce montée qui fit pousser des cris. A la base, d'abord, c'était un carré de carton bleu figurant un temple avec des portiques, colonnades et statuettes de stuc tout autour, dans des niches constellées d'étoiles en papier doré; puis se tenait au second étage un donjon en gâteau de Savoie, entouré de menues fortifications en angélique, amandes, raisins secs, quartiers d'oranges; et enfin, sur la plate-forme supérieure, qui était une prairie verte où il y avait des rochers avec des lacs de confitures et des bateaux en écales de noisettes, on voyait un petit Amour, se balançant à une escarpolette de chocolat, dont les deux poteaux étaient terminés par deux boutons de rose naturels, en guise de boules, au sommet.

Jusqu'au soir, on mangea....

[Flaubert is very hard to translate: I have concentrated on meaning rather than style, and some of the humour is lost.]

The table was set up in the cart shed. On it were four sirloins, six chicken fricassées, some casseroled veal, three gigots and, in the centre, a lovely roast sucking-pig, flanked by four *andouilles à l'oseille*. At the corners stood carafes of brandy. Bottles of cider were sending their thick froth up round the corks, and all the glasses had already been filled to the brim with wine. Great dishes of yellow cream, swaying gently at the slightest movement of the table, showed on their smooth surfaces the newly-weds' initials in flourishes of coloured sugar. A *pâtissier* had been brought in from

Yvetot to do the tarts and nougats. Because he was just setting up in business in the area, he had taken care with the things, and he himself contributed to the dessert a *pièce montée* which made people exclaim. Its base, first of all, was a square of blue cardboard representing a temple, with porticoes, colonnades and stucco statues all round in niches sparkling with gold paper stars. A castle keep in Savoy cake stood on the second tier, surrounded by tiny fortifications of angelica, almonds, raisins and orange quarters. Finally, on the top tier, which was a green field with rocks and jam lakes and nutshell boats, could be seen a little Cupid balanced on a chocolate swing whose poles were surmounted by two real rosebuds as finials.

They ate all day ...

Kalach, Kolatch, Kulitch - Challah?

By Josephine Bacon

Despite the fearsome warnings against the adoption of heathen customs which appear throughout the Old Testament, it is obvious that Jews down the ages have copied to a lesser or greater extent, the rituals of other religions and incorporated them into their own. Certainly, idolatrous practices - sacrifices to alien gods, including human sacrifice - were repugnant to the upholders of biblical orthodox Judaism, but it may be surprising to learn that not all the other faiths were reviled. The Bible has nothing but the highest praise for Cyrus and Darius, whose religion, of which little is known, is considered to be monotheistic. Did the Jews adopt certain religious practises from this faith, and from that of the Persian race which again conquered the Holy Land in post-biblical times, the Sassanians, whom the Jews also greatly admired? The Sassanian women are alleged to have taught Jewish women certain customs of dress.

Despite the barriers of the dietary laws, which did much to prevent Jews and non-Jews eating together, the Jews learned many dishes from their neighbours. Thus, it is very possible that cheesecakes entered the Jewish culinary repertoire through the Greeks. *The Deipnosophists*, contains many references to the elaborate cheesecakes which the Greeks served as wedding cakes. Could these be the precursors of the cheesecakes of middle Europe? Boiled chicken with dillweed was a popular Roman dish which was adopted by Jews under the Roman rule of Judæa. Roman breads of many kinds have spread throughout the world. The best known is the "bracellus", shaped to represent the crossed arms of the Roman at prayer. This has become the bretzel or pretzel. The shape is still hung as a sign outside baker's shops in Denmark, much as it must have been in Ancient Rome. Similarly, plaited loaves were baked for festive occasions in Roman times. These became popular for important occasions in many cultures, including Judaism.

In later times, Jews continued to adopt the dishes of the nobility, provided they did not conflict with the Jewish dietary laws, since Jews were forced to consort with the nobility in many parts of the world, due to the calling forced upon them of banker and money-lender. Whether it was in mediaeval times or earlier that the most important non-Jewish contribution to Jewish culinary tradition was adopted is not known. In any event, the plaited or braided loaf known as the *challah* in Hebrew, was adopted by all Jewish communities except those of the East (Babylonia, North Africa and the rest of the Middle East). The special bread, ceremonially blessed and eaten at the first meal of the Sabbath, on Friday evening and on other festivals, replaced the representation of the shew-breads, the 12 breads which constituted the meal-offering and which were laid out as a sacrifice in the Temple. These breads, symbolic of the 12 tribes, were displayed on a magnificent table on a cloth and beneath a canopy. The Bible explains that they were to be made of the finest flour, but they are always described as round, never braided, or even snail-shaped. It is these breads which are copied for consumption on the Sabbath by all the Jewish communities which have not adopted the challah.

To see the extent to which this shape of bread has been adopted by other cultures, it is interesting to compare Savella Stechishin's description of Kalach in *Traditional Ukrainian Cookery* with what Freda Reider *(The Hallah Book)* has to say about the Challah. Stechishin describes the "Kalach or kolach" as " a braided, ring-shaped bread. The name is derived from a Ukrainian word, 'kolo', meaning a circle, which is an old symbol of eternity and general wellbeing. The kalach, like the challah, is a feature of various religious and family rituals. There are numerous methods of ornamenting the kalach, some more elaborate than others".

Reider claims the ancestry of the challah to date back to the shew-bread and even before this to the manna that fell from heaven during the forty years in wandering in the desert. She adds "Jews from central and eastern Europe, known as Ashkenazim, regard challah as an absolute necessity for celebrating the Sabbath. In fact, tradition mandates that if one cannot afford both wine and challah for the Sabbath, the choice must be challah". She describes the origins of the word as referring to "a small portion of prebaked dough that Jews of the Temple period gave as a weekly Sabbath offering to their priests, the Kohanim... When the Temple was destroyed, the bread-offering to the priests ceased. To commemorate the ancient law of setting aside challah, Jews to this day separate a small portion of prebaked dough which they bless and burn... The small piece of separated dough is now called 'challah', which means 'offering', and the sweet white bread itself is now also known as challah". Yet, Reider goes on to admit that "the braided challah, which dates back to the fifteenth century, emerged primarily in the Ashkenazic European communities. This shape was not necessarily Jewish in origin. It is thought to have been modelled after the twisted white breads baked throughout the central Europe and Slavic countries".

In actual fact, the word *challah* is unknown outside the *Ashkenazi* community, and the piece of prebaked dough removed and set aside to be burned as an offering is called the 'terumah' in other Jewish communities.

All this points to the fact that not only the bread itself, but its very name, are derived from eastern European sources, the more so, since as Reider points out, "Very large hallot were often referred to as *koilitchen*". This is nothing more than the Yiddish pronounciation of "Kulitsch".

The kulitsch, which is often stuffed with raisins and glazed with icing sugar, was baked for Christmas in Bohemia, Moravia, parts of Poland, Byelorussia and the Ukraine. The name persists for an Easter bread in Russia itself, but the bread is no longer baked in the traditional shape. On Christmas Eve in the Ukraine at least - and perhaps elsewhere in the Christian orthodox tradition- a kulitsch is placed on the table and candles are lit, making it look even more like a Jewish Sabbath celebration, though in the Christian case, the candles are placed on the bread itself.

In Jewish circles, the bread is plaited for the Sabbath, but formed into the snail shape described by Stechishin for New Year and the other autumn festivals known collectively as the High Holidays. It is usually coated with an egg glaze (a milk glaze would make it *milchig*, i.e. only consumable at meatless meals) and sprinkled with poppy-seeds or sesame seeds. For Purim, raisins are added and hundreds-and-thousands sprinkled on the bread which adhere to the sugar-glaze with which the bread is coated. The same applies for the large marriage challot, which are more elaborately braided than the normal breads. The braids are usually four-ply, incidentally. The only time in the year when challah is not eaten, is when the sabbath falls during Passover, when unleavened bread (matzo) is eaten instead.

The riddle remains: how could such an important traditional ritual item have come from non-Jewish (and almost certainly from heathen) sources? I would be interested to hear any other explanation, but would profer the daring hypotheses that either the challah was originally adopted by the Sadducees, the Jewish nobility who fraternised strongly with the Romans and who eventually came to constitute the priestly class, or that it is the result of the influence of the Judaizing sects, *subbotniki*, or even of the Khazars. It was at the very time that the challah became current in Jewish households that relations between the Jews and their neighbours was closest and most of the Jewish population of Europe was concentrated into the area historically known as "Red Russia", around the River Dnieper. This was also the area in which the Khazars had their kingdom. Could the challah be a legacy of Khazars both for the Jews and their non-Jewish neighbours? Then in the mid-17th century came the massacres orchestrated by Bogdan Chmielnicki, the worst until the pogroms. Jews from the Dnieper region were scattered all over Europe, to Poland, Romania, Hungary, Germany.

Did they take the challah with them?

There are other customs connected with the eating of challah. It is very often dipped in salt. "Chleb-sol" (bread-salt) is the Russian word for hospitality and the two are also inseparably linked in Russian tradition as the two staples of life. Another interesting custom is that some communities do not cut the challah with a knife but only break it, and they throw the pieces at the diners, to remind them that bread does not come from the hand of man but from God.

Another riddle is why the German and Austro-Hungarian Jews refer to the challah as *barches*, a word obviously derived from the Hebrew *berachah*, meaning "blessing".

It remains as a curious fact that the Jewish religion, always so quick to distance itself from other faiths in custom and practice, should have adopted a symbolic food from another culture as part of its most important ritual.

The Black or Hell Banquet

by Prof. Phyllis P. Bober

Annals of inventive gastronomy contain scattered accounts of banquets that read like Hallowe'en horrors, mock or all too real, at which guests are served with every manner of black or even loathsome thing to eat in settings designed to evoke funeral services at the least or afflictions of Hell itself, at worst. It is my task to trace a family-tree, so to speak, the *stemma* of these macabre feasts and to suggest their inspiring model in classical antiquity. A few writers on culinary history have already suggested possible prototypes in ancient literature and practice, but no one to my knowledge has hit upon the actual source.

Most famous – or infamous – among such paradoxical *jeux d'esprit* is the "black" banquet offered up by that "prince of gastronomes" of the *ancien régime*, Grimod de la Reynière. It took place on February 1, 1783, a date made significant in that it ushered in the period of Lent; from the Middle Ages, association of the "Dance of Death" with Carnival offered an appropriate context for the type of repast planned with rather malign humour by the host. It helps to remind ourselves that Grimod was embittered by malformed, webbed fingers he could only use with prosthetic devices as well as by class-conscious distress over his mother having married beneath her into a family whose wealth came from hog-butchery and charcuterie. His were not the imaginings of a cheerful and well-adjusted personality.

As he himself hinted, the invitations – ostensibly to his own obsequies – may have been issued as a test of friendship. The entire affair certainly became one. We learn of it in the *Mémoires* of Bachaumont and alternative sources which have conflated several reports and occasions. Having heard rumours of his death, guests presented themselves before a door hung in mourning to find a bier draped in black in the entrance hall and a footman in *livrée de deuil* who opened the door upon their host at a festive board. This was but climax to two earlier sepulchral banquets, one commemorating a Mlle. Quinault, when those invited were bidden to the interment of a *gueuleton* and arrived to find that each was honoured with his coffin behind him, that funeral tapers were lit in the darkened space in place of candles, and that a funereal chant announced every dish.

The other spells out the depths of his ingenuity and his perverse flaunting of genealogy: once more expectations aroused by invitations so extraordinary that Louis XVI is said to have acquired one to frame. Bordered in black to resemble funeral notices, these were sent to three hundred guests, although only twenty-two were actually to dine: the rest, following normal Renaissance and eighteenth century protocol, were to observe the festivities which began in anything but a festive setting, billed as the funeral and obsequies of M. Balthazar Grimod de la Reynière, Esquire, Advocate to Parliament and drama critic. Arriving at the appointed hour – nine p.m. for supper at ten – guests who passed a first check-point were challenged by a sentry who demanded if they were to be received by M. de la Reynière, "oppressor of the people" (obviously "père") or M. de la Reynière, "defender of the people". Responding appropriately, the diners passed into a guard-room filled with heralds in mediæval garb who conducted them to a second screening by a fearsome apparition in chain mail and concealing helmet. In the next anteroom they faced an interrogator whose report and final receipt of their invitation/passports gave them access to yet another room in which choir-boys burnt funereal incense. Passing into darkness, they finally reached the banquet-hall, eerily lit by candles and antique lamps, to encounter a table set with a catafalque as centrepiece, while each guest had his (or her in two disguised cases) own coffin placed upright behind his chair.

Barbara Wheaton, in her splendid book on *Savouring the Past*, devotes some perceptive paragraphs to Grimod's conceit. She quite rightly interprets his "macabre theatre" as aggression and warped humour, not only because guests on one occasion were held captive until almost dawn, but because a course was entirely of pork dishes while charcuterie was prominently featured in food, cutlery and decorations as travesty of Grimod's less than elite descent from that hog-butcher grandfather. She speculates that Grimod's inventiveness depended in at least several limited respects upon Petronius' *Satyricon*, including Trimalchio's silver skeleton given pride of place at his banquet. Likewise, André Castelot, in his commentary on the dinner of 1783, suggests that inspiration may have come from Herodotos' story of an ancient Egyptian *memento mori* in which a skeleton was paraded among diners to remind them to "eat, drink and be merry, for..." Such small, hinged skeletons in bronze were normal accompaniments at modest Epicurean feasts in Roman days.

Evidently galvanised by Grimod's ingenuity, the nineteenth century novelist, Huysmans, has his hero of *A rebours*, Des Esseintes, host a much more creatively "black" funeral feast for himself at which even the garden lying outside a dining-room draped in black echoed the same mournful colour. Its paths had been gravelled in coal, its little pool edged with basalt and filled with ink, its plantings made dark in cypress and pine. The dining table was decorated with baskets of violets and scabiosa set on its black cloth, while lighting was supplied by chandeliers of votive candles and candelabra putting forth green flames. A hidden orchestra played dirges for guests served by nude negresses, their stockings of silver cloth strewn with teardrops. The food as well was dark and sombre and served on plates bordered in black: turtle soup, black Russian rye bread, black olives, caviar, smoked Frankfurt boudins noirs, poutarges of mullet, coulis of truffles, and sauces for game the colour of liquorice juice and boot-blacking; desserts included chocolate creams, puddings and fruits such as raisins, black cherries and plums; the drinks in dark glasses featured the most deeply coloured wines: Tenedos, Roussillon, or Port; all finished off with coffee, walnut liqueur, *kvass*, porter and stout. Alberto Capatti, in turn, writing of Fillia's Futurist inversion, suggests that his monochrome meal of "white desire" was inspired by the Huysmans passage (*A manger des yeux*, 1987, p. 79, n.8); its colourless food — at least to receptors of hue in the eye — as the offspring of a literary trope.

After considering these relatively modern representatives of the genre, let me emphasise two aspects of a much more venerable history: that there is a long tradition of macabre, black dining in connection with Carnival introducing Lent (and this was the timing of Grimod's exploit on February 1, 1783); and that the grandfather of them all appears to be the "Hell Banquet" of the Roman Emperor Domitian (81-96 A.D.)

I believe that the "mortuary banquets" orchestrated by Grimod de la Reynière in pre-Revolutionary play-acting were not intended as Wheaton suggests to evoke Trimalchio's feast, but to replicate Domitian's malign exploit designed to terrorise alleged senatorial enemies (who ultimately must have been pleased when he suffered *damnatio memoriæ*).

(NOTE: Her refs: G. Desnoiresterres, *Grimod de la R. et son groupe*, Paris, 1877, for the first dinner; Ferdinand Hofer (ed.) *Nouvelle biographie générale*, s.v. "Grimod de la R." for the second.)

But first, some documentation for the practice of offering macabre feasts at Carnival and the onset of Lent: I cite one of the most famous, given by Lorenzo Strozzi at Rome in 1519. It was attended by four cardinals, and guests also included the Venetian envoy, Sanuto, who reports it. Although all the mise-en-scène for a "death banquet" was present (skeletons in the four corners of a black-draped hall, and light from votive tapers set next to each), skulls decorating the table were culinary art and broke open to reveal roast pheasant within, while sausages were contained in the bones of the centrepiece.

During the Italian Renaissance it did not require Carnival to indulge in similar titillating experiences of gastronomy. It is beguiling to read of sixteenth century dining societies in Florence. Artists and other citizens belonged to these mannerist confraternities in which monthly banquets had to be dreamt up by designated "presidents". Vasari tells us of several that make one wish to be like Mark Twain's *Connecticut Yankee at King Arthur's Court*. I, for one, would dearly love to be transported back in time to witness an invention of Andrea del Sarto for the Company of the Cauldron. He presented an octagonal church like the Baptistery, edible in all its parts: mosaic floor of jelly, porphyry-looking columns of sausage with bases and capitals shaped in Parmesan cheese, marzipan tribune, and a central choir-desk of cold veal bearing a pastry choir book with notes formed of peppercorns. The choir was the true chef d'oeuvre: its main body consisting of roasted thrushes, their beaks open as if in song, while two large pigeons served as the basses and six larks as the sopranos, all gowned in surplices of thin pig's caul.

A different Company of the Trowel (which specialised in such culinary architecture) was responsible for yet another of our black banquets, this time reproducing the terrors of Hell itself. This must certainly have gained affective power from processions representing the Triumph of Death at Carnival time; think of one of 1511 praised — again by Vasari — for its maskings designed by Piero di Cosimo. The guests were greeted by Ceres at the threshold of the underworld, the goddess questing after her stolen daughter Proserpina. The guardian dog, Cerberus, made it plain that Proserpina would not be relinquished by his master, but Pluto invited them all inside to his wedding feast. Entering through the gaping mouth of Hades, jaws of a huge serpent, hinged to open and close for each couple in turn, guests found themselves in a circular room gloomily lit by one small candle. A hideous devil with pitchfork showed them to their places at a black-draped table, while their host declaimed that the torments of Hell would be suspended for the time being in honour of his wedding. About the walls of the room were pictured the "holes" of the damned, their varying tortures periodically revealed by "flames" which could be made to flare up beneath them. At one point, when Pluto retired, all light was extinguished as the poor wretches filled the darkness with dreadful "screams". Food was in the guise of the most repulsive creatures — ostensibly serpents, lizards, toads, newts, spiders, frogs, scorpions and the like; inside these deceptive exteriors delicious tidbits lay concealed. Service of such dishes came on a fire-shovel, while wine was poured by a "devil" from an ugly sort of rhyton into drinking cups that were actually glass-melting ladles. Guests being Italians, the wines were choice and described as "most delicious," and skeleton bones replacing fruit at the dessert course, represented the confectioners' art, made of sugar or marzipan. But all of this proved merely a curtain-raiser for a splendid banquet to follow with proper lighting, servants and *trionfi*. Climax of this true *festa* brought a ship full of delicious confections, the crew of which led the company into upper salons to enjoy a comedy called *Filogenia*. Festivities ended at dawn as all returned to their homes "lightheartedly".

These examples are sufficient to show the long life of the funereal or Hell banquet in various "black" manifestations. As already noted, ancestor of them all – despite the fact that certain feasts feed off one another – appears to be the terrifying Hell banquet of Domitian. His guests were commanded to attend without their usual attendants. A stele beside each recliner bore his name as if it were a grave stone. The lamps were of a votive type hung in tombs and all the black food set out on black dishes resembled viands sacrificed at funerals to the *manes* of the departed. Slave boys who served and danced were painted black, while the Emperor discussed topics related only to death. No one else seems to have spoken; according to our source, there reigned a silence bidden by fear. Even more fear shook the guests when they were imperiously dismissed with strange slaves to escort them home in the absence of their own. Each expected to become one more victim of Domitian's murderous rule, but trembling turned to relief at being invited back to a magnificent feast at which the servitors (now cleaned of their black paint) enacted one's personal *genius* and the stelæ were now honorifics of silver. At the end, all received costly gifts of the vessels used at this compensating dinner.

Perhaps Domitian's frightening joke, recounted by Dio Cassius, has its own ancestry in some Hellenistic production. I would be very grateful for any reference that would extend this sketch of a venerable conceit.

The Bayeux Tapestry Shish Kebab Mystery

by Robert Chenciner

Rather like the Turin Shroud, the Bayeux Tapestry has enjoyed an almost religious veneration since it was first displayed in the library in Bayeux in 1842, freshly relined and restored. Having long put off the pilgrimage, which is an essential part of the itinerant vocabulary of every student of textiles, my visit to Bayeux took place last December in 1989. The Bayeux Tapestry - in fact, as is well known, it is a wool embroidery on fine linen tabby - was moved during 1982-3 into a long dark hall where it is displayed at least 30 cm behind glass in a long "U" shaped stand. While slowly walking the 70 metre length I found that, as always, having the real thing in front of my eyes, made me look at it more carefully than at a photograph. With a well-known object, it requires extra effort not to dismiss it as familiar.

It was natural to follow my interest in food and look more closely for a Norman feast. The first relevant scene was a side view of the trundling onto the boat of two wooden barrels, a large one in a cart and a smaller one on a man's back and a later badly drawn front-view of a man carrying it off again [1] - early examples of French imported wines, (surely not well - liners as suggested elsewhere-[2]). This led to preparations for a banquet in William's honour which took place in Hastings [3]. Wadard, one of William's intendants, supervises the cooks. Wadard is identified in the Doomsday Book as a major tenant of Odo, Bishop of Bayeux [4], half brother to William [5]. One of the cooks is looking after shish kebabs of meat cubes and a small fowl, spread out like a spring chicken, being grilled over a box-shaped container with three shelves and rings protruding on each side of the top supported by a low (about 20cm) tripod over a fire. He is picking up or turning over a rissole or piece of bread with tongs. Two other assistants pass what looks like the skewered meat to the waiters who remove the meat (including rabbits) onto a shield-table before serving it to the guests. This grilling contraption looked strange - the barbecue was the first puzzle.

Calls to the current recommended UK authorities on the period at the York Archaeological Trust produced comments. Neither the metalwork nor the manuscript authorities for this period knew of a similar object or drawing of the barbecue [6]. However, from cuts on bone remains there is evidence of butchering at York from Roman times. Yet this does not confirm that meat was cut into cubes, like those seen here, rather that it was jointed and boned. Also the Norman Vikings may have eaten differently from the York Vikings and Anglo-Saxons.

The existence of kebabs - then and there - was the second puzzle. If there is a gastrologic parallel to Darwin's law of survival of the fittest - survival of the tastiest - then it is odd that the kebab, allegedly introduced by the Normans, only became popular in Britain in the early 1960s following the immigration of Turkish Cypriots. This contrasts with rabbits which were introduced into England by the Normans [7]. Perhaps a more likely date for the introduction of kebabs to France was around 1722, when an exchange of cultural embassies followed Ottoman Turks who had settled in Lyon, and Constantinople absorbed the Rococo style which (in my opinion) ruined the Ottoman decorative arts.

The word kebab is probably of Persian origin meaning pieces of cooked meat. It appears in an ironic contemporary poetic parody of Hafiz, the 14th century poet, describing the burning of a pining lover's heart. Shish is a Turkish word meaning a skewer. It may have been mentioned in al-Jahiz's 10th century book on suitable dishes for a gentleman to eat. The earliest occurrence of these words is not known at present [8]. When the reliable de Clavijo, the Spanish envoy, visited the court of Tamerlane at Samarkand in 1404, he attended many feasts. He records roasted sheep, torn into pieces by hand; sides of horse, pilaw rice with meat, but no shish kebabs. N. Halici - the Turkish food researcher - suggests that shish kebabs were used by migrating Turks in the 11th century because the scarcity of dried fuel made it necessary to cook smaller cut pieces of meat more quickly [9].

After a brief description of the textile, it seems worth examining a puzzling range of discrepancies in published work, verbal reports and observations. These include the style of drawing of the Tapestry, physical changes, the history of the object, its condition and copyability. It is regrettable that several of the various deductions are of a negative or excluding nature, which can only provide an incomplete part of a logical argument.

The Bayeux Tapestry is difficult to examine, especially as it was not possible to see the back, except for a black and white detail photograph [10] and the front is perhaps 30 cm behind glass. Above the long band is crudely stitched a white band with Arabic numerals from 1 to 58 dividing the 70 plus metre band into different scenes. The style of the script of the numbers appears to date from the 18-19th centuries. The band itself is about 50 cm (45.7 to 53.6 high - a normal variation for an embroidery, - and there are several patches of restoration which appear to have been made at least on two different occasions as well as what appeared to be re-outlining and infilling (but not double thickness) restoration. Judging from the colours, viewed under unspecified artificial light, one restorer used apparently chemically dyed wool, which was only introduced after 1865 (in contrast to the 1842 restoration date given).

THE BAYEUX TAPESTRY SHISH KEBAB MYSTERY

TAPISSERIE DE BAYEUX

The unrelieved cheap woollen thread used in embroidering such a monumental work is also surprising and untypical. Earlier hangings, called "web" in Beowolf, are of gold or silk, as are those found in other ecclesiastical texts. The earlier and maniple of Saint Cuthbert in Durham cathedral of 934 [11] and the "casula" Saint Harlandis and Saint Relindis are also worked in gold [12]. And the contemporary will of Matilda, queen of William the Conqueror, made in the year of her death -1083 - only mentions gold embroidered tunic, mantle and girdles [13]. From a contemporary source it was written that "the English women excel all others in needle-work and in embroidering with gold" [14]. And furthermore this embroidery was "called by way of eminence 'English Work'" [15]. From exchequer records it seems that much silk was purchased by Norman prelates and that English embroidery enjoyed increased support after the Norman Conquest [16]. This makes it surprising that there is no gold wrapped thread - even picking out the notables - as it is generally thought that Bishop Odo commissioned the Tapestry, and he and his brother Count Robert are portrayed in it.

The kebab question also led to a closer at the poor style of other depictions in the embroidery.

In both Oriental and European [17] embroideries the outline is normally drawn in charcoal or ink on the background cloth, not by the embroiderer but by a designer, sometimes using a stencil for repeated designs. "The celebrated Dunstan (909-988) when a young man was considered as an artist of some degree of eminence for drawings of this kind' [18]. Strutt continues: "It is highly probable (though I speak indeed from conjecture alone) that other artists made their living in this way." Several examples of brilliantly drawn Opus Anglicanum embroidery [19], dating from the 13th and 14th centuries which employ this method of design. I have an English 15th century example of this where the drawing is clearly visible even after repeated washing. However in the Bayeux Tapestry, there is no trace of the original drawing, just pricked through holes [20] and some outline stitching visible on the back [21]. This is a usual method of copying, though not necessarily of designing, embroidery. Dr Budny has inspected about 20 known surviving other Anglo-Saxon and Anglo-Norman embroideries which are of course smaller than the Tapestry. None of them appear to have under-drawing - as far as could be determined without harming the embroidery, but they do have brown or red outline stitches visible on the back. As there was no paper in Northern Europe [22] during the 11th or 12th centuries, a cartoon would have to have been drawn on vellum and then pricked through onto the eight linen strips, twenty five foot plus long, which were subsequently joined together. There is no satisfactory explanation for not simply drawing the original design directly onto the linen and then sending the linen to be embroidered. Odo was both a bishop (also thought by Dr. Budny to be probably a Benedictine, with their great tradition of art patronage) and Duke William's half-brother, and so would have had access to both court and ecclesiastical designers. The majesty of the whole conception is at odds with much of the detail found in the infills.

The designer of naturalistic drawings of figures, animals and so on, was usually a book illustrator. It is hard to believe that this was so here. Wilson confirms that "the coarse detail of the Tapestry is very different from the fine lines of Anglo-Norman penmanship" [23]. In further comparison, even the minutely carved contemporary walrus tusks - far harder to work - are of far higher quality than the Tapestry.

What is strange, however, is that in Wormald's essay on the Style & Design [24], the comparative material, though similar in form, is different in style. The fragment from Montfaucon's authoritative engraving by Benoit [25] of 1730 appears to be of a similar but much more refined work. Equally, the woven border from an 11th century chasuble at Bamberg is of much more elegant style. It is possible to embroider (by definition, with a needle) far more accurately and expressively than to weave, which is restrained by the grid of warp and weft. This is especially so in the case of curved lines. While laid and couched work is admittedly the crudest and fastest sewn form of filling an embroidery, the outlines in "stem and outline stitches" [26] are capable of greater accuracy. From the vast array of 626 human figures, 190 horses and mules, 35 hounds and dogs and 506 other various animals [27], it must be significant that the six examples in Stanton and in Wilson chosen for their similarity to other 11th century works, are so much cruder in style than their alleged models.

The contemporary but badly damaged Oslo fragment [28] certainly shows that this technique of embroidery in wool was found elsewhere, but both one of the recognisable faces of the stacked corpses and the tree form have more vigour than the floppy examples in the Tapestry. Wilson considers anyway that it has little relevance here beyond showing that such a hanging existed in north Europe at this period, with an embroidery technique only surviving in Iceland after the 12th century [29].

Next, a widespread stylistic detail found in the infills of costumes, which implies mistakes in re-embroidery or copying from only an outline: the badly drawn folds of the hems of the costume bear little relation to any designed of the period. It is precisely these folds which are used as the key factor to differentiate styles in the far more difficult contemporary technique of Champleve enamels, made in northern Europe, or, for example in drawings like that taken from the Winchcombe Psalter [30]. Decorative art must be seen in context: "...the art of Anglo-Saxon manuscripts is intimately related to works of art in other media, such as stone ivory carving, decorated metalwork and embroidered textiles" [31].

In Stenton every essay on the decorative arts objects portrayed in the Tapestry is qualified. Nevinson, Stenton's costume specialist [32], states: "this account should perhaps end with a note of warning not to place too great reliance on the Tapestry for-giving conclusive evidence on the history of dress ... [it] must raise doubts about the accuracy of his (the designer of the Tapestry as copyist) pictorial representation of his contemporaries." There Nevinson echoes Strutt's doubts of Montfaucon's engravings expressed in 1775 when Strutt wrote that "the work and the habits so far as one can judge from the representation seem to be of a much more modern date" [33]. Though by 1796 Strutt thought it was "at least half a century later" [34]. Strutt stuck illuminated manuscripts in his widely sourced book illustrating both costume and armour in England [35]. Sir James Mann even makes excuses for "certain inevitable shortcomings ... in using the Bayeux Tapestry as a guide to the arms and armour of the time", questionably citing the embroidery technique and (hardly) small scale [36]. Allen Brown again used the excuse of embroidery as an inaccurate medium to justify the "predominating pessimistic of the value of the tapestry for the study of architecture" [37] in his additional essay for the 1965 edition of Stenton, ignoring other numerous examples such as the gothic arcading in the Toledo Cope [38], or the church in the Pienza Cope [39]. A recently recognised stone sculpture fragment from Winchester before the destruction in 1093 (69 cm high by about 40 cm) is sadly lacking all details of faces and hands of the two figures and the dog, but there are some similarities in the armour and it also seems to come from a frieze [40].

The linear measurement of the Tapestry varies, especially the height. Since 1730, the size of the Tapestry appears to keep changing. Montfaucon - pre 1730 - gave the length as 68.69 metres (221 pieds and the height as "a little less" than two pieds or 68.69 cm [41]. According to Strutt, the eye-witness Ducarel gives the measurements as "1'11" in height by 212' in length [42]. Leve in 1919 gave the length as 70.34 metres. The 1940-41 German measurement was 68.45 metres long with no height given. Both differed from the 1946 measurements of Verrier of the Monuments Historiques of 70 metres by 50 cm. By 1983 it had shrunk again to 68.38 metres. In fairness, it is difficult to measure a long piece of linen, but the variation in the height is puzzling.

The numbering of the scenes written on a band stitched to the Tapestry also varies implying a remounting alteration. Kendrick of the Victoria & Albert Museum wrote in 1904 of "The numbers 1-79, [used in his description of scenes from the Tapestry] correspond with those marked at a late period in ROMAN figures along the upper border of the Tapestry" [43]. This differs from the ARABIC numbers 1-58, written on the cloth stitched above the band there today, and from the 73 scenes described in Stenton.

The history of the Tapestry has remarkable gaps. In Bertrand's account [44] there is no record of the Tapestry until 1476. Then more silence until 1724 when a sketch was sent from Normandy to M. Lancelot, a most distinguished member of the Academie Royale des Inscriptions et Belles Lettres who is quoted as writing "... I have ... been unable to discover whether this sketch represents a bas-relief ... sculpture ... fresco ... or possibly a tapestry." Bernard de Montfaucon, the antiquary, was collecting material for his five volume work on the French monuments. He got a baroque style drawing of the first 30 feet (pieds) from Foucaut [45]. Montfaucon says that the drawing is 30 pieds by one and a half pieds. In 1729 Montfaucon dispatched Antoine Benoit, "one of the ablest draughtsmen of the time", to Bayeux cathedral to copy the Tapestry [46]. The drawing follows the 11th century style and is identical in content to the Tapestry with gaps in the now restored embroidery and epigraphic discrepancies. For example he missed out the curious cross of the "d" [47] for the letter "th" which appears in the name "Gyrth" [48]. Wilson confirms, too, that the letters in the text on the Tapestry are a mixture drawn from inscriptions and manuscripts, implying that someone connected with the embroidery was indeed widely read.

In 1752 Andrew Ducarel, the archaeologist, was apparently not allowed to see it [49], but he later obtained a set of the plates in Montfaucon which Ducarel published in *Anglo-Norman Antiquities* in 1767. However Strutt quotes from Ducarel as an eye witness [50]. Next mention is made (without a reference) in 1792, when the unsatisfactory story is told of attempts to use the long linen strip as a (most inconvenient) waggon cover [51] and a little later, according to Wingfield Digby, to decorate "The Chariot of the Goddess of Reason" [52]. In 1794 on the 9th of Fructidor the Tapestry was spread out in the "Temple of Supreme Being" and the dust removed. Two weeks later it was inspected again "so as to compare its condition with the description and drawings of Montfaucon" - the results were not provided by Bertrand. Nothing more was heard until 1803 when the Minister of the Interior got it sent to the Musee Napoleon in Paris where "this fragile record of our history" attracted Bonaparte's attention mainly because of the comet incident, mystically repeated as he prepared to invade England from Boulogne. It was then returned and kept "coiled round a machine like that which lets out the buckets to a well" [53] which Kendrick thought "barbarous" [54]. By 1818 Charles Stothard, the draftsman working for the Society of Antiquaries of London, and Dawson Turner both stated that it had suffered greatly since the drawings were made in 1729. It was eventually exhibited at the Bibliotheque Publique in the Place du Chateau in Bayeux in 1842, following restoration supervised by Lambert the librarian and subsequently photographed by Percy Hennell (on black and white film subsequently hand coloured, called a "colour photograph") [55]. In the 1860's Theophile Gautier wrote "How remarkable that this fragile strip of linen should have come down to us undamaged through the centuries...", and Wingfield Digby confirmed "that the Bayeux Tapestry is in an extraordinary sound state of repair, if one considers its great age ... and the chequered course of its history". Weirder still, "in 1941 the (occupying) German authorities had it transferred to the Abbey of the Premonstrants at Juaye-Mondaye, where four experts studied it from June 23 to July 31. No trace has been found of the photographs and drawings that were made at the time" [56].

To add some practical notes on the condition of the Tapestry: some items from my modest collection of embroideries in laid and couched technique have been mounted and restored during the past twenty years. From observation it is possible to say that wool being heavier than silk would tend to deform and break the background cloth more than silk. Also whereas much heavier metallic threads would rip the silk even more, these (in Opus Anglicanum) are always backed by a strong canvas, other Anglo-Saxon and Anglo-Norman examples are unbacked [57]. The Tapestry must have been worn away or ragged after the following severe treatment. In 1476 it was recorded that the Tapestry was each year hung around the nave of Bayeux cathedral for eight days at the Feast of the Relics and Ducarel confirmed in 1752 that this continued until then [58]. If this happened between 1100 and 1750, the 70 metre long band would have been unrolled, hung up, taken down and rerolled 650 times. Also in 1794 it was reported that dust had to be shaken out when the Tapestry was unrolled. Such dust acts like sandpaper on wool. The various comments on the condition of the embroidery are confusing. By way of illustration, I have an eighteenth century Ottoman silk laid and couched embroidery, nearly disintegrated but cleverly patched, which indicates that old textiles were valued although in far worse condition than the Tapestry. Experience of buying old carpets and occasionally copies of old carpets shows that at about the turn of the century, patching and obvious restoration have been used to artificially age a rug.

Wingfield Digby does not appear to have had the experience of employing any professional restorers when he speaks of the execution of the Tapestry as a "formidable undertaking" [59]. When reproducing laid and couched work in silk, which would take longer than wool (being thinner), Caroline Turner, the embroidery and textile conservator, estimates that it would take two hours to work a square foot of fresh linen with embroidery covering a third of the area, as in the Tapestry. The dimensions of roughly 220 by 1.7 feet make an area of about 375 square feet. A professional embroiderer can do ten hours work a day, so there were only 75 person-days work involved here. The embroidery was made in eight sections [60] so the work could have been done in about ten days on 20 inch portable frames similar to the Turkish frame [61]. The weight of wool needed is only about 50 kilograms or 30-40 English fleeces. (Typically three kilograms of raw wool a fleece reduces by half after combing, washing and spinning) [62]. The ease of copying this type of embroidery is eloquently confirmed by the existence of the little known Tapisserie of the Chateau de Pirou depicting the Norman conquest of Sicily, made in 1930, which was not on view when I visited Bayeux.

While not questioning the early documents related to the original existence of a Bayeux Tapestry [63], there appears to have been ample opportunity to make a copy or over-embroider damaged parts simply because it was more acceptable to display a textile in good condition. The contributions of Stenton's distinguished authorities on the Decorative Arts and Wilson's most recent additions not only "present a problem because of the unique nature of the Tapestry" as he generously concedes, but also suggest a cultural hotch-potch, reminiscent of the Iconography of the notorious Billy & Charlie figurative metal objects "found in the Thames" in the 1860's. However the inconsistencies seem rather those caused by mistakes made in a quick copy. Of course that would only have been made with a motive - either the obvious prestige in preserving such a unique treasure or as substitution for the original or routine mending.

Stimulated by the shish kebabs portrayed in such great detail on the Tapestry, a further series of questions has been raised which might encourage those in charge of the Tapestry to have an independent carbon dating test carried out to confirm that what is on display is indeed the same as that described in the inventory of the ornaments of Bayeux Cathedral on the Feast of Relics, July 1st 1476 [64]. Since it began operating in 1984, the Oxford Archaeological Institute's carbon 14 test only needs 30 milligrams of textile - a small postage stamp sized piece of linen or a small length of woollen thread - and will give a date 95% certain to be minus 120 years, quite sufficient for our purpose [65]. It is likely that there is a lot of re-embroidered restoration, which could also be put into dated periods by analysis. Without damaging the front of the Tapestry, dye analysis of each woollen thread end sticking out at the back of the embroidery would show:

1. If different yellow dyes were used in the yellow and green coloured woollen threads, implying different dates.

2. If chemical dyes which are post 1865 are present [66].

3. If the DNA of cochineal insects (producing a red dye) confirmed, say, an Armenian origin and so a later date [67].

In addition, the characteristic sheep breeds can be determined from quarter inch long pieces of wool cut from ends sticking out on the back of the embroidery [68]. There are significant breed changes between the middle ages and the 18th century. Also infrared light and/or photography might show if there were traces of original drawing [69].

Even if carbon dating, dye analysis and wool analysis were to confirm it as mainly original, there should be a plan published showing the restored areas; but the Bayeux Tapestry stylistic mysteries would still remain unsolved.

References

1. Wilson, Sir D., *The Bayeux Tapestry*, 1985 pl 46. Referred to as W below. 2 W p 184.
3. Stenton, Sir F., *The Bayeux Tapestry*, 2nd Ed. 1965 pl 48. Referred to as S below.
4. W p 186.
5. Montfaucon vol 1 p 371ff.
6. Verbal reports, Drs. P. Ottway, D. Tweddle, H. Kenward.
7. W p 187.
8. Preliminary verbal report, Prof. M. Zand.
9. Verbal report.
10. W p 196.
11. Kendrick, A., *English Embroidery*, n.d., c.1905 p 12. Referred to as K below.
12. W p 201.
13. K p 13.
14. Strutt, Joseph, *A Complete View of ... Dress in England*, 1796 ed., vol 1, pp 73-4, quoting *Gesta Gulielmi Ducis apud Duchen* p 211. Strutt, the first English costume historian, who was also an engraver, wrote this detailed scholarly three volume work with 143 coloured plates, first published in 1775.
15. Strutt, vol 1, p 74, quoting *Anglicum Opus. Guil. Pictavens*, p 211.
16. Strutt, vol 2, p 88.
17. S p 43.
18. Strutt, vol 1, p 74, quoting 'Osbornus, de viti Dustani', *Anglia Sacra* vol II, p 95. Dr. Budny has translated Osbernus and quotes this and others in a broader discussion of Saint Dunstan in B pp 143-146. See note 29.
19. K pl III-XIX.
20. W p 10.
21. Verbal report M. Budny.
22. Verbal report K. Holmes and S. Fairbrother - paper conservators.
23. W p 208.
24. S p 32ff figs 1-21.
25. S S p 32 fig 1.
26. S p 40.
27. S p 42.
28. S Fig 22.
29. W p 206.
30. Budny, Dr. M., *The Cambridge Guide to the Arts in Britain*, 1988 p 122. Referred to as B below.
31. B p 146.
32. S p 75.
33. S p 70.
34. Strutt, vol 2, p 143.
35. S p 56.
36. S p ?
37. S p 76.
38. K pl X.
39. K pl XIII.
40. W p 207, fig 5.
41. S p 53.
42. Strutt, vol 2, p 143, quoting Ducarel p 79 and Appendix p 2.
43. K Introduction.
44. S p 76 ff.
45. Montfaucon, Bernard de, Monuments de la Royaume Francoise, 5 vols, c.1733. vol 1, pp 371-379 pls XXXV-XLIX.
46. Montfaucon, vol 2, pp 1-32 pls I-IX.
47. W p 204.

48 W pl 63-64.
49 S p 90.
50 Strutt, vol 2. p 143.
51 S p 90.
52 S p 52.
53 S p 52.
54 K p 21.
55 S note 38a p 55.
56 S p 96.
57 Verbal report Dr. M. Budny.
58 Mlle. Simone Bertrand in S p ?.
59 S p 42.
60 S p 42.
61 *Flowers from Thrace to Tartary*, Chenciner & Marko, 1981.
62 Verbal report J. Powell.
63 *The Anglo-Saxon Chronicle* may be "laconic, short and pious", and only refer to the consecration of Westminster Abbey, the death of Edward, the accession of Harold, the approach of Haley's comet and the Battle of Hastings, and the *Gesta Normannorum Ducum*, written after 1070, tells a slightly different story of the imprisonment of Guy de Ponthieu and of the death of Harold at the beginning of the battle, but the most detailed contemporary account is by William of Poitiers in *Gesta Willelmi Ducis Normannorum et regis Anglorum* (W pp 18 & 19, notes 23 & 26). There is also one surviving record of a commemorative hanging presented to the church at Ely on the death of the Ealdorman of Essex at the Battle of Malden in 991, by his widow (W p 201). But, frustratingly neither its size nor shape are recorded.
64 K p 20.
65 Verbal report Dr. R. Howsley.
66 Verbal report Dr. H. Bohmer.
67 Verbal report Dr. M. Budny.
68 Verbal report M. Ryder.
69 Verbal report Dr. M. Budny.

Iguanas, Chocolate, Muskrats, and a glimpse at Cochineal

by Dr. Sophie D. Coe

When Columbus arrived in the New World, he found that everything there was different. As different as day from night, he said, mentioning the trees and their fruit, the grasses, and even the stones (Dunn & Kelley, 1989, p.93). To fit all these things into the categories established in the Old World was a major intellectual task, and we will only deal with a small corner of it. The process of accommodating New World foodstuffs to the requirements of the Roman Catholic Church as to abstinence and fasting will be used as an illustration of the arbitrary limitations human beings put on their food.

These requirements, although they changed over the centuries, and were specifically based on what would now be called community standard, not the views of the scholars of the time, were basically two. On days of abstinence one could eat the normal number of meals, but they could not contain meat. The question to be addressed, therefore, became what is meat, and what is not meat. On days of fasting one could drink, but only eat one meal. The question was, was it food, or was it drink? Conveniently, one of our New World controversies concerns the first question, whether or not the flesh of the iguana was meat. The second question addresses the culinary position of chocolate, food or drink, a controversy which proved far more protracted.

Thomas Aquinas defined meat as coming from warm blooded animals that lived and breathed on the earth, while fish, or what had better be called non-meat, lived in the water, and was cold-blooded. Mammals and non-mammals, we would say today, but we must remember that it is not the opinions of systematists and taxonomists that counts officially, but the beliefs and practices of the country. Reptiles and amphibians are fish in this classification, because even though they do not all live in water, they are cold-blooded, and everything that was not certainly and definitively meat, was fish. For those who had to abstain from meat in the New World, one of the things that fell into this category were the large lizards of the *Iguanidæ* family, which aside from a few outlying species in Fiji and Madagascar, are exclusively natives of the New World.

There are two edible genera of iguanas in Mexico and Central America, *Iguana* and *Ctenosaura*. The former is known as the green iguana, and can be up to six feet long, although most of that is tail. It eats tender leaves and fruit, although it is not averse to small birds and mammals, and prefers to spend its time in the trees, preferably over a river. If disturbed on its perch it falls into the river, where it is a competent swimmer, thus confirming its "fish" status in the eyes of the Spaniards. The other species, or complex of them, belong to the genus *Ctenosaura*, and are usually called black iguanas. They are not nearly as aquatic as the green iguana, preferring to live in dry rocky areas. They are fierce, and tend to bite, but some people consider them superior eating.

The native peoples of Mexico and Central America used the iguanas for food without distinguishing between the species, as far as we know. The bones are found in lowland archaeological sites in large quantities, being obviously a major food source along with deer, turkey, and dogs.

Not only was the iguana food for the people, it was also food for the gods. One of the surviving Maya ritual books gives us pictures of iguana offerings, which consist of a high-rimmed plate holding two symbols for maize, topped with a schematic drawing of the iguana's crest. We do not know exactly how this iguana was cooked with maize. It may have been used as a filling in a tamale, a steamed maize dumpling wrapped in a leaf, or perhaps as iguana meat boiled in epazote-flavoured water, which was then thickened with maize dough and ground toasted squash seeds, a recipe published in a Chiapas cookbook in 1988 (*Comida Familiar Chiapas*, 1988, p.76). Perhaps it was just pieces of roasted iguana on top of plain maize tamales, because at least one archaeological excavation revealed that 70% of the iguana bones were darkened by heat, meaning that they had been prepared directly over the fire, not in liquid.

The iguana was also one of the four standard offerings to the four directions, the other three being a fish, a turkey, and a haunch of meat. According to present scientific terminology, this means that each direction is represented by a different taxonomic class. In this case Maya classification and ours seem to coincide, recognising the differences between reptiles, fish, birds, and mammals, even though we refrain from attaching them to the cardinal points as the Maya did.

There is another, and more striking, coincidence, between the Maya and the Spaniards as far as the iguana went. From the invaluable description of Bishop Landa we learn that in sixteenth century Yucatan there were two war captains, one hereditary, and one elected. Landa tells us nothing about dietary constraints endured by the hereditary chief, but the elected one was allowed no meat during his three year term. In place of the meat he ate fish, and it is emphasised in the text that iguanas are classed as fish.

Fish, and therefore very probably iguanas, were very high status food among the Maya. This has been shown by carbon pathway analysis of the bones of the inhabitants of Lamanai, Belize, during the Maya Classic period, AD 300 to AD 900. It was found that the male buried in an élite tomb had enjoyed unusual access to sea food, which was not even available to the woman buried in an élite situation, although she had had an unusually varied diet as far as vegetable food went. The same prestige is attached to sea food in a later piece of invective from highland Guatemala, in which one lord is slandering another. His enemy, he says, only eats cacao dregs and water flies, while he, the speaker, enjoys fish and little fresh shrimp.

It is tempting, but unlikely, to suppose that the Spaniards asked the Maya if that creature over there was meat or fish. They certainly made much of the iguana. Gonzalo Ferdinando de Oviedo spent a good deal of time depicting its terrifying aspect, and praising its delicious taste. He said that it was better than the best Spanish rabbit. Unfortunately the rest of his description leads one to doubt whether he had ever laid eyes on the animal, and confirms the judgment of one of his contemporaries that he was a great liar. In the first place he claims that the eggs have a yolk and a white like a hens egg, which they do not. The eggs are very delicious, and have a thin skin, as he says, but they are very definitely all yolk. Nor are they round, as he says they are, being in reality quite long ovals. Whether or not they must be fried in water rather than in oil, as he says, I do not know.

Ferdinando de Oviedo, and all the other early authors, stress the iguanas aquatic habits, even though as we have seen only one species behaves in this fashion. It was all part of affirming their "neutrality", as Oviedo put it, which meant their position as non-meat. It was not politic of Oviedo to compare the meat with that of rabbit, other authors carefully suggested that it was like frogs' legs, and the *Nuevo Cocinero Mexicano en forma de Diccionario* originally published in 1888, went further still in advising the reader to cook it like shark.

This problem of applying community standards rather than those of modern systematic biology still occurs today. In 1988 there was an article in the New York Times describing the custom of the inhabitants of the Downriver district of the state of Michigan, who eat the muskrat, *Ondatra zibethicus*, on Good Friday. They are convinced that they have a special dispensation to eat this mammal because it swims in the water like a fish. The archdiocese of Detroit begs to differ, saying that there is no dispensation, and that the animal is meat. As far as I know muskrat is still eaten Downriver on Good Friday.

The question of the iguana being acceptable on the table during days of abstinence was actually not such a difficult one. The question of cacao drinks, and especially chocolate, was far knottier. In the first place there was a multitude of cacao drinks, ranging from substantial maize gruels with a little cacao beverage floated on top of them, to the true chocolate, made with cacao, water, and a little honey. In the second place the cacao drinks were psychoactive, and they were the first non-alcoholic drinks of this nature that the Spaniards had ever encountered. It is worth remembering that tea and coffee became widespread in Europe during the latter half of the seventeenth century, one hundred and fifty years after the endlessly misquoted and misunderstood banquet of Motecuhzoma, which included the drinking of chocolate.

The Spaniards quickly became enamoured of cacao beverages. They spoke of them as giving strength to the body, of enabling one to travel for a whole day after having drunk a single cup in the morning, and as stimulating rather than befuddling. Perhaps it is only because the monastic orders published biographies of deceased members, that it seems that the religious were particularly addicted to it. In obituary after obituary we read of the austerities of the deceased, how he did not drink chocolate in the morning, or perhaps did not use it at all until he was over eighty and the drink was prescribed for medicinal reasons. But with all this emphasis on the singularity of those who did not take chocolate, it is obvious that most religious did take it, and in large quantities. When could they do so legitimately, and what were the approved formulations?

This quickly became the subject of debate and polemic, with popes Gregory XIII, Clement VIII, Paul V, and Urban VIII all being asked to give their opinions. To give a sample of the sort of reasoning involved, I will quote from the early stages of the debate.

> "And because I wish to remove doubts, or at any rate not to raise them, I must warn those countries where this drink is used, that one must be careful with it on fast days. When it is drunk as medicine there is no doubt that it can be used without hesitation. The doubt comes when it is used as sustenance, which it gives greatly. In the year 1591 they printed a book in Mexico called *Problemas de las Indias*, and the doctor who wrote it concluded that chocolate and wine broke the fast because they were sustaining. The Viceroy of Mexico sent me this book so that I could examine it, and I approved it, because when they brought it to me it did not have that conclusion... Then the author added it, and it was printed without further examination. I would not

condemn those who drink chocolate saying that it broke the fast of the church, any more than I would condemn those who drink wine: because it is a clear truth that drink does not break the fast. I was always ashamed that my name was burdened with such a great lie as saying that wine broke the fast, and the same goes for chocolate. I have seen the opinion which was given to Pope Gregory XIII by the learned and saintly Doctor Atzpilcueta Navarro, on the request of the Procurator of the Province of Chiapas, where this drink began, and as the request was urgent, the Pope answered twice, that it does not break the fast. I do not say this to give permission, but to give the truth." (Augustin Dávila Padilla, in Suárez de Peralta, *Noticias Históricas de la Nueva España*, p.344)

Despite this positive statement, the controversy continued. Tomás Hurtado, who published his work on chocolate and tobacco in 1645, said that when the Spaniards consulted Gregory XIII they did not mix as many things with chocolate as they did in his day, they just used cacao, sugar, and chili. This was a sizable exaggeration, as any reader of the lists of additions to Pre-Columbian cacao drinks will agree. But by Hurtado's day they were adding not only spices and sugar, but also milk, eggs, and broth, and in Hurtado's opinion, although not in that of some of his colleagues, these were sustaining, and therefore food and prohibited.

When chocolate was introduced to France in the late seventeenth century, the controversy followed. If it was a drink, priests could take a cup before saying mass, which they could not do if it was food. The Jesuits, who were elsewhere accused of trying to monopolise the cacao market in parts of the New World for financial gain, insisted that it was a drink; the Jansenists took the opposite tack.

If anybody thinks that the much quoted adage "Liquidum non frangit ieiunium" must have settled the question by our century they are wrong. In 1935 a Discalced Carmelite published a thesis on the ecclesiastical regulations having to do with fasting and abstinence (Parra Herrera, 1935). There we read that drinks, taken to assuage thirst and facilitate digestion, are permissible on fast days. But when we look at the list: wine, beer, tea, coffee, lemonade, liquors in general, and soft drinks, we do not find chocolate among them. Chocolate, ever difficult, is said not to be usually taken as a drink, and therefore not permitted if taken in what are called notable quantities. Thus in 1935 we have an unspecified chocolate recipe contradicting centuries of judgments which had put chocolate on the drink side of the fence rather than on the food side.

Catholicism is not the only religion to have trouble with chocolate. Joseph Smith, the founder of the Church of Jesus Christ of Latter Day Saints, received a revelation prohibiting the use of hot drinks, usually narrowly interpreted as meaning tea and coffee, to his flock. Once biochemistry had identified the alkaloids contained by these drinks, they were considered the substances prohibited. Arch conservatives have sought to have Coca Cola banned as containing caffeine, but nobody has ever breathed a word against chocolate, which contains a goodly dose of caffeine, as well as other alkaloids, and continues to be served at church functions. Perhaps it was the novel psychoactive qualities of the ancient cultivars of cacao prepared in strong solutions that the Spaniards found so noticeable, and a small dose of cacao, flavouring a large cup of hot milk and sugar and marshmallow, has no effect that the Mormon church can identify as that of the prohibited alkaloid.

The last New World product we will touch on is cochineal, which is really a dye for food, rather than a food itself. *Dactylopius coccus* is a small insect that looks like the mealy bug that gets on ones houseplants, but produced the brilliant and expensive dye that made the "red-coats", or more precisely the higher ranks of the "red-coats" red. This was another product discovered in Mexico by the Spaniards, and it was so highly valued that it was considered the third most important export, immediately following gold and silver. The discovery of aniline dyes destroyed much of its function, but it continued to be used in one small field, that of food colouring. It was in this rôle that it fell foul of Old World rules, specifically the eleventh chapter of Leviticus, verse 42, where we are told not to eat what goes on its belly, creeps on the earth, and has more than four feet. This marks one of the major gulfs between New World cuisine and that of the Old World, or at least the European portion of it. The steadfast refusal of Europeans to even consider eating insects, cuts the world off from a copious source of nutrients, to everybody's detriment.

Perhaps the main use of these problems raised by the New World products is to lead us to think twice about the rules and regulations with which are food is surrounded. We may think that we are wonderfully liberated to explore all the gastronomic possibilities, but in reality everybody has conscious or unconscious limits. As the discovery of the New World forced the Old World to reorganise its thinking on some subjects, perhaps we should use this opportunity to give another thought to what we eat and why.

Bibliography

Anon, *Comida Familiar en el Estado de Chiapas*, Banrural, Mexico, 1988

Anon, *Nuevo Cocinero Mexicano en forma de Diccionario*, facsimile published by Miguel Angel Porrua, Mexico, 1986, original published by Ch. Bouret, Paris, 1888.

Dunn, Oliver, & James E. Kelley, Jr., *The Diario of Christopher Columbus's First Voyage to America 1492-1493*. University of Oklahoma Press, Norman, 1989.

Ferdinando de Oviedo, Gonzalo, "Sommario della naturale e generale istoria dell'Indie Occidentali" in Giovanni Battista Ramusio *Navigazioni e Viaggi*, vol. V, Giulio Einaudi, Milan, 1985.

Holusha, John, "Where the Muskrat is a Delicacy for Lent", *New York Times*, Friday, April 1, 1988

Hurtado, Tomás, *Chocolate y Tabaco, Ayuno Eclesiastico y Natural*, Francisco Garcia, Madrid, 1645.

Parra Herrera, Antonio, *Legislacion Eclesiastica Sobre El Ayuno y La Abstinencia*, Universidad Catolica de America, Estudios Canonicos, Numero 92, The Catholic University of America, Washington, D. C., 1935.

Suárez de Peralta, Juan, *Noticias Históricas de la Nueva España*, Manuel G. Hernandez, Madrid, 1878.

On the Edge of the Feast
Outsiders in early Greece

by Andrew Dalby

A beggar at a country farm

The simplest human household described in the Odyssey is that of Odysseus's pig-farmer Eumaeus. Odysseus himself, disguised as a vagrant on his return to his own island,[1] is an unexpected visitor to it.

Eumaeus's being an isolated farm with valuable livestock, Odysseus is first threatened by guard dogs. Eumaeus brings him safely to the house, which is imagined as having a single room and little if any furniture: it is shared by Eumaeus, his slave and his labourers. Here the stranger is at once given food and wine:

> 'Stranger, it would not be right for me, even if one worse than you should come, to slight a stranger: before Zeus everyone is a stranger and a beggar.'[2]

> He went to the sties, where his tribes of pigs lived. He took two from there, brought them out, sacrificed them both, singed them and chopped them and stuck the meat on spits. Well, he roasted it all and brought it and put it before Odysseus, hot on the spits; he sprinkled white barley-meal on; he poured honey-sweet wine into a mug, and himself sat down facing him, and to encourage him said: 'Eat now, stranger, what servants have to hand: piglets, but the fat sows are eaten by the suitors...'[3]

Eumaeus talks while his guest eats and drinks greedily in silence. This was not a regular meal but some food hastily prepared from what was at hand because the stranger was hungry. But at length Eumaeus's labourers return; Odysseus shares their meal, being placed near the hearth and honoured with the best portion of meat.

The aside 'what servants have to hand' may excuse the absence of bread, the invariable constituent of Greek domestic meals throughout ancient times. Bread is included in all other complete domestic meals in the *Iliad* and *Odyssey*. Eumaeus's next unexpected visitor, Telemachus, arrives before breakfast on the following day; thus bread and some meat remain from the previous dinner:

> The pig-farmer put before them plates of roast meat that they had left uneaten the day before, and hurriedly piled bread alongside in baskets, and poured honey-sweet wine into a mug...[4]

A beggar in town

A *pto:khós*, a 'beggar' or 'vagrant', in the *Odyssey* was not a man who begged for food and offered no return. Odysseus had been helping Eumaeus to prepare the breakfast: he expected, if he remained at the farm, 'to obey a directing master in everything,'[5] and said that the option would be a hard one: in other words, to go on getting his food there he would have become a farm labourer. At a big house in a town, with its noisy feasts, such a man might have other opportunities. Here they are, sketched first by one of the boisterous diners when Odysseus, still incognito, has come back to his own house:

> 'Stranger, well now, would you wish to be a labourer if I took you, on a far-off field...? But if you have learnt bad ways you will not want to go to a farm but will choose to cringe around the town to get the fodder for your starving belly.'[7]

And here Odysseus himself depicts, to Eumaeus, what he may have to do in town to make his way:

> 'I should soon do well whatever they wanted ... no other man could rival me at service, laying a fire, splitting logs, carving and roasting meat, pouring wine, and the sorts of things that the worse do to serve the good.'[8]

This amounts to three alternatives, really: one offered, one sketched by Odysseus himself, one mentioned as a taunt: farm work, household work, or remaining a 'beggar' and living on patronage and odd jobs, as the unpleasant Irus did. Very similar options present themselves to poor people in less-developed countries now: hard work on the land, paying badly; service, paying badly; or the search for patronage, an unsettled, unofficial sort of life, benefiting from the occasional stroke of luck.

But it was not so simple. A beggar started out 'without family, without law, without hearth'.[9] Whatever his aspirations he must first find a family and enter the bounds of its law: for we are not so very far yet from that kind of society in which 'each man gives law to his children and his women'[10] (the two plurals cover the two subordinate relationships in a patriarchal household, assuming that 'children' includes slaves, as it does commonly in later Greek). His first step of all must be to gain entry to a house.

Now in a town the rules of hospitality were different from those the country-dweller Eumaeus claimed to observe, as Odysseus's son Telemachus, not giving away his father's disguise, says to Eumaeus:

> 'Take this unhappy stranger to the town for him to scrape his meal there: *whoever wishes* will give him crust and cup. I cannot look after all men.'[11]

In a town, then, not every householder would offer a welcome, and those that did might think their grudging hospitality abused:

> 'Have we not enough other wanderers, troublesome vagrants, cleaners-up of feasts?'[12]

The beggar must ask advice[13] and make his choice of houses to approach: if not driven off by stones or dogs, he progressed as far as the doorway, and there he sat unless invited inside. The porch was the place for him even if, like Irus, he considered himself to be the house's only beggar. Between him and his future were two barriers none the less real for being invisible. One focus of the hall before him was the 'equal feast',[14] the dining and drinking of the 'Achaeans';[15] he would be drawn towards that from some distance.

> 'I know that many men are having a feast inside, because the smell rises up, and there is the sound of music, which the gods have made companion to the feast.'[16]

Surrounded by the feasters, but separate from them, was the household, whose focus was the hearth.[17] There was interaction between the feasters and the household, but it was limited. The housewife sat near her husband's chair; the women might join in conversation with the feasters;[18] bards, like other recognised craftsmen (see below), were offered food;[19] male and female slaves and attendants served food and wine;[20] the *Iliad* seems to show us that a boy might be relegated from feast to hearth if he had no father there;[21] servants, on the other hand, might be favoured with a special position:

> First of all godlike Telemachus saw the pig-farmer coming into the house, and so he quickly nodded to him to call him; [Eumaeus] looked around and took the folding stool where the steward used to sit carving all the meat for the suitors as they feasted in the house. He got it and carried it towards Telemachus's table, opposite, and there he sat down, and a squire cut a portion [of meat] and brought him it with bread from the basket.[22]

Not part of the men's feast, then, were women, servants and those without connections: outside both feast and hearth were the dogs[23] and the beggars.

In the doorway a beggar like the disguised Odysseus, visible to the feasters, hoped for an act as generous as that of Telemachus (who of course knew that this vagrant was his father):

> Telemachus called the pig-farmer over and said to him, taking a whole loaf from a fine basket and as much meat as he could hold in his cupped hands,
> 'Go and give the stranger this and tell him to go around all the suitors, begging.'[24]

With this invitation Odysseus went the rounds, 'starting from the right', asking each man for some food to put in his bag, at last returning to squat at the threshold, with his bag in front of him as a plate, and eat.

It would be an unusually bold man who, as night fell, made his way across the first invisible barrier without invitation and took part in the household work;[25] for indeed if he aimed at employment he was a possible threat to those already employed, and should expect enmity particularly from them. Odysseus faced the jealousy of the established beggar Irus, of the goatherd Melanthius[26] and of a housemaid, Melanthius' sister:

> 'Stranger, are you still here in the house begging from men? ... There are other feasts of the Achaeans.'[27]

Even on a quite different occasion, when well-dressed and looking his best, Odysseus when entering Alcinous's house in Scherie needed Athene's magical concealment to cross the room to the hearth and the queen, whose protection he had been advised to seek.[28]

Story-tellers

While many details may be attributable to the demands of the plot, the consistency of the *Odyssey* allows the reader to observe that, as is natural enough, a stranger's welcome depended on what he had to bargain with. A beggar sat in the doorway, 'for who goes out of doors to invite a stranger?'[29] ... No one would invite a beggar to consume him.'[30]

But a man of acknowledged skills, 'one of those who are public workmen, a seer or a healer of sicknesses or a maker of shields, or an inspired poet, who gives pleasure by singing,'[31] like an accepted labourer or servant,[32] would be invited to find his share of food on an equal footing with those at the hearth. In the passages just quoted Eumaeus, responding to the just suspicion that he is behind Odysseus's presence in the big house as a beggar, puts up a smokescreen of platitudes which conveniently bring out the social distinction.

The maker of the *Odyssey*, himself a poet close to the oral tradition, took several opportunities to specify what reception would best please an oral poet, 'honoured by the people'.[33] Among the Phaeacians we are to observe that Demodocus was sent for by name to the King's house and provided with a lyre, a table, a bowl of wine and a basket of food;[34] as if that were not enough, Odysseus on one occasion sent him over a portion of boar spare rib from the nobles' feast.[35]

Women outsiders

There are no female beggars in the *Odyssey*, as it happens. But the shame of vagrancy might come to a whole household,[36] and certainly might come to women as much as to men. It is reasonable to take the myth in Plato's *Symposium* (early 4th century B.C. – much later than the *Odyssey*) as extending the epic evidence and specifying one way a female vagrant might earn her food:

> The gods were celebrating, Craft's son Resource among them. While they were at dinner, Poverty came begging, as she would when a feast was on, and hung about the door. Resource became drunk on nectar (wine did not yet exist), went into Zeus's garden and sank down to sleep; and Poverty, deciding in her resourcelessness to have a child by Resource, lay down beside him, and there she conceived Eros.[37]

There were other ways. The story of the goddess Demeter, who came to Eleusis as a destitute old woman in the long central myth of the anonymous 7th or 6th century B.C. *Hymn to Demeter*, indicates what work might be expected of a beggar woman who took service. Demeter sits beside a well, the outdoor location where she would be most likely to meet other women, and asks to be advised 'to whose house, man's or woman's, I may go ... I could nurse well a newborn child, holding it in my arms, and keep house,[38] and make up the master bed in an alcove of the well-built rooms, and teach the work of a woman.'[39]

The *Odyssey* as a source

This paper cites many of the passages from the *Odyssey* that were used earlier this year by Elizabeth Minchin in her article on Homeric hospitality in *Petits propos culinaires*. The contrast between Elizabeth Minchin's use of the material and mine can be brought out by quoting from her summary of Odysseus's reception by Eumaeus and by the occupants of his own house:

> Eumaeus is a good and conscientious host. His care and concern for his beggar-guest contrasts with ... the violent treatment which the 'beggar' will receive at the hands of the suitors when he makes his way to the palace – by rights his home. The suitors, unlike Eumaeus, judge him by his appearance alone: they conclude that he is not of their kind. They feel free, therefore, to exploit the beggar as a source of entertainment, they make him the butt of their ridicule. They are as discourteous as hosts as they are as guests.[40]

It is reasonable to ask whether two such different evocations of the culture described in this single source, a Greek epic of the eighth century B.C., can both be valid. They can be. Central to the nature of the kind of storytelling represented by the *Iliad* and *Odyssey*, as also by the greatest Icelandic sagas, is a more-than-divine objectivity. The narrator is aware, if he wishes, of the tiniest detail of the thoughts, aims and deeds of every character, man, woman or god; he reports on all, switching focus as he pleases, as if from an immense height. The world he makes us see is, so to speak, complete. We are free to interpret it in terms of the good and bad behaviour of individual characters, as Elizabeth Minchin does, or of the demands of different kinds of social interaction, as I have tried to do. Neither approach is sufficient on its own: both, one hopes, contribute to the understanding of this particular society, imaginary and yet inextricably linked to the real society of early classical Greece.

Notes and References

1. *Odyssey* book 14.
2. *Odyssey* 14.56-8, cf. 14.402-4. The rule might fall heavily on a poor farmer with no neighbours (*Odyssey* 16.82-4) as a sensitive traveller would realise (*Odyssey* 17.18-19).
3. *Odyssey* 14.73-81.
4. *Odyssey* 16.49-52.
5. *Odyssey* 17.21.
6. *Odyssey* books 17-18.
7. *Odyssey* 18.357-364, cf. 17.222-8.
8. *Odyssey* 15.308-324.
9. *Iliad* 9.63.
10. *Odyssey* 9.114-5, said of the Cyclopes.
11. *Odyssey* 17.10-13.
12. *Odyssey* 17.376-7. My italics.
13. For advice sought and offered in similar circumstances compare *Odyssey* 15.307-312, 15.509-512 and 7.18-36 with the *Hymn to Demeter* quoted below.
14. The phrase is Iliadic, used both of human meals (*Iliad* 1.602, 23.56) and of divine (1.468 etc.).
15. *Odyssey* 20.182.
16. *Odyssey* 17.269-271, cf. 10.10-11.
17. *Odyssey* 6.303-315. In weighing the relative power of 'feast' and 'hearth' we may recall Vatin's free paraphrase of these lines: 'Ne t'y trompes pas, dit ... Nausicaa à Ulysse, mon père est le maître, mais c'est ma mère qui décide.' C. Vatin, *Recherches sur le mariage et la condition de la femme mariée à l'époque hellénistique*. Paris (Boccard) 1970.
18. *Odyssey* 6.308-9, 19.399-412, 18.206-291, cf. 17.90-98.
19. *Odyssey* 8.474-483.
20. *Odyssey* 1.109-160.
21. *Iliad* 22.492-9. Telemachus's position is oddly close to this. His father is presumed dead; his mother must choose her second husband outside the family, so that he risks loss of his inheritance: and he does not dine with the suitors but apart, where Eumaeus might pull up a stool and sit with him, see next quotation.
22. *Odyssey* 17.328-335.
23. *Odyssey* 10.216-7.
24. *Odyssey* 17.342-6.
25. *Odyssey* 18.306-345.
26. *Odyssey* 18.1-31, 17.217-222.
27. *Odyssey* 20.178-182.
28. *Odyssey* 7.139-145.
29. If elaboration is needed, Hesiod provides it (*Works and Days* 342-3): 'Invite your friend to a feast, but let your enemy alone: most of all invite whomever lives near you.'
30. *Odyssey* 17.382, 387.
31. *Odyssey* 17.383-5.
32. *Odyssey* 15.376-9.
33. *Odyssey* 8.472.
34. *Odyssey* 8.43-70, cf. 254-262.
35. 'Chine' is the traditional translation. *Odyssey* 8.474-8.
36. Tyrtaeus quoted by Lycurgus, *Against Leocrates* 107.
37. Plato, *Symposium* 203b.
38. Nursing and housekeeping were jobs for women too old for childbearing and sex, cf. *Homeric Hymn to Demeter* 101-4, *Odyssey* 1.435, 2.345-361.
39. *Homeric Hymn to Demeter* 138-144.
40. Elizabeth Minchin, 'Homer reflects on hospitality' in *Petits propos culinaires* no. 35 (1990) pp. 42-49.

Tradition and Innovation in the Pacific Northwest Outdoor Feast

by John Doerper

The scene was as pretty as an impressionist painting: a verdant lawn shaded by the grey branches and leafy canopies of giant, centuries-old oaks. Beneath the trees, on tables spread with colourful cloths, bouquets of flowers glowed in the afternoon sun. Now and then, the rays of the sun struck bottles and glasses of wine, with which each table was liberally supplied, shooting kaleidoscopic flashes of red and gold across the glade.

On one side of the dell the lawn had been pulled up, leaving a strip of bare earth some ten feet wide and fifty feet long. A bed of glowing oak coals stretched down the middle of the strip. To either side of the coals, which seemed to burn especially hot in the 100 degree (°F) heat of the day, green alder poles, their bark seared by the heat, were lined up – a well-spaced row to either side. Metal ferrules supported the poles, tilting them slightly towards the coals. Each pole was crowned by a whole butterflied salmon, flesh side towards the fire, skin side to the air.

An inimitable aroma of flowers, fresh woodland air, oak coals, hot alder, and seared salmon permeated the air. "The coals smell almost better than the salmon," said one cook. "Wait till it gets chilly tonight," interjected another, "they'll hang around the fire and finish up the beer." The beer, dispensed straight from the cask, was Bridgeport Ale from a small, "micro" brewery in Portland, Oregon, which brews only real ale. A good-natured argument erupted, on whether beer or wine go better with barbecued salmon.

The flattened salmon, closely grouped together, formed an elongated funnel. The heat pushing up and through the gaps between the fish evenly cooked the flesh. Several cooks monitored the salmon and as soon as each was deemed done, they rushed the fish to a serving buffet where people were lined up to load their plates not only with freshly barbecued salmon, but with other traditional foods of the Pacific Northwest outdoor feast as well: hot corn on the cob, salad, steamed mussels and clams, freshly baked rolls, and fresh fruit. A Dixieland band played lively tunes.

The sun began to set over the western mountains and the light turned soft and mellow, much as the chardonnay, pinot gris, pinot noir, and amber ale in our glasses, as I sat down to eat with Willamette Valley vintner Bill Blosser, innkeepers David Campiche, and sommelier Phil de Vito (whose wine cellar at the Salishan Lodge has long been recognised as the best in Oregon).

Our meal, simple as it seemed, had the weight of tradition behind it. Fastening butterflied salmon to alder poles and cooking it over an open fire was invented by the Indians of the Northwest Coast, long before the first white man landed on this shore. The modern addition – setting the sticks into metal ferrules instead of sticking them into the ground – was minimal. The Indians cooked their salmon plain, without condiments, but Rollie Toevs, who supervised the cooking, admitted to lightly sprinkling the salmon with salt and pepper to enhance the flavour. But he added no barbecue sauce, a practice widespread at backyard and community barbecues throughout the Northwest. (So much so, that an infant Northwest barbecue sauce industry has sprung up in the last year or two.) Steamed clams also go back to Indian times, though the clams are no longer steamed in seawater but in a broth of wine and herbs. Steamed mussels, though very popular at Northwest feasts, are a relatively new addition – they became popular about a decade ago, when they were introduced in Seattle by François Kissel, a French chef. Before that, mussels were referred to as "those ugly blue things on the rocks"). Sweet corn came to the Willamette Valley with the first settlers, in the 1830s, and has remained popular. To keep it at its sweetest and best it is picked just before cooking (lest its sugar change to starch). Serving a fresh salad with barbecued fish or meat is actually a Californian custom which spread north. It is always made from fresh seasonal ingredients. In our feast, vine-ripened tomatoes and sweet onions dominated the salad, because lettuce had bolted in the summer heat. The fruit, tree-ripened peaches, was also seasonal. It was too early for pears and apples, and you simply should not serve cold storage fruit at such an event.

Despite the bounty, this summer feast was not, however, complete. Later this year, in fall, (that is right now, as we sit here to discuss food and eating) foods out of season in summer are added to the feast: freshly gathered oysters, barbecued in their shells, swimming scallops (also cooked in their shells and eaten whole, with their roe), shrimp and prawns, simply boiled in herbed water, and Dungeness crab, cooked in seawater, cracked, and served with melted butter. Also missing were rice, potatoes, pasta, and cheese, because they were not considered suitable for a salmon barbecue.

But the feast, despite its traditional framework, exhibited several very unusual aspects. First, the location. We were on the grounds of Linfield College in McMinnville, Oregon, at the apex of the annual Pinot Noir Festival, a gathering of experts which brings together winemakers, technicians, the wine press, and connoisseurs from all over the world

– California, France, Germany, Australia – wherever the pinot noir grape is grown. The wines also came from all over, and ranged from simple village wines to mature beauties. Blanc de noir sparklers, and related varietals like pinot gris and chardonnay rounded out the picture. At first glance, there was nothing unusual about this, except that Linfield College started as a religious school and has been affiliated with the American Baptist Churches, USA, since its founding in 1849. Because American Baptists are not known for a love of alcohol in any form, this was very unusual indeed, and may signal a trend of a more liberal attitude by the traditional hellfire and brimstone, churches. (The festival is in its fourth year.) Also unusual was the presence of beer at a wine festival. But Northwest winemakers have unquestioningly accepted brewers of real ale as their own, ever since this cottage beer industry got its start in 1981, perhaps because Oregon real ales came to life in 1984 when a vintner, Dick Ponzi of Ponzi Vineyards near Portland, started the Columbia River Brewing Company (which brews Bridgeport Ales). But the presence of beer also proved that Oregon vintners do not fear that beer would ever replace wine as the Northwest's favourite food beverage, recognising that there is a place for both (with beer treated mostly as a hot-weather or after dinner drink).

More unusual than the presence of beer, however, was the fact that the tables held twice as many red wines than whites, since seafood dominated the feast. Earlier in the day, during a luncheon of seared tuna and roasted quail, much ado had been made about matching seafood and pinot noir, but during the evening's feast, everyone took it for granted. (Even though Americans, as a group, prefer white wines to red with almost any food.)

In Northwest cooking there is a new stance, an attitude that cookery must be good to be simple. While this was true even ten years ago, much has changed in the Northwest during the last decade. Foods still tend to be simple – barbecued salmon, roasted meat, grilled chicken – but the sauces, condiments and other accoutrements have become more complex. Clams and mussels are often steamed with ginger root and sake instead of parsley and white wine. Fresh Dungeness crab still comes with drawn butter, but it is also served with ginger or with fermented Chinese black beans. Smaller fish may be served whole, steamed or grilled, instead of being breaded and fried (the traditional method). Even the fact that lamb is beginning to replace beef as the favourite backyard barbecue meat proves that local palates are becoming more sophisticated. Curiously, this sophistication is coupled to an anti-European attitude (despite the increasing popularity of European-style wines). Throughout the Northwest, French restaurants suffer from a lack of business while Chinese, Korean, Southeast Asian, and Mexican restaurants prosper. Wild Ginger, a Seattle restaurant, combining the styles of different Asian cuisines with fresh local products, is doing a land office business. Of the European-style restaurant cuisines, only Italian cafés are doing well – perhaps because of their down-to-earth approach to cooking, perhaps because of the strong, rustic flavours of the food. For there is no question that the Northwest has discovered strong flavours. Pungent herbs and condiments like lemongrass, Thai basil, cilantro, wasabi, fermented black beans, or chile paste are added to a great number of dishes, from delicate sanddabs to hearty venison. Salsa, fresh or cooked, but always pungent with red or green chiles has also become a favourite Northwest condiment, showing up on oysters on the halfshell, on fresh fruit, and with all sorts of fish, fowl, and meat.

But, despite the many changes, a certain amount of conservativism pervades public and backyard barbecues. I have selected a few recipes to show the range of preparations.

The Recipes:

Barbecued Riesling Salmon

Besides using barbecue sauce (often sweet from added fruit) on their salmon, Northwesterners like soaking salmon in a marinade heavily laced with salt and brown sugar before smoking or barbecuing the fish. Here's a more refined version:

(Serves 6)

1 5-pound fillet of salmon, marinated for 12 to 24 hours in a late harvest (Spätlese or Auslese) Riesling

1. Wipe the fillet dry. Let sit in a draft of air for a few minutes until a light glaze forms on the flesh side.

2. Place salmon fillet skin-side down on barbecue grill over a bed of very hot grapevine cuttings, alder or fruit wood coals, or charcoal. To obtain a good smoke flavour, grill the salmon with the lid on (my barbecue, a cast-iron Japanese hibachi, has no lid – I cover the salmon with a large, inverted gold pan – the kind you use for washing gold nuggets from creeks). Cook until the fish flakes easily with a fork. (About ten minutes per pound and inch of thickness).

Serve salmon hot from the grill with freshly baked bread and raw summer vegetables. Accompany with dill sauce.

Dill Sauce

    3 tablespoons vegetable oil (I use almond oil)
    1 tablespoon zinfandel vinegar (or another first-rate California wine vinegar)
    1 tablespoon sugar
    Salt and freshly ground white pepper to taste
    2 tablespoons Dijon mustard
    3 tablespoons minced fresh dill

Blend all ingredients together. Serve with smoked or barbecued salmon.

"The Recipe" for a Neighbourhood Salmon Feast

Up and down the Coast, the most popular salmon barbecue sauces contain tomato ketchup and Worcestershire sauce in varying quantities. Here's the recipe many consider the "standard" from which others are adapted:

    (Dresses one ten pound salmon)

    1/2 pound butter
    2 tablespoons prepared mustard
    1 clove garlic, crushed
    1/4 cup tomato ketchup
    Dash of Worcestershire sauce
    4 tablespoons soy sauce
    Dash of pepper
    1 tablespoon lemon juice

Mix ingredients together; heat over low heat. Stir to combine ingredients. Baste salmon one to two hours before cooking, then occasionally as the salmon cooks over the hot coals.

Salmon in Oregon Hazelnut Butter

Tony Kischner of the Shelburne Restaurant in Seaview, WA, uses a more sophisticated approach for salmon:

    (Serves 6)

    3 tablespoons unsalted butter
    6 7-ounce salmon fillets (preferably chinook)
    Salt and freshly ground pepper to taste
    1 1/2 cups fish stock
    1 1/2 tablespoons lemon juice
    1/2 cup hazelnut butter*

1. Select a baking sheet large enough to hold the fillets and deep enough to hold liquid. Coat with the unsalted butter.

2. Lightly salt and pepper the salmon fillets. Lay them into the pan; add the fish stock and lemon juice. Place a dollop of hazelnut butter on top of each fillet.

3. Bake salmon in preheated 500°F oven for 10 minutes.

4. Remove salmon from oven; place fillets on individual heated plates.

5. Pour the liquid from the baking sheet into a sauté pan and bring to a boil. Add the remaining hazelnut butter to the pan and simmer until the sauce has thickened.

6. Divide the sauce equally among the fillets and serve immediately.

Hazelnut Butter

    1/2 cup whole unsalted butter, softened
    1/3 cup ground roasted hazelnuts
    1 shallot, minced
    1 teaspoon minced garlic
    1 tablespoon parsley, minced

Combine all ingredients in small bowl until well blended. Set aside at room temperature.

Mussels in Pinot Noir Butter

It's a toss-up whether Northwesterners like salmon better than clams, or vice versa. But you can be sure they will be steaming their clams in a kettle instead of baking them in a pit of kelp, the way New Englanders do. Using sake, Japanese rice wine, instead of white wine has become very popular. You drink either chilled white wine or sake on the rocks with this dish. Unless you prefer a young pinot noir from a lesser vintage. Of course, it's quite permissible to steam clams or mussels in pinot noir:

    (Serves 4)

    4 dozen mussels
    1 1/2 cups Oregon pinot noir
    1/4 cup finely minced shallots
    1/4 cup freshly squeezed lemon Juice
    1/2 pound unsalted butter, cut into small cubes
    1 cup fresh salicornia (pickleweed – sold in Seattle markets as "sea beans")

1. Pick over mussels. Discard any that do not close when touched. Scrub mussel shells well. Debeard.

2. Heat 1 cup pinot noir in large stainless steel or enamelled pot. Add mussels. Cover, steam mussels open. Discard any shells that do not open.

3. In the meantime, cook remaining 1/2 cup of wine, shallots, and lemon juice in a heavy (non-aluminium) skillet. Reduce over low heat until liquid is almost gone. Stir in cooking juices from mussels. Reduce over medium to high heat until liquid thickens. Caution: in the final stages, liquid may thicken very rapidly. Do not let it burn!

4. Remove pan from heat and add 1 or 2 small cubes of butter. Add remaining butter a cube at a time. Stir steadily with wire whisk until blended. Butter sauce should have the consistency of home-made mayonnaise (neither too solid nor too liquid). (The warm skillet should retain sufficient heat to do this smoothly – if temperature drops too much, return skillet to low heat). If butter separates from sauce (curdles), whisk rapidly to emulsify.

5. Chop or break pickleweed into 1/8-inch pieces.

6. Remove mussels from shell. Discard upper shells. Make small beds of chopped pickleweed in lower shells. Place a mussel on each bed and cover with sauce. Serve warm.

David Campiche's Clam Cakes

David Campiche, innkeeper at the Shelburne Inn in Seaview, Washington, serves what may well be the best breakfast on the Coast. Growing up on the Coast when razor clams were common, Campiche likes to serve them to his guests, though they are quite scarce now and he often has to dig the clams himself.

    (Serves 6)

    4 cups potatoes, parboiled and grated
    1 medium yellow onion, chopped
    1 small red onion, chopped
    6-8 fresh razor clams, chopped
    6 beaten eggs
    1/2 cup all-purpose flour
    1 tablespoon finely chopped fresh thyme
    2 tablespoons finely chopped fresh oregano

3 tablespoons chopped fresh chives
1/8 teaspoon cayenne
Salt to taste
1 stick unsalted butter, melted, and more butter as needed for frying

1. Parboil and grate potatoes. Chop onions and combine with clams, eggs, potatoes, thyme, oregano, chives, and butter.

2. Heat a small amount of butter in frying pan. Fill a large spoon with clam mixture, drop into pan, and fry at medium heat. Cook 3 to 4 minutes on each side, until golden brown. Serve hot.

Razor Clam Pie

Cathy Wandell also gave me this recipe. I had finished three books on Northwest cookery before she told me about this dish, an old favourite on the Coast. I was crestfallen. How could I have missed it? I began to check other recipe books on the foods of the Northwest. No clam pie. I began to ask around. No one in Seattle had ever heard of it. But folks on the Coast knew all about it. Why hadn't they shared the recipe with me? Because this pie served as a famine or leftover dish in the past, when razor clams were plenty. The cooks didn't believe anybody writing a cookbook could be even remotely interested in such a humble dish:

Clam Mixture:

1 large onion, chopped
2 tablespoons butter
1/2 pint chopped clams
1 - 2 stalks celery, chopped
1 large potato, diced
1 tablespoon parsley flakes
1/3 pound bacon, cubed and cooked

Sauce:

2 tablespoons butter
3 tablespoons flour
1/2 cup vermouth
1/2 cup evaporated milk
1/2 teaspoon salt
1/4 teaspoon freshly ground pepper
1/8 teaspoon nutmeg
1 dash Tabasco sauce

Pastry, Top and Bottom Crust:

1 1/2 cups flour
1/4 teaspoon salt
6 tablespoons butter
2 tablespoons shortening
4 tablespoons cold water

1. Sauté onion in 2 tablespoons butter for 10 minutes. Add clams, vegetables, drained bacon, and cook for 5 more minutes.

2. In a saucepan, melt 2 tablespoons butter. Stir in flour, then vermouth and stir till smooth. Then pour in milk and again stir till smooth; stir in salt, pepper, nutmeg, and Tabasco sauce.

3. Combine sauce with clam mixture. Pour into 10-inch pie shell lined with crust and cover with remaining crust. Bake for 10 minutes at 400°F, then for 40 minutes at 350°F. Let stand for 1/2 hour before cutting.

Below-the-Salt Cookery

by Christopher Driver

'My most embarrassing moment', to borrow a phrase from that well known periodical called Digester's Read, was positively courted. Imagine the white sahib in the Blackwell's of Madras, five years ago, glancing along the well-stocked shelves of cookery, plucking out a ten-rupee paperback, and wondering for at least five minutes whether I had the crust to present it at the till. The Kama Sutra, the Good Brothel Guide - these would have been easy compared with that - in hungry India - but we symposiasts are nothing but brazen. I can still see and hear the little giggle of the young woman who took my money, but never mind: here is the book whose moment has come for this year's theme: *Tasty Dishes from Waste Items* by Aroona Reejhsinghani (Bombay, 1973, reprinted 1978, therefore clearly meeting a felt need in circles which have lost the struggle to keep up with the Patels).

I cannot claim to have eaten the dishes whose recipes are printed below but 'every one is tried and tested and guaranteed to work', according to the back cover, and Mrs. Reejhsinghani is an experienced nutritionist. Lunchers at the Symposium cleared the dish of water melon rind salad - whether or not they noticed the label. She is versatile too, as author of *Housewife's Guide to Chinese Cooking* and *Woman's World* ("Want to know how to be fashionable and beautiful? The author tells you in detail, offering innumerable helpful hints on how to make the best of what you have got").

'What you have got', in the culinary context, is the rinds of water melon, the banana skins normally reserved for the predicaments of Cabinet ministers, the pods of 'fresh young peas' (where can these be found in London?) and the heads and tails of pomfret or other fish, fully adequate for fish fingers, Bombay-style. The recipes speak for themselves, and if they do not sound precisely finger-lickin' good, let alone *vaut le pélerinage*, the genre is much closer to European models than present cookery book buyers realise. Nothing in Reejhsinghani is as disgusting as the attempts printed in various British wartime cookery books, to synthesize something that could be described as 'mayonnaise'. For that matter nothing is closer to *Tasty Dishes from Waste Items* than the kitchen procedure of the ingenious chefs de cuisine for whom Nicolas Freeling worked in bottom-rung hotels in French seaside resorts, operating the culinary maxim or system: *rien ne se perd*. Of course, bottom-rung cookery in India stands far lower than Freeling's hilarious *Kitchen Book* (1970), and indeed far lower than Reejhsinghani: few Indians could afford ten rupees for a cookery book, and only a minority could read it (outside the state of Kerala, where the literacy rate compares rather well with modern Britain).

I read this book not sardonically but wistfully. We have learned to use her spices, but where are these carrot and radish leaves which Reejhsinghani recommends - never mind the green banana skins (bananas, not the bland yellow plantains Fyffes send us) and the jackfruit seeds? We shall have to manufacture our own 'waste items'. Cooks of the industrial world, unite: you have nothing to lose but your processor blades.

Carrot leaves bhajee

2 cups top leaves of carrots, cleaned and sliced. 2 medium onions, sliced. 1 small piece ginger. 4 green chillies, sliced. ¼ tsp. turmeric powder. 1 medium tomato, sliced. Salt and chilli powder to taste. ¼ cup moong dal.

Put 2 tblsps. oil in a pan, heat it and fry onions, ginger and chillies till soft. Put in all the spices, dal and leaves and cook till dry. Put in tomato and ¼ cup water and cook till done.

Spicy peapods no. 2

Pods of 250 grams fresh and tender peas. 1 tblsp. mango powder. ¼ tsp. pepper. Salt and chilli powder to taste.

Wash the pods and boil in salted water till tender and completely dry, put in 1 tblsp. oil and all the spices and cook for a few minutes. Serve cool. After you have eaten the pods throw out the hard portion from the mouth.

Watermelon rind salad

1 cup grated white portion of watermelon. 25 grams roasted and pounded groundnuts. 1 tblsp. grated coconut. ¼ tsp. mustard seeds. 1 green chilli, minced. A handful of sliced coriander leaves. Salt and chilli powder and lime juice to taste.

Heat 1 tblsp. oil and put in mustard seeds, when they stop popping, remove from fire and mix in the rest of the above ingredients.

Mixed peel salad

Steam peels of marrow and pumpkin and slice into pieces. Mix in sliced cucumber peels. Add sliced tomato, onion, lime juice, little coconut milk and salt. Sprinkle grated coconut and coriander leaves on top before serving.

Fish salad no. 2

Flesh of 2 heads and tails of boiled pomfret. 1 small each of sliced cucumber and tomato. 1 hard-boiled egg, minced. Salad dressing. Potatochips.

Mix together fish, egg and salad dressing. Take crisp reddish leaves and decorate with vegetables and potato chips.

Feasts of the Fur Traders

by Dorothy Duncan
Executive Director, The Ontario Historical Society Canada

For thousands of years Canada, as it is known to-day, was a wilderness of forests, plains, mountains and waterways. The primeval forest was home to hundreds of thousands of Native Peoples who did not consider it hostile, but a life-sustaining environment. About four hundred years ago the first explorers from Europe and Great Britain appeared looking for a northwest passage to China and India and their rare and valuable trading goods - silks, spices and gold. There was a great deal of disappointment and frustration that a harsh, rocky and forested land blocked their path, but it soon vanished with the realisation that there was "gold" of another kind to be found there. By coincidence, gentlemen in the Old World wanted fine hats made of fine felt and good felt could not be made of anything but animal hair or fur. The best felting material ever discovered was the soft downy undercoat of the beaver. This explanation from an expert helps us to understand the singular function of the beaver in providing hats so prized that men pursued him across oceans and continents:

> To be of good quality, thick and heavy, the beaver-pelt must come from an animal taken during the winter, and taken in as hard a climate as possible. Then the skin carries two kinds of fur; close to the skin is a thick mass of beaver-wool, down or duvet as the French called it; on top is a glossy fur of long guard hairs. It was the beaver-wool above all which the felters wanted but it was difficult to get the beaver-wool out from a prime winter's skin without also tearing out the guard hairs and thereby completely destroying the skin. English and French felters liked to get their beaver-wool from skins from which the guard-hairs had already been removed and this made them dependent on coat beaver. These were skins which the Indians had worn for a season and in the process lost their guard hairs and become thoroughly greasy. The custom of wearing beaver, an art of doing so in such a way as to impart a maximum of grease, was peculiar to the northern Indians of Canada. [1]

This then was the "gold" of the Canadian interior and the reason that great commercial empires grew from the search for furs in the Canadian wilderness - the XY Company, the Hudson's Bay Company, the North West Company and many more. Much has been written about the trade and the men who took part in it, but I would like to highlight some of the occasions when there was a time for relaxation and feasting despite the bitter rivalries and the rush to a wild frontier that developed as the search for furs expanded to meet the demand of Old World markets that appeared to have no limits. The North West Company designed one of the most ingenious plans to bring out the furs despite the geography and the climate of Canada, and yet at the same time we have evidence that they took time to relax in the midst of getting the job done.

Due to the short Canadian summer and the difficulty of transport in this unsettled wilderness, it was impossible to bring the furs from the western interior to Montreal in the east and return before the waterways were frozen. Therefore, an inland headquarters was built, first at Grand Portage and later at Fort William and the month of July was chosen as the time of the Rendezvous. As soon as the ice melted in the lakes and rivers, the fur trappers and traders from the interior started for Fort William paddling their beaver pelts in their small 'canots du nord', a journey, in most cases of over a thousand miles. At the same time, the partners and merchants of the North West Company left Montreal with the trade goods that were to be exchanged for the furs at the Rendezvous. They were paddled in great 'canots de maître' by French Canadian voyageurs, who as well as paddling had to carry the packages of trade goods (one hundred pounds per package) on their backs over the 35 portages between Montreal and Fort William. These enormous Montreal canoes carried about two tonnes and it took just over a month of steady travel to cover the distance of about 900 miles.

In July the two groups began to assemble - the fur brigades from the west and the merchant partners from the east. It is not surprising then that the annual Rendezvous became a legendary time of feasting and celebration. The population of Fort William grew to about 2000 persons and included the English and Scottish merchants and their clerks, the French Canadian canoemen, men and women of the First Nations who were guides, advisors and often providers of specialised needs such as survival food for the chain of forts and posts stretching into the interior.

The central building at Fort William was the Great Hall and these two descriptions give us an insight on how they appeared to travellers of the period:

> In the middle of a gracious square rises a large building elegantly constructed, though of wood, with a long piazza or portico, raised about five feet from the ground, and surmounted by a balcony, extending along the whole front. In the centre is a saloon or hall, sixty feet in length by thirty in width, decorated

with several pieces of painting and some portraits of the leading partners. It is in this hall that the agents, partners, clerks, interpreters and guides, take their meals together, at different tables. The kitchen and servants' quarters rooms are in the basement. [2]

The dining hall is a noble apartment, and sufficiently capacious to entertain two hundred. A finely executed bust of the late Simon McTavish is placed in it, with portraits of various Proprietors. A full-length likeness of Nelson, together with a splendid painting of the Battle of the Nile also decorate the walls. [3]

From accounts of other fur trading posts we have descriptions of meals as reported by travellers, and this one helps us to picture a dinner there although this actually describes Fort Vancouver:

At the end of a table twenty feet in length stands Governor McLoughlin directing guests and gentlemen from neighbouring posts to their places, and chief traders, traders, the physician, clerks and the farmer slide respectfully to their places, at distances from the governor corresponding to the dignity of their rank in service. Thanks are given to God, and all are seated. Roast beef and pork, boiled mutton, baked salmon, boiled ham, beets, carrots, turnips, cabbage and potatoes, and wheaten bread, are tastefully distributed over the table among a dinner set of elegant Queen's Ware, furnished with glittering glasses and decanters of various coloured Italian wines. [4]

During the month of the Rendezvous dignity appears to have been aside once the sun began to set. Days were spent in the Committee House at meetings where the business of the trade was carried out in great secrecy, but the nights were spent dining and roistering in the Great Hall. Dinners of "buffalo tongue and hump that had been either smoked or salted, thirty pound lake trout and whitefish that could be netted in the river at the gates to the Fort, venison, wild ducks, geese, partridge and beaver tails would be augmented with confectioners' delicacies that had been packed all the way from Montreal in those great canoes." [5] Traditionally five toasts honoured the fur trade, and these were given in the following order: Mary, the Mother of all saints; the King; the fur trade in all its branches; the voyageurs, their wives and children; and absent brethren. A classic ritual marked the peak of these memorable evenings. Armed with a paddle, everyone sat on the floor in two long rows and singing lustily, paddled an imaginary great canoe across the floor. This must have been one of the sights of Canadian history that should be more permanently recorded.

With the ten gallon kegs of rum running low and dawn fingering the windows of the Great Hall to find the partners of the North West Company, names that mark and brighten the map of Canada, leaping on benches, chairs, and oaken wine barrels to "shoot the rapids" from the tilted tables to the floor, and singing the songs of home. Mounting broad bladed paddles, the gentlemen in knee breeches and silver buckled shoes pounded around the hall in impromptu races, shoving boisterously, piling up at the corners, breaking off only to down another brimming bumper of spirits. [6]

These were the memories they carried with them on the long journeys back into the interior as they pursued that little animal that was the basis for vast commercial empires as well as a fashion trend that our ancestors enjoyed.

End notes

1. Rich, E.E., "Pro Pelle Cutem", *The Beaver*, Spring, 1958, page 12.
2. Russell, A. L., Papers on Fort William in Thunder Bay Historical Society Papers, Thunder Bay, 1915, page 15.
3. MacKay, D., *The Honourable Company*, Toronto, 1949, page 204.
4. Hind, H. Y., *Narrative of The Canadian Red River Exploring Expedition of 1857*, London, 1860, pages 25-30.
5. Harmon, Leslie F., *Forts of Canada*. Toronto, 1969, page 205.
6. *Ibid.*, page 205.

Butter Before Guns

by Hugo Dunn-Meynell

The year was 1943, and I was sixteen years old.

As a schoolboy, I had survived the worst of the *blitzkrieg* - curled up nightly on a concrete floor. The legacy of this has been a lifetime capacity to sleep whenever I wish, and a feeling of being at home in cellars.

I now found myself licking stamps in a large building in the City of London. Every ten days, I was expected to take my turn at 'firewatching'. This involved sleeping in the office vaults until the air-raid sirens sounded. Then I grabbed some ancient binoculars and climbed on to the roof, which had a fine view across London Bridge, and a telephone to the nearest hosepipe.

The "V1", a flying bomb colloquially known as the "doodle-bug", was Hitler's latest secret weapon: when its fuel ran out, it dived and one had to take cover. This "buzz-bomb" was superseded by huge "V2" rockets, one of whose descendants was eventually to land on the moon, a possibility that did not occur to us in the nineteen-forties.

V1s and V2s were normally dispatched from the French Channel ports in daylight; Heinkel bombers provided our after-dark *frissons*. So, there was usually a tranquil period between 5.30 when the office closed, and around 9 o'clock, when the anti-aircraft guns began their work. We devoted this period to feasting.

The War historians, when they mention food at all, usually say that there wasn't much eating to be done. Do not believe it. A little ingenuity, street cunning, and tenuous connections with useful people, enabled us every ten days to sit down to a reasonably enjoyable supper with the added piquancy that, for all we knew, it would be our last.

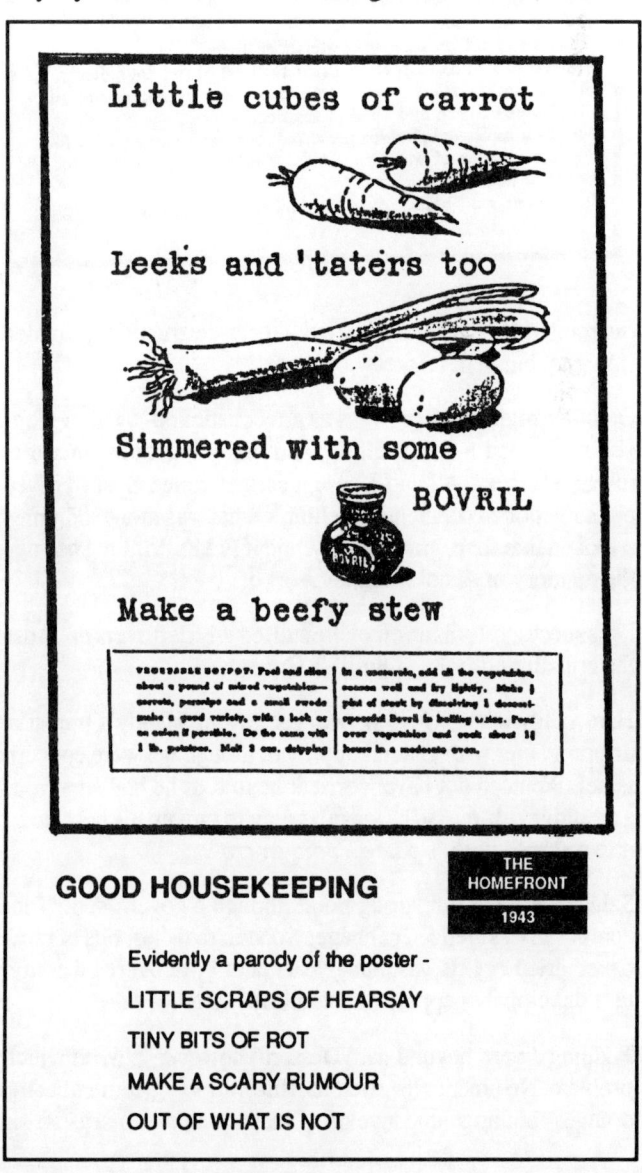

GOOD HOUSEKEEPING — THE HOMEFRONT 1943

Evidently a parody of the poster -
LITTLE SCRAPS OF HEARSAY
TINY BITS OF ROT
MAKE A SCARY RUMOUR
OUT OF WHAT IS NOT

Ours was a monastic life, since the Government ruled that firewatching was men's work. Our team consisted of Richard, an archetypal pinstriped managing clerk, who every day struggled to London from seafront Brighton, then a "sealed" town with heavily mined beach where secret preparations for the D-day invasion were in progress. Dick, of course, never told us about these. "Careless Talk Costs Lives", the posters said, but occasionally he threw out dark hints of "pretty big stuff", and then looked guilty for a while; Jimmy ("invalided" from the Army after nasty injuries at Dunkirk, and subsequently "bombed out" of the hospital where they were trying to put him together again - "like Humpty Dumpty", he said cheerfully, amazing a succession of beautiful girlfriends with the scars and stitches); Paddy (cockney, 1914-18 sergeant-major, and proud parent now of a 40-year-old of similar rank); another veteran named Fred, our janitor, a bad-tempered fellow with a rather boring flow of monosyllabic expletives. His language both shocked and fascinated me: how could the sole adjective in his vocabulary be used to describe everything, from wartime stout and Hermann Goering to Vera Lynn and (most respectfully) "the King and Queen, God bless 'em"? Fred's redeeming feature, however, was a hot line to one of the few surviving fish-and-chip shops in E.C.3.

Edgar, another WW1 veteran, was First Reserve, though being also a Home Guard officer, he was technically exempt from firewatching.

So there we were, Jimmy with one eye, Richard and Fred lame, Paddy ancient, Edgar seldom present, and Hugo wet behind the ears. By common consent, my contribution to the Defeat of Tyranny was to orchestrate the culinary talents of the duty quartet, both in the procurement of agreeable things to eat, and in the preparation.

Before the day of our shift. I would try to persuade my mother that she had sufficient ingredients to bake a dried-egg cake, using saccharin tablets and - when desperate - medicinal paraffin in place of butter.

FAVOURITE WAR-TIME RECIPE

AUSTERITY CHRISTMAS PUDDING

- 3 ozs. Self-raising Flour.
- 3 ozs. Breadcrumbs.
- ¼ lb. Chopped Dates.
- 3 ozs. Raw Carrot, grated.
- 1 level teaspoon Bicarbonate Soda.
- ½ teaspoon Almond Essence.
- ¼ Nutmeg, grated.
- 2 tablespoons Dried Egg.
- 3 ozs. Cooking Fat (Dripping or Suet).
- ¼ lb. Chopped Prunes.
- ¼ lb. Sultanas.
- 4 ozs. Raw Potato, grated. Pinch Salt.
- 1 large tablespoon Golden Syrup.
- 1 tablespoon Marmalade.

Procedure for making :

Soak prunes in water over night.
Rub fat with flour.
Draw water off prunes, stone and chop them.
Add breadcrumbs to prunes, dates and rest of dry ingredients.
Stir in finely grated raw potato, carrot and apple, marmalade, Golden Syrup and almond essence.
Mix to a moist dough with the dried egg reconstituted with four tablespoons of water.
Leave to stand overnight.
Put into greased basin, cover and boil for at least 3 to 4 hours.

But first, there was soup, prepared over the office gas-ring once the afternoon tea-break was over. I quickly learned how to achieve miracles with simmered potatoes, carrots and parsnips. The mixture was painstakingly sieved, since electric blenders would not be available for another 10 years; at an advanced stage I added a can of *Heinz Cream of Tomato*, coaxed from one of the counter staff at Jolly's Snack Bar in Cannon Street. They had a corner in that particular comestible, evidently stockpiled at the time of Munich, in much the same way as my uncle William had laid down '33 Clicquot. All of this was enlivened by some splendid herb (was it thyme?) from Richard's Sussex garden, which apparently thrived on bombardment.

Our entrées varied considerably. If Fred's city contacts were "frying tonight", slabs of skate might come our way, with masses of chips. Sometimes, we ate spaghetti - no onions for the sauce, nor, of course, Italian tomato purée, but *Bovril* came in handy, and occasionally there were leeks. Mrs. Paddy grew chives in her Hackney windowbox, and unrationed "soya link" sausages (warranted 10% real meat), fried to near-destruction, provided a substance that would have given them hysterics in Bologna, but kept us pretty buoyant.

On other nights, my prowess as a reconstituted-dried-egg omelette-maker was stretched to the limit. The leathery yellow needed a lively filling, and many ingenious mixtures were tried in turn. Soyer would have admired my resourcefulness. A Lend-Lease meatloaf called Spam proved popular, and was our introduction to the American phenomenon of 'contents labelling': what was monosodium glutamate, we wondered? "National Cheddar", though it looked like soap, grated tastily, and if Fred's drinking partner could produce a bit of smoked haddock, we honoured the memory of Arnold Bennett, sort of.

Less successful was an omelette stuffed with leftovers of "Austerity Christmas Pudding", enriched with Marmite and the crunch of crumbled Smith's Crisps.

Ham sandwiches, 1/- (5 pence) each from Mandy's upmarket snack bar in Leadenhall Market and fried crisp in dripping, met with general approval, though we were concerned lest we offended Jimmy, whose second name was Israel. We need not have worried: he told us he had survived "the Beaches" (Dunkirk, remember) for two days on a mouldy pork-pie, so he wasn't going to turn up his nose now at more palatable bits of pig than ever found their way into a shared poilu's *pâté de porc en croûte*.

Salads were not our strong point, though a government "food flash" each week besought us to eat more of them, composed of shredded cabbage, wooden radishes, bits of cold spud, no garlic, and occasional chunks of tomato and baked dried egg. It was many years later I discovered that my parents' gardenful of nasturtiums could have yielded us a deliciously peppery and colourful summer salad.

Puddings were beyond us. "Dessert" however, a word which in those days meant fruit, was never too much of a problem. No pineapples, melons, (fuel rationing, remember), grapes nor (since none of us could claim to be pregnant) oranges; but an abundance of whatever came into season, since there were no freezers and the canning factories' output went to the armed forces, a priority we never questioned. The American government once or twice sent California prunes: we devoured them *au naturel*. Once I made a finale of "chocolate truffles", based on soya flour, "preserving sugar" and cocoa powder. They were greeted with similar excitement to the news of El Alamein.

There was always beer of some sort, Edgar occasionally contributed a bottle of claret, and coffee (sugarless) was limitless. The per capita tea ration was, I believe, about three times our average consumption in Britain today.

I need hardly say that 'Black Market' food and drink did not feature. It could be bought quite easily, we knew, but it would never have occurred to us to tap into the system; just not cricket. I was to be amazed, on my first forays into then-occupied Europe, to learn that patronising Le Marché Noir was there regarded as a demonstration of patriotism; but of course we wanted our leaders to win the war, and many of the Continentals didn't much care.

We had visitors, the guardians of neighbouring buildings mainly. One night, Paddy arrived with his son, who had access to Rainbow Corner, the G.I. canteen in Shaftesbury Avenue. They brought with them some peculiar stuffed buns called hamburgers.

Our conversation was mostly about food. Dick, who pined for decent cheese more than filet steak, told us (so often that we could have screamed) how twelve months after the Fall of France, a client had taken him to Simpson's in The Strand, where special customers could still cajole a wedge of Camembert. Jimmy's mother had worked wonders at Passover. Paddy and the missus occasionally struck lucky at a jellied eel stall in the Old Kent Road.

From Edgar, we heard the story of the very discreet "Court Martial" of a titled Home Guard private whose crime of stealing ammunition had to be reconciled with his remarkable skill at potting delectable rabbits. A school-friend of mine who had already managed to get into uniform, called one night clutching an unlabelled bottle of real Navy grog: he's an Admiral now, and I'm not surprised. Jimmy's much decorated kid brother, who held the RAF's record for more sorties over Berlin than anyone else, once turned up with a huge can of peaches. Occasionally, Edgar and Fred would reminisce about the Flanders trenches: I recall their discussing the relative merits of two Madamoiselles from Somewhere-or-other, Fifine and Marie-Therèse, barmaids whose various services they had both patronised some quarter-century earlier. "I liked Fifine best," said Fred, "She worked *wiv* yer, if y'know wot I mean..."

When daylight came, we breakfasted at Jones' Dairy in Crooked Lane near the old Billingsgate Fish Market – both now vanished. The excellent Minister of Food, Lord Woolton, recognised that fish-porters needed fuel, so Mr. Jones and his pretty wife were able to do us pretty well, though the excursion mopped up the whole of our nightly "subsistence allowance" of 4/6d (translation, 22½ pence). At Christmas, we even got **real** fried eggs, plus a big kiss each from Mrs. J.

Came the day when I took the King's Shilling and said goodbye to my motley of fellow anti-incendiaries. My diet improved, except at the times I had to take over as Ship's Cook.

I seldom go to the City these days, and it is usually to visit wine cellars or (I blush) attend Livery banquets. But as I pass along Cannon Street, my mind always turns to our Jerome K. Jeromesque camaraderie of nearly half a century ago. I, of course, am the only survivor, but I like to think of the others enjoying the Paradise they deserve - of Dick making up for the lost Camembert years, and Paddy and son sharing celestial *Big Macs*. I'm sure Jimmy was quickly forgiven the ham sandwiches, though Edgar may have had to do some explaining about the rabbits. As for Fred, no doubt he is reunited with the industrious Fifine.

Brandade de Morue en Tenue de Guerre

This creamy salt cod "in battledress" is, though I say it myself, a splendid version of a classic French dish, made entirely from ingredients readily available throughout the grim 'forties. If the potatoes were omitted, it could fairly claim to be an authentic "brandade de morue", but in that case one really ought to have encased the mixture in a croûte – which would have been difficult in the era of National Wheatmeal flour and an acute shortage of fats.

I have long since mislaid my Wartime recipe, but I have based this one on those of Elizabeth David, Pierre Koffmann and Richard Olney's Time-Life series.

Ingredients

    1000 g salt cod, soaked overnight in running water
    500 ml milk
    500 ml water
    2 sprigs of thyme
    2 bay leaves
    300 g light olive oil
    5 garlic cloves, crushed
    800 g potatoes
    Freshly ground pepper

Method

Bake the potatoes (Gas mark 5) in the oven. When they are cooling, cut them into halves lengthwise and carefully scoop out the flesh, taking care to leave the "shells" intact: put these briefly back into the oven to make them crisp, then put aside in a dry place to cool.

Mash the potato well, with a fork, using no seasoning, and put it aside in a covered bowl.

Put the milk, water and soaked cod in a saucepan with the thyme and bay leaf. Bring to the boil, then simmer on a low heat for 10 minutes. Take the pan off the heat and leave to cool. Strain off the cooled liquid and reserve it. Skin, bone and flake the fish while still warm.

Heat the oil in a saucepan. When it is sizzling, add a little of the cod and stir well with a wooden spoon. Add a little more cod, stir well and repeat until you have used all the cod. Make sure the fat stays very hot and that the fish absorbs it all. Stir in the garlic and parsley, and mix well.

Put the fish mixture into a china bowl. Using a wooden spoon, slowly mix in the mashed potatoes. The mixture should be smooth, with the consistency of very thick cream. If it is not, add some of the stock. Add pepper, and taste: the pepper flavour should be very pronounced. Pile the mixture into the potato shells and decorate with tiny sprigs of parsley.

You will probably have some Brandade left over: it goes well with crispbread.

Salt cod, in common with the best oysters, is not normally sold in England until September.

Food for Family and Friends from Shrove Tide to Easter

by Johanna M. P. Edema and Katinka (Christina A. M. I.) Hermans

Introduction

For ages Shrovetide and Easter were sober Lent's festive companions, each marked by its own set of special foods. But what happened to these habits when at Vaticanum II the Roman Catholic Church lifted its food bans for Lent? Did housewives till that very moment hold on to their traditional foodways? Or did they change them long before? After World War I for instance? And if so, why? These are the questions behind this investigation into tradition and innovation in food habits among farmers' wives in the rural area of St. Oedenrode.

However, there was precious little recorded about the food habits these women practised at that time of the year and even less about the rationale behind their clinging to tradition or inventing new foodways. This called for a so-called qualitative study of a small but well-chosen population using the open, tape-recorded interview-technique. [1]

A preliminary study of literature and of previous investigations into the rationale of tradition and innovation in food habits [2] (part 1) generated the questions for the interview-manual we used eventually in our field-work in St. Oedenrode.

The results of investigation are described in the second part of this paper, which is rounded off with a customary chapter, 'Conclusion'.

I. The literature on fast, feast, food

Introduction

Literature referred to here falls into three different categories. There are in the first place publications dealing with the Church's ideas on food in relation to fast and feast. Then there are authors whose main interest lies with food-lore and cooking. Finally there are those who see food and cooking from the point of view of the mistress of the house. The different findings are described in the following paragraphs. Together they generated the basic questions for the investigation into tradition and change in the food habits in St.Oedenrode during the last eight decades.

The Catholic Church

Turning the pages of the Bible and reading them properly, one cannot but understand how it came about that the Church developed such mixed feelings on the subjects 'food', 'fast' and 'feast'.

In Genesis we read that immediately after his creation God gave Man for food all the seedbearing plants and the seedbearing fruits of all the trees (Gen.1:29). However once Man got the Garden of Eden to live in, to cultivate and to preserve, God forbade him to eat from one specific tree, the tree of knowledge (Gen.2:17). But Adam and Eve could not resist temptation and ate from the fruit of the forbidden tree. From then on Man had to live off the produce of the fields which had to be earned by hard labour (Gen.3:19). It was only after the Flood and when Noah had discharged his mission, that God decided to add all the animals that live on earth, in the sky, and in the waters to the list of foods Man is allowed to eat (Gen.9:1-3).

In other parts we learn about meals, dinners, suppers, picnics and of proper foods for special occasions and grand feasts. Among others in (Gen.18:6-9) (Adam and Sarah preparing a meal for visiting angels), (1 Sam.20:27-29) (David's absence from Saul's table), (Matt.14:19-21) (the miracle of the loaves and fishes), (Matt.26:26-29) (the establishment of the Last Supper), (John2:1-11) (marriage at Cana), (Luke15:23-25) (the prodigal son's return). There are furthermore passages where the virtues of living on a meagre fare are extolled such as in (Matt.3:4), where the austere diet of John the Baptist is described. And the virtue of offering food and drink to those who are starving, and the deadly sin of overlooking those in need of sustenance (a.o. Matt.25:35,42; Luke16:19-24).

The Scriptures' various messages on food, fast, and feast set the scene within the Church for heated debates on the rival merits of fasting and feasting - increasingly so when Christianity became shot through with an ardent desire to detach the soul from the world and to help it grow impervious to life's pleasures such as appetising food.

In medieval times one of the many debates on fasting arose around the locusts and wild honey, the only food John the Baptist was sustained by in the desert (Matt.3:4). Because the consumption of these two foods suggested that he lived not only on meat but on a delicacy as well, purists among the scriptural commentators became uneasy about John's virtues. However, his reputation could be saved by declaring that the kind of locust he ate was an unpalatable plant or tree-pod and that wild honey was anything but sweet and delicious. (Henisch,1978,p.2,8).

At that time other debates bore on the virtues of fasting for the individual Christian and as a commendable means to cleanse and discipline society. With regard to Lent these debates resolved themselves into a number of very specific and strict rules in order to prepare the soul for Easter. These forbade the consumption of meat, butter and eggs, sometimes cheese and milk even, and allowed the ingestion of only one single meal a day, which had to be postponed till after the hour of vespers. (Henisch, o.c.,p.29-44). Where Lent lasts for forty consecutive days, these rules were very harsh indeed. But as time went on, the Church made more and more exceptions to them such as permitting the use of eggs (Mennell, 1985,p.28). Milk, butter and, cheese followed in due course and, in the middle of the 20th century, meat and meat products as well. At that moment the Church ceased to use food rules when preparing its flock for the feast of Easter.

The Church's involvement with Shrovetide is of quite a different order. In the first place because Shrovetide does not figure on the ecclesiastical calendar. It is therefore to be assumed that the Church would have dealt with the three days of Shrovetide as just an ordinary Sunday, Monday, and Tuesday, if only their flock had nowhere and never been inclined to transform these days into feast-days of their own making, with singing, dancing, eating and all that stands for merriment. But the people of North Brabant were not that obedient.

According to Meurkens (1983) in North Brabant Shrovetide was up till 1850 synonymous with special privileges for the unmarried youth, such as singing to fellow-villagers and strangers for money, dancing and going courting. But the situation changed in about 1850, when the well-to-do saw fit to try and curtail these quite boisterous public feasts and to promote domestic order. Shortly afterwards the clergy too adopted this ideal. So much so, that the Bishop of 's-Hertogenbosch introduced in 1881 in his diocese a Forty Hours Devotion for Shrovetide. Since then the faithful of North Brabant were each year summoned to come to their parish church [3] as often as possible and to pray that they would resist the temptations of Shrovetide and not be led astray. With temporary success, however. For the next year saw the establishment of the first association for the organisation of festivities at Shrovetide by the inhabitants of 's-Hertogenbosch the very town where the Bishop himself resided (Rozema,1983,p.183). But till circa 1955 Shrovetide remained a very subdued affair in the rural part of his bishopric.

For Easter the Church seems never to have laid down any food rules. And in view of human nature, it would not have served the purpose. For the long sad journey of Lent in the guise of lack of flavour and abstinence asks for a happy ending with a feast surrounded with plentiful as well as nice food.

But where one man's meat is another man's poison, the Church allowed and allows its members a free hand on the point of selecting the foods that should grace their tables at ecclesiastical high-days. And wisely so. For otherwise housewives might not be able to cater to the likes and dislikes or their families - not even to such idiosyncrasies as a preference for strict adherence to traditional Easter Fare only, or the opposite: abhorrence of all that is traditional at Easter. And that would put the very joy out of this feast of feasts.

Folklorists and authors of Cookbooks

Writers of popular books [4] on Dutch food-lore in several parts of the Netherlands recorded 9 food specialties for Shrovetide and 13 for Easter, but did not provide the corresponding recipes. Those were found in the Amsterdam, the Hague and the NCB Cookbooks, three widely used Dutch cookbooks [5]. Especially those for Shrovetide specialties seemed of interest.

Now it became plain that the folklorists used two different names for one Shrovetide specialty - a bread baked in the Dutch oven. This brought the number of Shrovetide specialties back to 8. These are prepared either in a skillet, a griddle, a deep-fat fryer or a Dutch oven.

Heidenreich's Manual on the Methodology of Food Preparation (Heidenreich, 1979) gives the basic recipes for 5 of these 8 Shrovetide specialties (Table I)

Table I. Basic recipes for Shrovetide specialties

Ingredients		Pancakes	Batternuts	Doll's pancakes	D. Oven Bread
flour	(gr)	200	200	200	200
milk	(dl)	3.5	1.5	2.5	1.5
egg	(piece)	1	1	1	1
yeast	(gr)	10	10	8-10	10
salt	(gr)	3-4	3	3	3
d. fruit	(gr)	-	100	-	100
c. pork	(gr)	50-100	-	-	-
apples	(p)	2	-	-	-

Legend: batternuts = deep-fryed balls of a batter
 D. Oven Bread = bread baked in a Dutch oven
 d. fruit = raisins, currants, and / or candied peel of the fruit of *Citrus medica* proper
 c. pork = cured pork

Source: Heidenreich, 1979.

These basics were supplemented with the following notes on the respective batters:

the batter for Pancakes runs off the spoon as a thick cord.
" " " Doll's pancakes runs off the spoon as a broad ribbon.
" " " Batternuts drops off the spoon in pieces.
" " " Dutch Oven Bread ditto

and with the following rules for adaptations:

use for a thick batter at most 2 eggs / 1000 gr flour,
" at most 20 gr butter / 100 gr flour,
" between 50 - 100 gr filling / 100 gr flour,
" 8 gr yeast / 100 gr flour in case the filling is heavy,
count 1 egg for 0.5 dl milk,
count 100 gr butter for 0.5 dl liquid

As a higher amount of yeast makes for a quicker rising batter, it is interesting to note, that the Heidenreich recipes contain less yeast than three editions of the Amsterdam and The Hague respectively. The amounts found in two editions of the NCB-cookbook are even higher still. It looks as if the authors of the NCB-Cookbook thought that quick rising batters would be a real boon for the prospective readers, the housewives in rural North Brabant.

A further comparison of different editions of the three mentioned cookbooks proved, that after World War II housewives were supposed to use wheat flour for all these specialties. But between the wars this was the case only for Batternuts and the Dutch-oven Bread, whereas equal amounts of buckwheat and wheat flour were prescribed for the remaining 5. That this mixture was not advised for Batternuts and Dutch-oven Bread relates to the lack of gluten in buckwheat. This implies, that a batter of wheat flour mixed with buckwheat will not rise well in deep-fat nor in the oven.

For Lent the NCB Cookbook contained 6 menus. Their respective nutritive value per person was calculated and compared with the energy requirements of farmers, farmhands and the like which Bonnema formulated in 1947 (Table II).

As it turned out, one of the menus (Menu F) surpassed Bonnema's standard by 150 Kcal. But the other five fell short of that standard - Menu A by no less than 900 Kcal and Menu E by 500. It does not seem possible that these deficiencies could ever be made good by adding sugar to the dessert, for 900 Kcal asks for no less than 225 gram and 500 Kcal for 125 gram sugar. So when a housewife put these meals in front of her husband it was a very frugal one indeed - perhaps even too frugal for his spiritual well-being.

Table II, Calculated") nutritive value per person in Kj and Kcal respectively of 6 NCB-menus#) for Lent. (rounded)

Menu		Kj	Kcal
A:	main course with boiled eggs, dessert	4570 Kj	1070 Kcal.
B:	main course with fried eggs, dessert	7400	1750
C:	main course with scrambled egg, dessert	6820	1610
D:	main course with fish, dessert	7190	1700
E:	main course with fish, dessert	6090	1440
F:	main course with pulses, dessert	9030	2070

") The calculations of portions per person are based on the NCB-Cookbook and on Heidenreich (1979); their content on the Nederlandse Voedingsmiddelentabel (1987)

#) The recipes of the desserts of the first five menus don't contain sugar, which should be served separately. An average amount of sugar per portion is 15 gram and contains 250 Kj or 60 Kcal.

The folklorists linked the cock- and hen-shaped rolls, the breaded ring, and the cracknels specifically with the decorated pole that children carry on Palm Sunday on their round through the village, the so-called Palmpaas.

These figured breads were all ovenbaked as were the Easter specialties which the folklorists enumerated such as hare- and man-shaped rolls, twisted rolls, snipped rolls and loaves filled with a dried fruit with a mixture of dried fruits and/ or rolls of Dutch almond paste.

The housewife in her kitchen

The notion 'food' in connection with 'fast' turns the mind automatically to ideas such as frugality, abstention, dullness, monotony, and merit. But when 'food' becomes linked with 'feast' and the feast is Easter, it evokes visions of well-laid breakfast-tables, baskets filled with all kinds of crisp new breads, bowls with coloured eggs, the choicest jams and marmalades in brimful jars and a festive atmosphere. Or one sees in one's mind's eye a daintily laid table and smells the delightful aromas of a delicious meal concocted from all the fresh meats, fruits and vegetables that spring offers.

But when Shrovetide comes nearer with Lent in it's wake, a housewife's mind will turn to her larder, her purse, her stock of recipes, her family's likes and dislikes, their physiological needs, and last but not least her and her family's diary. That is of course nothing out of the common. For there is no session in kitchen without a swift checking of the mouths to fill, a glimpse in the storeroom, a glance at the stock of habitual menus [6], a quick inventory of the physiological needs of the eaters, a hasty survey of appliances and utensils, a rapid calculation of the available time, fuel and labour, and need be and time and season permit a dash into the vegetable garden, the poultry-house, the rabbit-hutch or a trip to the shops with money in the pocket. Not even the most ordinary day of the year will witness one housewife-on-duty who skips this ritual. And for ages the prudent housewife has gone through all these motions well before Lent knocked at her door, for some of her mainstays in preparing nutritious meals for her family figured on the Church's list of foods forbidden for Lent.

In so far as these forbidden foods are perishable, the housewife had to rid her larder of them. This was in particular a dilemma for the quite prosperous housewife, who used in her kitchen meat and pork of home-fattened pigs. It was a little bit easier for the housewife who ordered these commodities at the butcher's. But mirabile dictu, it was easiest by far for the really poor housewife who had to live from hand to mouth and never had a piece of meat or pork in her larder.

But when just before Ash Wednesday one had still some meat or pork in the larder that would not keep till Easter, one had no choice but to concoct with these ingredients some more or less copious meals at Shrovetide. However, once done, the housewife and her family might well turn this invention into tradition and ever after have that kind of meal during Shrovetide (Henisch, o.c.,p.38)

Lent, however, lasts only 40 days and the outcome is Easter, a feast which the Church never burdened with lists of forbidden foods. So to the end of Lent the housewife can freely stock her larder with Easter specialties or the ingredients for them.

A housewife's many activities

Everybody has but one head, one pair of hands, one pair of feet and needs some 8 hours for recuperation per day. This implies that nobody can put more activities into one day than he or she can cram into 16 hours, be it a work-, a Sun- or a Holy-Day.

Providing her family with at least three meals a day and cups of tea or coffee in between is a task a housewife has to perform. But a number of other domestic tasks compete for her time, energy, knowledge and skills. And so do all kinds of social institutions that the household or she herself is connected with. The Church, for instance, and kinsfolk, a circle of friends, occupational activities, public or corporate affairs, sports or recreational associations, the educational system and so on (fig.1).

Fig.1. The matrix of a housewife's economic web

warp of activies	domestic life	kin	friends	church	educat. system	work	affairs		sports a.o.
							public	corp.	
weft of assets									
capital (goods)									
time									
vital energy									
ready money									
knowledge									
skills									

(adapted from Edema, 1985,p.39)

It is self-evident that the more time and energy, money even, she is or feels obliged to spend on a particular day on those kinds of activities, the less time, energy and perhaps money she has left for the preparation of meals, snacks, and beverages. Which implies that her ways with food are not determined by the money she can spend on ingredients, the appliances she has at her disposal, the nutritional knowledge she possesses and her cooking skills. Consequently a housewife may be forced to change her foodways on some particular days, because she has to adjust her time-table. Or she might change them because on exactly these days the pressure on her time and energy is for some reason less than before. In other words, changes in a housewife's time-table may well account for changes in the food habits within her domestic circle. Which hypothesis implies that data gathered by interviewing housewives on their reasons for sticking to or changing their foodways, will fit the matrix of figure 1. But the very same reasons will at the same time point to the basic rules by which the interaction between the members of a single household is guided.

The housewife and the members of her household

The members of a household interact in accordance with unwritten, but substantial rules. Foodways are often a manifestation of these rules and confirm them at the same time. When, for instance, parents are of the opinion, that their son is of marriageable age and he brings a girl home, the two will be treated to drinks and snacks that underline their adulthood. And by doing just that the parents demonstrate that they are willing to launch him into matrimony. Or when a housewife likes her children to participate in activities the Church organises, she will set the mealtimes to the Church timetable.

These and many other food-related interactions between the members of a household relate to the social values the household as a social institution incorporates (Edema 1983, 1985, 1988).

These values are at their most concise

> to manifest a proper esprit de corps [7]

> In this context the adjective 'proper' means three different things. Firstly that the individual member of a household is entitled to the other members' support and protection. Secondly that the household as a group has to support the common cause in money or in kind. Thirdly that in due time children, born within the group are launched into the world (e.g. into marriage).

- to watch over the spiritual well-being of the individual members (e.g. by obeying the Church's rules or by using food as balm for wounded feelings),

- to watch over the physical well-being of the individual members (e.g. by distributing food according to each one's appetite and nutritional need),

- to stimulate its members to participate in institutions outside the household appropriate to their age or sex, (e.g. by offering food and drink to visiting kin, friends and potential suitors and fiancées),

- to socialise each member of the household to behavioral codes which the household as such, as well as significant sectors of the larger society, approve of (e.g. the Church, the School, the Community, the Labour Market).

Because foodways are so closely linked with social values - which in everyday life crystallise into norms, goals, and expectations (Van Doorn & Lammers, 1976, p.177) - an investigator may find here the reasons why housewives are unable to find the time and energy for new and more time-absorbing foodways. Or he may discover that his interviewees looked for the earliest opportunity to curtail on specific days some of their customary activities in order to find room for new and more time-absorbing foodways, because one or more of these values were at stake.

Conclusion

This overview of the literature generated the following questions about tradition and innovation in food habits from Shrovetide up to and including Easter in general and among farmers' wives in St. Oedenrode in particular.

Are todays farmers' wives of St. Oedenrode familiar with the foods the folklorists mentioned as specialties for Shrovetide, Palm Sunday and Easter? Which of them do or did they ever prepare themselves? What ingredients do or did they use?

What happened in the last 50 years with Shrovetide in St. Oedenrode? Did the Forty Hours Devotion survive or was it supplanted by Carnival? And what happened during those 50 years to the food habits at Shrovetide?

Did housewives before Vaticanum II serve special menus during Lent? And if so, what happened afterwards?

What happened during the last 50 years with regard to Palm Sunday, what to Easter? And what to the traditional food habits on these days?

How did tradition and change relate to the housewives' economic web? And to the five social values the household incorporates?

II. From Shrovetide to Easter in St. Oedenrode

Introduction

The above questions formed the backbone of the interview-manual for the investigation in St. Oedenrode. But they were supplemented by three written aids. One contained 22 cards, each one bearing the name of a food the folklorists mentioned as a specialty for this time of the year. The second was a compilation of all the ingredients the authors of the three consulted cookbooks enumerated in the recipes for these 22 foods. The third was a list of the materials Nannings (1932) and Naaykens (1978) described as traditional ingredients for the composition of a Palmpaas.

For the selection of our respondents we had to rely on two inhabitants of St. Oedenrode. They were able to introduce us to 18 farmers' wives who met our requirements which were, that they were born and bred in the rural fringe of the town St. Oedenrode, had lived there all their married life, belonged to the Roman Catholic Church. As the oldest was born in 1901 and the youngest in 1958, it was assumed that their collective recollection of food habits at Shrovetide and Easter would cover the entire period between 1910 and 1990.

This assumption proved correct. Those born between 1900 and 1925 started to talk about how things went in their youth, followed that up with data about the time their children were still at home and came in the end to the present time. Yet when an interviewee was born between 1930 and 1945 she started with here and now and turned from there to what was customary in her youth. But when born between 1945 and 1960 our respondent would talk merely about the present. Such differences between older and younger housewives did not really come as a surprise as the youngest interviewees had been married less than ten years, whereas previous research (NN,1963) had born out that women need ten to fifteen years in order to turn from a novice in matters of marriage and household into a dyed-in-the-wool housewife.

Specialties, old and new

None of our respondents was familiar with 5 of the 22 foods mentioned by authors of Dutch food-lore as typical fare for Shrovetide and Easter. The following were the foods in question: the smoutebol, the doughnut, the two "Dutch-oven" breads, and one oven-baked bread.

Table III. Foods for special occasions

name of food	Occasion									
	St	PS	Eas	Xmas	NYE	TAF	C-Bd	Fday	Sday	YR
1. Pancake (pork)	x									x
2. " (apple)	x									x
3. Battemuts	x				x	x				
4. Waffles	x					x	x			x
5. Doll's pancakes	x					x	x			
6. Stuffed rolls	x		x	x				x	x	
7. Cock-shaped rolls		x	x							
8. Chicken- " rolls		x	x							
9. Man-shaped roll			x							
10. Hare-shaped roll			x							
11. Easter-loaf			x							
12. Loaf with succade			x					x		
13. Loaf w. raisins			x	x	x			x	x	
14. Loaf w. currants			x	x				x	x	
15. Rusk-buns			x					x		x
16. Twisted rolls				x				x	x	
17. Snipped rolls								x	x	

Key:
- St = Shrovetide
- PS = Palm Sunday
- Eas = Easter
- Xmas = Christmas
- NYE = New Year's Eve
- TAF = The Annual Fair
- C-Bd = Children's Birthday
- Fday = Feastday
- Sday = Sunday
- YR = now and again

That nobody had ever heard about the smoutebol was the most remarkable, for the interviewees were very familiar with the battemut and a smoutebol is nothing but a battemut deep-fried in lard. One explanation would be that the tradition of deep-frying batter-balls was invented after oil had become relatively cheap. Another might be that deep-frying in lard was such a tricky business that salad oil took its place as soon as it appeared on the market and the old habit of deep-frying in lard has been completely forgotten since then.

Asked if they ever used the remaining 17 foods at either Shrovetide, Palm Sunday or Easter it turned out that the twisted and snipped rolls (nos 16, 17) were never put to that purpose. But the stuffed rolls, the Cock- and the Chicken-rolls did double duty: the first were served at Shrovetide as well as at Easter, the figured rolls both on Palm Sunday and Easter. The remaining 12 did single service from Shrovetide till Easter: the pancakes, battemuts and waffles at Shrovetide, the breads and rolls at Easter (Table III).

From the data of Table III it can be concluded that none of the Shrovetide specialties is that special, that it is merely served at Shrovetide. And neither are three out of the four special loaves for Easter.

Ingredients, old and new

In the course of time the ingredients used for four of the five Shrovetide specialties of Table III underwent some change (Table IV)

They are directly linked to some developments which the farming system underwent in this part of the Netherlands. Up to World War II buckwheat, potatoes and rye had been the main crops here, whereas some cows and one or more pigs had made up the farmer's livestock. As a careful housewife was not supposed to buy what was produced on the farm, every St. Oedenrode farmers' wife would stock her store-room with buckwheat and rye and the meat, sausages, pork and lard, a pig would provide her with and she would buy as little wheat flour, salad oil, molasses and sugar as possible. She would, for instance, only buy wheat flour when she had to fry batternuts for neither buckwheat nor rye flour could give her batternuts the required lightness.

This kind of background information makes it clear that in 1920 the old farming system was still in full swing, but by 1950 the first changes had already occurred. And ten years later the farmers' wives relied on the food-industry for all the ingredients they needed for preparing the specialties of Table IV. The data for 1990 demonstrate moreover, that the St. Oedenrode housewives are even very much abreast of modern ideas about the nutritive value of different flours and oils. That the farmers became at the same time more prosperous, is also born out by Table IV: in 1920 molasses and sugar were used as sweeteners of only two out of four specialties, but in 1950 all four were accompanied by a sweetener and icing sugar was added to the list of customary sweeteners.

Table IV. Flours, cooking fats, and sweetenings for 4 Shrovetide specialties before and after 1960

year	c.1920	c.1950	c.1960	c.1990
Pancake with pork	buckwheat lard -	b.wheat+rye b.wheat+wheat wheat lard molasses	Self-raising fl. margarine salad oil molasses	wheat whole wheat 4 grain mix (#) margarine molasses sugar
Pancake with apple	buckwheat b.wheat+wheat lard salad oil molasses sugar	wheat margarine salad oil molasses sugar	baking fl. margarine molasses sugar icing sugar apple syrup	wheat whole wheat 4 grain mix (#) butter margarine sunflower oil molasses sugar icing sugar apple syrup
Batternuts	wheat salad oil	wheat salad oil icing sugar	baking fl. salad oil icing sugar	baking fl. battermix (#) sunfl. oil icing sugar
Doll's pancakes	buckwheat sugar	bwheat+wheat icing sugar	bwheat+wheat icing sugar	D's pc-mix (#) icing sugar

(#) proprietory mixes available in the Netherlands

Tradition and invention in Shrovetide specialties

Reminiscences of the older interviewees and data on present food habits bear out that pancake with pork and pancake with apple as its substitute were the real traditional Shrovetide specialties. In some households it constituted the main course of the cooked meal at noon and was served between the soup and a dessert of buttermilk-cum-barley or something similar. In others it replaced at the uncooked 6 o'clock meal the customary plate of warmed-up leftovers of the cooked meal that had been served that day at noon.

Because Shrovetide fell around the time that the housewife had started her spring-cleaning and the farmer his ploughing, sowing, and harrowing, a labour-saving pancake-meal came in very handy indeed. The more so where Shrovetide was the time of the Forty Hours Devotion, because that implied that every member of the household had to go as frequently as possible to the Church for an hour of prayer. As a matter of fact, the bachelor sons and the unattached daughters did not mind changing their clothes a few extra times during those days for they might well see or even speak to a promising person of the opposite sex on the church-path or the church-square. Such a chance was not to be despised at a time when the Church did not allow co-education and mixed societies, frowned upon dancing and merrymaking at annual fairs and earmarked Shrovetide for labour and prayer and nothing else [6]. But in the 60's major changes occurred in Dutch society at large, which in due course affected life in St. Oedenrode as well.

At that time industrialisation pressed on in the Netherlands, wages boomed. and in agriculture specialisation, intensification, mechanisation became the order of the day. From that time onward the farmers of St. Oedenrode introduced labour-extensive and capital-intensive husbandry, primarily based on the fodder-industry, instead of the traditional system of labour intensive, but capital extensive mixed farming.

That and the growing demand for well-trained employees and skilled labourers outside agriculture caused many farmers' sons and daughters to turn to a vocational training for gainful employment outside father's farm and mother's kitchen, which made it possible for them to contemplate marriage at a much earlier age than former generations in St. Oedenrode had dared [8].

Small wonder that the need for new forms of entertainment cropped up. Of this the founding in 1957 of the first St. Oedenrode Carnival Society was an overt sign, because in less than no time 10 more followed.

This development implied that housewives had to drop the traditional Shrovetide pancake as soon as Shrovetide took on a new meaning. For a pancake with pork as the main course of a meal might be up to the mark as a Shrovetide specialty as long as that period was set aside for labour and prayer. But it would never do for a housewife to serve pancakes as a snack [9] - not even to her family let alone to visitors. So when the notion took root, that Shrovetide should be set aside for the cheerfulness of the carnival procession, the sociability of surprise visits of family, friends, and neighbours, and the pleasure of card-playing in the afternoons or nights with some friendly couples, housewives had to look out for a convenient as well as appropriate snack. This they found in the traditional habit of New Year's Eve, when they fried a large batch of batternuts that took care of the evening itself as well as of every visitor who cared to call and offer his congratulations on New Year's Day. And if they thought the batternuts too rich and too sweet for the occasion, they found recourse in the less rich apple fritters, the less rich and sweet waffles - specialties of the annual fair - or the savoury stuffed rolls - a Christmas specialty. Some housewives with young children started even with doll's pancakes - also a specialty of the annual fair. But quite soon they discovered that that habit was too impractical for such a restless time as Shrovetide had become. Later on, when these children and their friends were old enough to keep carnival, their mothers invented for their benefit some new Shrovetide specialties, because now they had to see to it that the young would not publicly disgrace themselves by getting the worse for drink. Remembering the old saying the stomach takes alcoholic beverages best on a bottom of batternuts, they made a still larger batch of batternuts. What is more, they prepared as well a nourishing (pea-) soup and / or a good-sized (macaroni-) casserole and / or a supply of pan-fried chicken. With all that in their larders, they would be able to serve the young merry-makers (among them perhaps a future son or daughter in law) a square meal, when the latter cared to drop in for a bite. And taking into account that in St. Oedenrode tradition demands that one has fried eggs after an evening at the pub or a social event in some meeting-room, they would moreover lay up a good number of eggs and might put some stuffed rolls in the freezer for good measure.

As soon as the oldest generation among our interviewees perceived in what direction the changes went, they took the cue from the next younger generation of housewives and exchanged the batternut or the apple fritter or the waffle for the pancake with pork as well.

The youngest housewives had already grown up with the idea of keeping carnival and held on to that habit after they got married. Some did not even break the habit of keeping carnival with their former school-friends, others made merry with their husband and a few friendly couples. But since they were now housewives and mothers they had to take their young children to the procession and to the curly-heads' dance or another festivity for the very young, to arrange for a baby-sitter and last but not least to stock the larder with a good number of eggs and the freezer with savoury snacks and a number of square meals.

The above-mentioned data lead to the self-evident conclusion that shortly after the first St. Oedenrode Carnival Society was founded the most dramatic changes occurred in the St. Oedenrode Shrovetide specialties. Till then housewives were preoccupied with work and Church. But in the 60's they exchanged work and prayer for work-free afternoons, spending the time and energy thus recovered on the members of their families, their kin and friends, the friends of their grownup children in particular, and on public amusements such as the Carnival Procession.

The covert reasons for these shifts lay in the fundamental economic and social changes the farmers' families underwent in the 50's. Till that time it was a blessing in disguise when farmers' children married when they were well into their thirties. But after the 50's marriage could be contemplated at a much earlier age. And a housewife could at least try and foster just that by stimulating her offspring to participate in the right manner in the Shrovetide activities by having snacks and meals ready for the merry-makers, by joining in the festive atmosphere at any rate by taking the afternoons off, and by lending the young merrymakers a sympathetic ear when they might need one.

Tradition and invention between Shrovetide and Easter

In relation to Lent proper neither specialties nor special menus were mentioned. In the memory of our interviewees it had just been a period of frugal meals. And that had been singularly hard on the farmers. For Lent fell in the season when the farmer had to plough, sow and harrow. In order to illustrate this, many a tale was told about farmers passing out in the field or coming home for a piece of pork. And that notwithstanding he had to pray for such a lapse and even to pay 15 cents!.

It is interesting to note that similar stories were not told about farmers' wives. Lent was not only a time of hard work for the farmer but for his wife as well. For Lent stood formerly for a very thorough spring cleaning, which included among other things chimney sweeping, whitewashing, putting the winter clothes in moth-balls, making the summer clothes ready for wear, so that at Easter the house would be spick and span, the summer clothes put on, the stove put out and everybody in high spirits, but shivering with cold.

In relation to Good Friday one single specialty was mentioned. This was the old habit of having that day stockfish with a sauce of rape-seed oil. In later years fresh fish with brown butter supplanted the stockfish. But some kept at least to tradition and graced the dinner-table on Good Friday with a menu with fish, because 'every rule gets abolished, why not hang on to this one.' But nobody seemed to long for a return of all the former frugality of Lent.

Up till the early 80's Palm Sunday was just another Sunday but for the consecration of the bunch of box twigs people brought along in lieu of palm-branches, the Palm procession during High Mass, and in the afternoon the palming of the rye. But when in the 60's the importance of rye as one of a farmer's main crops diminished and corn or another fodder was more and more sown on the rye-fields, the farmers discontinued the habit of solemnly planting consecrated box twigs at the corners of the rye-fields. That made the resemblance of Palm Sunday to an ordinary Sunday even more pronounced.

However, in 1982 the Church started the Palmpaas ceremony, apparently for at least three different reasons. The first was undoubtedly to try and catch the interest of young children, the second to strengthen ties between the Church and the individual families and the third to create a certain link between the youngest and the oldest generations of the congregation, the infirm included.

The first reason is an obvious one, because the Palmpaas is a very festive sight and has interesting details such as figured rolls. The third is as obvious as the first as the children bring their Palmpaas in procession to the Roman Catholic Old People's Home and to the houses of the infirm.

The second reason is less overt but nevertheless present, for the Palmpaas has to be put together at home in accordance with an instruction leaflet which the children bring home from school and which is prepared by the Church's Palmpaas Committee, a group of active laymen and women. The instructions relate among others to the kind of decoration to use, figured rolls, twisted bread, fruit, ribbons, etcetera.

From the farmer's wife's point of view the invention of the Palmpaas caused her to invest more time, energy, ready money, knowledge and skills in Palm Sunday than ever before, part of which she spent more or less directly on her children, the rest more indirectly on the Church and the larger society.

Tradition and invention in Easter Specialties

The Easter loaf and the four figured rolls are proper Easter specialties (Table III). But it is definitely beside the truth to assume that the figured rolls are a well-worn tradition. Our data bear out in fact that figured rolls were not used before 1982, when the ceremony of the Palmpaas came into being and brought a need for figured rolls in its wake, for a Palmpaas is not complete without a Cock- or Chicken-roll on top and is often embellished with a braided bread-ring or a cracknel as well.

It was certainly a matter of housewives' luck that the Church had not hit on this particular idea twenty years before, when bread was still home-baked from rye flour. That flour gives a very sticky dough that does not handle well. It would therefore have been very difficult for farmers' wives to produce the required rolls, let alone a braided bread-ring. It was just the Church's luck that it had not perceived the need for an innovation such as the Palmpaas two or even one decade earlier, because in the early 80's mothers of young children were quite familiar with the idea that bread could be freely selected from the baker's varied supply.

The Church was not instrumental in the invention of other Easter novelties such as Easter breakfast, Easter brunch, Easter eggs, and Easter egg hunting. Those skills farmers' wives and daughters learned at the NCB Cooking-schools and special courses for housewives. For years farmers' wives were not able to use these skills, because they had to tread the Church path twice in the morning and once in the afternoon. Till Vaticanum II therefore they kept to the tradition of serving Easter eggs and currant loaves after Lauds at the 4 o'clock high coffee.

But the rules for Easter were lifted and the farmers' wives started to turn their hands at painting Easter eggs, preparing an Easter breakfast or brunch, cooking a fine dinner with for instance savoury patty shells or a savoury fruit & chicken salad as a starter, special cuts of meat and different vegetables as a main course, and a Bavarian Cream or a Charlotte Russe for dessert. And last but not least to lay the table with an Easter tablecloth and Easter napkins, and to decorate a twisted branch of the *Corylus avellana Contorta* with coloured or painted blown eggs and ribbons.

Our respondents' opinions on the merits of these changes differed slightly, but when summarised read as follows: 'Formerly one put on one's new clothes on Easter Sunday and went several times to Church and on Easter Monday one paid a visit to one's parents and parents-in-law. And that was it. Work on the farm never stops. Now Easter unites the family, because there is time for doing things together. And there is still Easter Monday for seeing kin and friends. A pity, that commercialisation set in in such a big way. The same as what happened with Christmas. One has to be on one's guard'.

It seems plausible that when farmers' families worked as well as lived on their own farms the lives of the individual members converged so much that a trip to the Church was a legitimate means to see and speak to more people than just family, kin, and near neighbours and was welcomed as such.

But when the agricultural system became thoroughly modernised, it became difficult for the farmers' families to maintain their esprit de corps as long as the Church claimed such large parts of their Sundays. For now the lives of the individual members diverged so much, that the family had to set time aside for doing things together in order to foster that we-feeling, that feeling of belonging together and of shared responsibility without which a family is not a family (Lumpkin,1933,p.26-29) and no day of the week lent itself so well to this purpose as Sunday and no days of the year so well as feast days like Easter. The withdrawal at Vaticanum II of the old rule - that one dare not break one's fast before Mass, had to attend Mass twice in the morning and Lauds in the afternoon - came at least in this part of the world at a time when it was most needed.

Conclusion

The above data make it abundantly clear that before the 50's the St. Oedenrode list of specialties or Shrovetide up to and including Easter, was very short indeed and contained only meal-time items such as pancakes and breads. Not that the St. Oedenrode farmers' wives were unfamiliar with the more snack-like specialties the folklorists mentioned, but they used these on other occasions such as the annual fair, Christmas or New Year's Eve. Till the 80's however, figured breads were an unknown item.

The introduction of new specialties occurred first at the end of the 50's, when the farmers' wives started to exchange snack-like specialties such as batternuts, apple fritters, and stuffed rolls for the traditional Shrovetide meal-time item pancakes. By that time they had already wrought some minor changes in the ingredients they used for batternuts as well as pancakes. The latter changes relate to the fact that the farmers' wives got less and less buckwheat and rye flour directly from the farm, but had to buy their flours at the grocery instead and could select there what suited them best.

Changes in the farming system were also instrumental in the introduction of the first mentioned changes. Because of these changes the farmer's wife had to spend more time, energy, money, knowledge and skills on her family, kin and friends and even on social activities such as the Carnival Procession than ever before. She managed to do so by cutting down on the time she formerly spent in the Church and on her domestic duties, cooking excluded.

Vaticanum II did not bring about much change in the food habits the farmers' wives in St. Oedenrode practised during

Lent, but they were now allowed to look after the physical needs of their families properly, that is to provide them at this time of the year as well with nourishing meals, thus setting themselves free from the fear that their husbands would pass out during their work. Some, however, kept to the habit of serving fish at dinner on Good Friday.

In 1982 the Church introduced the ceremony of the Palmpaas on Palm Sunday thus familiarising farmers' wives in St. Oedenrode with figured rolls, braided bread-rings and cracknels. These they bought at the bakers' in order to put the required Palmpaas together at home.

After Vaticanum II the traditional Easter eggs and Easter bread were no longer served after Lauds, but in the morning as part of an elaborated breakfast or brunch. It became also a tradition to serve later in the day a nice and elaborate dinner.

Conclusion

The conclusions of Part II do not do full justice to the last question of Part I 'How did tradition and change relate to the five social values the household as an institution incorporates?'. But by rephrasing that question, it too is answered.

Firstly, once industrialisation and modernisation set in on the farms, the farmers' children could contemplate marriage at a much earlier age than a generation earlier. And a housewife could try and foster just that by stimulating her offspring to take an active part in Shrovetide activities, at the same time impressing upon them that they had to behave well. When framed in terms of the social values which the household incorporates this conclusion reads: in order to manifest a proper esprit de corps, in the 60's farmers' wives in St. Oedenrode had to spend much time, energy, ready money, knowledge and skills on activities, that would help their offspring to participate in age and sex appropriate activities outside the household and to behave there in accordance with the prevailing codes so that they may be launched into matrimony at the appropriate time.

Secondly compliance on the part of the farmers' wives with the Church's innovation of the Palmpaas has also to be understood as acting in accordance with the social value, that the members of the household be stimulated to participate in activities outside the household, but in this case for small children.

Thirdly the introduction of an elaborate Easter breakfast or brunch and of Easter dinner is an overt sign that at the time of Vaticanum II the modernisation of the farming system had gone so far already that time, energy, money, knowledge and skills had to be set aside for activities favouring the family's esprit de corps - so much so that on Easter Sunday the Church had to give way to the domestic circle.

These conclusions make clear that the rationale behind tradition and change in food habits has first of all to be sought in the interconnectedness of a housewife's economic web and a household's basic social values. Secondly developments within the economic sector these households are connected with and in the third place in other social institutions such as the Church.

For it might well be true, that the changes Vaticanum II brought about in the Church's teachings for Shrovetide up to and including Easter were a prudent answer to rising conflicts between two social institutions, namely Church and Household.

Notes

1) Such a small-scale qualitative study based on a well-selected homogeneous sample from a close-knit society is not to be confused with a pilot study from a heterogeneous population. The latter's results have still to be verified by a large-scale quantitative investigation, the former's do not.
2) See Edema, 1988.
3) In North Brabant every church of the dioceses has its own Forty Hours Devotion. This may well be due to the more or less veiled controversies between the secular clergy and the regular priests with regard to their pastoral rights and duties. These date back to the middle of the 19th century, when the rulers of neighbouring countries began to perceive them as 'the ordained body-guards of Rome' and did not want them to reside on their territories, which started an influx of regular priests into the predominantly Roman Catholic province of North Brabant. (Bax,1983,p.150).
4) Consulted were Engels-Geurts (1988), van Hoeven (1983), Keuper & Harmsen (1988), van Lamoen (1987), Lotgering-Hildebrand (after 1940), van Oirschot (1979), Stam-Dresselhuys (1980), Streekrecepten (after 1967).
5) Wannèe (1938), Stoll (1938) and the NCB-kookboek (1938) belong in this category as the first two are

extensively used in teacher training courses for home economics, while the latter was composed by teachers in home economics and intended for the rural population of North Brabant.
6) Da Costa Senior & Duister (1986) discovered that to a housewife individual recipes are of no use as long as she has no idea of how to piece them together into menus for proper meals.
7) The term 'esprit de corps' is from Katherine Lumpkin, an anything but well-known author in academic circles. In the 80's Anne-Marie Rocheblave - Spenlè granted her nevertheless the title of precursor of role theory, as she was the first to apply the concept 'role' systematically (Rocheblave,1962,pp15/6). But she used it for a specific problem and not a general one. This and the circumstance that she had not taken recourse to statistics but applied the case study method throughout, may well account for the fact that her name does not figure on the list of role theorists.
8) This and the fact that sons and daughters are preferably employed at their father's farm or other enterprise and in their mother's household respectively, made courting a time-consuming business. Both factors might at least partly explain why our oldest respondents were all over 30 when they got married, which was before 1960. The younger repondents married between 1960 and 1970 but were between 25 and 30, whereas the youngest, who married after 1970, were not yet 25 years old.
9) At least in Dutch society serving pancakes implies that the table has to be set with plates and cutlery and that the baking has to start shortly before everyone is seated. But batternuts can be taken directly from the bowl and eaten with the fingers and therefore offered to anyone who cares to call. (see also Mary Douglas,1975, pp.249-276).

Bibliography

Bax, M., (1983) 'Ritualisering en versobering in een Brabantse dorpsparochie'. In: Koster, A., Y. Kuiper & J. Verrips, (eds.), - *Feest en ritueel in Europa*. VU Boekhandlel/Uitgeverij, Amsterdam, pp.133-157.

Bonnema, C. J., (1976) *Eenvoudige voedingsleer*, Nijgh & van Ditmar, Rotterdam / Den Haag.

Da Costa Senior, R., & W. Duister, (1986) *Varieren met en vervangen door peulvruchten in de maaltijden*. Dep. of Human Nutrition, Agr. University Wageningen, M.Thesis No.86-37 (unpubl.)

van Doorn, J. A. A. & C. J. Lammers, *Moderne Sociologie*, Het Spectrum, Utrecht/Antwerpen, 1976

Douglas, Mary, *Implicit Meanings*: Essays in Anthropology. Routledge & Kegan Paul, 1975.

Edema, J. M. P., (1983) 'The Social Sciences and Research on Food Habits in the Netherlands'. In: Teuteberg, H. - J., & Johanna M. P. Edema (eds.), *Nutritional Behaviour As a Topic of Social Sciences*. Publ. AGEV Vol.2. Ernährungs-Umschau 30 Suppl.

Edema, J. M. P., (1985) 'Foods habits, their determinants and their malleability'. In: Diehl, Joerg M., & Claus Leitzmann (eds.), *Measurement and determinants of food habits and food preferences*, Euro-Nut Report no.7. Uitg. Ned. Institut voor de Voeding, Wageningen.

Edema, J. M. P., (1988) 'Food Legumes and Cultural Fixation'. In: Nils-Arvid Bringèus u.a. (hg.) *Wandel der Volkskultur in Europa. Festschrift für Günther Wiegelmann*, Münster, BD.I., pp.445-458. (Beiträge zur Volkskultur in Nordwest-deutschland 60)

Engels-Geurts (1988), Wil & Netty, *Traditionele feestgerechten het jaar door*. Zuid Hollandse Uitgeverij, Weert.

Heidenreich, J. C., H. H. F. Henderson, L. Y. Bossinade, & H. Toors, (1979) *Receptenleer*. Nijgh & van Ditmar, Den Haag.

van Hoeven (1983), *Streekgerechten van Libelle*. Spectrum, Utrecht/Antwerpen.

Keuper, R., & H. Harmsen (1988), *Potdeurmekare; Oude Achterhoekse gerechten en eetgewoonten*. Gherre, Gaanderen.

van Lamoen, Jo, (1987), *Van Poempaaipap en preioot; Brabantse streekgerechten en wetenswaardigheden*. In de Toren, Baarn.

Lotgering-Hildebrand, R., (n.d.; after 1940), *Ieder zijn meug; Smulboek van Nederlandse volksgerechten*. Libellen-serie, Bosch en Keuning, Baarn.

Lotgering-Hildebrand, R., (1938) *Het Coöperatieve Kook- en Huishoudschoolboek*. Coöp. Groothandelsvereniging De Handelskamer 'HAKA' G. A., Rotterdam.

Lumpkin, Katharine Duprè, (1933) *The Family; A study of Member Rôles*, Chapel Hill, Univ. of North Carolina Press.

Mennell, Stephen, (1985) *All Manners of Food; Eating and Taste in England and France from the Middle Ages to the Present*. Basil Blackwell, Oxford.

Meurkens, Peter, (1983), 'Feesten van het oude Kempenland' (Feast in former Kempenland, now the province North-Brabant). In: Koster, A., Y. Kuiper & J. Verrips (eds), *Feest and ritueel in Europa*. Amsterdam, VU Boekhandel/ Uitgeverij, pp.158-175.

Naaykens, J., (1878) *Noord-Brabant in Grootvaders tijd.*, Kruseman, Den Haag.

Nannings, J. H., (1932) *Brood- en Gebakvormen en hunne beteekenis in de folklore*. Uitgever ??.

NCB-Kookboek, (1924,1938,1980). Uitgave Noord-Brabantse Coöp. Boerenbond, Tilburg.

NN [Edema, J. M. P.], (1963) 'Vrouwen van boeren en tuinders in gezin, huishouding en bedrijf. In: *Agrarisch Plan voor Noord-Holland*, Dl.I pp.173-199. POA nv., Alkmaar, 1963.

van Oirschot, A., (1979), *Van water tot wijn, van korsten tot pasteien*. Uitg. Brabantse Dag, Heeze, 1979.

Rocheblave- Spenlè, Anne-Marie, (1962) *La notion de Rôle en psychologie sociale*, Paris, Presses Universitaires de France.

Rozema, Hanneke, (1983) 'Veredeling en vreemdeling'. In: Koster, A., Y. Kuiper & J. Verrips (reds.), *Feest en ritueel in Europa*, VU Boekhandle/Uitgeverij, Amsterdam, pp.178-199.

Stam-Dresselhuys, J. P., & J. C. Wessels-Nijenhuis, (1966/1980) *Oud-Nederlandse Streekrecepten*, Zomer & Keuning, Wageningen.

Stoll, F. M., & W. H. de Groot, (1924,1938,1980) *Recepten Huishoudschool Laan van Meerdervoort*. Gebr. van Cleef, Den Haag.

Streekrecepten. (n.d.; after 1967). Uitgave van het Nederland Zuivelbureau, Den Haag.

Voedingsmiddelentabel, Nederlandse, en aanbevolen hoeveelheden energie en voedingsstoffen. (19..) Uitg. Voorlichtingsbureau voor de Voeding, Den Haag.

Wannèe, C. J., (1924,1938,1980) *Kookboek van de Amsterdamse Huishoudschool*. H. J. W. Becht, Amsterdam.

The Politics and Social Implications of Tableware for Feasting

by Elizabeth Gabay

The term 'feast' is today very much confined to religious festivals. The Concise Oxford Dictionary defines a feast as a 'Joyful religious anniversary; moveable, immovable feast: one that recurs on different, same, date; moveable feast: meal taken at no regular time; annual village festival; sumptuous meal, especially public one given to many guests; partake of feast, eat and drink sumptuously from the Latin festus meaning joyous'. The feasts of early history have continued in the traditions of dinner parties and large dinners. Here is a 19th century definition of a feast as a 'dinner of invitation' as described in *Food and Feeding* by Sir Henry Thompson Bart around 1900.

> And of this entertainment, the dinner of invitation, there are two very distinct kinds. First, there is the little dinner of six or eight guests, carefully selected for their own specific qualities, and combined with judgment to obtain a harmonious and successful result. The ingredients of a small party, like the ingredients of a dish, must be well chosen to make it 'Complete'. Such are the first conditions to be attained in order to achieve the highest perfection in dining. Secondly, there is the dinner of society, which is necessarily large; the number of guests varying from twelve to twenty-four.
>
> The characteristics of the first dinner are - comfort, excellence, simplicity and good taste. Those of the second are - the conventional standard of quality, some profusion of supply, suitable display in ornament and service.

Mrs Beeton in the 1861 edition of her *Household Management* defines the value of dining in society.

> Dining is the privilege of civilisation. The rank which a people occupy in the grand scale may be measured by their way of taking their meals, as well as by their way of treating women. The nation which knows how to dine has learnt the leading lesson of progress.

We are told that 'Mrs Beeton aims at teaching the newly rich how to dine if they wish to be accepted by society and how to give a dinner - if accepted.' that 'The size and arrangement of the dining-room, the quality of the plate and china, the quantity and elaborateness of the food and the time at which one dined - seven or half-past in the higher, six in the middle and midday in the lower ranks - all indicated with a fair amount of accuracy just where the party-giver stood in the social and economic scale.' [1] It is interesting to note the importance given to the timing of dinners in the mid 19th century. Meal times were already changing in the 18th century when breakfast was added to the midday and evening meals.

Until the 17th century medieval attitudes lingered; 'table service' was an action, laying a table and preparing to serve a meal, rather than the collection of vessels on which food was placed. Sir Henry Thompson's reference to 'suitable display in ornament and service' points to the importance of tableware for feasting. In medieval times guests brought their own tableware, while on display on a sideboard or buffet would be the host's gold and silver plate - ceremonial dishes, basins, ewers and cups. These sideboards could be elaborate and etiquette prescribed the number of shelves the dresser should have according to the status of the master of the house. At the lower end of the social scale two shelves were specified for a baron, the number increasing with rank. Paintings of royal feasting show dressers with eight rows, marking the supreme royal dignity. This display of plate was to illustrate the host's wealth and power. Rank and wealth were further emphasised in the actual serving of food, as Harrison, a poor clergyman in the 16th Century wrote:

> 'The beginning of every dish notwithstanding being reserved unto the greatest personage that sitteth at the table: to whom it is drawn up still by the waiters as order requireth, and from whom it descendeth again even to the lower end, whereby each one may taste thereof. ...When they have taken what it pleaseth them, the rest is reserved, and afterwards sent down to their serving men and waiters, who feed thereon in like sort with convenient moderation, their reversion also being bestowed upon the poor which lie ready at their gates in great numbers to receive the same.'

By the end of the 16th century a small dining room was slowly being introduced. Feasting no longer meant that the whole retinue and household participated. Feasts became more specialised, no longer occurring everyday for public display, becoming the opportunity for a particular statement, entertaining an important person, patronage and social influence. By the 18th century it was already possible to dine in a dining room 'privately' and still create good effect with elegant tableware. The court of Louis XIV, 'The Sun King', and his successors continued with the great formality

1. Elizabeth Burton, *Early Victorians at Home 1837-1861*, Longmans, 1972.

of the medieval traditions with public, ritualised banqueting.

Over and above location, timing and who was invited, the quality of the plate used for serving food was also carefully considered. We are told that in the 16th century food was served 'in silver vessels, if they be of the degree of barons, bishops and upwards'. Pewter was used for lesser folk. The overall impression of the feasting table by the end of the 16th century and at least to the middle of the 17th was relatively subtle. Finely worked pewter reflected candlelight in its dull surface. Glasses would have echoed the smokey-grey colours, their etched and cut decorations creating patterns. The brilliant blue and white of Chinese porcelain was finding its way onto the table and a further splash of colour was provided by the scarlets and crimsons of a Turkey carpet covered with a white cloth spread upon the table. Amidst this rather subtle beauty there would have been, on the tables of the wealthy at least, lavish gold and silver 'salts' and the use of some of the display gold and silver plate on the table.

The importation of porcelain from China throughout the 17th century introduced to the Western table bright, translucent wares that were thin and elegant, strong and cheap. European craftsmen were influenced by the growing number of Chinese imports. Their dominance in the Western market lasted until the end of the 18th century when home produced porcelain and creamwares were able to successfully compete. The acceptance of dining off ceramic services seems to have developed in 16th century Italy with the use of maiolica wares in the 'rustic' villas of the Italian nobility. Museum displays [1] illustrate well the standard of beauty which these earthenware services attained with their beautiful and elaborate paintings in brilliant blues, greens, oranges and yellows. As with silverware, these more ornamental plates would have been more for display than for eating from. It was to take some time before the idea of eating from anything other than silverware would be acceptable at society dinners. As late as 1663, Samuel Pepys could note with genuine disapproval that a function as formal and important as the Lord Mayor's banquet at the Guildhall was furnished only with wooden plates; the City Corporation plate had been melted down during the Civil War, and there was still no intermediate material for dining off. The Restoration of the Monarchy in 1660 ushered in a boom period for English silversmiths, due, no doubt, partly to a general desire to replace the enormous quantities of wrought silver converted into coin for payment of both armies during the Civil War and partly to satisfy an urge for a luxurious mode of living.

Many of the innovations and fashion trends in tableware of the 17th and 18th centuries were influenced by science and technology and at the ultimate level indicated significant achievements and were treated as symbols of wealth and power. The display of the feasting table was becoming more subtle in its forms of advertisement. The qualities of porcelain, which make it so attractive, especially today, is its delicate translucency. When Chinese porcelain was first introduced to Europe, however, the initial attraction was its smooth pure white surface. In comparison to painted maiolica and the dull coloured pottery then available, Chinese porcelain would have looked dramatically bright. European potters made items with a white glaze - the most commonly known being delft-ware - but these imitations were very subdued and clumsy next to the imported porcelain wares. The problems in making porcelain lay in the need to locate the right ingredients, including china clay, and to be able to fire the earthenware at a very high temperature. Until hard-paste or true porcelain was discovered, soft-paste porcelain was made which in England was and is sometimes known as English Bone China due to the addition of ground bone to the clay in an attempt to give a porcelain type translucency.

Competition to make true porcelain, to rival that imported from China, was keen. The first to make the discovery were J. F. Boettger and E. W. von Tschirnhausen in Dresden in 1708. The importance given to the art of making porcelain can be seen in the way in which heads of state jealously guarded the means of making true porcelain and the fierce rivalry in design and style. Royal permission had to be granted for the making of soft-paste porcelain in France where the factory at Sèvres had a monopoly. It was the aim of every European country to produce porcelain to equal that of the Chinese. By about 1720 the Saxon factory of Meissen had succeeded in locating the necessary China clay and china stone in its own territory, making possible the production of true hard-paste porcelain. The same materials were not discovered in France until the last quarter of the 18th century and until then craftsmen had had to produce artificial or soft-paste porcelain.

Workers from factories were forbidden to leave, under threat of great punishment, in case valuable trade secrets were passed on to rivals. Some did manage to leave, but in France the Royal monopoly tracked errant workers down. By mid 18th century many heads of States were eager to sponsor a porcelain factory in their territory even if only as a status symbol. Painters and designers were headhunted. In 1766 a royal edict was issued which encouraged the establishing of further French porcelain factories - possibly to promote research into the materials of true porcelain. This relaxing of the monopoly brought about more competition than anticipated, and rival factories began to flourish under the patronage of members of the Royal family and other powerful courtiers.

1. Victoria and Albert Museum

Political statements of power and the extent of scientific and cultural civilisation were made on the top feasting tables of Europe. The value attributed to these porcelain dinner services took the place of the lavish gold and silver gifts of the medieval monarchs. Court sculptors designed figurines, court painters created pictures. The latest fashionable influences whether in the style of neoclassicism, Arcadian or rococo were translated to these porcelain dinner services. Famous contemporary characters and actors were portrayed in figurines. Many large services, vases and centre pieces were given by Louis XV as diplomatic gifts. The Empress Catherine II, thanks to the encouragement of the British ambassador, ordered many services decorated either with a crowned EII (Ekaterina) or, as in the case of a service made by Wedgwood with a little frog, the emblem of the Palace de la Grenouillère where the service was to be used.

These services were not ordered and given for beauty alone. Their very presence indicated money, technology and patronage of the arts. Monograms on every plate confirmed ownership. The paintings of rural England on the Wedgwood service facing guests of the Empress of Russia would constantly accentuate the commercial presence of such a powerful country. Wedgwood was an active publicist of his own wares, obtaining English Royal and Society patronage. The use of quality tableware was not unremarked upon and attention was drawn to the porcelain in use.

> Dr Swan dined with Lord Gower this week; after dinner your Brother Josiah's Pottworks were the subject of conversation for some time, the Cream colour Table services in particular. I believe it was his Lordship who said that nothing could exceed them for a fine glaze etc.

The power behind the giving of porcelain dinner services can be regarded in much the same way that umbrellas, diaries and pens with corporate logos are treated today even if in a somewhat different league. When Napoleon was 1st Consul he became interested in the former Royal porcelain factory, and some very large impressive services were made as presents to various foreign diplomats and heads of state, including the Tsar of Russia, Pope Pius VII and 'Count of Livourne, King of Etruria'. In 1761 Frederick the Great of Prussia chose to reward his General Mollendorff by giving him a complete dinner service. Matching cutlery handles, table figurines and decorations are all part of this service, decorated in white and gold in the latest fashion (influenced by the excavations at Pompeii and Herculaneum) with scenes from Classical mythology [1]. Catherine II of Russia gave lavishly decorated porcelain table wares from The Imperial State Porcelain Factory to many of her court favourites. As early as 1735-7 Augustus III of Saxony gave to his court favourite, Count Sulkowsky, a dinner service whose pattern was to become very popular with its moulded basket work pattern.

Many of the dinner services of the 18th century were extremely elegant. During the first half of the century the designs were simple and very much influenced by the work being produced in China. By the second half of the century the designs of the factory at Sèvres were leading the market. Many were illustrated with precise botanical drawings executed with a great feeling for design and reflecting the expansion of science in another field. An advertisement for Derby Porcelain in 1756 describes just such a service: 'A Curious Collection of fine Figures, Jars, Sauceboats, Services for Desserts, ... all exquisitely painted in Enamel, with Flowers, Insects, India Plants etc.'.

Not all designs were so tasteful. One set from 1778-9 is ornamented with sphinxes in bright turquoise, gold and white and strongly reflected the current interest in Egypt [1]. Even contemporaries failed to be impressed by the artistic qualities of some table ware. A particularly famous ornate service was given in 1763 by George III and Queen Charlotte to her brother, the Duke of Mecklenburg-Strelitz. Horace Walpole, who saw the service, was not enthusiastic,

> ... I saw yesterday a magnificent service of Chelsea China which the King and Queen are sending to the Duke of Mecklenburg. There are dishes and plates without number, an epergne, candlesticks, salt-sellers, sauce-boats, tea and coffe equipages, in short, it is complete and cost twelve hundred pounds! I cannot boast of our taste; the forms are neither new, beautiful, nor various.

A sale of 1782 lists the necessary items for a complete dinner service. "60 table (dinner) plates, 24 soup plates, 20 oval dishes in sizes, 1 pair tureens and Covers, 4 sauce boats and stands and a salad dish." It is interesting to note that there are no side plates. The oval dishes of varying sizes were flat, uncovered vegetable dishes. Dinner services for the middle classes remained in a different league until the end of the 18th century. Until then it remained cheaper to continue importing these wares from China and these included many more serving dishes which presumably wealthier households already possessed in silver and gold. European potters had not mastered the skill at successful mass production until the end of the 18th century thus ensuring the rarity and value of their quality dinner services.

Novelty shapes were also made and teapots from the first half of the 18th century were made in the shapes of 'a seated

---

1. Victoria and Albert Museum

camel with square 'howdah' on its back, a squirrel holding a nut or a fully rigged ship to commemorate the capture of Porto Bello in 1739'. Commemorative uses were also popular. Mugs, jugs, plates and glasses were produced for Royal births, marriages and deaths and military victories. After the Duke of Wellington's victory over Napoleon at Waterloo, he was given a Berlin dinner service by King Frederick William III of Prussia in 1819. This dinner service was used every year at a special banquet on Waterloo Day to celebrate the victory.

At the same time as technical and artistic advances were being made in the production of china dinner services, early Georgian technical advances in the making of quality glassware in the 1730's led to more adventurous glass cutting by the 1780's. Taxes levied on glass were calculated on the weight of the final product rather than on its value and it became profitable to sell lightweight vessels decorated with more elaborate ornament such as gilding and enamel. The glassware of the 18th century was crystal clear and the thicker, heavier (and more expensive) glass was intricately cut to refract the candle light and to glitter (a tax levied on enamelled glassware in 1777 increased the popularity of cut glass); fine porcelain dinner services gleamed in the candlelight, their delicate gold patterns and white translucent backgrounds shining, the colours of each individual service creating a whole different look on each table. Glasses with colour twists in the stems were displayed and were often chosen to create a complete look. Gold and silver decorations and centrepieces were prominently displayed often of superb craftsmanship.

The different courses in the formal pattern of serving dinner required many different dishes and specific dishes were made to serve fish, salad and fruit. The elaborate medieval salts and been replaced by the epergne (English) or surtout (French) centre piece which often included a chandelier, baskets of sweetmeats and nuts and other elaborate scenes. At times the central table decorations would include mirror lakes, fountains, gardens and paths of coloured ground marble with porcelain figurines of shepherds and shepherdesses wandering in an Arcadian setting. In 1748 the English Ambassador, Sir Charles Hanbury Williams, at the court of Augustus III in Dresden reported a banquet at which were seated over 200 guests at one table and with a centrepiece in the form of a fountain "at least eight foot high, which ran all the while with rose water ..."

By the beginning of the 19th century the usage of porcelain dinner services had filtered through to the lower ranks of society. By 1773 it was necessary for Derby to acquire a retail outlet in London, though porcelain dinner services were still very much a luxury and something worthy of a mention. Samuel Johnson wrote to Mrs Thrale in 1777 concerning a visit to the china factories at Derby. 'The Derby China is very pretty, but I think the gilding is all superficial, and the finer pieces are so dear, that perhaps silver vessels of the same capacity may be sometimes bought at the same price...'. Indicating that even at this late date universal use of porcelain for special dinners was not taken for granted.

From being of great political importance, table services and table manners had become the key to social standing, as mentioned by Mrs Beeton. Nineteenth century literature is full of references to dining habits and their subtle messages are largely lost to todays readers. In *Deerbrook* by Harriet Martineau published in 1839, there is great social competition between two families and at one stage in the story they vie with each other in holding various entertainments. The new dessert service is regarded as an additional honour to the dinner.

> On the day of the Rowlands' great dinner-party, when all was to be so stately for the Hunters, when the new dessert service was procured from Staffordshire, the fish had not arrived from London.

The purchase of the dessert service has equal standing with the food to be served. The separation of dessert services from dinner services reflects the earlier importance of the dessert course at formal banquets when it was often regarded as the highlight of the meal. Eighteenth century dessert services consisted of far more than serving dishes and dishes to eat from. Porcelain openwork baskets, leaf shaped dishes, plates and tureens elaborately covered in relief flowers and fruit shaped bowls and covers were all included. Porcelain figures supporting candlesticks and baskets for comfits were also part of services designed to grace the dessert table taking the place of the earlier elaborate sugar centrepieces. Nineteenth century dessert services were simpler and did not include the figurines. It also became traditional to remove the table Cloth for this final course to reveal a polished mahogany table.

Later in the century ownership of a dinner service is something of a necessity and not regarded as a novelty purchased. In George Eliot's *Middlemarch* published in 1871-2 she describes English provincial life in the 1830's. Her comments on social standing presumably reflect attitudes prevalent throughout the 19th century. When describing the fragile boundaries of social distinction, the following comment is used to sum up the superiority of one neighbour over another. "...but in no part of the world is genteel visiting founded on esteem, in the absence of suitable furniture and complete dinner-service." (my underlining) With this damning phrase, Mrs Garth is reduced to a lower rank in society. It was not however always essential to buy the full service as listed in the catalogues. Selected items could be purchased to compliment any existing silverware items.

As the use of dinner services progressed through society, so too did the idea of feasting change from being the elaborate almost public form of entertaining to smaller family scale entertaining. It was just as important to impress your neighbours and to maintain your position in the rural community as in the wider stage of European politics. Smaller dinners suited the new expensive tableware as none but the extremely wealthy could afford enough settings for vast dinners. The Royal Doulton Catalogue gives us some idea of what a 'complete dinner-service' would entail in 1869. (see page 104).

There were some who bemoaned the use of porcelain which could so easily be broken by a clumsy servant. Some writers even advocated that porcelain dinner services should be used every day to accustom the servants to handling such delicate ware.

And the aim behind this complete dinner service? In 1872, 'G. C.' wrote in *The Round Table* about entertaining.

> One of the greatest elements of success in a dinner party is the uniform harmony which should exist in all the 'mise en scène', so to speak, of the dinner. The plate, the dinner and dessert service, the glass etc. go a great way towards making the dinner table look pretty and inviting; and those who aspire to a reputation for good taste, have ample scope to attain it in selecting these things.

Feasting throughout the early modern period was to continue as one of society's means of establishing power, wealth and status. Feasting as such was not held for the enjoyment of food; meals and dishes were created for novelty and to impress and continued to be served on a dinner service that would indicate wealth and position. Order of service and method of serving followed trends in fashion. Table etiquette indicated, and still does, the familiarity of the diner with grand scale entertaining. Even today we can still laugh at the confusion of others or be horrified ourselves at the daunting thought of the vast number of cutlery lined up on either side of a plate.

Selected Bibliography

Cushion, John, *Continental Porcelain*, Charles Letts Books Ltd. 1982.
Godden, Geoffrey, *Godden's Guide to English Porcelain*, Granada Publishing 1978.
Godden, Geoffrey, *British Porcelain - An Illustrated Guide*, Barrie & Jenkins Ltd. 1974.
Honey, W. B., *Old English Porcelain*, 3rd Edn. Faber & Faber 1977.
Sheaf, Colin and Richard Kilburn, *The Hatcher Porcelain Cargoes - The Complete Record*, Phaidon Christies Ltd. 1988.
Sterner, Gabriele, *Pewter through 500 Years*, Christies 1979.
Towner, Donald C., *English Cream-coloured Earthenware*, Faber & Faber 1957.
Vose, Ruth Hurst, *Glass*, The Connoisseur 1975.
Wilkinson, O. N., *Old Glass: Manufacture, Style, Uses*, Ernest Benn Ltd 1968.
Wilson, Anne C., *Food & Drink in Britain*, Constable 1973.

White Foods in Anatolian Feasts

by Nevin Halıcı

In Anatolia the rich culinary tradition of the old Turkish folk kitchen still lives very much to this present day. From birth to death, there are some traditional foods for every special occasion of an individual's life, as well as for every religious and social event. In Anatolian folk cuisine, every food is related to the event for which it is served. For instance, everywhere in Anatolia when you visit a woman who has just given birth, you will be offered a hot sherbet juice called *lohusa şerbeti* (convalescence sherbet). *Lohusa şerbet* is firmly believed to increase the mother's milk. You can be equally sure that it is *hedik* (boiled wheat) that you will get when you pay a visit to the feast of the first appearance of a tooth of a baby. *Hedik* is served so that the child's teeth are as healthy, shiny and straight as the wheat grains.

Although many culinary customs and traditions are the same, there may be some differences due to local floral characteristics and historical developments in the Anatolian regions. In Konia yoghurt soup, pilav with meat, *irmik helvası* (semolina helva), okra soup, pilav, *zerde* (rice pudding with saffron), and *hoşaf* (compote) are traditional wedding feast foods. In Izmir, however, the wedding food is yoghurt soup, chickpeas with meat, pilav with meat, *keşkek* (dehusked wheat with lamb or chicken) and *zerde*.

During my research in the region of Marmara, the Aegean, the Mediterranean, South East Anatolia, and part of Central Anatolia, I have come across very rich examples of the Anatolian culinary folk culture. I have had the opportunity to be present at some important occasions, some of which I heard of or experienced for the first time, but I have enjoyed them all. None, however, appeared as interesting to me as the one in the South East Anatolian region which established links between the food consumed and colours. This relationship may be found among other countries' culinary traditions as well.

Almost everywhere in Anatolia Sultan Nev-ruz (March 20-21), and Hıdırellez (May 6) are celebrated as spring festivals. With various festivities and picnics people welcome spring. For food they take their regional *börek* (pastry with minced meat or cheese filling), *çörek* (special bread), *köfte* (meat balls), *yaprak sarması* (stuffed vine leaves), *lahana sarması* (stuffed cabbage), yoghurt, eggs, cheese, seasonal vegetables, fruits and nuts.

As there are certain beliefs regarding the occasions of Sultan Nev-ruz and Hıdırellez, there are also certain customs and traditions that must be observed regarding the food consumed during these festivals and feasts. For instance, at Nev-ruz you are expected to eat seven different kinds of food whose names all start with 'S'. During Hıdırellez it is believed that if you step in a green field, eat fresh lettuce, onions, plums or any other green vegetable or fruit, you will be refreshed and your body rejuvenated. If you eat food that requires peeling like potatoes and eggs, it is believed that within that year all your troubles will also be 'peeled' off. To drink the milk of a milking sheep is considered conducive to getting rid of all kinds of ailments. There are several regional traditions of this sort.

During 1986, while conducting my research in the South East Anatolian region, everyone I interviewed mentioned that the Sultan Nev-ruz and Hıdırellez feasts required them to wear white clothing and consume white food. This is essential for a bright and happy year. According to the traditional story, which is believed to originate from Hıdırellez, 'Khıdır' (a mythical figure in this region) and Elijah (a judaic prophet) were two brothers. One day they did something which displeased God. As a result God separated the two, making one the Lord of the Lands and the other the Lord of the Seas. They could come together only one day each year. On that day Khıdır and Elijah would be together all day and would depart agreeing to meet again the following year. The first meeting place was Antakya (ancient Antioch). On that day both brothers wore white clothing. "That is why we too wear white clothing and eat white food; so that we spend a year in happiness and hope." (Source: Vardiye Alkan, age 80, Siirt). "On that meeting day, high in the sky above, a white bird would fly and wish all good things for those who wear white clothing and eat white food. For those who don't, the holy bird wishes bad things." (Source: Müslime Avşaroğlu, age 56, Dıyarbakır).

Accordingly, the main food items consumed during the Hıdırellez celebrations are eggs, milk, yoghurt, cheese, *sütlaç* (rice pudding), *lahana sarması*, *yaprak sarması*, and pilav with *zerde*. In Dıyarbakır the special white sweet, *şeker lokum kurabiyesi* (flour, butter, icing sugar) is widely served as a Hıdırellez food.

During my travels in the region I have noted that white food consumption is not confined to the Hıdırellez and Nev-ruz feasts, but is also observed in other feasts, possibly originating from Hıdırellez beliefs. For instance, during the two main Islamic feasts of Ramadan and Kurban, almost everywhere in the region you must have *zerde* which is consumed in the family and served to visitors. In Mardin, *zerde* is replaced by the very similar *sütlaç*. Only in Mardin is it considered praiseworthy to prepare and serve white foods - rice, pilav, *sütlaç, zerde, muhallebi* (rice flour pudding), etc. during the Miraç Kandili, feast of the Ascension (Mirac) of the Prophet Muhammed, to friends and relatives alike. In Siirt it is customary to give eggs to each other as presents during spring feasts.

Among the Christian inhabitants of Mardin it is also customary to serve white coloured food. "During the Easter morning celebrations, we go to church for morning prayers before eating. We pray and have holy wine and bread there; the bread is eaten after dipping it in the wine. When we return home, we have our feast meal which often includes ribs, pilav, boiled and coloured eggs, Easter *çörek* and *lebeniye* (yoghurt soup prepared and cooked with dehusked wheat) with grape syrup called *pekmez*. *Lebeniye* eggs and Easter çöreks are distributed among our friends and neighbours. Our Muslim friends serve white coloured *sütlaç* or rice pudding with *zerde*; we serve *lebeniye* to our friends. *Lebeniye* with *pekmez* is considered a sign of happiness and joy; it also symbolizes the purity of the Virgin Mary". (Source: Eliza Donat, age 55, Mardin).

In conclusion it can be clearly stated that in the South East Anatolian region white coloured food is considered essential for a bright and happy life and, therefore, is used extensively during all the festivals and feasts. It is safe to assume that similar beliefs are current among the people of the East Anatolian region also, because of their proximity. Since I noticed this relationship between the colour white and food, I have heard from many people that white food is consumed in other regions of Anatolia also. For instance, in the city of Tokat, in the Black Sea region, a white baklava is prepared and served during special occasions. This indicated that once a comprehensive study is conducted throughout Anatolia, more examples will be available and this relationship will be more firmly established.

This is a recipe which is not to be found in any printed cookery book.

Nergisleme (Dıyarbakır)

In the South East Anatolian region the Spring festivities start in the city of Siirt with Cigor (çikgör = come out and see), which is the first Monday in February, and continue until the end of May. The gathering of the traditional narcissus during these celebrations is considered the harbinger of spring; these flowers will in turn adorn the spring tables at home.

Those who have not gathered enough narcissus flowers or have been too lazy to collect any, will celebrate spring with this salad called ner*gisleme*, which is named after the flower. Because the salad includes eggs, which are at the top of the white food list, those who eat it will have a bright and happy year. As they peel off the shell of the egg, they themselves will peel off their troubles during the year.

How to prepare *nergisleme* for three people:

    6 eggs
    1 water glass of chopped spring onions
    1/2 water glass of chopped parsley
    1 teaspoon red pepper
    salt to taste

Boil the eggs until hard; cool them in cold water; peel and chop them.
Clean, wash, rinse and finely chop the spring onions and parsley.
Place the eggs, onions and parsley in a salad bowl. Add salt and red pepper according to taste and serve. If desired, lemon and olive oil mixture may also be added.

N.B. I wish to extend my heartfelt thanks to Mr. Taçgey Debeş who has kindly translated this paper for me.

Texas Barbecue: A Feast for all Classes

by Sharon Hudgins

Introduction

It is said that in Central Texas, the subject of cooking meat over fire arouses as much passion as football, politics, or sex.[1] That passion focuses on the Texas culinary phenomenon known as "barbecue" (also spelled "barbeque," "bar-B-que," "bar-B-cue," "bar-B-Q," and "BBQ").[2]

The word itself has several meanings in Texas. As a verb, it refers to a particular cooking method for meat. As a noun, it denominates both the meat cooked by that method and a social gathering (public or private) at which the meat is served. As an adjective, it describes the meat cooked by that method ("barbecue[d] beef," "barbecue[d] chicken"); any sauce used for basting and/or as an accompaniment to the meat ("barbecue sauce"); occasionally a bean dish ("barbecue beans"); the device in which barbecue is cooked [3]; the type of meal at which the meat (including specific accompaniments) is consumed ("a barbecue dinner"); the type of restaurant that specializes in cooking and serving barbecue (often called "a barbecue joint"); and a type of cooking contest ("barbecue cook-off").

The word "barbecue" has many of these same meanings outside of Texas. When a Texan uses the word, however, he or she is referring specifically to the particular type of barbecue cooking and barbecued meat known as "Texas barbecue." This barbecue differs from the barbecues of other regions in the kind of meat preferred, the way the meat is cooked, the type of sauces associated with it, and the side dishes that accompany it. Not all these characteristics are unique to Texas barbecue—but, taken together, they constitute a type of cooked meat (and a type of meal) that is recognized by both Texans and non-Texans as "Texas barbecue." This recognition even by outsiders legitimizes the widely shared belief that Texas barbecue belongs in a category all its own.

The consumption of barbecue in Texas is not limited to any one socio-economic, racial, ethnic, cultural, or religious group. Nor is it restricted to any particular location [4], season, or social event. Texas barbecue is cooked and eaten indoors and outdoors, at home, at restaurants, at feasts–by rich and poor, blacks and whites, Hispanics and Anglos, Protestants, Catholics, and Jews. In Texas, barbecue is often served at baptism celebrations; family and school reunions; birthday dinners; "coming out" and graduation parties; wedding rehearsal dinners and receptions; company picnics; church socials, fund raisers; Memorial Day, Fourth of July (Independence Day), and Labor Day picnics; political functions and inaugural balls. Its appeal extends to big-city lawyers and small-town laborers, to wealthy socialites and hard-scrabble farmers, to airline pilots and ranch hands. From cradle to grave, Texas barbecue is a food for all classes.

Barbecue: Origin, Definitions, and Development

The oldest known cooking method is heating food by holding it over an open fire or burying it in the embers. Both activities initially took place outdoors; later, as people became more settled and built (or adapted) temporary or permanent dwellings, cooking became an indoor activity in many regions (especially in colder climates). Outdoor cooking has continued to exist, however, in those places where climate and social, economic, or cultural factors favor, encourage, or necessitate it.

In the United States, the word "barbecue"—as a cooking technique—loosely refers to several ways of cooking over an open fire or over embers. As a general term, it does not distinguish among broiling, grilling, spit-roasting, or smoking over a fire. Such distinctions are made, however, by people from different socio-economic/ethnic/racial groups, and in different geographic regions of the country.

The English word "barbecue" is said to derive from the Spanish *barbacoa*, which comes from Taino, the language of the now-extinct Arawak Indians of the West Indies. [5] The word was first used in the New World in the seventeenth century to describe a raised lattice or grill of green wood, placed over or near an open fire, on which the Indians spread meat, fowl, and fish to be preserved by smoke-drying. [6] A grisly woodcut published in Paris in the previous century (1575) depicts a similar lattice being used by Indians in Brazil to smoke-cook butchered humans. [7] Later Spanish explorers along the south-eastern coast of North America also observed Indians using this kind of wooden rack to smoke meats over open fires. [8]

The first recorded mention of the word "barbecue" in the North American colonies dates from 1610, when the Virginia

Burgesses passed a law that forbade "the shooting of firearms for sport at barbecues, else how shall we know when the Indians are coming." [9] During the eighteenth century in North America, the term was firmly established as applying to both the meat (usually a whole animal carcass) roasted over an open fire, and the social gathering at which the meat was cooked and consumed. [10] In 1769, George Washington wrote in his diary: "Went up to Alexandria to a barbicue[sic]. Back in three nights." [11]

Stuart Berg Flexner, in *LISTENING TO AMERICA*, points out that by 1800 a "barbecue" had also come to mean

> ...a political rally at which barbecue was served—a good way to attract and hold a large group of people through a long series of speeches. For example, William Henry Harrison, Whig candidate for President, held a mammouth political barbecue in 1840 at which party workers and prospective voters consumed 18 tons of meat and pies (he won the election). [12]

During the nineteenth century, barbecue in America continued to be "an outdoor food served at political rallies and picnics, sold in pastures and backyards." [13] Around 1900, individual small-time entrepreneurs began setting up barbecue stands on street corners of American cities, in the backs of already established meat markets (butcher shops), and along the roads in rural areas. Roadside barbecue stands became increasingly popular as more and more Americans acquired automobiles in the first third of the century. Many street-corner stands evolved into small, unpretentious restaurants often affectionately (and accurately) referred to as "barbecue joints." [14]

After World War II, large numbers of Americans began moving to the suburbs, into single-family dwellings with a grassy yard around them. The 1950s ushered in the era of the "backyard barbecue" at which the man of the house (almost never the woman [15]) cooked steaks, hamburgers, hot dogs, or chicken on a small portable grill in the yard behind the home—often on weekends, and only for the family and/or a small group of friends. According to Flexner, "by the late 1950s [these events] were called *cookouts* (this word originating in the southwest U. S. around 1949)." [16] Many people also call them "barbecues"—especially in regions that do not have a firmly established, or specifically defined, commercial or cultural barbecue tradition. Barbecue purists (of all sorts) tend to wince when the term is applied to the cooking technique of searing meat quickly over a high flame, or grilling it rapidly over very hot coals, on a backyard grill.

Texas Barbecue Defined

If only one type of cooking method could be designated as typically Texan, it would be the method of smoke-roasting meat that Texans call "barbecuing." The resulting product, known as "Texas barbecue," has specific characteristics that distinguish it from cooked products labeled "barbecue" by people in other parts of the world.

Texas barbecue is meat that has been smoke-roasted at a low temperature (approximately 140°F. to 200°F., and in some cases, up to 250°F.) for a long period of time (several hours, or even days) in a closed pit or over an open pit. In both cases, the meat is cooked by indirect heat, not over a direct flame. The hot smoke cooks the meat, gradually infusing it with the aroma and flavor of the particular type of wood used for the fire. [17] The open-pit method produces lightly-smoked meat. The closed pit method (actually preferred by most Texans) makes a heavily smoked meat. The resulting product is meat that is slightly charred on the outside, still juicy on the inside, and so well cooked that it almost falls apart when sliced.

Because the meat is cooked in some form of pit (open or closed, above or below ground, indoors or outdoors), Texas barbecue is often called "pit barbecue." Both open and closed pits (outdoors, below ground) were used originally by the Indians of Texas, and later by settlers who moved into the territory of Texas from Mexico to the south and from the eastern and southern regions of the United States. Outdoor pit barbecuing was favored on ranches and cattle drives, and at any large outdoor gathering, such as picnics and reunions. Indoor pit barbecuing developed around the turn of the century at small-town meat markets in Central Texas. [18]

For outdoor pit barbecuing, a rectangular pit is dug about five to six feet deep, three to four feet wide, and as long as is necessary to accommodate the amount of meat to be cooked. The pit is heated by means of (a) wood coals transferred to the bottom of the pit from a fire built outside the pit; (b) rocks heated in a fire outside the pit, then placed in a layer in the bottom of the pit; or (c) a fire built in the pit and allowed to burn down to coals.

For closed-pit barbecuing outdoors, the meat (sometimes wrapped in burlap or other heavy cloth) is lowered into the pit. A wire grid might be placed above the hot rocks or coals to support the meat, or a layer of sand or dirt spread over the coals before the meat is added. The pit is then covered with a lid of sheet metal, or filled with dirt or heated rocks; sometimes hot coals are also placed on top of the dirt-enclosed meat. The meat remains in the pit for several hours (usually about eighteen hours) until it has been thoroughly cooked. If the pit has been completely filled in with dirt/

hot rocks/embers, the meat is steam-roasted in its own juices. [19] If the pit has been covered only at ground level with a lid, more smoke can form in the pit (from the meat juices dropping on the wood coals or hot rocks), and the meat will be thoroughly smoke-roasted. In the latter case, the meat is often turned several times in the pit while it is roasting.

For open-pit barbecuing outdoors, the pit construction and heating method is the same, but the meat is placed on supports (a metal grill or thin tree branches) laid across the opening of the pit at ground level. [20] The wood coals are positioned in the pit at least two feet below the grill, and the meat is hot-smoked over the embers.

Indoor closed-pit barbecuing is the type used by most of the barbecue restaurants in Texas. (A few have the pit located outdoors; and a few use the indoor open-pit method whereby the meat is smoke-roasted on a grill placed over an open pit. In all cases, the "pit" is constructed above ground.) Commercial barbecue pits are a type of oven usually made of brick, built ten to twenty feet long and waist high, with a heavy sheet-metal lid to close them. [21] A fire is built at one end of the pit (the firebox), and a smokestack regulated by a flue is at the opposite end. The meat to be barbecued is placed on a grill between these two elements. Smoke and heat from the fire are pulled up through the flue or fan vent in the oven, surrounding the meat and cooking it in the manner of a modern convection oven. [22] The entire cooking process usually takes ten to thirty-five hours, depending on the type of meat, amount of meat, and temperature of the smoke.

In Texas, the woods used for barbecuing are mesquite, scrub oak, post oak (cut during the winter when the sap is low), pecan, seasoned hickory, or any other hardwoods available locally. Each produces a different kind of aromatic smoke and hence a different flavor in the meat. On the plains and prairies of Texas, where wood is scarce or not available at all, early settlers and ranch hands barbecued with fires made of dried cattle dung ("cow chips" or "prairie coals"). [23]

The three types of meats that predominate in Texas barbecue are beef brisket [24] (the favored cut for barbecue), beef and pork ribs, and sausage (pork or beef-pork mixtures). [25] Other meats used for barbecuing in Texas are beef clods [26], beef steaks, beef tenderloin, chuck roasts, pork loin, ham, kid, goat, lamb, turkey (domesticated and wild), chicken, venison, quail—and even soft-shell turtles, armadillos, and rattlesnakes. It is said that Texas is a place where people barbecue everything except ice cream.

The meat is seldom marinated before cooking, because the method of cooking is so effective for tenderizing the meat (one of the functions of a marinade). Marinades can be used for flavoring the meat, but many barbecue cooks claim that marinades draw the natural moisture out of the meat while cooking (a result not to be desired). They prefer to use a "dry rub," a spice or mixture of spices—chili powder, paprika, black pepper (but little or no salt, which draws out moisture)—rubbed onto or massaged into the meat before cooking. [27]

Basting the meat while cooking is a matter of personal choice. Non-sugar-based sauces (commercial or homemade) are sometimes used ("mopped on the meat") throughout the cooking process. Sauces containing sugar (which can caramelize and burn during cooking) are brushed on the meat during the last thirty minutes of cooking time. [28] Many barbecue cooks refuse to baste or sauce at all, because basting necessitates opening the oven and letting the smoke escape, thus destroying the proper conditions for smoke-roasting.

A Great Debate in Texas centers on whether barbecued meat needs any sauce at all. Purists cook without sauces and serve the meat without sauce. Others—cooks and eaters alike, and certainly the majority of them—consider barbecued meat incomplete without an accompanying sauce (served with the meat after it is cooked). Commercially bottled barbecue sauces and homemade sauces (often using commercial sauces as a base) contain such ingredients as tomatoes (or tomato ketchup), lemon juice, vinegar, water, brown or white sugar, Worcestershire sauce, Tabasco sauce, onion, garlic, jalapeño peppers, salt, Texas-style chili powder [29], black pepper, cayenne pepper, paprika, mustard, black coffee, whiskey, butter, and meat drippings. Recipes for barbecue sauces are often closely guarded family or business secrets. [30]

The foods traditionally eaten with Texas barbecue are as well-defined as the cooking process for the meat. Together with the cooked meat, they constitute what is recognized as a barbecue meal, whether it is consumed at a feast, at a restaurant, or at home. The classic accompaniments ("side dishes," although they are usually served on the same plate as the meat) are pinto beans (small speckled brown beans), cole slaw (cabbage salad), potato salad, and sometimes corn-on-the-cob. Garnishes include sliced white onions, sour and/or sweet pickles, and jalapeño peppers. Most barbecue restaurants serve only sliced commercial white bread, but cornbread and sourdough biscuits are more traditional and can be found at large barbecue feasts and at home-cooked meals. Favoured desserts are pecan pie, fruit (especially peach) cobbler, fried pies (with fruit fillings), and homemade ice cream (especially vanilla). The drinks traditionally consumed with Texas barbecue are very cold beer, scalding hot coffee, and iced tea (often sweetened).

Texas Barbecue: Origins and History

Within Texas, barbecue has its own regional characteristics, influenced by the different peoples who settled in various parts of the territory. Native American Indians were the first inhabitants, followed by Spanish soldiers and colonists in the sixteenth and seventeenth centuries, and later by Mexican settlers, the last two groups populating the western and southern regions along the Rio Grande and northward to Central Texas. The Indians, Spanish, and Mexicans were the first people in Texas to use pit-cooking techniques, barbecuing wild game such as buffalo and venison, and later the sheep and goats which the Spanish introduced into the area.

Around 1800, small bands of settlers came to east and south east Texas from the lower South of the United States and the Louisiana Territory, bringing with them a preference for pit-smoked pork and small game, along with hot-spicy seasonings. [31] In the 1820s and 1830s, Anglo-American settlers from the upper South of the United States (Tennessee, Kentucky, Missouri, Arkansas) moved into northeast Texas, eventually pushing farther westward into north-central, north, and west Texas, where they encountered the Mexicans and Indians already living there. By that time, the initial Anglo-American preference for pork had been supplanted by one for beef. The Anglo-Americans adopted several Mexican ingredients and cooking techniques, including pit-roasting/smoking, and created their own tradition of west Texas ranch (or cowboy) cuisine. [32]

Blacks who came to Texas from the southern part of the United States, both before and after the Civil War (1861-1865), brought their own food preferences and knowledge of southern barbecuing techniques. After the Civil War, many blacks settled as farmers and laborers in east and north-central Texas; others went to west Texas where the men could find employment as cowboys, ranch cooks, and chuck wagon cooks (cooking outdoors for the cowboys during cattle round-ups and cattle drives). [33] Today, many of the descendants of these black settlers operate their own barbecue restaurants in Texas, or work as barbecue cooks for restaurants and catering services.

Central Texas was populated by Anglo-Americans from the upper South of the United States, who began arriving in the 1830s, and by German and Czech immigrants who settled in the region between 1830 and the early 1900s. (34) It was in Central Texas that meat smoking techniques brought by the Germans and Czechs were combined with pit-cooking methods to produce what is today known as "Texas barbecue."

Around the turn of the century, German and Czech butchers in small towns in central Texas devised a profitable way to use up their unsold and less desirable cuts of meat. In addition to making sausages out of the meat scraps, they built enclosed barbecue pits in the back of their meat markets, and began smoke-roasting the meat they could not otherwise sell (tougher cuts, such as brisket and shoulder clods). Customers at the meat market could not only purchase fresh cuts of meat at the front counter, they could also eat hot-smoked meats in the back room of the shop. Originally the barbecuing of meats was a way to attract customers into the shop (and sell more meat) on Saturday market days. The idea was successful, and barbecuing soon turned into a daily commercial operation. The combination of meat-market-and-barbecue-pit became a Central Texas institution. [35] Even today, many of the oldest and best Texas barbecue restaurants are run by families with German and Czech surnames.

The Central European influence on Texas barbecue is evident not only in the smoking of the meat, but also in the traditional accompaniments of potato salad, cole slaw, and heavy desserts. The Anglo-American influence is evident in the preference for beef over pork (also a function of Texas' being a major cattle-producing state), and in the preference for white breads and rich desserts. Mexican influence is seen in the use of hot-spicy barbecue sauces and jalapeño peppers, as is the Indians' contribution in the form of corn for cornbread and corn-on-the-cob. This combination of local products, transferred food traditions, and adapted techniques produced the type of meal now known as "a Texas barbecue dinner."

Texas Barbecue Feasts

Feasts are held for many reasons - religious, social, political, seasonal - and certain foods are often associated with specific feasts. In Texas, barbecue is usually the food of choice to be served at large outdoor gatherings (and many indoor ones as well) [36], regardless of the reason for the gathering or even the time of year.

In Texas, the eating of barbecue is not restricted to any one socio-economic class, race, or ethnic group. That fact that barbecue is the main food served at a feast - or even the focus of that feast - does not say anything about the status, race, ethnicity, or religion of the participants. A barbecue can be the wedding reception for a Houston millionaire or the company picnic for a group of insurance salesmen. It can serve as the focus for a church social in an East Texas black community, or a round-up dinner on a West Texas ranch. In each of these examples, the meats and accompaniments would all fit into the category defined as "Texas barbecue."

The social status of a barbecue (the gathering) is determined not by the food served but by the guests allowed to attend. A Dallas high-society barbecue will be distinguished from a small-town high school graduation barbecue by the people invited to each gathering, even though the meals served at both functions would be practically the same. Barbecue as a food thus cuts across socio-economic lines and is a type of meal that is eaten by all groups, regardless of status.

Public barbecues (such as local festivals), some "political" barbecues, and barbecue-cooking contests ("cook-offs") are feasts that almost anyone can attend. At these functions, people from different socio-economic, racial, ethnic, and religious groups gather to eat a food enjoyed by all. The especially casual atmosphere of large public barbecues encourages the mingling of people of all types and classes (although members of the very highest and very lowest classes would not be likely to attend).

Texas barbecue *as a food* therefore has little or no sociological status. *As a feast*, it can be used to demonstrate status (exclusivity based on invitation) or, conversely, the conscious blurring of class distinctions (in the case of public barbecues). The attributes of Texas barbecue as a non-status food and as a feast consumed by all classes (eating together at the same feast) probably derive from Texas barbecue's origin on the frontier.

Frontier life was too difficult, dangerous, and lonely for class distinctions (based on food or most other factors) to have much importance. Ranches were located many miles apart, and even small settlements and towns risked being attacked by Indians. Everyone living on a ranch or in a small frontier community ate essentially the same foods. Any occasion—the start of a cattle drive, a national holiday, the return of absent community members—could serve as the reason for butchering and barbecuing a steer, which was then eaten at a festive gathering attended by all (including "people from miles around"). A public barbecue feast could also be an affirmation of the economic success and well-being of the local community—a celebration of the surviving of another year of potential illnesses, crop failures, livestock diseases, droughts, and Indian raids.

As Texas became more settled, and as commercial barbecuing took root in Central Texas, barbecue continued to be regarded as a food that was eaten by all classes. Likewise, barbecue has a long history of acceptance by all of Texas' racial and ethnic groups, as has already been shown. Similarly, neither of the state's two dominant religions (Protestant and Catholic) prohibits the eating of any of the foods traditionally served at a barbecue meal. (Some Protestant churches forbid the consumption of alcohol, however.)

During the second half of the nineteenth century, "Barbecues...flourished in Texas where they had appeared as early as 1836 and had become a common form of entertainment at Fourth of July celebrations, rodeos, county fairs, and almost any public gathering." [37] Old Settlers' Reunions were also a popular form of get-together at which barbecue was served. According to Texas food historians Ernestine Linck and Joyce Roach, "Family reunions in Texas are rather recent - Texans had to wait several generations for families to multiply - but there were Old Settlers' Reunions. Nearly every town had a designated place for the reunion..." [38] - usually a patch of land outside the town, with a good water supply (river or stream) and plenty of shade for shelter from the Texas sun. The meat for these barbecues was donated by individuals or organizations in the community, and an expert barbecuer was selected (or brought in) to do the cooking (open or closed pit in the ground). Side dishes were prepared by the women of the community. These feasts lasted up to three days, and included such entertainments as bronco riding, roping, fiddling, and square dancing. [39]

Big Texas ranches also held barbecues as a feast to celebrate the end of the annual work cycle. Ranch owners and foremen, present and former ranch hands, old and new friends, and members of adjacent communities gathered at the ranch in early autumn to consume large quantities of barbecued meat and other traditional foods. Another function of these feasts was to demonstrate the wealth and power of the ranch's owner(s). A contemporary example is the annual XIT Rodeo and Reunion held each September in Dalhart, home of the XIT Ranch. The feast is on a scale that appeals to Texans' love of anything BIG:

> ...a two- to three-hundred-foot trench, about five feet deep and four feet wide is dug. Covered over with sheet metal, then dirt, the pit holds the coals of fifteen cords of mesquite on which are laid as much as 12,000 pounds of beef to feed up to 10,000 people. After the meat has smoked for thirty hours or so, the ranch hands bring in a front-end loader to scoop off the dirt, then lift off the sheet metal and take the meat from the coals. [40]

One description of this monumental feast calls it "the only place in the world where they barbecue with bulldozers, backhoes, and dump trucks laden with animal carcasses." [41]

Huge public barbecues for thousands of people are not uncommon in Texas. A Labor Day barbecue at Bay City attracted 18,000 people, topped by 20,000 who attended a barbecue at the local nuclear plant's open house. Company and industrial barbecues can be equally large—for example, an IBM picnic in Austin at which barbecue was served to 17,000 people. [42] Barbecue for these large gatherings is catered by commercial barbecue firms (restaurants or catering services specializing in barbecue). Usually they smoke the meat before the event, then transport it to the gathering—or bring large portable barbecue smokers to the event and cook the meat on site.

Political barbecues are neither a purely Texan phenomenon nor a recent one. Evan Jones has observed that in the United States "Electioneering and barbecuing became virtually synonymous in the eighteenth and nineteenth centuries." [43] But since the 1960s, Texas political barbecues have received much media attention because of their direct link with presidential politics and their use by two United States presidents (Lyndon B. Johnson and George Bush) to entertain (and impress) world leaders.

Political barbecue feasts can be used to raise funds for the party (e.g., $1,000-a-plate barbecue dinners, by invitation only); to increase the candidate's media visibility; to win votes (large public or private barbecues); and to demonstrate the largesse (and power) of a winning candidate. During Lyndon Johnson's time in the White House, he turned the presidential barbecue into a national media event:

> The Lyndon B. Johnson outdoor barbecue has become a tradition, literally eaten up by Eastern writers who claim they have seen nothing like it since Franklin D. Roosevelt fed hot dogs at a Hyde Park picnic to King George VI and Queen Elizabeth of England. [44]

Johnson's barbecue feasts at the LBJ Ranch near Stonewall, Texas, were famous for their combination of good food (in copious amounts), informal manners, and high-ranking guests.

The barbecues were catered by Walter Jetton ("The Kingpin of the Barbecue Men") from Fort Worth, and the dessert was often Lady Bird Johnson's homemade peach ice cream. Foreign dignitaries and other guests were flown in by private plane, and "typical Texas hospitality" was dispensed in large doses. In 1964, when Johnson entertained West Germany's Chancellor Ludwig Erhard with a Texas barbecue feast at the ranch, the meeting became known as "The Spareribs Summit." [45]

The current United States president, George Bush, has continued the tradition. Although born in Connecticut, Bush has been a Texas resident for many years. On the eve of the July 1990 economic summit meeting in Houston, he hosted a Texas barbecue for the prime ministers of Great Britain, Canada, and Japan, and the representative of the European Community, in addition to 5,000 other guests. The feast consisted of 7,000 pounds of barbecued meat (brisket, sausage, chicken, and ribs); 1,250 gallons of barbecue sauce, pickles, and jalapeño peppers; 500 pounds of onions; 3,000 pounds of cole slaw, potato salad, and beans; over 5,000 servings of fruit cobbler and carrot cake; and 650 gallons of lemonade and iced tea. The evening's entertainment included country-and-western music, horseshoe pitching, armadillo races, and a rodeo. The foreign dignitaries also received gifts of custom-made ostrich-skin cowboy boots, Western belt buckles made of silver with gold inlay, and "ten-gallon" cowboy hats. [46]

The appropriate attire for most Texas barbecues—from the presidential level on down—is American Western: blue jeans, cowboy shirts, denim skirts, cowboy boots. Even at high-society barbecues, the attire tends to be *expensive* Western fashions, not tuxedos and formal gowns. The casual style of dress—even when achieved at great expense—is another way of expressing a casual attitude toward social class (or other) distinctions. A Texas newspaper reporter observed that "For those who attend their first LBJ barbecue, there is an unaccustomed informality that breeds friendship and understanding." [47]

As in earlier times, however, the feast functions not only to display the host's hospitality and largesse, but also his power. [48] The informality of the event (even though carefully orchestrated) sends subtle messages of power and confidence to the guests, especially to those who are not accustomed to such casualness at official functions. It is the host's way of saying: "I am so much in control (of my country/state/clan/tribe/self) that I don't need to pretend to high manners and false fronts". This is a form of reverse snobbism, or down-scale ostentation, which (if successful) makes the guests feel inferior because of their own expectations of a more formal setting or event.

In the case of presidential barbecues, the President's unspoken message to his foreign guests is that he (and by extension, all Americans) are just "down-home folks"—socially unpretentious members of a frontier society whose strength (of character) lies in its openness, its cultural uniqueness, its New World attitudes. Foreigners tend to romanticize the American West, and presidential barbecues in Texas serve to perpetuate the myth of a society in which the head of state is equally at home in the White House or on the frontier.

Historically, Texas barbecue feasts were gatherings of people who knew each other, or who at least lived in proximity to each other. The late-twentieth-century barbecue cooking contest - known as a "barbecue cook-off" - is a different sort of feast which attracts a variety of people from many locations (including other states and countries) who are not necessarily (or even likely) acquainted with each other. Brittin and Daniel point out that the barbecue cook-off is a "favorite excuse for a social gathering...upwards of 25,000 Texans gather yearly at the Taylor International Barbecue Cook-Off held in Taylor, Texas."[49] All classes can, and do, attend barbecue cook-offs (except the very highest "old-money" types who generally do not socialize with members of classes lower than their own).

Barbecue cook-offs are sponsored by local Chambers of Commerce, various civic organizations, charities, and other groups. Information about the locations, dates, sponsors, and prizes is published in local newspapers and special-interest publications such as the monthly *GOAT GAP GAZETTE*. The March 1990 issue of *GOAT GAP GAZETTE* lists fifty-seven upcoming barbecue cook-offs between March and November, thirty-three of them in Texas. [50]

The titles given to these cooking contests reflect the Texas penchant for exaggeration and hyperbole:

Texas' Richest Bar-B-Q Cook-Off (San Antonio)
Taylor International Barbecue Cook-Off (Taylor)
World Championship Barbeque Goat Cook-Off (Brady)
Super Bowl of Brisket (Abilene)
World Championship Barbecue Beef Cook-Off (Pecos)
International Barbecue Society Tournament of Champions (Grand Prairie) [51]

Most barbecue cook-offs require the contestants to pay an entry fee, ranging from about $10 up to $300 (although most fees are under $100). Some sponsors provide the meat (and even the wood) for the contests; others require that contestants bring their own meat and fuel. Prizes vary from trophies to thousands of dollars. Except in rare cases, the cook-offs are open to the public (as contestants and as guests). Often the guests are admitted free; sometimes a small entry fee is charged (especially if a charity is sponsoring the cook-off). Parties, dances, games, races, and arts-and-crafts fairs can also be part of the cook-off's activities. Additional food is for sale during the day (remember, barbecue takes several hours to cook). After the judges have tasted the meats and determined the winners, most contestants usually give the leftovers away to family, friends, and anyone else around. At charity events, the leftover meat is usually sold to the guests for a nominal price.

A unique feature of barbecue cook-offs (in Texas and in other states) is the custom-built portable barbecue oven or "smoker." At most cook-offs, pits or holes in the ground are not allowed, so contestants must bring their own barbecue cooking equipment. In Texas, that means portable "pits" constructed on the same principle as the original stationary ones built into the back rooms of Central Texas meat markets at the turn of the century.

Some of these smokers are merely large metal boxes (often stainless steel) containing the requisite firebox, grill, grease drain, and smoke outlet. Others are true examples of contemporary Texas folk art (in addition to being fully functional barbecue ovens). Joe Amyx of Denton has constructed a barbecue smoker in the shape of a "jackalope," a mythological southwestern animal that is a cross between a jack rabbit and an antelope.[52] Amyx's jackalope cooker (named "Texas Jack") has the firebox in the animal's haunches (mesquite wood is put into the smoker via the jackalope's "cottontail"), the opening for the grill on its side, and the smoke outlet through the ears. Realistically shaped brass genitals (male) form the grease drain.

Ray Green of North Main Barbecue in Euless cooks meat in a five-foot-high armadillo-shaped smoker named "Bubba" (with the firebox in the head, the grill access on the side, and the smoke outlet through the tail). The same company also has a pistol-shaped smoker, which has the firebox in the gun's handle, the grill in the ammunition chamber, the grease drain through the trigger, and the smoke outlet through the barrel. Steam locomotives and railroad cabooses are also popular shapes for barbecue smokers. Ronnie Wright of Haltom City owns a 27-foot-long "Orange Thunder Cadillac barbecue smoker/rolling bistro"[53], an orange 1970 Cadillac Eldorado convertible with a barbecue smoker built into the rear end. Sam Higgins of Arlington built a barbecue smoker out of two old-fashioned, enamelled cast-iron bathtubs, hinged together; with a grill placed inside. " 'Cook a brisket in this baby,' he says [in a paraphrase of Kipling], and you'll end up with meat 'tender as a mother's heart, moist as a goodnight kiss, and lean as a cowboy's wallet.' " [54]

The construction of these folk-art barbecue smokers can be attributed to several factors: the natural human desire for display, the financial incentive (and prestige) of winning a cook-off award for "showmanship" or "most elaborate booth," and/or simply a good sense of humor. Some of the owners of these elaborate (and costly) smokers also cater parties, reunions, and other barbecue feasts, in order to recoup their investment or even make a profit. [55]

Barbecue cook-offs, although usually open to the public, are a way in which individuals can establish status within the particular, well-defined limits of a competitive event. They establish status, however, *only* as cooks, not as members of a certain socio-economic class. Almost all barbecue cook-off contestants - and guests - come from the vast American middle class, but they range from lower-middle-class blue-collar workers (truck drivers, construction workers, members of road crews) to upper-middle-class white-collar professionals (doctors, lawyers, teachers, airline pilots). In all cases, the contestants must have enough money to spend on cook-off entry fees, travel, portable barbecue smokers, and perhaps camper vans, in addition to enough leisure time to attend cook-offs. The majority of them would certainly be characterized as extroverts.

Texas Barbecue at Restaurants and at Home

In addition to large feasts, the two other places where Texans eat barbecue are at barbecue restaurants (often) and at home (much less often). Contemporary barbecue restaurants in Texas - the culinary descendants of the meat-market-cum-barbecue pit established in Central Texas at the turn of the century - are a sociological phenomenon of their own, a discussion of which is beyond the scope of this paper. Suffice it to say that because Texas barbecue is a food consumed by all classes, the blurring of class distinctions is also evident at almost all Texas barbecue restaurants (except for those relatively few barbecue restaurants that strive to be "up-scale"). In the parking lot of any good barbecue restaurant in Texas, you are likely to see a dirt-splattered Cadillac, several pick-up trucks, a Mercedes Benz or BMW, two or three station wagons, and a couple of motorcycles. Inside, company presidents rub elbows with office boys; millionaires eat at the same table with secretaries; blacks and whites, professors and policemen, state legislators and garbage collectors, all stand in a cafeteria line together to purchase plates of barbecue and "trimmings."

Most Texans have little incentive to cook barbecue at home when it is so easily available at large public gatherings and (relatively inexpensively) at barbecue restaurants (1,465 of them in Texas, nearly one-fourth of all the barbecue restaurants in the entire United States).[56] Authentic Texas barbecue also requires special cooking equipment (if you don't want to dig a pit in your backyard), and much time to prepare. It is possible, however, to purchase small, inexpensive, home-size smoker-grills, on which one can smoke-roast meats to produce fairly authentic-tasting Texas barbecue at home. This is the only solution for transplanted Texans like myself (currently a resident of Germany) and for anyone else outside of Texas who would like to eat "Texas barbecue" at home.

Following are seven recipes for the components of a complete Texas barbecue meal, all of which can be prepared at home. I have developed the recipes from a comparison of several classic Texas ones, in addition to doing extensive field research in the area (i.e., I have eaten Texas barbecue throughout the state, during much of my life). I have also tested these recipes many times. These are the recipes I use whenever I prepare a Texas barbecue dinner at home.

NOTE: ALL VOLUME MEASUREMENTS IN RECIPES ARE BASED ON STANDARD 8-FLUID-OUNCE AMERICAN CUPS.

HOME-COOKED TEXAS-STYLE BARBECUE

The best way to make Texas-style barbecue at home is to use the kind of enclosed barbecue grill known as a "smoker" or "smoke cooker," with a lower pan for the charcoal fire and a separate pan for water between the fire and the grill. Follow the manufacturer's instructions for heating the grill with charcoal. For a more authentic Texas flavor, soak pecan shells, mesquite wood chips, or hickory wood chips in water for 30 minutes to 1 hour before you begin cooking, then place them on the coals before adding the meat and closing the smoker's lid.

Rub the meat all over with a little vegetable oil, then coat all surfaces of the meat with plenty of black pepper and/ or chili powder, rubbing the spices into the oil and the meat. Place the meat on the grill rack, cover the smoker, and smoke the meat according to the instructions that came with the grill. Usually it takes at least 6 hours to smoke 5 pounds of beef, depending on the thickness of the cut. The cooked meat should be well done but not dry, tender and almost falling apart when you cut it.

Slice the meat thinly and serve it with barbecue sauce spooned on top, if desired. Authentic accompaniments are pinto beans slow-cooked with onions and chili powder, potato salad, cole slaw, sliced onions, pickles, and jalapeño peppers. Wash it all down with plenty of cold beer.

HOT-SPICY TEXAS BARBECUE SAUCE

(One of several thousand recipes for barbecue sauce)

3 to 4 medium-size onions, finely chopped
3 to 4 fresh jalapeño peppers, chopped
(or 1 tablespoon crushed dried red pepper flakes)
8 large cloves of garlic, minced
1 cup strong black coffee
1 cup Worcestershire sauce
1 cup tomato ketchup
1/2 cup dark brown sugar, firmly packed
1/4 cup cider vinegar
1/4 cup Texas-style chili powder. See note 29.
1 teaspoon salt
1 teaspoon finely ground black pepper

Combine all ingredients in a medium-size saucepan. Bring to a boil, reduce heat to very low, and simmer, uncovered, for 30 minutes, stirring occasionally. Let mixture cool in the pan for 30 minutes at room temperature, then puree in 2 batches in blender or food processor. Serve warm or at room temperature, as an accompaniment to barbecued beef or sausage. Leftover sauce can be refrigerated up to 4 days, or kept frozen up to 3 months. Makes 5 cups.

(Recipe adapted from Black Jack Barbecue Sauce, published by the Phillip Morris Company.)

TEXAS RANCH BEANS

1 pound dried pinto beans
1 pound salt pork or bacon, cut into small cubes
2 medium onions, chopped
2 large jalapeño peppers, finely chopped
4 large cloves of garlic, minced
1/4 cup Texas-style chili powder. See note 29.
1 teaspoon finely ground black pepper
Salt to taste

Sort the beans, discarding the bad ones and any rocks. Wash beans thoroughly; drain. Put beans into a 6-quart stockpot and add enough cold water to cover. Soak beans overnight.

Drain beans thoroughly in a colander and rinse once more. Return beans to stockpot. Add all remaining ingredients except salt, plus enough cold water to barely cover the ingredients. Stir well.

Bring the mixture to a boil over high heat. Reduce heat to low and let beans simmer, uncovered, for approximately 6 hours, stirring only occasionally. Add a little more water if needed during cooking. Thirty minutes before the cooking time is finished, add salt to taste. Makes 10 to 12 servings.

NOTE: I prefer another equally authentic version of these beans, made by a Spanish/Mexican technique. Wash and soak the beans as directed in the recipe above. Cook the beans alone—in just enough water to cover them and without adding other ingredients—for about 2 to 2 1/2 hours, until the beans just become tender but are not yet soft. In a large skillet, make a sofrito by sauteing 1 large onion (chopped), 1 bell pepper (chopped), 2 medium tomatoes (chopped), 2 jalapeño peppers (chopped), and 4 large cloves of garlic (chopped), in 1/3 cup of vegetable oil (or melted lard) until all ingredients are soft and well combined. Stir in 3 tablespoons of Texas-style chili powder and saute for 2 minutes more. Add the sofrito to the beans, along with 1 teaspoon each of salt and freshly ground black pepper. Stir well. If more liquid is needed, add some water or beer, but do not let the mixture become too liquid (it should be very thick). Let the beans continue to simmer, uncovered, for 30 minutes to 1 hour. Add more salt, if needed, just before serving. Makes 10 to 12 servings.

NOTE: In *EATS: A FOLK HISTORY OF TEXAS FOODS*, Ernestine Linck and Joyce Roach give this description of how to cook Mexican Beans (pinto beans cooked Mexican-style), in a quote from Daisy Atkins (*WAY BACK YONDER*. El Paso, Texas: Guynes Printing Co., 1958, p. 11): "One of the best ways to cook Mexican beans is to dig a pit, build a fire in it of wood that makes plenty of coals, after the ground is well heated, remove the fire, place a container with a tight lid, in which the beans have been brought to a boil—well seasoned with salt bacon or ham. Now put the container in pit, cover with dirt - build a fire on top. After a night there the beans are ready to eat. Sure have a grand flavor as no steam can escape."

TEXAS POTATO SALAD

7 to 8 medium-size boiling potatoes
1 teaspoon salt
1 large onion, finely chopped
2 hard-boiled eggs, finely chopped
1 whole pimento (canned or bottled), finely chopped
1 large dill pickle, finely chopped

Dressing:

1 cup mayonnaise (preferably homemade)
3 tablespoons American mustard
1 tablespoon apple cider vinegar
1 teaspoon black pepper
1/2 teaspoon salt

Wash potatoes thoroughly and place in a large saucepan with enough cold water to cover them, plus 1 teaspoon of salt. Bring water to a boil over high heat, reduce heat to low, and simmer, covered, for about 20 minutes, until the potatoes are tender but still firm.

Drain potatoes well. While potatoes are cooling, make the dressing by whisking together mayonnaise, mustard, vinegar, salt, and pepper. When the potatoes are cool enough to handle (but still warm), peel and dice them into a large bowl. Pour the dressing over the potatoes, and toss gently to mix well. Let the potatoes sit for 5 minutes, then add the chopped onion, hard-boiled eggs, pimento, and dill pickle. Toss again to mix well. Makes 6 servings.

TEXAS CHILE COLE SLAW

One 2-pound cabbage, cored and finely shredded
1 medium onion, chopped
2 to 3 fresh green chile peppers, finely chopped*

Dressing:

1/2 cup corn oil
3 tablespoons apple cider vinegar
1-1/2 teaspoons mustard seeds (black or yellow)
1-1/2 teaspoons salt
1/2 teaspoon freshly ground black pepper
2 to 3 cloves of garlic, pressed

*Such as jalapeños or serranos

Place shredded cabbage in a large bowl and pour enough boiling water over it to cover completely. Let cabbage sit for 5 minutes. Drain thoroughly in a colander. In a large bowl, toss cabbage with onion and chile peppers, mixing well. Make dressing by whisking together oil and vinegar, then add salt, pepper, mustard seeds, and garlic. Pour dressing over salad and toss to mix well. Chill well before serving. Makes 6 to 8 servings.

NOTE: Many Texas recipes add sugar to the salad dressing, to offset the acidity of the vinegar.

JALAPEÑO CORNBREAD

2 tablespoons corn oil
2 cups yellow cornmeal
4 teaspoons baking powder
1-1/2 teaspoons salt
1 egg
1-1/2 cups milk

2 jalapeño peppers (fresh or canned), finely chopped
1 cup cooked, drained, whole kernel corn
1/2 to 1 cup shredded Cheddar cheese

Put the oil into a 9-inch square baking pan (or 9-inch square/10-inch round cast iron skillet; be sure to use a skillet that can be put into the oven). Place the pan in the oven and turn the heat to 450°F. Let the oven and the oil heat while you prepare the other ingredients.

In a large bowl, combine the cornmeal, baking powder, and salt. In another bowl, lightly whisk the egg and combine it with the milk. Add the liquid mixture to the dry ingredients, and stir only until the batter is smooth. Stir in the chopped jalapeños, cooked corn, and shredded cheese.

Very carefully remove the hot baking pan (or skillet) from the oven, and set it on top of the stove. Pour the batter into the pan, over the hot oil. Return the pan to the oven, and bake at 450°F. for 20 to 25 minutes. Serve warm or at room temperature. Cut into squares or wedges for serving. Makes 16 squares of cornbread (approximately 2 inches square).

NOTE: For a less hot-spicy version of this cornbread, omit the jalapeño peppers.

TEXAS PECAN PIE

1 cup white sugar
2 tablespoons flour
1/2 teaspoon salt
3 eggs
1 teaspoon vanilla extract
1 cup light corn syrup
2 tablespoons melted butter
1-1/2 cups coarsely chopped pecans
One 9-inch unbaked pie crust shell (recipe follows)

Preheat oven to 375°F. In a small bowl, stir together the sugar, flour, and salt. In a medium-size bowl, beat the eggs lightly. Stir in the vanilla extract, corn syrup, melted butter, and finally the sugar mixture. Stir to mix well. Sprinkle the pecans in an even layer over the bottom of the unbaked pie shell. Pour the liquid mixture into the pie shell, on top of the pecans.

Bake on the rack in the lowest third of the oven, at 375°F. for about 40 minutes, or until the filling is firm. During baking, the pecans will rise to the top of the pie. Let the pie cool completely, on a wire rack, before cutting it. Makes one 9-inch pie (6 to 8 servings).

BASIC PIE CRUST

1-1/4 cups all-purpose white flour
1/2 teaspoon salt
1/4 cup butter, chilled
1/4 cup solid vegetable shortening, chilled
1-1/2 to 2 tablespoons ice water

Measure the flour by lightly spooning it into the measuring cup. Mix flour and salt together in a medium-size bowl. With a fork or pastry cutter, work the chilled butter and solid vegetable shortening into the flour, until the mixture is the consistency of coarse crumbs. Add the ice water gradually, while you toss the mixture lightly with a fork. Work the water into the dough, gently with your fingertips, just until the dough holds together in a compact ball. The dough should not be wet or sticky. Wrap the dough in plastic wrap and refrigerate it for 30 minutes.

Roll the dough out on a floured surface, to form a circle 11 inches in diameter and 1/8-inch thick. Line a 9-inch pie pan with the dough, being careful not to stretch the dough as you put it into the pan. (For a crisper bottom crust, lightly butter the pan before lining it with dough.) Trim the edge of the dough, leaving 1/2 inch extra around the rim. Fold this extra dough under, to make a double thickness around the rim. Crimp the pastry around the rim, with a fork or with your fingers. Fill the pie crust shell with Texas Pecan Pie filling, as directed.

Footnotes

(1) Patoski, p. 148.
(2) The western cattle brand $\overline{BQ}$ (a symbol read as "Bar-B-Q") is also occasionally seen. In the spoken language, the term "barbecue" is sometimes shortened to merely "Q" (pronounced "kyoo").
(3) Texans usually refer to "the pit," "the smoker," "the grill" - with the adjective "barbecue" implied. People outside of Texas, including some Europeans, use the noun "barbecue" when referring to the cooking device itself.
(4) Authentic Texas barbecue, catered by Walter Jetton's in Fort Worth, has been served all over the United States, including at the White House (when Lyndon B. Johnson was president). Hamilton, pp. 82-83; Hughes, p. 18.
(5) Webster's New World Dictionary of the American Language, 2nd Edition. Most etymologists now discount the suggestion that "barbecue" derives from the French *de barbe à queue* (from head to tail), referring to the roasting of whole large animals. Lobel, p. 261.
(6) Farb, p. 192; Flexner, p. 490; Jones, p. 73; Tannahill, pp. 265-266. Stuart Berg Flexner, in *LISTENING TO AMERICA*, also points out that "The English word buccaneer comes from French *boucanier*, hunter of wild oxen, literally "he who cures meat," from French *boucan*, a grill for smoking dried meat, and originally referred to European adventurers who had been hunters of wild cattle in Haiti...(the French got the word *boucan* from the Tupi Indians of Brazil and Paraguay, from the Tupi word *mocaen*, barbecue frame; it is similar to the Spanish word *barbacoa*, which gives us the word barbecue)." Flexner, p. 442.
(7) Tannahill, p. 266. Woodcut identified in note on p. 419 as "*Comment les sauvages rôtissent leurs ennemis.*" From André Thevet, *La Cosmographie Universelle*, Vol. 2., Paris, 1575.
(8) Jones, p. 73.
(9) Johnson and Staten, p. 198.
(10) Flexner, p. 490.
(11) Johnson and Staten, p. 7.
(12) Flexner, p. 490.
(13) Johnson and Staten, p. 8.
(14) Johnson and Staten, pp. 7-8. During the 1920s, "barbecue" also acquired a slang meaning, especially among blacks. It was used to describe a sexually attractive girl or young woman—the term being derived from the song "Struttin' With Some Barbecue," recorded by Louis Armstrong in 1927. Flexner, p. 491; Johnson and Staten, pp. 63, 122.
(15) In the United States, cooking barbecue has been (and still is) traditionally a male activity. In the past, the frontiersman shot the game, then brought it home or to the camp, where he butchered and roasted it outdoors. Butchering is a male domain, and the association of butchering and barbecuing (on the range or at meat markets) has continued up to the present. Also, men had the strength to hoist whole carcasses of buffalo or beef into cooking pits. The tradition also derives from ranch and cattle-drive cooks, who were almost always men. Another factor is the cultural division of labor (and space) that assigns women to the kitchen (indoors) and men to the outdoors. Today, as in the past, almost all cooks at barbecue restaurants, barbecue catering services, outdoor picnics, and home barbecues are men. This is also the case at barbecue cook-offs, although an increasing number of women are entering the cook-offs (a reflection of the blurring of sexually-defined roles in America).
(16) Flexner, p. 491.
(17) The technique should not be confused with cold-smoke curing of meat.
(18) Brittin and Daniel, pp. 12-13; Johnson and Staten, pp. 178-179. See following section on "Texas Barbecue: Origins and History."
(19) Both Eckhardt (p. 74) and Jones (p. 80) describe how this technique is used in South Texas and along the Rio Grande to barbecue a whole beef's head. Jones claims the technique came from Mexico via Spanish soldiers.
(20) Brittin and Daniel, pp. 12-13. A photograph (c. 1912) from the Institute of Texan Cultures shows an outdoor open barbecue pit in Texas, with old Ford automobile axles laid across it to support the meat!
(21) Eckhardt, p. 68.
(22) Brittin and Daniel, p. 22; Eckhardt, p. 28.
(23) Brittin and Daniel, p. 24.
(24) A cut of meat from the breast of a steer, just behind the foreleg. Made up of two main pieces of meat, it is surrounded by, and marbled with, fat, which bastes the meat during the long, slow barbecuing process, and which keeps the meat moist and gives it a rich flavor. Brisket loses about half its weight while cooking. Johnson and Staten, p. 217.
(25) Brittin and Daniel, p. 28.
(26) The top of the beef shoulder, weighing about eighteen to twenty-five pounds.
(27) Johnson and Staten, pp. 209-210.
(28) Brittin and Daniel, p. 28.
(29) A commercial spice blend of ground ancho (dried poblano) peppers, ground cumin, oregano, garlic powder,

black pepper, and salt.
(30) In 1990, the owner of an Arlington, Texas, barbecue restaurant filed a lawsuit against his former manager when the manager left the restaurant - and allegedly took the restaurant's secret barbecue sauce recipe with him - to work at another barbecue restaurant in the same city. McDonnald, p. 1.
(31) Hooker, p. 38.
(32) Linck and Roach, pp. 3-5.
(33) Linck and Roach, pp. 93-96.
(34) Linck and Roach, p. 67; Mikulencak, p. 38.
(35) Brittin and Daniel, pp. 12-13; Johnson and Staten, pp. 178-179.
(36) With the invention of the portable barbecue smoker, it is no longer even necessary to dig a hole in the ground. The pit can now come to the barbecue, wherever its location.
(37) Hooker, p. 270.
(38) Linck and Roach, p. 154.
(39) Linck and Roach, pp. 146-147, 154.
(40) Linck and Roach, pp. 145-146.
(41) Brittin and Daniel, p. 14.
(42) Johnson and Staten, p. 213; Patoski, p. 148.
(43) Jones, p. 74.
(44) Hughes, p. 18.
(45) Brittin and Daniel, p. 14; Hughes, p. 18. A few months after Johnson's death, his wife held a combination cattle auction (to sell off the family's cattle) and barbecue feast at the LBJ Ranch. The Lyndon B. Johnson Presidential Library in Austin, Texas, produced a film about the event, entitled *The Last Auction*, edited by the author of this paper and released in 1973.
(46) Dowd, p. 3; "Mild Beefing Poses Juicy Topic," p. 3; "VIPs Enjoy Some Texas-Style Entertainment," p. 3. The reporting of these barbecue feasts in the national press tends to emphasize the large-scale aspects of such feasts ("thousands of pounds of this, hundreds of gallons of that"), perpetuating the image of Texans as people who do everything "in a big way."
(47) Hughes, p. 18.
(48) Presidents from Texas are not the only ones who use feasts in this way. In recent times, both Jimmy Carter and Ronald Reagan hosted barbecues (Southern-style and California-style, respectively) for officials and foreign dignitaries.
(49) Brittin and Daniel, p. 14.
(50) *GOAT GAP GAZETTE* (5110 Bayard Lane #2, Houston, Texas 77006), Vol. 17, Issue 11, March 1990, p. 7. The Kansas City Barbeque Society (11514 Hickman Mills Drive, Kansas City, Missouri 64134) publishes a newsletter humorously entitled *The Bullsheet*, which also lists upcoming barbecue cook-offs.
(51) Barbecue cook-offs outside of Texas and similarly named: The Annual Memphis in May World Championship Barbecue Cooking Contest in Memphis, Tennessee; the International Barbecue Festival in Owensboro, Kentucky; and the Annual World Barbecue Championship in Lisdoonvarna, County Clare, Ireland.
(52) Similar to the German *Wolpertinger*, a mythological animal well known not only to German children, but also to German hunters who have drunk one too many glasses of *Schnapps*.
(53) Evans, pp. 1, 6.
(54) Goodrich, p. 1.
(55) The cost of building or purchasing a custom-made barbecue smoker in the United States can run from a few hundred dollars up to forty thousand dollars. Brittin and Daniel, p. 15.; Johnson and Staten, pp. 198-207.
(56) Johnson and Staten, p. 17; Texas Restaurant Association Statistics for 1988.

Bibliography

THE BRADY STANDARD, Brady, Texas, Vol. LXXX, No. 50, September 1, 1989, p. 1, and special insert: "Goat Cookoff Souvenir Edition of *THE BRADY STANDARD*," pp. 1-24.
Brittin, Phil, and Joseph Daniel. *TEXAS ON THE HALF SHELL*. New York: Doubleday, 1982.
Butel, Jane. *FIESTA!* New York: Harper & Row Publishers, 1987.
Butel, Jane. *FINGER LICKIN' RIB STICKIN' GREAT TASTIN' HOT & SPICY BARBECUE*. New York: Workman Publishing, 1982.
Dowd, Maureen. "In Texas, Prologue With Barbecue and Armadillo Sprints," *INTERNATIONAL HERALD TRIBUNE*, July 10, 1990, p. 3.
Eckhardt, Linda West. *THE ONLY TEXAS COOKBOOK*. Austin, Texas: Texas Monthly Press, Inc., 1981.
Evans, Christopher. "The Bad Boy of Birdville," *FORT WORTH STAR-TELEGRAM*, Section 5, January 7, 1990, pp. 1, 6.

Farb, Peter, and George Armelagos. *CONSUMING PASSIONS: THE ANTHROPOLOGY OF EATING*. Boston: Houghton Mifflin Company, 1980.

Flexner, Stuart Berg. *LISTENING TO AMERICA*. New York: Simon and Schuster, 1982.

GOAT GAP GAZETTE, Houston, Texas, Vol. 17, Issue 11, March 1990, and Vol. 18, Issue 2, May 1990.

Goodrich, Terry. "All Fired Up," *FORT WORTH STAR-TELEGRAM*, Section 4, April 14, 1990, pp. 1, 16.

Hamilton, Andrew. "He's Kingpin of the Barbecue Men," *SATURDAY EVENING POST*, April 21, 1956, pp. 49, 82-85.

Hawkins, Nancy, and Arthur Hawkins. *THE AMERICAN REGIONAL COOKBOOK*. New York: Greenwich House, 1984.

Hooker, Richard J. *FOOD AND DRINK IN AMERICA*. New York: The Bobbs-Merrill Company, Inc., 1981.

Hudgins, Sharon. "Germans in Texas: Finding Freedom in the Lone Star State," *SPOTLIGHT MAGAZINE*, Munich, West Germany, April 1990, pp. 52-55.

Hudgins, Sharon. "Texas Barbecue: Where There's Fire, There's Smoke," *SPOTLIGHT MAGAZINE*, Munich, West Germany, October 1989, p. 17.

Hughes, Eddie S. "Jetton Stars at LBJ's 'Spareribs Summits'," *THE DALLAS MORNING NEWS*, Section 1, September 20, 1964, p. 18.

Johnson, Greg, and Vince Staten. *REAL BARBECUE*. New York: Harper & Row, Publishers, 1988.

Jones, Evan. *AMERICAN FOOD: THE GASTRONOMIC STORY*, 2nd ed. New York: Vintage Books, 1981.

Kansas City Barbeque Society. *THE PASSION OF BARBEQUE*. Kansas City, Missouri: Pig Out Publications, 1988.

Lewis, Peter H. "The Open-Pit Barbecue: A Texas Tradition in Good Hands," *NEW YORK TIMES* article reprinted in *THE STARS AND STRIPES*, European Edition, February 15, 1988, p. 14.

Lich, Glen E. *THE GERMAN TEXANS*. San Antonio, Texas: University of Texas Institute of Texan Cultures, 1987.

Linck, Ernestine Sewell, and Joyce Gibson Roach. *EATS: A FOLK HISTORY OF TEXAS FOODS*. Fort Worth, Texas: Texas Christian University Press, 1989.

Lobel, Leon, and Stanley Lobel. *ALL ABOUT MEAT*. New York: Harcourt Brace Jovanovich, 1975.

McDonald, R. Robin. "Recipe for a Lawsuit," *FORT WORTH STAR-TELEGRAM*, Section 1, February 20, 1990, p. 1.

Madigan, Tim. "Kreuz Market: A Texas Shrine," *FORT WORTH STAR-TELEGRAM*, Section 5, October 25, 1987, pp. 1, 8.

Mikulencak, Mandy. "Hej Slované!" *TEXAS HIGHWAYS*, Vol. 35, No. 8, August 1988, pp. 36-43.

"Mild Beefing Poses Juicy Topic—Is Otto's the Superior Barbecue?" Associated Press article, *THE STARS AND STRIPES*, European Edition, July 10, 1990, p. 3.

Patoski, Joe Nick. "The Barbecue Brothers," *TEXAS MONTHLY*, October 1986, pp. 148-149, 211.

Pinkard, Tommie. "Barbecue Texas Style," *TEXAS HIGHWAYS*, February 1984, pp. 30-37.

Richhart, C. L. "Walter Jetton's Chuck Wagon Apt To Be Spotted on Any Range," *FORT WORTH STAR-TELEGRAM*, October 11, 1964.

Sheraton, Mimi. "The Authentic Texas Barbecue," *NEW YORK TIMES* article reprinted in *THE STARS AND STRIPES*, European Edition, July 23, 1978, pp. 10-11.

Tannahill, Reay, *FOOD IN HISTORY*. New York: Stein and Day, 1973.

Texas Restaurant Association Statistics for Calendar Year 1988. Photocopied information from office of the Texas Commissioner of Agriculture, Austin, Texas.

"VIPs Enjoy Some Texas-Style Entertainment." Associated Press article, *THE STARS AND STRIPES*, European Edition, July 10, 1990, p. 3.

WEBSTER'S NEW WORLD DICTIONARY OF THE AMERICAN LANGUAGE, 2nd College Edition. New York: William Collins + World Publishing Company, Inc., 1974.

Wells, Carolyn. *BARBECUE GREATS: MEMPHIS STYLE*. North Kansas City, Missouri: Pig Out Publications, 1989.

Acknowledgements

I would like to say a special word of thanks to the following people for their assistance in providing information for this paper:

L. M. Weldon, for documenting on photographs several of the unusual custom-made barbecue smokers to be found in and near Fort Worth, Texas; and L. M. and Ruth Weldon for providing many of the books and articles listed in the bibliography.

Jo Ann Horton, Editor, *GOAT GAP GAZETTE*, Houston, Texas.

Jim Hightower, Texas Commissioner of Agriculture, Austin, Texas.

Carolyn S. Wells, Pig Out Publications, Kansas City, Missouri.

Pecos, Texas, Chamber of Commerce.

And last, but certainly not least, to Tom Hudgins, transplanted Texan, for cooking the authentic Texas barbecue, beans, and potato salad that we eat at our current home in Germany.

Notes of Fasting and Feasting in Thailand

by Philip Iddison

Fasting is a daily occurrence for the Thai Buddhist monk who traditionally eats no food from noon until dawn of the following day. Fasting for the majority of the population is perhaps only an exercise in avoiding meat on the regular Buddhist holy days which occur at roughly eight day intervals.

Thailand is however not exclusively Buddhist. In the south there is a substantial Muslim minority who observe the fasting month of Ramadan, whilst in the north animistic beliefs are still strongly evident. Christianity also has its adherents and festivals; frozen turkeys have a ready sale in late December in Bangkok! The Chinese community of southern Thailand has a vegetarian festival each October which calls for considerable culinary skill creating look-alike meat dishes from bean curd and bean curd skin (*fong tao hoo*), wheat noodle dough and vegetables.

If feasting is defined as a significant alteration in the routine consumption of food, in Thailand it occurs at the expected major events in the individual human cycle, birth, marriage, death and also at communal events such as the dedication of a temple, the culmination of the rice harvest or the end of Ramadan, *Eid al fitri*.

Carl Bock recounting his travels in Siam in the nineteenth century gives an outline account of a northern Thai, then considered Laotian, wedding festivity for a minor prince:-

> "All the morning I could see large quantities of provisions being carried into the Chow's palace - rice, curry, pork, buffalo meat, vegetables, roasted capsicums and an endless supply of arrack."[1]

This menu would not be amiss at a similar occasion today but Bock also records that the wedding ceremony was named after the betel-nut (*mahg*) which was an essential part of the celebration but whose use is currently slipping into oblivion under the onslaught of more fashionable stimulants.

Thais generally eat a simple diet of rice and noodles, a little meat and fish, vegetables and fruit. A temple festival or family celebration provide the reason to invest effort, time and money in preparing different food to the routine, perhaps a large batch of steamed *khanom* for the ordination of a monk or the sacrifice of a pig to appease the spirits (consumed afterwards by the celebrants). Descriptions of celebrations of this sort in northern hamlets practising swidden (slash & burn) farming in 1957-8 follow:-

> "On the night before the threshing was to start the ceremonial fans (*taling*), a part bottle of wine, three or four desserts (*khanom*), *miang* (tea leaf), several cigarettes, a banana shoot, an unhusked green coconut, an egg, red rice seeds, and several bundles of each kind of rice grown that year were taken out to the threshing area ...the edible items are eaten or taken back home again to be eaten later.

> [at another hamlet] a dog is tied up and carried to the field, where a small spirit house is constructed. The dog is offered to the spirit alive, and again after being killed and the meat prepared "with rice", with words of invitation to eat and of request that the spirit (*phi*) help the rice threshed be bountiful. After leaving the food on the spirit house for a while, it is assumed that the spirit has eaten all it wishes so the remainder is requested from the *phi* and eaten by the owner and his friends.[2]

Subsistence farming does not permit elaborate ceremonies or waste.

Chinese festivals have been adopted into urban Thai life and introduce specialities both in the market at Chinese New Year and on specific occasions such as *Cheng meng* (visiting ancestor's graves), *Tuan yang* (Dragon Boat Festival) and *Chung chiul* Moon Cake Festival). These festivals have been subtly transmuted to have their own Thai flavour.

These brief notes are concluded by descriptions of three dishes and a cuisine which illustrate various aspects of Thai festive food both home grown and adopted from other cultures.

Khanom Sai Sai

Vandee Na Songkla[3] identifies this as a celebratory dessert for an engagement ceremony in times past. Today the neat little pyramidal banana leaf packages are commonly seen for sale as a street snack or for home consumption.

On a double layer of banana leaf (*bai tong*) shaped ready for folding as detailed in the figure, assemble the following:-

- a soft paste of glutinous rice flour (white or black) and jasmine flower water
- a filling of shredded coconut and palm sugar (*nam tan peep*) cooked to a sticky consistency and scented with night jasmine (*mali*)
- a topping of coconut cream thickened with rice flour and seasoned with salt

Fold up the banana leaf, apply a coconut frond strap and pin with coconut palm mid-rib. Steam for 10-15 minutes. Alternative fillings are banana or pumpkin.

The effort and intricacy of this dish encourage large scale production for an end product consumed in seconds!

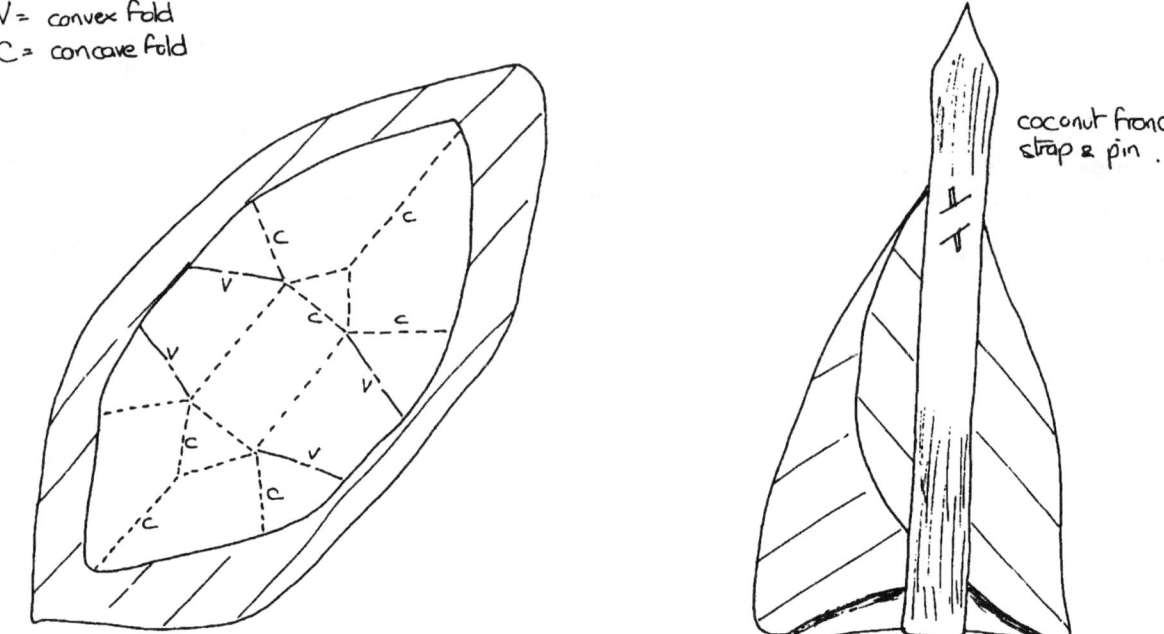

Folding diagram for *Khanom sai sai*

Ba Chang

The Dragon Boat Festival is a fairly low-key event in Bangkok except for the appeerence in the Chinese community of *ba chang* on the morning of the fifth day of the fifth lunar month. These dull green tetrahedra bound with pink or blue plastic raffia contain a wonderfully fragrant savoury rice dish, irresistable! They celebrate the suicide by drowning of the Chinese poet Chu Yuan. His followers attempted to provide sustenance for him in the after-life. They cast food into the river where it was promptly eaten by the fish and turtles with the result that the poet's spirit requested the food be packed into bamboo tubes stoppered with leaves and tied with silk threads.

The Thai-Chinese have selected bamboo leaves as the outer wrapping; they are large, up to 45 X 8 cm. and are imported from China. Three of these are oiled and laid on top of each other ready to be folded round the filling. This consists of a variety of ingredients according to the taste of the cook. The essentials are glutinous rice, salted egg yolk, Chinese sausage, processed pork mix (*moo tang*), dried black mushrooms (*hed hom*) and chestnuts. Substitutes and additional choices are peanuts, sweet taro cream, salty peanut cream, dried shrimp, sweet bean paste, black pepper, garlic and pork meat, fat or skin.

The package is bound and steamed to be eaten cold, the bamboo leaves imparting a delightful fragrance to the whole concoction, worth waiting all year!

Khanom Wai Prachan

The Moon Festival occurs on the full moon of the eighth lunar month and is celebrated with the consumption of mooncakes. In Thailand the favourite filling for these is durian paste with optional salted egg yolk, displacing the various bean pastes, dried fruits and lotus seeds used in other Chinese communities. Durian has achieved considerable notoriety and friends should not be encouraged to bite into a durian mooncake without being made aware of its contents. For the initiate the flavour seems to be addictive in about 70% of cases and makes black bean paste seem very mundane. Mooncakes come in a selection of sizes from a single bite to family sized specimens and 1989 saw the creation of a huge specimen for which the recipe follows:-

Line a dish 630 centimetres across by 12.5 cm. deep with pastry made from 580 kilos of flour and 100 kilos of oil, reserving enough for a lid and Chinese style decorations. Bake the case for 4 hours before filling with 2,300 kilos of durian paste (*mon thong* variety). Carefully distribute 100 kilos of melon seeds and 5,000 salted egg yolks through the fruit paste. Assemble the lid and rebuild the oven round it, bake until done and allow to cool for two days. [4]

The mooncake weighed 3180 kilos and about 10,000 portions were sold for charity.

Arhan Jay - Vegetarian Food

The vegetarian festival celebrated during the first nine days of the ninth lunar month in the southern provinces of Trang and Phuket represents the synthesis of Chinese and Indian customs into the Thai culture. The self mortification and endurance tests undergone by the celebrants hail from India with parallels in Malaysia. Festivities are centred on Chinese temples and the adoption of a vegetarian diet originates in China, understandable as the festival was started by immigrant Chinese tin miners in the last century. There appears to be no other tradition of vegetarian cuisine in Thailand, Thai food is characterised by the inclusion of small quantities of meat, fish or their products in all savoury dishes.

The vegetarian food consists of the abundant fruit and vegetables and also the imitative food products already mentioned. Vandee Na Songkla gives an outline description of the preparation some of of this food :-

> "Pork entrails-like: place a 20 cm. long and 1 cm. diameter bamboo stick in boiling water and remove. Flatten the dough and cover the bamboo stick. Tie the dough with cord along the bamboo stick. Dip the bamboo-dough in almost boiling water until well done. Let cool. Take off the stick and slice into pieces as entrails. Fried egg-like: mix the fresh *fong tao hoo* with salt, soy sauce and sugar together; leave it for 20-30 minutes. Roll the *fong tao hoo* mixture into a circle. Heat peanut oil until smoke coming and fry the *fong tao hoo*. Serve with sauce."[5]

NB. All words in italic are transliterations from Thai.

References

(1) Carl Bock, *Temples and Elephants. Travels in Siam 1881- 1882*, republished by OUP 1986.
(2) Chao Rai Thai, *Dry Rice Farmers in Northern Thailand*, Ph. D. thesis by Laurence C. Judd published in Bangkok 1977.
(3) Vandee Na Songkla. *Thai Foods from Thai Literature*, Book II (from *Karb Hea Chom Kreaung Wang* of King Rama VI).
(4) *Bangkok Post*, September 1st & 4th 1989.
(5) Vandee Na Songkla, *Thai Chef Cuisine*, Book 2.

Fasting and Feasting Among Oregon's Russian Old Believers

by Mary Wallace Kelsey

The Russian Old Believers, who have come to Oregon by circuitous routes, have a fascinating pattern of fasting and feasting. Fasting may be as often as 200 or more days a year, with each major fast period followed by feasting.

History

The Russian Orthodox Church in the 17th century split over some changes in doctrine made by Nikon, patriarch of the church, who wanted the Russians to follow more closely the Greek Orthodox beliefs. The Old Believers, not liking the changes, fled to Siberia to avoid persecution during the reigns of Peter The Great and Nicholas I. [3,11,16]

In the 1920's, the Russian government forced the Old Believers to relinquish their land and belongings. Some of them moved into China; one group to Harbin, in Manchuria, and a smaller group to Sinkiang Province. When the communists took over China, both groups fled to Hong Kong where the Tolstoy Foundation and the World Council of Churches helped to relocate them. [3,4,5,11]

Families from both Chinese groups of Old Believers were sent to Brazil, to farmland near Ponta Grossa. On their way to Brazil through Los Angeles, some of them met Russian Molokans who spoke of land in Oregon, U.S.A. [3] The Old Believers found that labour was cheap in Brazil, but material goods were high cost. The land they were located on was poor, and by the time the Old Believers learned how to make things grow, they found that the Brazilian economy would not support them. Remembering what they'd heard about Oregon, the group sent scouts there and then decided to move. [6,16]

Meanwhile, a third community of Old Believers had gone from Russia to Turkey. About the same time as the Chinese colonies were being relocated, many of the Turkish Believers moved back to Russia at the invitation of the Russian government. Those who were afraid to return found that they hadn't enough marriage partners, so had the Tolstoy Foundation move them to New Jersey to be near other Russians in the United States. [4] New Jersey was too well populated, however. Hearing of the group in Oregon, they asked to be sent there as well.

It was relatively recently - 1962 - that the Old Believers started moving to Oregon. By 1969, about 300 families had arrived. [6] Now their number is estimated to be more than five thousand, [16] but we will not be sure how many until the data from the recent census-taking has been processed. The Russian name usually used by the group for themselves is *Staroveri* [6,12].

Fasting

The Oregon Old Believers have kept their beliefs and practices, a main feature of which is fasting from all animal products, as well as oil, with a few exceptions. Fasts are followed by feasts; this has been classified as cyclical by anthropologist Margaret Bentley. [3]

Abstention from oil is an interesting distinction of the fast periods. There are two possible reasons given for this avoidance. In ancient Greece, oil was stored in animal stomachs which, of course, contaminated the oil with an animal product. The idea may have been passed to the Russian Orthodox Church along with other aspects of the religion. Richard Morris, an anthropologist who has lived in the Oregon Old Believer Community, points out that the Russian word for butter, *maslo*, means either butter or oil. He suggests that the interpretation of the law forbidding butter includes oil as well because of the undistinguishable name. [11]

Some fast days are not as strict as others, allowing the use of oil, and fish is permitted on some days. The following chart for 1980 is similar to that used annually. The Old Believers use the Julian calendar, and each homemaker has a calendar giving her the fast dates and prohibitions. She is responsible for keeping the family on the appropriate fasting schedule.

FAST SCHEDULE SCHEME FOR 1980 (Bentley, 1983)

Fast	Dates	Food Prohibitions
Pre-Christmas	Nov. 28-Jan. 6	no meat, dairy products, eggs.
	Nov. 28-Dec. 19	vegetable oil allowed daily. fish Tues., Sat., Sun. only.
	Dec. 19-Jan. 6	fish Sat., Sun. only. oil Tues., Thurs., Sat., Sun.
Easter	7 weeks before Easter	no meat, dairy products, eggs. oil Sat., Sun. only. fish Palm Sun., Annunciation.
Peter-Paul holiday	starts 7 weeks after Easter, ends July 12	no meat, dairy products, eggs. vegetable oil allowed daily. fish Tues., Thurs., Sat., Sun.
Uspenskii	Aug. 14-Aug. 28	no meat, dairy products, eggs. vegetable oil Sat., Sun. fish Aug. 19 only.
Wednesdays, Fridays	(except for 6 fast-free weeks)	no meat, dairy products, eggs. no vegetable oil, no fish.

Foods allowed during fasts are fruits, vegetables including legumes, and grain foods. Some of the Old Believers will eat nuts while fasting, but will avoid peanut butter because it is too oily. One informant volunteered that this seemed a silly idea - eating whole peanuts but shunning crushed nuts. [1] Two other women, when asked what they'd taken in their lunches to school on fast days, remembered peanut butter sandwiches. [7,9]

Colfer [5] says that the most pious Old Believers eat only bread and water on fast days, and perhaps nothing on Wednesdays and Fridays. This is the only source found for that information.

Even though some Believers avoid nuts during fast periods because of the oil content, everyone seems to eat sunflower seeds. Morris suggests that this is an example of creative interpretation of the rules. [11] The growing of sunflower seeds in one's yard is said to be a distinguishing feature of Old Believer homes in the community.

The elementary school teachers reported that students brought only bread and fruit to school in their lunches on fast days. [10,15] A young woman who is employed at the local health clinic said that on fast days, she doesn't go home to lunch because there wouldn't be any food there. Instead, she walks to a nearby grocery store to buy a piece of fruit. [9]

There are some vegetarian foods available at shops and restaurants in the community. However, because the other primary minority group is Mexican-American, many of the foods are prepared with oil and would need to be avoided by fasting Russians. The main reason for not patronising restaurants, though, is that strict Old Believers do not eat food prepared by non-Believers, nor would they eat from dishes that outsiders might have used. The utensil problem is solvable in the "fast-food" restaurants which use disposable items, but there is still the difficulty of eating food prepared by people out of the faith.

Typical fasting meals eaten at home include vegetable soups, kasha, potatoes and *pirog* (or *piroshky* - individual *pirog*s) with vegetable fillings. Bread is a staple, served plain or with jam on fast days. Fruit or starch-thickened fruit juices (*kisel*) might also be eaten.

Beverages called *kvas* are served, too. *Kvas* is often made from fruits such as apples, pears, peaches or prunes. Both fresh and dried fruits may be used. It is also made from beet juice, and one reported by Morris [11] was flavoured with onions and pickles. In Russia, *kvas* may be made from dark rye breads. The Oregon Old Believers seem to eat primarily white breads. One informant said that her mother *had* to eat dark breads during hardships in other countries, so now that she could have white bread in the United States, that's what she prefers. [1] Unfortunately, refined white bread and other grain products have been something to strive for since ancient Egyptian, Greek and Roman times.

Some of the Old Believers who spent time in Brazil eat the nutritious combination of beans and rice on fast days. One woman said that her husband wanted plain beans at home, because when he visited the Alaskan Old Believers on fishing trips, he ate more rice there than he cared for.

Two young women said they make their own *tofu*, soybean curd, to eat on fast days. [7,13] I asked if this had been learned when the groups were in China, but neither had immediate family members who were old enough to remember China. The use of this food was learned in Oregon, where fresh *tofu* is available in most supermarkets.

Other sources report eating a great deal of pasta during fasts. [1] Of course, egg noodles would not be permitted and vegetarian sauces must be used. The older generations of Old Believers make their own pastas. [1,2]

Old Believers who must be hospitalised will sometimes eat food prepared in the hospital kitchen if the food is served on disposable dishes. Others will have their families bring in food for them. Either way, the fast periods must be observed. [13]

Feasting

All of the major fasts are followed by feasts for the Old Believers. The most important festival foods would feature animal products, which may have been denied the fasting Believers for as long as forty days.

Easter

As with both Russian and Greek Orthodox followers, Easter is the most important of holy days. For the Old Believers, the service observing Easter begins about three o'clock Saturday afternoon with readings of the Acts of The Apostles. At 11:30 p.m., there is a half-hour break until the resurrection service starts. The lights will be turned up, women will wear brightly-coloured clothing, and each parishioner will have a lighted candle. Coloured eggs are given to each member of the congregation, who go through a rite of having eggs blessed and greeting each other. If an egg cracked, it would need to be disposed of in a ritual manner because it is a symbol of the resurrection and cannot be thrown away. About six in the morning, everyone goes home for the first non-fasting meal in forty days. [4,11]

The Easter festival lasts for eight days. During this time, unclean acts such as washing clothes cannot be done. Johnson comments that teen-aged Old Believers may have many clothes to get them through this period. [3]

Informants were asked if traditional Russian Easter foods such as *kulich*, an egg-rich sweet yeast bread, and *paskha*, made with non-fasting foods such as cream, cottage cheese, butter and eggs are served in their homes currently. Two informants did not know these foods at all; one said that her aunt made them, but no one else in the family did. [1,2,9]

An interesting mix of traditional Russian foods and U. S. favourites may be used at Easter and other feasts now. A fish soup, *ukha*, *bliny* (pancakes), *golubtsy* (cabbage leaves rolled with meat stuffing), *pelmeny* (pasta dough with meat filling similar to ravioli, boiled or fried), *kotlety* (a type of ground meatball or loaf), and the aforementioned *pirog* or *piroshky* are some of the typical traditional foods. Homemade sausages are served, too, along with homemade cottage cheese. Fried chicken with potatoes and gravy, as well as lasagna have been mentioned as newer feast foods, and there are always soups like borscht and salads. It is usual to have several soups in the same meal. Pork chops or pork and potato stews are consumed on feast days by some families. [1,2,7,11,12]

Sabey [12] names more of the traditional pastries as festival foods than do other sources. His study was done shortly after the first Old Believers settled in Oregon, and one might conclude that some of these pastries are no longer prepared in modern Old Believers' homes.

Weddings

Wedding feasts last for three days following the ceremony. In preparation for the celebration, men will make 100-150 gallons of fermented fruit drinks, *braga*, (discussed on following pages) and prepare a shelter to hold tables which will seat about sixty people. Women will bake bread, make *kvas* and a multitude of *pelmeny*, similar to ravioli, probably with the favourite ground meat filling. Five-gallon cans of broth will be used in which to boil the *pelmeny*. Other soups will be cooked over fireplaces built by the men. [5,16]

The wedding ceremony takes place very early in the morning, the time most church services occur. After leaving the worship hall, the bridal couple and witnesses will proceed to the groom's home for the wedding breakfast [5,11]. The couple will be met at the door by the groom's parents who offer them bread and salt. This is a traditional symbol of acceptance and hospitality used at other times in the home as well as in church. Salt means essential quality, as in

Matthew 5:13, "The salt of the earth", while bread means a basic, healthy staple food available to all. [11]

After 10 or 11 a.m., when the witness breakfast is over, other guests start to arrive and by 2 p.m. about a hundred people will be drinking toasts to the newlyweds. Colfer says that the best time for a wedding is on a three-day holiday weekend. Otherwise, some guests must work days and then go to the celebration only in the evenings. [5]

At wedding feasts, the outsider guests and Old Believers who are not in good standing with the church community, or *sobor*, eat at a separate table at the back of the room. This table has its own serving dishes which would be used only by the outsiders. [11]

A few weeks after the wedding, the bride's father gives another feast, for one day only this time, and to which a smaller number of guests will be invited than for the wedding. This feast shows that all is well with the marriage and that the young couple still have the parents' blessings. [5]

Funerals

At the consoling dinner for friends and family of the deceased at a funeral, a porridge called *kutya* - a rather sweet kasha - is blessed with incense. Three spoonfuls of *kutya* are eaten first. The last course of the meal is *kvas*, usually made with fruit. After this meal, there will be remembrance dinners given three days, nine days, forty days and one year after the death. If the family is very poor, only the forty-day and one-year dinners may be given.

Hospitality

Braga, another symbol of hospitality, is usually made by the women, except for large celebrations such as weddings, when vast quantities of *braga* are made by the men. It takes about three weeks for the drink to be ready to consume [5]. *Braga* is usually made from berries, since most Old Believers grow their own berries. Oregon is noted for its raspberries, many varieties of blackberries, loganberries, and strawberries. Morris says the *braga* is sometimes as high as 28-proof in alcohol content. There are jokes about this and some Old Believers laughingly say that *braga* contains no alcohol, since they made it themselves and didn't add any alcohol! [11]

Hospitality requires that glasses be kept filled, and, because there are many toasts, much alcohol can be consumed at a feast. Usually *braga* is served with *zakuski*, appetisers, the way vodka is served in Russia. The food makes it easier to consume the drink without so many effects of alcohol. Often, in addition to eating, the group will play games so as to not drink too much. The love of drink supposedly comes from pre-Christian days in Russia, when Slavs drank mead, wine and beer. Purchased alcoholic beverages are forbidden to the Old Believers, although men in the Turkish group drink beer because their ancestors who went from Russia to Turkey 300 years ago did so. [11]

Non-Believer guests at family celebrations might sit at one end of the table, slightly removed from the family (although a high school teacher told me she had been the only one to eat when she was invited to dinner at the home of a student). Sabey also mentioned eating alone in the front room when he visited families on holy days. [12] The guest might have his own bowls of soup and salad, served in disposable dishes or on dishes kept only for non-Believer guests. The use of disposable dishes would be more likely, since washing outsiders' dishes would contaminate the sink. These dishes will be washed in the bathroom or laundry sink. The guest might be allowed to take a piece of food from a serving dish if he touched only his own piece; or, one of the women would serve him by jiggling a platter so that a portion of food fell on his plate. This action seems to absolve the server from actually sharing food with a non-Believer; the food dropped onto his plate. [11]

The traditions of fasting and feasting for Oregon's Russian Old Believers have continued for centuries. Some of the foods used in feasting are relatively new to the group, but the basic traditions seem to have remained the same. It is a challenge for the elders in the community to keep the young people from becoming acculturated as they are exposed to others in the public schools. Observers of the Old Believers have noted some slight changes occurring within the group, although not so much during the strict fasts.

1. A., C.* Informant - Russian Old Believers Community, Oregon. Personal interview. 1990
2. A., S.* Informant - Russian Old Believers Community, Oregon. Personal interview. 1990
3. Bentley, Margaret E.: *Diet and Culture Among Oregon's Old Believers*. M.A. thesis. Storrs, The University of Connecticut. 1981.
4. Brother Ambrose. Benedictine Abbey, Mt. Angel, Oregon. Telephone interview and videotape. 1990.
5. Colfer, Arthur M.: *Morality, Kindred and Ethnic Boundary. A study of the Oregon Old Believers*. Ph.D.

dissertation. Seattle, University of Washington. 1975.
6. Hall, Roberta L.: *Population Biology of The Russian Old Believers of Marion County, Oregon.* Ph.D. dissertation. Eugene, University of Oregon. 1970.
7. J., S.* Informant - Russian Old Believers Community, Oregon. Personal interview. 1990.
8. Johnson, Patricia White: *Dress and Acculturation Among The Russian Old Believers in Oregon.* Master of Science thesis. Corvallis, Oregon State University. 1982.
9. L., A.* Informant. Russian Old Believers Community, Oregon. Personal interview. 1990.
10. Lizotte, Ruth. Third grade teacher, Silverton, Oregon. Personal interview. 1990.
11. Morris, Richard A.: *Three Russian Groups in Oregon: A comparison of Boundaries in a Pluralistic Environment.* Ph.D. dissertation. Eugene, University of Oregon. 1981.
12. Sabey, Ralph H.: *Staraveri and School: A Case Study of Russian Immigrant Children in a Russian Oregon Community.* Ph.D. dissertation. Eugene, University of Oregon. 1969.
13. Schultz, Kathryn. Consulting Dietitian. Personal Interview. Corvallis, Oregon. 1990.
14. Untiedt, Jules A.: *Impingement Upon Old Believers in Oregon by Agents of Social Change.* Ph.D. dissertation. San Diego, California., United States International University. 1977.
15. Wigowsky, Paul. Elementary School Teacher, St. Paul, Oregon. Personal interview. 1990.

Film

16. *Old Believers.* Produced in Oregon by Margaret Hixon. 1979-810.

*Names of informants are not used in order to protect their privacy.

ANNUAL NUTRITIONAL CYCLE OF THE RUSSIAN OLD BELIEVERS (BENTLEY, 1983)

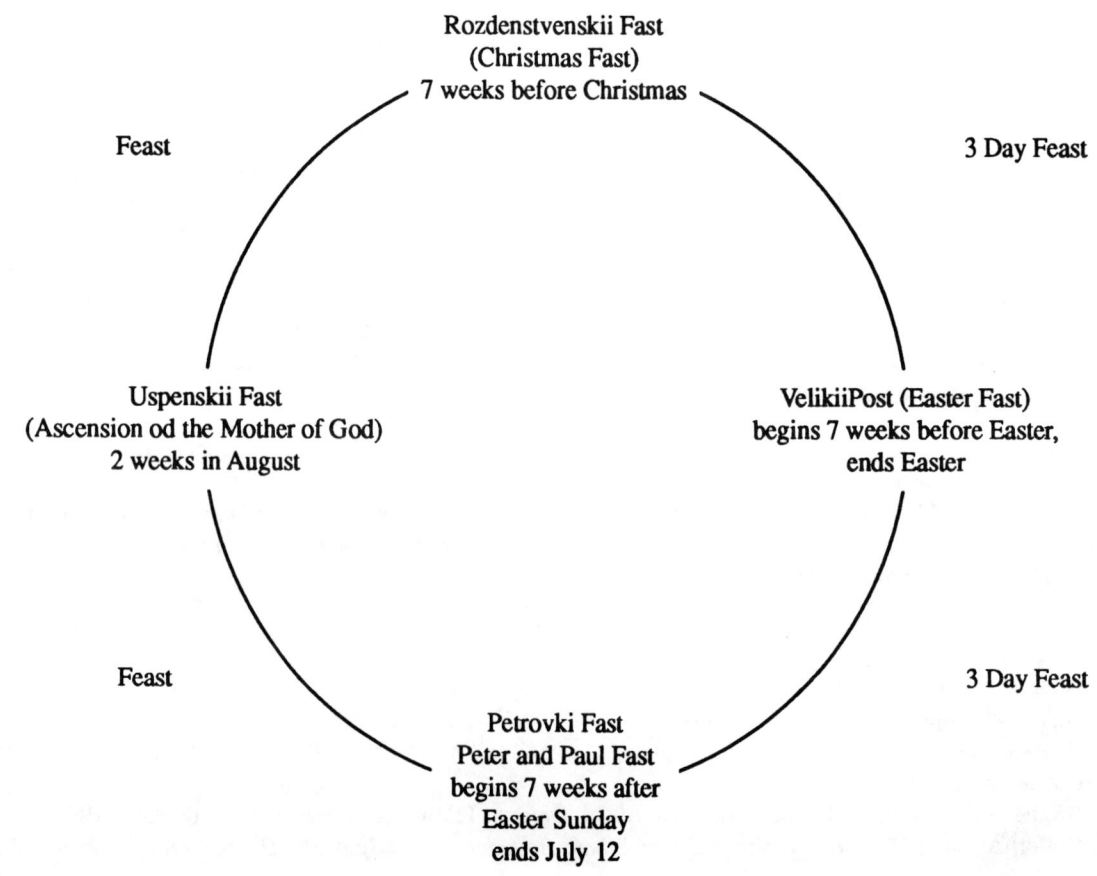

Fasting on Rumfordsche Suppe (circa 1791) and Woolton Pie (circa 1941). Feasting in Oxford, Capenhurst and Hammersmith.

Nicholas Kurti,
Brasenose College, Oxford.

I. FASTING

The two examples of fasting, or rather of eating not for enjoyment but to keep body and soul together, are separated by 150 years. The first is associated with the name of Sir Benjamin Thompson, Count Rumford and the feeding of the beggars of Munich while the second deals with feeding war-time Britain under the benevolent eye of the Minister of Food, Lord Woolton.

Sir Benjamin Thompson, born in the Commonwealth of Massachusetts in 1753, was a soldier, scientist and statesman who lived successively in America, in England, in Bavaria and in France. In Munich, where he was Minister of War in the service of the Elector of Bavaria, Prince Karl Theodor, he noticed the large number of beggars. He says in one of his essays that they "had been bred up from their infancy in that profession, and were... not only unacquainted with all kinds of work, but had the most insuperable aversion to honest labour, and had been so long familiarised with every crime that they had become perfectly callous to all sense of shame and remorse... To make vicious and abandoned people happy, it has generally been supposed necessary, *first* to make them virtuous. But why not reverse this order! Why not make them first *happy* and then virtuous!"

Rumford accommodated them in workhouses (men, women and even children over the age of five were expected to work 12-14 hours a day) and fed them on a "nutritious" soup of which I give the recipe:

The Ingredients (to feed 1200 people).

	Quantity (lb)	in 1800 £	s.	d.	in 1988 £
Pearl barley	71				
Peas	66	0	11	3	25
Potatoes	230				
Bread (Croutons)	70	0	10	2	17
Salt	20	0	1	2	1
Vinegar	47	0	1	5	4
Water	983				
	1487	1	4	0	47
Add fuel (88 lb Wood or 50 lb Coal)		0	0	2	1
		1	4	2	48

Preparation

As given in Rumford's Essay:

The method of preparing this soup is as follows: The water and the pearl barley are first put together into the boiler and made to boil, the pease are then added, and the boiling is continued over a gentle fire about two hours. The potatoes are then added (having been previously peeled with a knife, or having been boiled, in order to their being more easily deprived of their skins), and the boiling is continued for about one hour more, during which time the contents of the boiler are frequently stirred about with a large wooden spoon or ladle, in order to destroy the texture of the potatoes, and to reduce the soup to one uniform mass. When this is done, the vinegar and the salt are added; and last of all, at the moment it is to be served up, the cuttings of bread.

According to the above figures the daily diet of the inmates of the workhouse was an average 20 ozs. of Rumford's Soup, costing, at 1988 prices, about 4p. The daily calorie intake can be readily calculated and A.F. Dufton in a paper read at the 1936 meeting of the British Association (published in *The Lancet*, December 16th 1936, page 1535) gives 960 calories, far below the recommended standard of between 3000 and 3600. Dufton discusses "this startling comparison" with the help of "Human Vitality and Efficiency under prolonged restricted Diet" published in 1919 by the Carnegie Institution of Washington and of personal experiences while subjecting himself to a diet of Rumford's soup for 10 days and to a more generous diet (1300 calories) for a month. While he finds that the Rumford diet is not as absurd as it seems, it is hard to draw firm conclusions in the absence of information about the composition of the "workforce", the length of stay in the workhouse and the possibility of the Rumford soup not being the *only* food consumed.

While it would seem permissible to describe Rumfordsche Suppe as the basis of a fasting diet, Woolton Pie is in a different category. It is true that food in Britain between 1940 and 1950 comprised few gastronomic delights but it is often said - I believe with some justification - that neither before nor after that period did the British people have a healthier diet. Butcher's meat was rationed by price, 1 shilling and 2 pence worth per person per week, (equivalent to about £1.50 to-day), say 1lb. of the cheaper cuts, hence the encouragement to use root vegetables in traditional pies. The Ministry of Food's leaflets etc. often gave recipes for such vegetable pies, but I believe that the name Woolton Pie first appeared on the menu of the Savoy Hotel's Restaurant. I am very grateful to the Archivist of the Savoy, Miss Rosemary Ashbee, for valuable information and for material from the Savoy Archives.

Fig.1 is the luncheon menu for the 6th March 1941 where the Lord Woolton Pie is mentioned. Figs.2 and 3 are recipes from the Savoy files. I am not sure whether the amusing annotations are contemporary or more recent additions.

N.B. Both Rumfordsche Suppe and Le Lord Woolton Pie were offered at the Symposium for tasting at Sunday's lunch.

II. FEASTING

The three examples of feasting were not chosen for the originality or sophistication of the menus but because they were enjoyable dinners given under difficult conditions or in unusual places.

In August 1951 an international physics conference was held in **Oxford** and I was organising the Conference Dinner in Brasenose College. Rationing was still in force but, although there were no general shortages, choice was restricted. The menu (shown in Fig.4) looks rather pedestrian by to-day's standards but this was compensated by the quality of the dishes. Thus the Cumberland Sauce was prepared according to the excellent recipe in Elizabeth David's 12-page pamphlet *The use of Wine in Fine Cooking* published by Saccone and Speed, while the clotted cream had a coarse, almost gritty texture and a taste reminiscent of fresh milk, a far cry from the bland, smooth product that is sold nowadays under that name.

Harwell Cherry pie was served so as to remind the participants that the Oxfordshire village of that name had been famous for its cherry orchards long before it became a synonym of the Atomic Energy Research Establishment. There is an American equivalent: Livermore in California, an important research centre for nuclear weapons, had been renowned for many decades for its white wines.

Difficulties arose with the cheeses. Because of rationing the choice in the Oxford area was limited but, as a member of the Wine and Food Society, I was put in touch with suppliers in Yorkshire and in Cheshire. In Yorkshire I visited a Mrs. J.R. Hopper in Askrigg who helped us to obtain a fine Wensleydale cheese. As a *quid-pro-quo* we provided her with two peacock feathers which she needed to decorate a peacock pie displayed in an historic tableau at the Bolton Castle Festival. What an attractive barter: peacock feathers in exchange for Wensleydale cheese. The Cheshire contact, Colonel Geoffrey Hutchinson, a renowned cheese-maker in Malpas, was even more rewarding. He answered my enquiry in a truly jingoistic manner: "How refreshing to find an association wishing to show English cheeses, which are naturally the finest in the world even to-day, instead of throwing down all those foreign cheeses in messy portions on a fly-blown platter!" I visited his establishment and he provided the red and white Cheshire - both of them blue-veined, and the Stilton. I was shown round the establishment and tasted half a dozen of the white Cheshires. He congratulated me on my choice, remarking that the other half of that particular cheese was already earmarked for Buckingham Palace!

While the fare at the Conference Dinner was very British, the drinks were truly international and came from four suppliers. Kenneth Lloyd of Williams, Standring etc. supplied the Manzanilla and the Ch. Coutet (12/6 per bottle), the Lutomer Sylvaner, a fragrant wine though a bit too sweet for the salmon, came from Teltscher Brothers. Ronald

Avery, a good friend of Brasenose and of many of its members, provided the Bristol Milk, the Fine Champagne Cognac and the Irish Whiskey as well as the Ch. La Gaffelière. This St. Emilion which Ronald Avery feared was rapidly going downhill, was splendid - and we drank it in college for a few more years. Finally the 1934 Port came from the cellars of New College which, unlike Brasenose, laid in a good stock of ports in the 1930s and thus could offer its Fellows a generous allocation. Incidentally the charge per head was 25/- and I believe the subsidy was less than 10/-. Those were the days!

As a postscript to the above feast I give in Fig.5 the menu of another Brasenose feast some 4 years later. Note in particular the wide cheese selection and the 150 year old Vintage Madeira. However my main reason for mentioning that feast is that it prompted the creation and the serving of a new iced bombe. The origin of this delicacy and its recipe were published in the Times and the relevant part of the article is given below.

THE TIMES SATURDAY REVIEW AUGUST 8 1981

Imitative-Allusive names. Mont-Blanc de Marrons for the mountaineer; Barquettes de Marrons for the yachtsman; Toad-in-the-Hole for the zoologist; Pets-de-Nonne for the physician — why not something for the physico-chemist? I thought of this when in 1955 I arranged the menu for the banquet of a conference devoted largely to the physical properties of diamonds. This took place a few months after the American General Electric Company had succeeded in transforming graphite — the more common form of the element carbon — into its rare form, diamond. To remind the diners of that event I devised a bombe which attempted, through the gustatory rather than the visual sense, to illustrate this "allotropic" (from one form into another) transition.

Bombe Allotropique (graphite-diamant)

Serves six to eight

225 g (8 oz) plain or bitter (American semi-sweet) chocolate
255 g (9 oz) sugar
4 large eggs (4 yolks and 2 whites)
About 125 ml (6 fl oz) strong, black (high roast) coffee
60 ml (2 fl oz) dark Jamaican rum
450 ml (¾ pint) double cream
150 ml (¼ pint) milk
For the "diamonds"
Brown caramel made with 110 g (4 oz) sugar, chopped into small chips
For the "graphite"
85 g (3 oz) bitter chocolate, chopped

Melt 225 g chocolate, add slightly runny syrup made of 60 g sugar and finally enough black coffee so that, when cool, it has the consistency of thick cream.

Make a zabaglione (see recipe for Mousse Esme) using 4 egg yolks, 140 g sugar, 60 ml rum and 150 ml coffee. Let it cool. Mix the cream and milk, chill thoroughly and whip, fold in two whisked egg whites, add 55 g sugar, the chocolate-sauce, more rum according to taste, the bits of "diamond" and "graphite" and finally fold in the zabaglione. Freeze in a mould. Decorate with whipped cream and bits of "diamond" and "graphite".

Capenhurst in Cheshire is about 5 miles North-west of Chester. It is I believe unknown in gastronomic circles but it was the home of the UK Atomic Energy Authority's large plant to extract the rare, active isotope from natural uranium, for use in nuclear power plants and weapons. A committee of some 25 people called The Isotope Plant Design Committee (I.P.D.C.) served as a general advisory body and its 50th meeting, held in December 1952 in Oxford, was celebrated by a dinner in Christ Church. Six months later in June 1953 a dinner in the Grosvenor Hotel in Chester marked the start up of the plant.

The work of the Design Committee continued for another year and it held its last meeting, the 65th, on 21 May 1954, but such was the committee's attachment to the initials IPDC that the Design Committee was changed into a Dining Club which since then met occasionally for thirty years. It was decided that the last meeting of the Design Committee should be held in the Capenhurst Works and that it should be followed by the first meeting of the Dining Club in the Works Canteen.

This may seem an inauspicious venue for a Dining Club but there were good grounds for the choice. The chef who had prepared the dinner the year before at the Grosvenor Hotel apparently became tired of the irregular hours worked by a hotel chef and became Head Chef of the Capenhurst Works Canteen and welcomed the opportunity to practise his art in those austere surroundings but for the benefit of an appreciative gathering.

Fig.6 is the menu, and the meal was excellent, but there was one moment when the fish course threatened to become a fiasco. Late in the afternoon I called in at the kitchen to see how things were going. The chef was busy making the mayonnaise but it seemed to me to be barely enough for 4 people, let alone for 24. He explained that the Catering Manager refused to let him have more than half a pint of olive oil - he presumably thought that it was stupid to make mayonnaise when you can buy it in a bottle. By this time all shops in the village were closed but someone had a brilliant idea. Why not raid the First Aid Station and commandeer their stock of B.P. grade olive oil. We found nearly a litre of the precious stuff and the situation was saved. We kept our fingers crossed that no-one on the night shift would develop earache which required treatment with olive oil.

For the venue of the third example of feasting we go to **Hammersmith**, or more precisely to Brook Green, to St. Paul's Girls' School where the feasting took place. The Editorial Board of Interdisciplinary Science Reviews, or rather those of its 60 members, distributed over the world, who can manage it, meet once a year to discuss over a good meal the past and the future of the Journal. These meetings were usually held in London Clubs or Livery Halls and Cambridge or Oxford Colleges. At the 1987 meeting one of the Board members, Mrs. Heather (now Baroness) Brigstocke, then High Mistress of St. Paul's Girls' School, invited the Board to her school for the 1988 meeting. This was accepted with enthusiasm and Mrs. Brigstocke very flatteringly asked me to discuss the menu with her. Fig. 7 gives the result: it was a simple, 3-course meal but each of the courses was intended to make a point.

The first course demonstrated successfully that no wizardry is required to serve individual soufflés for 24 people, provided that the guests are ready when the soufflés are and that the dining room is not too far from the kitchen. (N.B. I proved by experiment that the latter condition is not critical. Having removed an individual soufflé from the oven I took it out into the cool evening air and after 60 seconds brought it to the dinner table. It did not suffer from this treatment).

The *Coq au Vin* was prepared from Elizabeth David's recipe published in the pamphlet mentioned on page 2 and showed that if you follow a good recipe conscientiously the result is equally good. The button onions, braised in butter, glazed in port wine, sugar and vinegar and added to the chicken at the moment of serving were particularly appreciated.

The last course, which I prepared myself and took to the school, consisted of two dishes: as a tribute to the High Mistress, I offered a *Bavarois à la Bruyère* which, as its name indicates, was flavoured with Heather Honey, served like a Charlotte surrounded with sponge fingers, topped with whipped cream and accompanied by a coulis of raspberries. This was also used to decorate the Bavarois with the inscription "To H.B. from I.S.R." The latter being the initials of the Journal.

The *Tarte* was dedicated to the "Paulinas". It differed from the traditional *Tarte Tatin* in two respects: 1) instead of short pastry I used a pastry made of flour, sugar, butter and ground, unblanched almonds, 2) Instead of sugar I sprinkled dark caramelised sugar between the layers of apples, and I cooked the tart longer than usual. The fresh taste of apples was thus lost, but as a compensation one had something like caramelised "apple cheese".

A meaningless but tantalising

ENVOI

When is a man's Fast a woman's Feast, or *vice-versa*?

LORD WOOLTON PIE.

1 lb. Pomme de Terre K.E.
2 " Carottes.
½ " E. Champignons.
2 Spring Onions.
1 Petit Poireaux.
2 oz. de Margarine ou Graisse de Volaille.
Sel. Poivre, Muscade, Persil Haché.
1 petit fagot fait avec: 1 small Bay-Leaf,
    1 petite branche de Thyme, Persil et Celeri.

Pêler les pommes de terre et les carottes, couper les en tranches de la grosseur d'un gros penny; bien les laver et les essuyer dans un torchon. Sauter les séparement à la Poêle avec un peu de graisse de volaille.

Faites de même pour les champignons en ajoutant les oignons et poireau emincés. Melanger le tout, assaisonner sel et poivre, un peu de noix muscade et persil frais haché grossièrement.

Remplissez avec cela un pie-dish, placer le petit fagot au milieu. Mouillez avec un peu de fond de Gibelotte ou avec de l'eau.

Laissez refroidir: couvrir avec une pâte faite moitié Beef-Suet ou graisse de volaille - moitié margarine.

Cuire au four pendant une heure et demie.

20.3.41.

K.E = presumably, King Edward potatoes.

SAVOY HOTEL LIMITED   COPY

LORD WOOLTON'S PIE

The creation of Monsieur Francis Latry, Chevalier de la Legion
                                                      d'Honneur
Maitre Chef des Cuisines, Savoy Hotel.

Peel two large potatoes, two large carrots, and one parsnip, and cut them into slices. Wash them separately in plenty of water and drain them on a piece of linen.¹ Mince the white of two leeks, throw them into a frying pan in which has been heated a good spoonful of chicken fat, beef dripping, or the rind of bacon cut into dice. When the leeks are getting coloured, add the carrots, and fry quickly, then the parsnips, and lastly the potatoes. Season with salt and pepper, a little nutmeg and chopped parsley.

Pour into a pie dish, and place in the middle one small leaf of laurel,² one small branch³ of thyme, one stick of celery, and one sprig of parsley, and sprinkle with a little chicken fat or margarine. Add a cup or two of giblet soup or water. Cover with a layer of paste⁴ made with half chicken fat or beef dripping, and half margarine, and bake in a moderate oven for one hour and a half.

1. "on a tea towel."
2. "one small bay leaf"
3. "sprig"
4. "pastry"

INTERNATIONAL CONFERENCE on LOW TEMPERATURE PHYSICS
OXFORD 1951

Conference Dinner

Brasenose College   August 27th

THE WINES

Manzanilla

Lutomer Sylvaner 1946

Château la Gaffelière 1934

Château Coutet 1947

Gould - Campbell 1934 Port
Avery's Bristol Milk Sherry

John Jameson 1910 Liqueur Whiskey
Avery's 1893 Fine Champagne
"Tia Maria" Jamaican Coffee Liqueur

THE FARE

Cream of Mushroom Soup

Scotch Salmon Mayonnaise

Roast Aylesbury Duckling
Cumberland Sauce   Garden Peas
New Potatoes

Harwell Cherry Pie   Cornish Clotted Cream

Assorted Cheeses
(Red and White Cheshire, Stilton, Wensleydale)

Dessert

Coffee

Diamond Conference
Oxford 1955
DINNER

■ ■

Melon

—

Meursault Perrières 1952	Lobster au gratin

—

Ch. Angludet 1949 — Fillet of Beef Wellington
New Potatoes   Green Peas

—

1953er Forster Jesuitengarten Auslese — Les bombes glacées au graphite et aux diamants

—

English Cheeses
(Blue and Red Cheshire, Lancashire, Leicester, Blue Vinney, Blue and White Wensleydale)

—

Fonseca 1934
Vintage Madeira 805 — Dessert

—

Rémy Martin V.S.O.P. — Coffee

Brasenose College   1st July, 1955

In Loving Memory of ISOTOPES PLANT DESIGN COMMITTEE Laid to Rest at CAPENHURST ON FRIDAY 21st MAY 1954
Aged 65 Meetings
"PER GRADUS AD ESS"

Hattenheimer Pfaffenberg Riesling 1946

Château d'Aux Talbot 1949

Fine Old Bual Madeira
Avery's Bristol Milk

Bisquit Dubouché 1914

Grapefruit

Scotch Salmon Mayonnaise

Aylesbury Duckling,
Cumberland Sauce,
New Potatoes,
Garden Peas,

Meringues Glacés.
Cheese & Biscuits
Fruit
Coffee
Petit Fours

INTERDISCIPLINARY SCIENCE REVIEWS

EDITORIAL BOARD
DINNER

Thursday 14th July 1988

St. Paul's Girls' School

Napa Valley
Chardonnay
Robert Mondavi
Winery
1981

Arbroath Smoky Soufflés

****

Coq au Vin

Domaine Cret des Garanches
Brouilly
1986

****

Bavarois à la Bruyère

Coulis de Framboises

Tarte des Demoiselles de Saint Paul
a variant on the
Tarte des Demoiselles Tatin

Royal Feasts

by Janet Laurence

This paper looks at medieval Royal Feasts, at their conduct, menus and significance.

Some idea of the scope of royal feasts in medieval times is given by the list of provisions for the feast given to Richard II and his uncle, the powerful Duke of Lancaster, at 'the Bishoppes place of Durham at London' on the 23rd September 1387: 111 pigs, 50 swans, 210 geese, eight dozen rabbits, three bushels of apples, 12 thousand eggs, etc., etc.. But it pales into insignificance when compared with the provisions for Archbishop Neville's installation feast in York in 1467[1]: 2000 each of geese, pigs and chickens, 100 dozen quails, 4000 each of wild ducks, pigeons and rabbits, 4000 cold tarts, 1500 hot pasties of venison, and much, much more (see Appendix for full details of both these feasts).

In the introduction to *Curye on Inglysch*, Constance B. Heiatt and Sharon Butler include a translation of the description of a feast by the late thirteenth century Walter of Bibbesworth. It runs: 'A fashionable yeoman who came from a great banquet has told us about the feast, how their service was ordered. Without bread and wine and ale, no one at a feast will be at ease, but the choicest of all three were provided there, he has told us. But it is worth knowing about the course which they had first: the head of a boar, larded, with the snout well garlanded, and enough for the whole household of venison fattened during the closed season. And then there were a great variety of cranes, peacocks, and swans, kids, pigs, and hens. Then they had rabbits in gravy, all covered with sugar, Viaunde de Cypre and Mawmenny, red and white wine in great plenty; and then quite a different multitude of roasts, each of them set next to another: pheasants, woodcocks, and partridges, fieldfares, larks, and roasted plovers, blackbirds, woodcocks, and song-thrushes, and other birds I cannot name; and fried meat, crisps and fritters, with sugar mixed with rosewater. And when the table was taken away, sweet spice powder with large dragees, maces, cubebs, and enough spicerie, and plenty of wafers.' [2]

Judging by the extant menus of the time, the description could apply to any of the great fourteenth, fifteenth and even sixteenth century feasts we still have details of. The items most conspicuously absent are those made with pastry. The Hieatt/Butler introduction already mentioned gives a brief but interesting analysis of such differences as did exist between the foods of these centuries, mostly a gradually increased use in dishes of spices and dried and fresh fruits, particularly the newly introduced oranges and lemons in the fifteenth century.

Richard II's court was famous for its extravagance. Warner, in his *Antiquitates Culinariae* reports: 'The prodigality of Richard was enormous. Two thousand cooks and three hundred servitors were employed in his kitchen - ten thousand visitors daily attended his Court and went satisfied from his table ... twenty-eight oxen, three hundred sheep, an incredible number of fowls and of all kinds of game, were slaughtered every morning'. [3] This makes his dinner at the Bishop of Durham's seem rather like slumming it.

The menus we have available for study from these times are those of royal tables or of the high nobility. But so universal had feasting apparently become by the beginning of the fourteenth century, that Edward II issued a proclamation in 1315 designed to restrain this conspicuous consumption. The Ordinance stated 'that, by the outrageous and excessive multitude of meats and dishes, which the great men of the kingdom used in their castles, and by persons of inferior rank imitating their example, beyond what their stations required, and their circumstances could afford, many great evils had come upon the kingdom, the health of the King's subjects had been injured, their property consumed, and they had been reduced to poverty; but the King being desirous to put a stop to such excesses, with the advice and consent of his Great Council, had ordained: That the great men of the kingdom should have only two courses of flesh meats served up to the tables; each course consisting only of two kinds of flesh meat: except Prelates, Earls, Barons, and the great men of the land, who might have an intermeat (une entremese) of one kind of meat if they pleased. On fish days they should only have two courses of fish, each consisting of two kinds, with an intermeat of one kind of fish, if they thought fit. And those who should transgress this ordinance should be severely punished.' [4]

This was restraint indeed! The greatest men of the kingdom confined to serving four different sorts of meat at their meals, and the ordinance says nothing about exceptions for special feasts; and the Prelates, Earls and Barons cannot have been too grateful for the addition of 'une entremese'. It is unlikely that the Ordinance was obeyed in every respect. And perhaps a wonder that it was not for almost another ten years that Edward was deposed in favour of his son, Edward III. But the Ordinance firmly equates style of eating with rank and, by implication, reserves feasts for the King. Something more than wealth is involved here. Feasts are a symbol of high office and the descriptions that are available of the conduct of these occasions demonstrate that much more was involved than the mere consumption of extraordinary quantities of food.

The serving of the food was ceremonious and involved the active participation of the highest ranking guests, who were appointed officers of the feast, positions that were no sinecures. Thomas Austin in his introduction to *Two Fifteenth Century Cookery Books*, gives details of Henry IV's Coronation Feast. He has taken them from Froissart's Chronicles and included details of the same event from Stowe's Annals and Hollinshed.

Henry IV's Coronation was the sacred acceptance of a dubious circumstance. Henry took arms against his cousin, Richard II, after he had been banished from England and then dispossessed of his lands, the vast Lancaster estates, after the death of his father, John of Gaunt, Duke of Lancaster, and Richard's uncle. Unpopular, surrounded by incompetent advisers and fatally inept politically himself, Richard was outmanoeovred and finally abdicated. The Estates of the Realm and the Lords Spiritual and Temporal consenting (giving legal substance to a claim dubious in blood and avoiding the dangerous precedent of rule by right of conquest), Henry assumed the crown as Henry IV, ushering in the House of Lancaster and paving the way for the Wars of the Roses.

Henry was crowned on Monday, 13th October, 1399 in Westminster Abbey with great ceremony. The High Constable for the Coronation was the Earl of Northumberland, the most powerful of the northern lords and one of Henry's main supporters in his dispute with Richard.

Those directly connected with the Banquet that followed in Westminster Hall were: Pantler, Thomas Beauchamp, Earl of Warwick; Marshall, the Earl of Westmoreland; Lord Chaberlain, Sir Thomas Erpingham. Sir Thomas supplied the king with water to wash his hands, both before and after the feast, being given the Basin, Ewer and Towels, etc., as a fee. Carver, The Earl of Somerset, apparently in right of his Earldom of Lincoln. To be Carver was a post of great honour and the Earl of Somerset was John Beaufort, Henry's half brother, born out of wedlock and legitimised when his father, John of Gaunt, Duke of Lancaster, married his mother, Katherine Swynford. Sir William Argentine, by reason of his tenure of the Manor Wilmundale, or Wymondley, Herts, served the King his first drink at the dinner, receiving the silver-gilt cup as his fee. Thomas, Earl of Arundel, was chief Butler, receiving the royal goblet as a gift. The City of London chose various of its citizens to serve in the Hall as attendants for the Banquet. William le Venour had the honour of making wafers for the king, Edmond Chambers was Larderer and Lord Grey of Ruthyn was Naperer (much ceremonious play was made with towels and linen at these feasts). These officials were appointed on October 4th.

At the Banquet sitting at the Royal Table were the two Archbishops and seventeen Bishops and the Earl of Westmoreland. The Prince of Wales and the Constable served the King from either side, bearing, respectively, the Sword of Mercy and the Sword of Justice. At the second table sat the five great peers of the realm. Thomas Austin identifies these as probably being the Dukes of Lancaster, York, Aumarle, Surrey and Exeter. The third table was for the principle Citizens of London, apparently the Lord Mayor and Aldermen. This table was at the left of the royal table. To the right of the royal table sat the Barons of the Cinque Ports. At a fifth table sat the forty-six Knights of the Bath that Henry had just created and a sixth held Knights and Squires of Honour (there is no mention of ladies at this feast. Henry at this time was unmarried - was it an exclusively male occasion?).

After the Banquet, during which the King's Champion, Sir Thomas Dymock had followed usual practice and challenged combat to any who dared maintain Henry was not a lawful sovereign, without having to fight, the King withdrew to his private apartments. There the Lord Mayor brought him a gold cup of wine, with another containing water to allay the wine (all food and drink was tested for poisoning, see the description of Archbishop Neville's installation below). Both cups were given him as his fee [5].

Some idea of the duties of the various officers at feasts such as this can be gathered from Warner's description of the enthronement of Archbishop Neville at York.

George Neville was brother to Richard Neville, the powerful Earl of Warwick, known as the Kingmaker since his critical support was given, at different times, to both Henry VI and Edward IV in the Lancaster versus York Wars of the Roses struggles for England's throne. George Neville had previously been appointed Bishop of Exeter. He was also made Chancellor of England and combined that office with his religious duties, first at Exeter and then at York, until pique caused him to fall out with the King and he was deprived of the Chancellorship in 1467. He was ambitious and one of the most powerful men in England. His enthronement feast reflects these facts. Warner includes an interesting account of the ceremonious serving of the meal:

Steward was the Earl of Warwick; Treasurer, the Earl of Northumberland; Comptroller, the Lord Hastings; Carver, the Lord Willoughby; Cup bearer, the Lord John of Buckingham; Sewer (title given to the organiser of the service), Sir Richard Strangwiche; Marshall, Sir Walter Worley and eight other knights for the Hall, also eight Squires, besides two other Sewers; Panter, Sir John Malyvery; the Sergeant of the King's Ewery, as Ewerer; Greystoke and Nevell, keepers of the Cupboard; Surveyor in the hall, Sir John Breaknock.

Sixty-two cooks prepared the feast, aided by a hundred and fifteen servants, including spit turners. Great ceremony was deployed in preparing the hall. In fact, four halls and a gallery were used in all. In the main Hall were seven tables. At the first sat the Archbishop, the Bishop of London, the Bishop of Durham and the Bishop of Ely, the Duke of Suffolk, the Earl of Oxford and the Earl of Worcester (it is to be noted that neither the King nor the Archbishop of Canterbury, Primate of all England, both of whom would have taken precedence over Archbishop Neville were present). At the second table, eighteen Abbots and Priors. At the third fifty-three Lords and Knights. At the fourth, the Deans and Brethren of the Minster. At the fifth, the Mayors and 'all the Worshipfull men of the said city.' At the sixth, the Judges and twenty-six learned men of law. At the seventh, 'threescore and nyne worshipfull Esquires, wearing the Kynges livery.' The ladies seem to have been confined to two separate rooms or halls. A 'Cheefe Chamber' (Chief chamber?) held three tables. At the first the Duchess of Suffolk, the Countess of Westmorland, the Countess of Northumberland and two of the Lord Warwick's daughters, plus the Duke of Gloucester (Edward IV's brother), who seems to have been the sole male in the room. At the second table, the Baronness of Graystocke, with three other Baronesses and twelve other Ladies, and at a third table the gentlewomen of these ladies. In a second chamber, two tables held various ladies, including the Countess of Warwick, Lady Hastings and Lady Strangwiche; the ladies in this room seem to have managed without a male to look after them. A Great Chamber held three tables with four bishops, the Earl of Westmorland, the Earl of Northumberland, two other Lords, ten Barons and fourteen gentlemen with the same number of gentlewomen. In a 'lowe Hall' were 'Gentlemen, Franklins and head Yeomen', four hundred and twelve in all, who were 'twyce fylled and served' (franklins were independent country gentlemen not bound by feudal services). In a Gallery were over four hundred servants, also 'twyce fylled and served'. The only officer of the Banquet who seems to have had a seat was the Earl of Northumberland, as Treasurer he seems to have had no direct duty at the actual Banquet. [6] Those in the low hall and gallery were probably served a separate menu from that given to the main participants in the feast.

At the Royal Feast at the wedding of the Earl of Devonshire (He married one of Henry's half nieces, the Lady Margaret Beaufort, whose sister Joan was Queen of Scotland. The marriage took place about 1431, during the early years of the reign of Henry VI whilst he was still a minor.) The bill of fare gives a three course menu after the style of the other menus given in the Appendix, then adds a two course menu 'Pro inferiori parte Auli' - for the inferior part of the Hall. The number of dishes for each course is less and the dishes themselves are generally not as lavish as those served to those in the main part of the hall (See appendix). [7]

In his description of the feast, Warner quotes instructions for the officers of a Banquet. These are immensely detailed. Both the salt and the bread are involved in complicated rituals and the salt is tasted with great ceremony by the Pantler. It is the Sewer's duty to check if the cooks are ready for the dishes to be served. When they are, the Marshall has to command the Carver, Sewer and Cupbearer to wash at the Ewrie. (Constant washing of hands by servers and guests continued throughout the banquet, necessary when much of the meal was eaten with the fingers. [8]

All the officers seem at some stage to have been involved in 'assaying' the wine and food served to the King or Guest of Honour, that is to taste it to check for poisoning. (Soon after Henry IV came to the throne, he and a large number of his court fell ill, it was assumed from something that was eaten, this despite assay.) Since treachery had to be watched for amongst the most powerful of the King's lords, attaching assay to the duties of the high officials would combine honour with going some way to ensure the food was untampered with.

The Carver had a duty to see that the Lord's trencher be kept clean and to carve a little of every dish for the Lord.

Placings in the various halls were the task of the Marshall. His difficulties were no doubt eased by the etiquette involved. Catherine Frances Frere in her introduction to *A Proper Newe Booke of Cokerye* quotes rules: 'A Duke may not keep the hal, but each estate by themselfe in chamber or in pavilion, that neither see other, Marques, Erles, Bishops and Viscounts, al these may sit at a messe [a messe was a dish containing sufficient food for two, three or four eaters]; a Baron and the Maior of London, and three Cheefe Judges and the Speaker of the Parliament, all these may sit two or three at a messe; and all other states may sit three or foure at a messe; also the Marshall must understand and knowe the bloode royale, for some Lorde is of the blood royall and of small lyvelyhood, and some knight is wedded unto a lady of roiall blood, she shall keep the estate of her Lord's blood - also the Marshall must take heed unto strangers and put them to worship and reverence, for if they have good cheere it is to your Souveraine's honour.

'Also a Marshall must take heede if the King send your Souveraine (master) any message, and if he send a Knight, receive him as a Baron, and if he sende a Yeoman, receive him as a Squire, and if he send a Groome, receive him as a Yeoman. Also it is no rebuke to a Knight to sette a Groome of the King's at his table.' [9] These precepts were for a regular Marshall of a major household, rather than for a temporary one appointed for a special banquet. The permanent household officers for various of the kings are detailed in the Ordinances and Regulations of the Royal Households. Those for Edward IV, who appears to have been careful of his honour, as befitted one who had claimed the throne through a superior blood lineage to Henry VI, are very detailed and cover every aspect of his day.

As a contrast to the lavish provisioning for Banquets, it is interesting to see what the Ordinances and Regulations for Royal Households set down for Edward IV's general meals: for breakfast, 2 loaves made into four maunchetts (presumably rolls), and two payne demayne (that is, the finest bread), one messe of kychyn grosse (a cooked dish?), dim' gallon of ale (dim' = demi = half? A half gallon is mentioned later in the account). At noon for his board, sitting alone, eight loaves, with the trenchers (plates of bread) and, say the Ordinances, his service of kitchen cannot be expressed at (as) certain. The Ordinances then quote Edward III as being served, when not with a crowd of people, with eight diverse dishes, the lords in hall and chamber with five, his other gentlemen in court with three dishes, besides potage (soup); and grooms and other with two dishes diverse. (The practices of the noble King Edward III are continually being cited in these ordinances, possibly because Edward IV was descended from Edward's second son, Lionel, Duke of Clarence through his daughter, Phillipa, which was the basis for his claim to a superior right to the throne over Henry VI, who was descended from Edward's third son, John of Gaunt, Duke of Lancaster. Harlan Walker has suggested, however, that it could be because the long and settled reign of Edward III was looked back on as something of a golden age when things were ordered as they should be, rather as we look back on Victorian times.) The Ordinances then continue detailing Edward IV's diet: Then the King's meat, two pitchers and dim' wine, two gallons ale. For supper, by himself, eight loaves, with the trenchers in all the kitchen, after the day, or after the stuff that is had within forth, two pitchers wine, two gallons ale, besides the fruter and waferer. Bread and drinking for the King's person between meals cannot be ascertained but by record of the ushers of the chamber, says the Ordinance, continuing: Item, nightly for the bed making one pitcher half gallon measure. The total annual cost of Edward IV's household was £13,000. [10]

So these feasts were much more than occasions for conspicuous consumption. They were an opportunity for the King to demonstrate his power: his most powerful subjects wait upon him, ensure his every comfort is observed, the ceremony and ritual that pertain throughout the life of all of noble birth is brought to its highest degree and the King's wealth is demonstrated by the lavishness of his hospitality. The same is true for feasts given by other powerful lords, both temporal and spiritual; sometimes, like George Neville, they were one and the same.

The nature of the food involved with these feasts can be seen from the detailed description of Henry IV's Coronation Menu in the Appendix. Much the same dishes appear in all the menus, with variations and substitutions. Sometimes the exact dish takes a little identifying but recipes can be found for most amongst the contemporary collections (*Forme of Curye* and the fifteenth century manuscripts). Three courses are almost invariably served (though there are apparently earlier royal feasts, such as the wedding of Edward III's son, Lionel, Duke of Clarence, to the daughter of the Duke of Milan when Stowe reports that thirty courses were served with the presentation of presents between each course). The pattern of the courses can roughly be categorised as moving from heavier dishes to lighter, the third course consisting of the smaller birds and little dishes, some sweet. But at this time sugar was used as a seasoning much as spices were and can appear at any point in the feast. It is unusual to see the same meat or dish appear twice in a menu.

Alcohol was served in the form of ale, wine (white and red) and hippocras, a spiced red wine that usually finished the banquet together with wafers, spices, comfits and other tit-bits. On fish days, the menu would consist entirely of fish, with tarts and other cooked items using almond milk and other non-animal ingredients; recipes will often give instructions for both versions. On meat days, the only fish dishes usually included are sturgeon and pike, sometimes lampreys. The menu for Henry IV's second marriage to Joan of Navarre at Winchester is included in the Appendix because it contains menus for three fish courses as well as for three meat courses.

At the great banquets the end of each course would be signalled with the presentation of a 'soteltie'. An opportunity for the creative chef to show off; these conceits, often made of sugarwork, could be very elaborate. The menu for Henry V's coronation feast is included for the detailed description it includes of the sotelties.

Medieval cooking was a skilled business. The spit, the pot, the chafing dish are all used and advanced techniques, for cooking eggs, for thickening stocks and using almonds, for frying and baking are called for. The recipes that survive contain few quantities and are more aide memoires than detailed instructions that could be followed by an untrained cook; considerable judgement in the exact quantities and use of many of the ingredients, including spices and other flavourings, are required. Basic foods such as bread and pastry do not have recipes, they would be part of a cook's training and day to day routine. And there seems to have been as much ritual in the preparation of food as there was in its service. Each bird has its particular method of preparation and its accompanying sauce. The same basic recipes for tarts and other dishes appear with very little change from manuscript to manuscript, only slowly evolving with changing fashion in the use of spices and dried fruits. Creative thought seems to have been confined to the 'sotelties'.

The lavishness of the feasts lay both in the sheer volume of dishes offered and the use of luxury items such as the great birds: peacocks, swans, cranes, bustards, etc., and the variety of tiny birds offered in the third course, the little singing birds, larks, thrushes, linnets and others as well as quails, pigeons, etc.

The sheer logistics of these feasts beggar the imagination. How large were Richard II's kitchens? How many fires were required to roast the number of meats and birds provided for Archbishop Neville's feast? Were the equivalent of camp kitchens erected? Or fires set up in the open? Did the right sauces meet up with all the right roasts? How many ovens heated over how many days were needed to bake all those hot and cold tarts and custards (another form of tart)? How many tempers snapped over the organisation of the cooking by so many? Where, indeed, did all the cooks come from? Did all the officials of the feast lend their own? Was York scoured of all its trained kitchen staff? These are details that don't seem to be recorded by any of the chroniclers. But enough has come down to us to paint a vivid picture of the ceremony and lavish provisioning of these Royal and noble feasts.

Notes

(1) The Reverend Richard Warner, *Antiquitates Culinariae*, pub. London, 1791, reprinted by Prospect Books, London, 197?, p93, gives the sixth year of Edward IV's reign as the date for this feast. Edward IV came to the throne in 1461 and 1467 is stated as the date for the feast in *Two Fifteenth Century Cookery Books* (see below). However Edward IV nominated Neville as Archbishop in 1464. He would have had to wait for the Pope's confirmation of the nomination but three years seems a long interval.
(2) *Curye on Inglysch*, ed. Constance B. Hieatt and Sharon Butler, published for The Early English Text Society by the Oxford University Press, London, New York, Toronto, 1985, p 3.
(3) Warner, *Antiquitates Culinariae*, p xxxii.
(4) *Ordinances and Regulations for the Government of the Royal Household*, printed for the Society of Antiquaries by John Nichols, London 1790, p viii.
(5) *Two Fifteenth Century Cookery Books*, ed. Thomas Austin, pub. for The Early English Text Society by the Oxford University Press, 1888, reprinted 1964 pp xi/xiii.
(6) Warner, *Antiquitates*, pp 93/106.
(7) *Two Fifteenth Century Cookery Books*, pp 63/64.
(8) Much play with knives is made during the ceremonies. Forks did not appear until the time of James I. Guests managed with hands and knives, spearing morsels from dishes laid on the tables. Plates were mostly trenchers cut from bread. Fingers were used daintily and there were strict rules of etiquette. Meat should not be dipped in the salt-cellar, diners shouldn't hog the best pieces, a gentleman looks after strangers, diners turn from the table to belch, eat only small pieces of meat, and not too many, and quietly. Don't scratch the head at meals, don't blow out crumbs, or spit, blow your nose on handkerchief not on napkin, don't pick your teeth with a knife, or your hands, don't touch food for others with putrified teeth, and many, many other precepts. *Manners & Meals in Olden Time*, ed. by Frederick J. Furnivall, pub. for the Early English Text Society, N. Trubner & Co., London, 1868, pp 71/81.
(9) *A Proper Newe Booke of Cokerye*, ed. Catherine Frances Frere, ibid, p xliv. Miss Frere gives no source for this account but it appears to be a paraphrase of that which appears in John Russell's Boke of Nurture, included in *Manners & Meals in Olden Times*, as above, pp 188/192.
(10) Ordinances for the Government of Royal Households, p 21.

Appendix

This Appendix consists of various menus for royal feasts, mainly belonging to the fifteenth century. For Henry IV's Coronation Feast, the dishes have been described, as succinctly as possible, using extant medieval recipes. After each description a reference for the recipe is given. For the sake of space, *Two Fifteenth Century Cookery Books* is described as: *2 15th Cent. Cookery Books*

(1) THIS IS THE PURVIAUNCE MADE FOR KINGE RICHARD, BEING WITH YE DUC OF LANCASTRE AT THE BISSHOPPES PLACE OF DURHAM AT LONDONE THE xxiii DAY OF SETPEMBER, THE YERE OF THE KINGE FORESAID .xij [A.D. 1387] (*Two Fifteenth Century Cookery Books*, pp. 67/68)

First begynnyng for a-chatry

Xiiij oxen lying in salte
IJ oxen ffreyssh
Vi^{xx} [six score] hedes of shepe fressh
Vi^{xx} [six score] carcas of shepe fressh
Xij Bores
Xiiij Calvys
Cxl pigges
CCC maribones
Of larde and grece, ynogh
IIJ ton of salt veneson
IIJ does of ffressh veneson

The pultry

L. Swannes
CCx Gees
L capons of hie grece [well fattened]
Viii dussen other capons
Lx dd [dozens] Hennes
CC copull Conyngges
IIIJ Fesauntes
V Herons and Bitores
Vi kiddes
V disson pullayn for Gely
Xij dd to roste
C dd peions
Xij dd partrych
Viij dd Rabettes
X dosen Curlewes
Xij dosen Brewes
Xij Cranes
Wilde fowle ynogh
VJ^{xx} [six score] galons melke
Xij galons Creme
XI galons of Cruddes
IIj bushelz of Appelles
Xj thousand egges

The first course

Veneson with Furmenty
A potage called viaundbruse
Hedes of Bores
Grete Flessh
Swannes rosted
Pigges rosted
Crustade lumbard in paste
And a Sotelte

The Second course

A potage called Gele
A potage de Blandesore
Pigges rosted
Cranes rosted
Fesauntes rosted
Herons rosted
Chekens endored
Breme
Tartes
Broke braune
Conyngges rosted
And a sotellte

The thirde course

Potage, bruete of Almondes
Stwde lumbarde
Venyson rosted
Chekenes rosted
Rabettes rosted
Partrich rosted
Peions rosted
Quailes rosted
Larkes rosted
Payne puff
A Dissh of Gely
Longe Frutours
And a Sotelte

(2) FEAST SERVED AT CORONATION OF HENRY IV 13th October, 1399
(Conuiuium domini Henrici Regis quarti, In coronacione sua apud Westmonasterium) (*Two Fifteenth Century Cookery Books* - pp 57/58)

Le primer cours

Braun en peuerarde

Meat parboiled, then sliced and cooked in spiced wine/broth with small whole onions, resulting in a thickish type of soup. RECIPE: *2 15th Cent. Cookery Books* p. 71.

Viaund Ryal

Red wine sweetened with honey, thickened with rice flour, spiced and coloured red with mulberries or saunders (an inodorous dye wood *Pterocarpus santalinus*, cf. *A Proper Newe Booke of Cokerye*, ed. Catherine Frances Frere, Glossary-Index p. 103). RECIPE: *2 15th Cent. Cookery Books* p 57.

Teste de senglere enarmez

Head of a wild boar, larded. In *Curye on Inglysch* p. 62 recipe 3 states: 'Cranys & herons schulle be enarmud wyth lardons of swyne & rostyd & etyn wyth gyngyuyr'. Maybe the larded meat, with the ends of the fat sticking out all over, was considered to resemble chain mail.

Graund Chare

Large piece of meat, probably boiled pork, beef or mutton, see *Curye on Inglysch*, glossary: grete, p. 193.

Syngnettys

Cygnets.

Capound de haut grece

Well fattened capon - a stuffing for a capon is made with parsley, pork fat or mutton suet, parboiled, chopped hardboiled egg yolks, ground pepper, ginger, cinnamon, saffron and salt, grapes in their season, cloves, boiled and chopped onions, a little chopped pork can also be added. The bird is stuffed, then roasted. RECIPE: *2 15th Cent. Cookery Books* p 41.

Fesaunte

Pheasant - killed by being allowed to bleed to death through the mouth, drawn, neck cut off, legs cut from the knee, bird parboiled, larded, knees placed in the vent, roasted, & 'reise hym upp, hys legges and hys wynges, as off an henne; & no sauce butt salt'. RECIPE: *2 15th Cent. Cookery Books* p. 116. Directions for boiling pheasants, partridges, capons and curlewes are given in the *Forme of Curye*; good broth with whole peppercorns, ground cinnamon, a good quantity, and when cooked pouder douce (a mixture of sweet spices) is added. RECIPE: *Curye on Inglysch* p. 106 No. 37.

Heroun

Heron - killed by being allowed to bleed to death after having been cut in the roof of the mouth, drawn through the vent, head removed, neck deboned and folded about 'the spite' (spit), the head being put in the gullet, legs broken from the knee to the foot, wings cut at the joint next to the body, bird put on a spit, legs bound to the spit with the skin of the legs, bird roasted 'reyse the legges and the wynges as of a crane,' sauced with vinegar, mustard and powdered ginger. RECIPE: *2 15th Cent. Cookery Books* p. 116.

Crustade Lumbarde

An open tart made with fine pastry, parsley, chopped dates, prunes, marrow, cream and eggs, seasoned with salt and sugar. RECIPE: *2 15th Cent. Cookery Books* pp 50 & 74.

Storeioun, graunt luces

Sturgeon, large pike. *2 15th Cent. Cookery Books* has a way of boiling sturgeon or turbot cut in wide pieces in salted water and served cold, a piece or two in a dish, with a green sauce and sprinkled with parsley leaves in vinegar, p. 117. A fourteenth century recipe for cooking sturgeon specifies veal and calves feet stock sweetened with honey (which Heiatt and Butler feel may have been an error) then, when the fish is cooked to powder, the bones to be taken out, the fleshed pressed well in a fair canvas and then laid in slices and served garnished with onions, vinegar and parsley. RECIPE: *Curye on Inglysch* pp 155/156.

A Sotelte

A decorative piece, a sugar sculpture or foods disguised to look like something else, a bird redressed in its feathers, etc. providing a decorative feature for the table, many very elaborate, often having some connection with the festive occasion on which they are served.

Le ij cours

Venyson en furmenty

Boiled venison served with furmenty, a porridge-like dish of boiled, hulled wheat, cooked with milk, sometimes with egg yolks, saffron and sugar added. RECIPE: *2 15th Cent. Cookery Books* pp 6 & 70.

Gely

Heiatt and Butler in *Curye on Inglysch*, Index p. 191, suggest that this is either fish or meat boiled and served set in its jellied juices. There is an elaborate recipe for making 'Gely' with calves feet, veal hocks and white wine. The stock is then used to cook 'faire sides of pigges' and small chickens, with the legs and feet left on. The cook is to take care that the meat is not cooked so much that it can't be sliced. Having removed the cooked meat, the broth is seasoned with salt, ground pepper, saffron (to colour it amber) and a good quantity of vinegar. It is strained through a linen cloth. 'Faire sidde ribbes' of the pork are cut and laid on a charger or dish, set in a cold place and the jelly is poured over. The dish is decorated with blanched almonds and pared ginger and left to cool. RECIPE: *2 15th Cent. Cookery Books* pp 86/87.

Porcelle farce enforce

Probably meat balls, which would be the farce, strongly flavoured, enforce meaning reinforced or strengthened, with parsley, which is the percelle but there are other possibilities. I have not been able to find a recipe for this dish.

Pokokkys

Peacocks. These birds were often served 'in their pride' at feasts, that is with the feathers on, the bird would flayed, the skin and feathers taken off in one piece, the bird roasted, then re-dressed to display his splendour. Directions for a Tudor banquet instruct it to be served as the last course: *A Proper Newe Booke of Cokerye*, ed. Catherine Frances Frere, intro. p. xxxvi. A fifteenth century manuscript states the peacock is to have its neck broken and throat cut, then flayed with the head still attached to the skin of the neck, the neck to be left unboned, the bird then drawn and roasted, the neck to be set above the spit, as he was when alive. When cooked he is allowed to cool, then the skin with its feathers is wrapped around the cooked body of the bird. Or he can be drawn and roasted as is a chicken - *2 15th Cent. Cookery Books* p.79.

Cranys

Cranes - prepared and roasted as herons above except that the legs are folded up at the knees under the thigh. And with additional suggestion that it can be sauced after having been minced. RECIPE: *2 15th Cent. Cookery Books* p. 116.

Venyson Roste

Roasted Venison. A fillet of venison is skinned and boned, parboiled, roasted on a spit and sauced. RECIPE: *2 15th Cent. Cookery Books* p. 81.

Conyng

A variety of rabbit. To be flayed, drawn above and beneath, parboiled, larded and roasted, head left on, and served with a sauce of ginger, verjuice and ground ginger. Very popular also served in gravy made from ground almonds, wine, broth of beef and mutton, strained, seasoned with ground ginger, cloves, maces and sugar. The animal then cooked in good fresh broth, apparently in its skin, the meat then picked off the bones and boiled up once in the syrup and served. RECIPES: *2 15th Cent. Cookery Books* p.80.

Byttore

Bittern, a marsh fowl related to the heron. Slain, prepared and roasted as for crane above but wings left on, no sauce but salt. RECIPE: *2 15th Cent. Cookery Books* p.116.

Pulle endore

A pullet gilded with egg yolk. I have not found a recipe for this, it was probably a fairly standard procedure. There are many recipes which call for gilding various foods with egg yolks.

Graunt tartez

Grand tart. Tarts could be made of meat or fish, often had dried fruits in abundance, sometimes fresh fruit such as apples and pears, Tart de brymlent mixes these with fish and dried fruit and is covered with pastry. RECIPE: *Curye on Inglysch*, p.137. The 'Graunt' could refer to the grand contents or to the fact that the tart was very large and so impressive. Large tarts were also tricky to bake in the oven.

Braun fryez

Slices of meat coated in egg and fine, manchet, flour, seasoned with sugar, saffron and salt, fried in a pan in fresh fat, sprinkled with sugar before serving. RECIPE: *2 15th Cent. Cookery Books* p.43.

Leche lumbarde

A sort of sweetmeat made from dates stewed in wine, pounded, then mixed with wine and sugar to a stiff paste (or hard boiled egg yolks mixed with honey to a stiff paste) then placed on a board. Slices of a stiff paste made from bread crumbs, ginger and cinnamon were added and a syrup of aromatic wine or spiced honey poured over. RECIPE: *2 15th Cent. Cookery Books* p.35

A Sotelte

(see above)

Le iij cours

Blaundesorye

A white soup made from milk of almonds, chicken or beef broth and wine, chopped chicken breast or white fish, garnished with comfits of red anise or with almonds. Or made without the meat or fish. RECIPES: *2 15th Cent. Cookery Books* pp 9, 21, 84.

Quynceys in comfyte

Preserved quinces. Quinces were enormously popular in medieval times and preserved both as a stiff paste that was cut into pieces and as a condiment that became the forerunner of marmalade.

Egretez

Egret, a kind of heron, killed by having its neck broken or the roof of its mouth cut, see heron, drawn as a hen (or scalded and then drawn), its wings removed by the body, also its head and neck by the body, legs to be folded as for the bittern, see above, then to be roasted, served with no sauce but salt. RECIPES: *2 15th Cent. Cookery Books* pp. 79 & 116.

Curlewys

Curlews. Killed as a crane (see above), wings cut off by the body, legs folded as a crane, nether lip and throat ball taken away, head put in his shoulder, roasted as a crane and no sauce but salte. RECIPE: *2 15th Cent. Cookery Books* p. 79.

Pertryche

Partridges. To be slain in the nape of the head with a feather (stabbed?), prepared, larded and roasted as for a pheasant, served sauced with wine, ground ginger, cinnamon and salt, or eaten with sugar and mustard. RECIPE: *2 15th Cent. Cookery Books* p. 78.

Pyionys

Pigeons. Roasted pigeons could be minced and served with a sauce of parsley, onions, garlic and salt, tempered with vinegar. RECIPE: *2 15th Cent. Cookery Books* p. 109.

Quaylys

Quails. To be served as a partridge with sauce gamelyne. Sauce gamelyne is a wine sauce thickened with bread, seasoned with ginger, sugar, ground cloves and little saffron. RECIPES: *2 15th Cent. Cookery Books*. pp 77 & 79. Lord Lisle, Governor of Calais under Henry VIII, sent several presents of quails to his King and Queen, the Queen 'loving and longing for them'. Lisle's agent and secretary in London, John Husee, wrote to Lady Lisle on 24th May 1537: 'Pleaseth it your Ladyship to be advertised that I have by this bearer received your letter, with the quails, the which came in season and were very welcome, both to the King's Highness and the Queen's Grace. For immediately as they came into my hands I rid in post to the court, with ij dozen of them, killed; and so they were anon upon vij of the clock presented until the King and the Queen's Graces, whose Highnesses, I assure your ladyship, were right glad of them, and commanded the one half of them incontinent to be roasted and the rest to be kept till supper. And those that were alive, Mr. Russell commanded me to kill them on Friday night, and to bring them unto the court upon Sunday. Those that shall be sent from henceforth must be very fat, and killed at Dover, and not to send past ij or iij dozen at once.' - *The Lisle Letters*, ed. Muriel St. Clare Byrne, selected and arranged by Bridget Boland, pub. The Folio Press, London, 1983, p 206.

Snytys

Snytes, a bird, to be killed as a woodcock or a plover. A plover has its skull broken, roasted with the neck whole and the bill in the shoulder and the legs folded as a crane, his wings cut and these and the legs raised as a hens, no sauce but salt. RECIPE: *2 15th Cent. Cookery Books* pp 80 & 117.

Smal byrdys

Small birds could be almost anything: larks, nightingales, thrushes, linnets, etc., etc.

Rabettys

See conyng above. Rabitts were roasted as Conyng. They must have been slightly different and there do not seem to be recipes for serving them any other way, such as in gravy as for the conyng above. But the duplication is a little curious. There is a recipe for conyng stewed and chopped and served with saffron and wine. This would have been a suitable method for this course but since the rabettys are not further defined, it would be dangerous to speculate further. RECIPE: *2 15th Cent. Cookery Books*, p.20.

Pome dorreng

Meatballs of ground pork made the size and shape of apples, gilded and made green with batter containing chopped parsley, cooked on a spit in front of a clear fire, or boiled then gilded with egg yolk and cooked on a spit. RECIPE: *2 15th Cent. Cookery Books* p.38.

Braun blanke leche

Minced meat cooked with sweetened almond milk, boiled then allowed to cool in a basin, turned out and sliced. The origin of our blancmange. RECIPE: *2 15th Cent. Cookery books*, p. 71.

Eyroun engele

A note on the menu for this feast as given in *2 15th Cent. Cookery Books*, p. 58, suggests these are iced eggs. The index corrects this to Jellied Eggs. There is a complicated recipe of Eyren Gelide given in Warner's *Antiquitates Culinariae*. p. 89, in which milk of almonds and cooked fish is pounded and spiced with cloves, heated and used to fill egg shells, a clove with a gilded head being stuck in the top. When cold and set, the shells are removed and the eggs set between slices of Leches Lumbard strewn with ground ginger and sugar.

Frytourys

Fritters made with a batter of eggs, ale, saffron, salt and slices of apple fried in oil and sprinkled with sugar. RECIPE: *2 15th Cent. Cookery Books* pp. 44, 73.

Doucettys

Sweet custard tarts, sometimes containing finely chopped pork, sometimes almond milk and sometimes cream, with egg yolks and sugar or honey and saffron or spices. The custard is baked in a pastry case. One of the recipes demonstrates the difficulties medieval kitchens had with cooking liquid mixtures in pastry, which could so easily leak. The instructions are to bake the case first then to ladle in the custard mixture from a dish fastened to the end of a pele, the long handled implement used for placing and removing items into and from the depths of an oven. RECIPE: *2 15th Cent. Cookery Books* pp 50 & 55.

Pety perneux

A mixture of yolks of eggs, sugar, ground ginger, raisins and minced dates in fine pastry cases, either baked or fried in fresh fat, sounds like an early version of our mince pies. RECIPES: *2 15th Cent. Cookery Books*, pp 51 & 74.

Egle

The only suggestion I can come up with here is Eagle but cannot find any mention of eagles being eaten. As a royal hunting bird the eagle must have been more valuable alive than dead. However, other menus do have an Eagle as a soteltie and it may be that this is what was meant here.

Pottys of lylye

Another conundrum. Pots of flesh? Curye on Inglysch gives Ly(u)re = flesh, also lye = mix. Or pots of lily? Lily was spelt this way in the fifteenth century but there is no evidence lilies were eaten. Could it mean pots containing something very white?.

A Sotelte

See above.

(3) HENRY IV's WEDDING FEAST Conuiuium Regis supradicti in nupcijs apud Wyntoniam (*Two Fifteenth Century Cookery Books*, pp 58/59). Served at his second marriage, in 1404, to Joan of Navarre, widow of John de Montfort, Duke of Brittany, in Winchester Cathedral.

Le j cours

Fylettys in galentyne
    Pork forequarter roasted without the skin until half done, cut into pieces then cooked with fried, shredded onions, in broth of beef or mutton with spices and vinegar and thickened with bread, served hot. RECIPES: *2 15th Cent. Cookery Books* pp 8, 82.

Vyaund Ryalle
Grosse chare
Signettys
Capoun of haut grece
Fesauntys
Chewetys
    Usually small, round pies made of fair pastry and filled with minced meat or fish and dried fruits and spices, sometimes fried instead of being baked. Again, early version of mince pies. RECIPES: *2 15th Cent. Cookery Books* pp 45,46,48,98.

A Sotelte

Snytys
Feldefare
Smale byrdys
Crustade
Sturgeoun
Fretoure
A Sotelte

Le ij course

Venyson with furmente. Potage
Gelye
Porcellys
Conynge
Bittore
Pulcynges farcez
Pertryche
Leche fryez
Braun bruse
A Sotelte

Le iij cours

Creme de Almaundys
Perys in Syryppe
Venyson Rostyd
Kyde
Wodecokke
Plouere
Rabettys
Quaylys

Ibidem conuiuium de pissibus [The fish courses]

Le j cours
Vyaund Ryal
Sew lumbarde
Salt Fysshe
Laumpreys pouderyd
Pyke
Breme
Samoun Rostyd
Crustade Lumbarde
A sotelte

Le ij cours
Purpayis en furmente
Gely
Breme
Samoun
Congre
Gurnarde
Plays
Lampreys in past
Leche fryez
Panteryse
Coronys for a sotelte

Le iij cours
Creme of Almaund
Perys in syrippe
Tenche enbrace
Troutez
Floundrys fryid
Perchys
Lamprey Rostyd
Elys Rostyd
Lochys & colys
Sturioun
Crabbe au Creueys
Graspeys
Egle coronys in sotelte

(4) A ROYAL FEAST AT THE WEDDING OF THE EARL OF DEVONSHIRE - A Ryal Fest in the Feste at the weddyng of the Erle of Deuynchire (*Two Fifteenth Century Cookery Books*, pp.63/64)

Le j cours
Furmenty with Venysoun
Vuyand Goderygge
Vele Roste
Swan with chawderoun
Pecokke
Crane
Vn leche
Vn Fryid mete
Vn pasty, cooperta
A sotelte: Ceruus

Le ij cours
Mammenye
Vyand Motlegh
Kede
Conyng
Herons
Chykonys endoryd
Venyson Rosted
I. leche
Vn Fryid mete
I. paste Crustade
A colde Bakemete
A sotelte: Homo

Le iij cours
Gely
Datys in comfyte
Fesaunt
Gullys
Poper
Mawlard de la Ryuer
Peionys
Pertryche
Curlew
Pomez endoryd
I. Leche
Payne Puffe
A sotelte: Arbor

Pro inferiori parte Auli [For the lesser part of the hall]

Le j cours	Le ij cours
Venyson en Brothe	Caudel Ferry
Spawdys [*Spaut or Spaud*: Shoulder] de Motoun	Pyionys
Kyde	Gullys
Doke	Rabettys
Chykonys Roste	Venysoun Roste
Pygge in Sawge	Doucetys
Venysoun bake	Vn Leche

(5) THE CROWNACON OFF KYNG HENRY THE FFYFTE (*A Noble Boke Off Cookry*, ed. Mrs. Alexander Napier, pub. Elliot Stock, London, 1882, pp.4/6), celebrated on a fish day.

The ffirste course

Venyson in brothe ⎫
Blank de serre ⎬ potage
Pyk, lampry poudred ⎭
Gurnard
Trout
Roche
ffried creves
Tartes
braun counterfet for lesshe with the ribe ther in a gret swan for suttellte sittinge upon a grene stok displaid with a skriptur in his bille - *Regardez Roy la droyt voy* and vi signetes growinge out of the sam stok under hir each on with a skripture
- for the ffirste *Theney la ley*
- for the second *Gardez la fey*
- for the third *Hors de court*
- for the ffourthe *Soit bannez tort*
- ffor the ffyfte *Eyez pete*
- ffor the sexte *des comunalte*

Then xxiiij swannys euychon of them a byll in the mouthe, - *noble honour and joy*.

The second course

Vyand Ryalle
gilly with swannys of braun ther in for the king and ffor other Estates
congur freche
halybut
Bace
molet
samon
sooles
egre, eles, and lamprous rost
place ffried
lamprey bak
fflampayn
lesshe lombard
Antelopes for suttellte with a scripture - *un sauvez plus maynteyn dieux*.

The iij course

Creme frez
dates in compost
carpes
perche
sturgion welkes
tenche in braissell
fflounders
porpas rost
lamprey roste
cloves de edewede
menewes fried
paynpuff
dowcettes
Egillis of gold displayde for suttelte withe a scriptur in their billes - *dest jour notable est honorable*

(6) THE FFEST OF NEVELL ARCHEBIFSHOPE OF YORK AND CHAUNCELER OF ENGLOND AT (ATT) HIS STALLACON IN YORK [1467]

Provisions (Quoted from Warner's *Antiquitates Culinariae*, pp. 93/95)

In Wheate	300	qrs.	Fessauntes	200	
In Ale	300	tunne	Partriges	500	
Wyne	100	tunne	Wodcockes	400	
Of Ipocraffe	one	pipe	Curlewes	100	
In Oxen	104		Egrittes	1000	
Wylde Bulles	6		Stagges, Buckes, and Roes	500	and mo
Muttons	1000				
Veales	304		Pasties of Venison colde	4000	
Porkes	304				
Swannes	400		Parted dysshes of Gelly	1000	
Geese	2000				
Capons	1000		Playne dysshes of Gelly	3000	
Pygges	2000				
Plover	400		Colde Tartes baked	4000	
Quayles	100	dozen			
Of the foules called Rees	200	dozen	Colde Custardes baked	3000	
In Pecockes	104		Hot pasties of Venison	1500	
Mallardes & Teales	4000		Hot Custardes	2000	
In Cranes	204		Pykes and Breames	608	
In Kyddes	204		Porposes and Seales	12	
In Chyckyns	2000		Spices, Sugered delicates, and Wafers plentie		
Pigeons	4000				
Conyes	4000				
In Bittors	204				
Heronshawes	400				

THE FEAST (*A Noble Boke off Cookrye*, pp. 7/8)

The ffirst course
Braun with mustard
ffurmente with venyson
hert poudred
ffessand in brayn
Swan rost
Ganetz
Gullez
capon de haut grece
heron roste
carpet in venison
pik in ereblad
leshe caute rialle
ffritur boyse
venyson bak
custad planted
chewetts riall with a suttellte

The second course
Gilly parti riall
viand rasens
venison in brakes
pecock in trapille
cony roste
roo reversed
lardes de venison
pertuches
leshe cipirs
ffritur napkyne
tarte in molde
wodcok
plouer
Goodwitts
red shankes
yarowe helpes
knottes
Oxene
Creme in purpull
chatowe dyuers riall with a suttellte

The third course
Bland desere
dates in comfet
neutes vert
Bittur rostid
Curlew rostid
fessand rostid
Railes rost
Egret rost
Rabettes
quailes
poums vert
Got whelpes rost
dotterelles rost
martynets rost
Gret birds
larkes rost
sparowes
ffreche sturgion
lesshe blaunche
ffritur cuspe
quinces bak
rosestis florishid
chamlettes withe a sutteltte

Feasting after Fasting in Archi Village, Dagestan, ASSR

by Dr. Magomedkhan Magoedkhanov, edited by Robert Chenciner

Archi is one of seven joined hamlets with a total population of 700, over 2000 metres up in the Great Caucasian mountains just downstream from a source of the Karakoisu river on the ancient shepherds' trek from Dagestan to Azerbaidzhan. The distinct and difficult language is a popular curiosity among philologists and there is even a grammar in English. *

In Dagestan, fasting, in theory, occurs at the usual time in the Islamic calendar - during the festival of Ramazan. In fact, the fast tends to be observed by older people, while, in contrast, the feasts are celebrated by all. There are also irregular instances of fasting. Firstly, after death there is spontaneous fasting related to mourning. Secondly, if family honour is offended by an internal scandal, the husband or wife - [Khanidasa barshi] - "don't speak or eat with each other" for one day. (Kuyada village is well known for this). Thirdly, enforced fasting was caused by famine from war or a bad harvest. If a dairy cow died from starvation, the woman owner will stay at home and not eat for a day. During the most recent famines from 1943-1947, pregnant women and children ate first. Virtually all food was taken for the Front, including the final reserves of dried meat over one year old. Some villages like Archi had to beg for food from other villages. Three women there died from eating earth from a population of about 200. There were also no shoes (no leather) and everyone had lice. They survived on boiled stinging nettles which are still enjoyed today (even though they are worried if foreign guests will eat such things).

The tragic stories of famine caused by the sharp proximity of war and cruel nature make their reaction - an almost aggressive enthusiasm for fasting - understandable. Any foreign guest will have endless feasts in Dagestan.

There are several opportunities for local feasts too. Linked with family survival, there are feasts for marriage, birth, circumcision (male), first tooth (boiled corn), and baby's first steps. Crop fertility is celebrated by feasts for the First Furrow and separating the grain from the chaff (crushed - as in Turkey - by wooden sled with protruding stones, pulled in a circle by bull). To ensure livestock fertility there are feasts firstly on the day selected for the ram to service the sheep (1:100 is the normal ration), secondly in winter when a shepherd leaves for the mountains with several people's sheep for the south facing specially preserved place with winter grass and thirdly on the day when sheep (or a cow) are butchered for drying.

The diversity of the village population in Dagestan is huge - 33 nationalities live in over 700 villages with from 300 to 10,000 inhabitants. So in different villages there may well be variations in both the feasts and the dishes, but that larger subject must be described elsewhere.

At the great local religious feast after the fast of Ramazan, there are both customs connecting the feast with an end to mourning and a large number of special prepared dishes.

The Imam, called the *Debir* in Archi after the 12th century saint who brought Sunnite Islam there, must announce the date two or three days in advance. A bereaved family are chosen and offer to prepare the ritual feast. As usual everyone is up and about at 6 a.m. In the morning separate groups of male elders (the *Jamat* or village council), men women, boys and girls go about the village. The group of elders first visit the *Debir*, followed by the younger men, the women, the boys and lastly the girls. Children take part as soon as they can walk. Next, only the men visit the cemetery to venerate their ancestors, and go on to the mosque to recite the festival *namaz* or prayer. They are now ready to visit the house of the bereaved (usually the most revered or youngest who died during that, or the previous year if there is none more recent). Both groups of men are the first to enter the house saying *Sob kIabul aba!* - "Let your fasting be noticed by God!", with the response *Ushutu yashi* - "Yours too." There the first meal, a breakfast of hot meat (mutton, beef or calf), potatoes and herbs has been prepared, described as *KIocg etIlas* - "putting down planks", that is the table. The younger the deceased the larger the feast. At the beginning and end of breakfast they pray the "Al fatiha" (Arabic) in memory of the dead person (who may be male or female). At this house there is no

---

* Non-English words:

Archi - in italic with an attempted phonetic spelling, including "kI" for a clicking "k" consonent, similarly "tI".
Avar - in [] brackets. Avar is one of the main languages of Dagestan, spoken by more than the 600,000 Avars who make up 30% of the population of Dagestan.
Russian - underlined.
These symbols may be combined if the word belongs to more than one language.

customary giving of [*saddaqah*] (Archi) + (Avar) sweet things. They then visit all the other houses in the village, staying about five minutes at each and only tasting what is on the table. Every household has prepared the dishes listed below, saving up the choicest ingredients throughout the year. Children follow the women who follow the men. On this feast day only necessary work may be done - no slaying of beasts or building. It is a public day with no private family meals. The feast ends with afternoon prayers.

The variety and preparation of the dishes is most elaborate, but at present we cannot understand whether there is a detailed symbolism employed in these twenty dishes or whether they merely reflect what is available. It is curious, however, that when the editor of this article shocked local custom by cooking and preparing dishes like omelettes, cheese pizza or schnitzel from the excellent local ingredients, they were completely unknown - and liked. This would indicate that there is the usual conservatism associated with their foods perhaps incorporating a now forgotten symbolic dimension. This would not apply to the main dishes and salads which frequently also appear in everyday meals, unlike several of the breads and sweets.

There are seven types of "bread":

1. Normal oven baked bread with yeast *klekl mulin kluali*.
2. Tandir oven baked bread without yeast *kluali*.
3. 5 mm thick pancakes *imts'o kluali*.
4. 15 mm pancake sandwiched between unleavened bread slabs *berku kluali*, from the Avar word [berkal], meaning "in everyday use".
5. 5 mm thick version of berku *khalakh kluali*.
   All pancakes are garnished with a melted piece of kurduk, fat-tailed sheep's tail on top and clarified butter on the bottom side.
6. Special Archi bread *boklirchi* from a beige malty tasting flour *daatsun*, made from ground dried grain which has been soaked in the river for seven days til it sprouts - this is also used to ferment [*buza*] the grey-beige fizzy cloudy sweet beer, of about 10 degrees alcohol strength. 2 glasses of [daatsun] are added to one glass of *bokh* flour which is mixed with water, without salt, into a dough and squeezed into hand-sized rolls. After baking the rolls have a crust with a sweet brown soft inside.
7. *ebkhl na kluali* Cornflour boiled in milk until it has the consistency of Kasha porridge. Add boiled dried mutton intestine fat, diced onion, raisins, chabrets and tumin coriander herbs. Sandwich 10 mm of the mixture between 3 mm sheets of rolled dough, then glaze with butter and bake.

Three main dishes:

1. Cold boiled meats - mutton, chicken, bull beef, veal on the bone which is lovingly chewed: *setetut akl*.
2. Plov *pulof* made in the following proportions. 1 glass rice *birinj*, 1/2 glass boiling water and 3 tbsp. clarified butter, one onion, 1/2 glass of boiled beans or 1/4 kg meat (beef or mutton, fresh or dried), add salt and pepper to taste.
3. Pilmeni *adzutib khungorto* slippery raviolis with Tvorok cottage cheese, meat or nettles. (In autumn the young nettle leaves are chopped and dried).

If available, there are fresh and pickled salads:

Salat is made from tomatoes or cucumber garnished with sliced onions, green herbs, vegetable seed oil, smetana, salt & pepper.
Whole garlic cloves.
Salted tomatoes and/or cucumbers.

There are seven sweets:

1. Tartii sweet 8" diameter *bizub kluali* made from eggs, clarified butter and sugar are baked the previous night and cut into rays, slices or squares next morning.
2. Archi sweet *khinkal* dumplings - little ones made of flour and eggs, usually just flour, and eaten with honey, *isib intsikl uvtib hankkorto*.
3. Halva *baakukl* made by adding flour to clarified butter and mixing in granulated sugar.
4. Sherbet (no word in Archi), made by mixing 2 glasses of boiled milk with 1 glass of sugar and 3 tbsp. of flour. This is then boiled with 1 tbsp. of butter. The longer it is boiled the harder the consistency of the white or beige toffee-like slabs.
5. *Holoklalo* is a beige rich sweet malty paste. Cold whip 1/2 litre of ground malt flour *daatsun* with 1/2 litre of Buza dregs *kholay* and 1 tbsp. sugar.

6. <u>Kompot</u> made from blackcurrants, apricots and/or rowanberries.
7. *Chelob* Rice boiled in just enough milk to swell the rice. It is put on a plate and a space made in the middle to fill with boiled butter alone or with *daatsun* malty flour, and [urbech] (ground apricot kernals, linen seeds or cannabis seeds) alone or with honey. [Urbech] is bought in from other villages.

Everything is eaten at the same time over a period of many hours. The popularity of this feast was so great that it continued to be celebrated throughout the Stalin period when even muslim funerals were forbidden. The next feast is on 15th May 1991.

The St. Joseph Day Altars of New Orleans

by Richard C. Mieli

edited by Stephen J. Christian

The Feast of St. Joseph is celebrated on March 19th, within the fast period of Lent. The tradition of the St. Joseph Day Altars was brought to New Orleans in the state of Louisiana by Sicilian immigrants over a century ago. According to legend, during a famine in Sicily St. Joseph, who was regarded as a protector of the holy family and a representative of the universal father, was prayed to by the peasants to end the famine. When the famine ended, the grateful peasants made offerings of food to the saint on his feast day. The reason that food was offered was because it was food that had been prayed for. The precise date of the famine which instituted the tradition of the Altars is not known.

New Orleans is noted the world over for its feasts and festivals, the most famous being Mardi Gras. Ash Wednesday ushers in the fast period of Lent, which culminates on Easter Sunday. Usually festivals do not take place during this period, due to the sacredness and reflectiveness of the meaning of Lent. The feast days of two important saints, St. Patrick on March 17th and St. Joseph on March 19th, occur during this time, however. Due to the significance of these saints, both feast days are celebrated intensely in the city. St. Patrick's Day in New Orleans features a huge, well-known parade, with jazz bands and the tossing of objects such as cabbages, potatoes, and onions from the floats. St. Joseph's Day has a more religious tone, but culminates on the following Saturday with a parade in the French Quarter that includes the tossing of fava beans, known as "lucky beans."

In Sicily, a family acknowledging the favours granted by St. Joseph prepares an Altar in the living room of their home. The Altar is decorated with flowers, candles, and elaborate breads. In front of the Altar a dinner is set that includes pasta, meat and fish dishes, vegetables, fruit, and pastries. The Altar is blessed by a priest before anyone is allowed to eat the food. Altars which I observed in New Orleans ranged from those in private homes and restaurants to those sponsored by the St. Joseph Guild and the Italo-American Organisation. The St. Joseph Guild is an association of individuals who are an extended community of the Sisters of St. Joseph. Members share in the spiritual, social and fund raising activities of the Guild.

Marie Cusimano, who lives in a modest two-family home in the Uptown area of New Orleans, has been preparing an Altar for over thirty years. She advertises her Altar in the classified section of a New Orleans newspaper, *The Times-Picayune*. The advertisement reads: "St. Joseph Altar, March 18th, 3-10 pm, Mr. & Mrs. Lawrence Cusimano 8131 Nelson Street." She has removed or covered all her living room furniture in order to display the Altar. When I arrived at her home I noticed a picture of St. Joseph on the door adorned by a red and white wreath; red and white are the colours associated with St. Joseph. Upon entering, I observed a display of food set on a tiered staging covered with a white cloth that took up two-thirds of the living room. A statue of St. Joseph was surrounded by elaborate breads shaped like chalices, representing the bread and wine of the Last Supper; a monstrance, or sacred receptacle, containing the Host; a beard and staff representing St. Joseph; and palms, symbolising generosity, justice and friendship. There were also candles, oranges, baked cookies, and red flowers distributed in various places on the Altar. The Altar had been blessed by the priest at 2:30 pm and opened to the public at 3 pm.

When I asked Mrs. Cusimano why she had prepared the Altar, she introduced me to her son who had come home for the holy day. Thirty-three years ago, after several years of marriage but without a child, she had made a novena to St. Joseph. Her son was born on St. Joseph's Day. The Altar was in response to the promise that she had made to the saint. As I left her home, she offered me a small bag containing bread and cookies. The customary donation was left in a box near the Altar.

The largest Altar I viewed was sponsored by the St. Joseph's Guild at 1200 Mirabeau Avenue. The building that displayed the Altar had a bouquet of palm fronds and bay leaves placed over the door. The palms represent generosity and friendship, and the bay leaves stand for protection and good luck. The food for the Altar covered several tables eight feet long, and included all types of bread work and pastries, main dishes such as whole baked fish and fava bean purées, and fresh fruit such as apples, oranges, and grapes. Candles and wine were placed among the food of the Altars. The baking schedule for this Altar was as follows:

The Baking Sxhedule for the St. Joseph's Guild Altar

Saturdays 9 - 3.30	Sundays 9.30 - 3.30
February 10	February 11
February 17	February 18
March 3	March 4
March 10	

Approximately 100,000 cookies were made for this Altar. All the food which had been donated was given to the poor, the needy, and the disabled after the feast day. As I left the viewing of the Altar, I was given a bag that contained a fava bean, a slice of bread, and nine different cookies representing the various kinds of cookies which had been baked.

Another Altar was viewed in Brocato's, a New Orleans pastry and ice cream shop. Elaborate bread work and pastry covered the Altar, which encompassed a space of about ten feet at the shop entrance.

The last Altar I viewed was sponsored by the Greater New Orleans Italian Cultural Society, at the Piazza d'Italia on Poydras Street. This is located downtown, near the French Quarter and many of the large hotels of the city. It appeared to attract more tourists than native New Orleanians. The Altar was blessed at noon on Friday, March 16th, and remained open on Saturday and Sunday 9 am - 9 pm. On Sunday entertainment was provided by orchestras from noon to 4 pm. On Monday a mass was held at 11 am, and at 2 pm food was given away.

A mid-city restaurant called "Katie's Restaurant," owned by Mary Leininger, displayed a St. Joseph Altar. On St. Joseph's Day, festivities at the restaurant began at noon with the visit of three children representing the holy family. The children knocked on the restaurant door asking for food and lodging, symbolising the plight of the holy family seeking refuge. The children were invited in and fed a meal that had been prepared for them. Traditionally, the children receive a taste of all the food, which has been blessed, from the Altar. This ritual was not open to the public, but once the ritual was concluded the public was invited to enter.

The food prepared for all the Altars usually had symbolic meanings; some, however, were traditional family recipes. One Altar had twelve fried whole trout, representing both the twelve apostles and the feeding of the multitudes. Oranges, which appear on most of the Altars, represent the fruit of the womb of Mary. Fava beans, the "lucky beans," are dried, roasted, and blessed, and given away with a piece of bread and cookies at most of the Altars. A legend holds that the fava bean became a staple during the famines and droughts in Sicily; as long as you have one, you will never go hungry.

Pasta dishes are the prevalent main dishes at the meals provided to the public. The tomato sauce is usually made with a fish base, anchovies, and pine nuts, topped with fried bread crumbs seasoned with sugar. The bread crumbs represent sawdust, symbolising the tradition that St. Joseph was a carpenter. Known as "modica," the bread crumbs are made by, sautéeing finely ground stale bread in olive oil until it is lightly browned, then sprinkling sugar over it. Modica is put on the pasta instead of cheese.

As St. Joseph's day concludes, the religious aspect of the festival comes to an end. The celebration continues, however, until the following Saturday, when a parade lasting several hours takes place in the French Quarter. Various items are thrown to the viewers, the most prized being the blessed "lucky bean." The parade participants march and ride on floats or in horse-drawn carriages and cars. This week-long feast during the fast period of Lent is truly in keeping with the philosophy of the city of New Orleans - the city that care forgot!

Bibliography

Burton, Katherine & Helmut Rupperger, *The Feast Day Cookbook*. D. McKay Co. Inc. NY. 1951.
Dolci, Danilo, *Sicilian Lives*. Random House-Pantheon Books, NY 1981.
Cole, Al, ed. *Viva San Giuseppe – A guide for St. Joseph Altars*. St. Joseph Guild, 1200 Mirabeau Street, New Orleans, LA., 1985.
Palao, Mike, *St. Joseph's Day in New Orleans*. La Mar Management Inc. New Orleans, 1979.
Simeti, Mary Taylor, *On Persephones Island – A Sicilian Journal*. Alfred A. Knopf, NY, 1986.
Simeti, Mary Taylor, *Pomp And Sustenance – Twenty Five Centuries of Sicilian Food*. Alfred A. Knopf, NY, 1989.
Smith, Denis Mack, *History of Medieval Sicily*. Viking Press, NY, 1968.
de Vries, Ad, *Dictionary of Symbols and Imagery*. North Holland Publishing Co. Amsterdam, London, 1974.

Italian American Digest. Spring 1990, 1608 S. Salacelo St., New Orleans, LA 70125.
Times Picayune. Sunday, March 11, 1990.

Dutch Treats or Festive Food in an Affluent Society

by Ileen Montijn

Dutch food in general has no great reputation. When Dutch specialties are praised, they are things like fish, asparagus, cheese - ingredients rather than prepared dishes.

Even worse than the reputation of Dutch food is the reputation of Dutch treats. (Ever since someone told the Dutch about this expression, which has no equivalent in their language, they have been very worried about it. It is invariably mentioned in newspaper articles which stress our national shortcomings; of these, there are many.) As a Dutchwoman, I am delighted at this chance to explain, and in such a learned setting too, about the real nature of Dutch treats. What I am about to tell you is certainly not learned at all, for most of it has been known to every single Dutchman from childhood.

No foodie, and very few food researchers, ever seem to refer to the large and booming tradition of very specific festive types of food in the Netherlands, mostly in the nature of sweets, which is accepted as part of life by every ordinary Dutchman. These treats appear regularly throughout the year, and throughout everybody's life-cycle, without anyone stopping to think about them. Banal as they are to us, they may seem strange and eccentric to people even a few dozen miles across the borders.

I shall describe some of these simple treats, which I think demonstrate that not only in pre-industrial, illiterate societies old and quaint food customs survive. Given the right economic and social circumstances, folklore like this may actually become more rather than less important, which has happened in the case of some of my Dutch treats.

Little Mice and Birthdays

The first treat in anybody's life, though he or she is not aware of this, is the *beschuit met muisjes*, rusk with little mice, which is offered to well-wishing visitors when a child has been born. The mice are white and pink sugar-coated aniseeds. They are, so food historians tell me, a very ancient food, having been used to decorate dishes even in the Middle Ages. They were called *trigy* then. Aniseed, of course, like fennel is a traditional cure for stomach disorders and colic in babies, though I am not sure that this fact is relevant.

Not only visitors, but also the young father's colleagues at work, and schoolmates of elder children are offered this exceedingly crumbly treat. Even grandparents living elsewhere may well treat their own friends to *beschuit met muisjes* in honour of their distant new grand-child. Once, there were regional varieties in the shapes of the rusks, and the colour and shape of the little mice differed according to whether a boy or a girl had been born. These subtleties have practically disappeared. But the custom itself is alive and kicking; both the rusk-industry and the Dairy Board (for butter) have used it in their commercial publicity. The manufacture of the little mice - which are sold as something to put on sliced bread, but aren't very popular in this capacity - must survive largely due to the birth-day-treat.

This brings us to the, entirely different, birthday treat. To a Dutchman this is such an ordinary custom that it seems almost embarrassing to explain about it. Anyone who goes to kindergarten, school or work outside the home is expected, on his or her birthday, to 'treat' (the verb *tracteren*, a transitive one as in the English language, is on this occasion used intransitively). It means giving something sweet or tasty to everyone with whom one is in daily contact - not just friends, but the whole crew, so to speak.

Healthy treats

In the beginning of this century, a large piece of gingerbread was tied to the arm of a schoolchild on its birthday with a festive ribbon; at school, everyone got a chunk to celebrate. By the middle of the century, the custom had evolved to the child bringing a large biscuit tin to school, filled with either biscuits or sweets, and ceremoniously (during class hours) going round to offer every class-mate, or school-mate if the school was small, a sweet. One sweet, mind you: never more. For the teacher, in those days, a cigarette or a more refined sweet such as a chocolate might have been brought.

In the early seventies, with growing awareness of the dangers of sugar to children's teeth, the birthday-treating custom became controversial. The impact of this new awareness was such that whole toffee-industries collapsed. Giving sweets to children came in some circles to be regarded as real maliciousness, if not cruelty. But birthday-treating survived. Producers of cheese, magazines for parents, even public health institutions, began giving away free posters with suggestions for "healthy treats" - cheese was usually an important ingredient. Lack of sweetness was compensated for by funny and elaborate design. These kinds of treats have remained popular, although the taboo on sweets has eroded to some extent. Nowadays, birthday treats at kindergarten and grade schools are often fancy affairs, sweet or savoury (usually both), full of animal faces, little flags, etcetera. But even plain bags of crisps are naively regarded by many parents as 'better' than sweets.

In offices, birthday treating has been the subject of less, if any discussion. My impression is that it has increased. The custom nowadays is that on one's birthday, one brings pastries, usually of a luxurious kind (not buns and the like) for the people one works with, to be eaten during coffee break. Having to buy forty pieces of pastry, costing the equivalent of twenty-five pounds, is by no means unusual. Those in higher positions send out their secretaries to buy them. The compensation of course is, that thirty-nine times a year you are treated by someone else. In quite a few offices, birthday gifts are the habit too. All this may seem quite childish, but it is a totally accepted part of office folklore. Someone refusing to take part in it would be regarded as a terrible spoilsport (and stingy into the bargain). Whole pastry shops in office neighbourhoods derive a large part of their turnover from the custom. Here and there, of course, people might bring a home-baked cake to share out instead of the bought stuff. In the home too, when visitors come for people's birthdays - and they always do, for birthdays are extremely important social occasions in all but the most degenerately blasé circles - pastries are an indispensable part of the proceedings.

Wedding cakes for weddings, Easter Eggs (taken up by confectioners with apparent near hysteria from two months before the date of Easter), those are things that are not unique to the Netherlands. English Christmas Pudding is only just creeping in, while German raisin-and-nut-bread for Christmas (*Weihnachtsstollen*) is a fairly established novelty. Bakers are now trying to push it for Easter as well. Like Mother's and Father's Day, this has perhaps not been invented, but certainly forced into general consciousness by commercial interests.

Abraham and chewy-chewy

Typically Dutch, I think, is Abraham. He is a large, flat, edible doll, once made of bread dough, nowadays more cake-like and elaborately decorated, or even mistakenly taken to be a kind of gingerbread man. He is a traditional birthday gift for a man who turns fifty. The basis for this is in the Bible, St. John, 9, v. 57: *Then said the Jews unto him, Thou art not yet fifty Years old, and hast thou seen Abraham?* The giving of Abraham dolls to people on their fiftieth birthday (and Sarah dolls to women, as a kind of consolation prize) has probably become more rather than less popular after the last war; some believe that the offering of an Abraham (not a Sarah!) to Queen Juliana on her fiftieth birthday in 1959 has been a boost. The custom seems to originate in the region of West-Friesland, but it has spread all over the country.

Gingerbread men were mentioned. Dutch ones are tall, and always baked in hollow moulds. There are also *speculatius* men (*speculatius* is a crisper, spiced kind of biscuit comparable to French *pain d'amandes* or Swedish *pepparkakor*). Both are closely bound up with Dutch Santa Claus. To go into the Dutch way of celebrating Santa Claus (*Sint Nicolaas* or *Sinterklaas*) would take us much too far here. Suffice it to say that the whole thing has nothing to do with Christmas, for the Saint's Day is celebrated on the eve of December 6th. He is a great giver of gifts to children and also of all manner of sweets. (All right, a bit more detail: *Sinterklaas* has none of your Santa Claus's undignified jocularity, he rides on a fine white horse over the roofs of all the houses, and is accompanied by his black helpers, all of whom are called *Zwarte Piet*, Black Peter. The gifts go into the children's shoes, put out in the evening by the chimneypiece. This little ceremony, shoe-setting, is accompanied by singing *Sinterklaas* songs).

Apart from things like nuts and oranges, *speculatius* and especially gingerbread are among the oldest edible treats from Santa Claus. Dutch gingerbread is chewy and has, or ought to have, more of an aniseed than a ginger flavour. It is called *taai-taai* or chewy-chewy. It is cheaper than *speculatius*, being made with rye flour, honey or syrup, and no fat, while *speculatius* calls for wheat flour and sugar, and preferably almonds. Both were traditionally baked in carved wooden moulds in various shapes, mostly human, but also representing biblical scenes, ships, and so on. A famous chapter in a Dutch novel of 1839 tells, with heavy irony, of a cozy gilding-party in a lower-middle-class family, spent decorating such cake figures for *Sinterklaas*.

Their industrial production began around 1880, leading, among other things, to great loss of variety in the moulds. But even today, all *speculatius* and chewy-chewy is sold in some traditional moulded shape, however rudimentary. Two accepted exceptions are gingerbread nuts, in the shape of little buttons or lumps, which Black Peter habitually strews around him, and filled *speculatius*. This last seasonal delicacy is filled with almond-and-sugar-paste, a kind of soft marzipan. Rising miles above the supermarket *Sinterklaas*-treats, this stuff can be delicious, and quite expensive.

Marzipan, once a great luxury, has risen to popularity too as a *Sinterklaas* treat. Most often, the material itself is produced industrially, and then kneaded by hand in pastry shops into brightly coloured little apples and pears or other shapes. There is a lot of jokiness about here, vaguely connected with Black Peter's habit of teasing people. So, for example, lots of driving licences, artfully reproduced in marzipan, are sold, supposedly to be offered as a gift to people who keep failing their driving tests. Greasy-looking sausages made of marzipan are popular too.

Edible letters

Until recent times, figures made of nothing but sugar - animals, Santa Clauses - were much more widely spread than marzipan because of their relative cheapness. They, however, are disappearing. Only a softer kind of sugar confection, *borstplaat*, made with cream and sold either in heart shapes or in little discs is still common in pastry shops. The hearts are perhaps the *Sinterklaas*-treat which is most often made in private kitchens. They are cloying but delicious if well made. Their commercial importance is clearly diminishing. The one-time popularity of these straightforward sugar confections must date from the nineteenth century, of course, when sugar became available on a large scale.

Chewy-chewy, marzipan, sugar animals, all of these are ancient enough to be mentioned in traditional *Sinterklaas* songs (which thanks to modern sound equipment, are to be heard in every shopping precinct around the country weeks before December 5th). Not mentioned in any of these songs, but in terms of industrial turnover probably the most important *Sinterklaas*-treat of all is chocolate letters. Last year, seventeen million manufactured chocolate letters were sold in the Netherlands, a country with under fifteen million inhabitants. The letters represent about seven percent of the total chocolate consumption. They are exclusively linked with Santa Claus; even to ask for one in a shop in spring or summer would be ridiculous.

Although there is a mention of chocolate letters for children in a novel of the eighteen-eighties, they did not come into general use until this century. One large manufacturer, Verkade, tells me they began production around 1905.

The whole idea of eating letters is an interesting one. Is it, as many people seem to think, a metaphor for learning? Apparently, bread or cake letters were made centuries ago. One other kind of edible letter is still to be found in Dutch Santa Claus food folklore, probably older than the chocolate one. It is made of flaky or puff pastry, filled with the marzipan-like almond filling used also for *speculatius* (see above). But it is typically a small-scale product, for it lacks all the conveniences of chocolate letters, being bulky, prone to breakage, and to spoiling and drying out. Only S and M shapes (for *Sinterklaas* and Mother) are generally available - and O's ('wreaths') for Christmas. Other letters can usually be made to order.

Of chocolate letters, on the other hand, almost the whole alphabet is mass-produced. It has to be, for the present-day custom is to give one's loved ones their first-name initial (or have *Sinterklaas* give it). This, coupled with the strict seasonality of the product, presents serious problems of supply and demand for both manufacturers and retailers. How many people's names begin with A, B, etcetera? Nowadays, pastry shops and supermarkets are saved the trouble of estimating how many of each letter they need to order. They are distributed by the producers in bulk packs containing assortments based on careful research. To every V, 0, I and F, for example, there will be five J's (most Dutch men are called Jan) and eight M's (as there are not only many Margriets but also a lot of Mummies). There are trends in this: one generation ago, the J was still topmost.

The letters are made by four or five big manufacturers, who begin production in the spring. They are cast in tin moulds, designed not only to preclude breakage as much as possible, but also to produce letters with the same weight, regardless of whether a J or a W is made.

The late 19th-century novel I mentioned, has children receiving their whole name spelt in chocolate. That would be regarded as extravagance now. But I am sure that the status of chocolate itself, being an expensive commodity, has played an important role in the popularity of the treat, which has grown spectacularly after the Second World war.

In the last few years, small confectioners have more and more taken to making specialty letters: ones made of marzipan, or of better-quality chocolate (although most industrial letters are of reasonable enough quality, considering what they might be). White chocolate, as everywhere, is up and coming, as popular taste seems to get sweeter and sweeter. In the 'seventies, not surprisingly, attempts have been made to market cheese letters, but they have failed - as have all attempts by manufacturers to sell chocolate ones outside the Netherlands.

There is one novelty in chocolate letters this year, an attempt to change the letter design which has been virtually the same since the 'thirties. At that time, sans serif letters became superseded by the present form, which I am told should be classified as bold Egyptian. Verkade, the largest producer, is now launching so-called 'digital letters' with a modern computer-type look. Such an innovation represents a considerable investment, as twenty new moulds need to be in working order for mass-production at once for the novelty to be saleable at all. The response by retailers, apparently, is most encouraging.

What the story of Dutch treats demonstrates, I think, is that the often-expressed opinion about national characteristics in food fading away in our time, is not quite true. The Dutch, like everybody else in the Western world, do of course celebrate with meals consisting of shrimp cocktails, steak-and-chips, and chocolate mousse. They eat more fast food and fewer of their traditional dishes. But in an affluent society, some old and quaint traditions can be kept up alongside all that. Industry and commerce, indeed, do all they can to exploit them. And so some of the most expensive folkloristic treats, like chocolate letters, thrive as never before. For as long as demand is big enough, and the article lends itself to attractive profit margins, modern industries are prepared to supply very awkward products.

ABCDEFG

HIJKLMNOPQRSTUVW

XYZ

Elements of Arab Feasting

by Charles Perry

'Muhammad ibn Abi al-Muammil used to say, "If people drank water with their food they would not suffer upset stomachs. The less they drink, the more they suffer. This is because a man does not know how much he has eaten until he takes some water... Doctors know that what I am saying is the truth, but they also know that if they adopted this view they would be out of work and lose all their fees."

'He used to say, "If it were not that water is cheap and bread is expensive, people would not be eager for bread and despise water. People are most full of praise for food when it is expensive or rare or out of season. These carrots of al-Sâfi and these green fava beans of al-'Abbâs are better than the pears of Khorâsân or the bananas of Bistân, but because people are short of understanding they only crave things as they are expensive and long for rarities...

' "I do not relish boiled carrots with vinegar and oil and *murri* (a condiment) over truffles in butter and pepper because they are cheap, but because their excellence is true and they are healthful. Who knows this, knows, and who knows this not, knows not." ' [1]

To us this passage sounds like the sober wisdom of a doctor or gourmet; in China or India it might have formed the basis of a school of diet. In the Near East, however, it is considered richly comic. The work it is quoted from is named *The Book of Misers*; to a ninth-century Baghdadi, it was self-evident that a host who refused to serve rare or expensive foods and even begrudged his guests their fill of bread was simply mean, and his theories of health and correct taste had to be laughably transparent hypocrisy.

That Muslims esteem hospitality is well known. Sayings honouring hospitality are among the most famous ascribed to Muhammad: 'The best among you is he who feeds people'. 'There is no good in him who is not a giver of hospitality'. 'Food for one is enough for two, food for two is enough for four, food for four is enough for eight'.

We tend to think this reflects the importance of hospitality in the harsh environment of Arabia. However, similar sayings can be found in most religions. There may also be a specific religious factor involved in the attitude toward feasting as well: the need to maintain a clear distinction between the day-time fasting and night-time feasting of Ramadan.

This may be partly why Islam, unlike some other religions, positively encourages meat-eating. On the last day of the Pilgrimage, Muslims - not only those in Mecca but all Muslims everywhere who can afford it - must sacrifice a lamb in memory of the sacrifice of Abraham. The Prophet is reported to have said, 'The lordliest food of the people of this world and of Paradise is meat', and to have praised his favourite wife saying, 'Aisha surpasses other women as *tharîd* [bread mixed with meat and broth] surpasses other dishes.' In Islam vegetarians, far from being considered especially pious, have often been suspected of heresy.

To the Prophet, a meal also represented not only the feeding of the guest but a religious grace, an occasion to enjoy the passionate spiritual brotherhood of Believers. There are also many traditions to this effect: 'Eat together and do not separate. Blessing is in society'. 'The best of food is that in which hands are many.' The most extreme statement in this line is attributed to the 11th of the 12 Shi'ite Imams, Ja'far al-Sâdiq: 'When you sit at the table with your brothers, sit long, for it is a time that is not counted against you as part of [the ordained span of] your lives.' [2]

To hospitality and religious brotherhood, the conquest of Persia added the elements of display and gourmet refinement. Ostentatious display had been known among the Bedouins, of course. A certain Hatim al-Ta'i gained fame by slaughtering all his camels merely to feed a casual guest. But traditions of the Prophet warn that he never saw a fattened sheep or ate from gold or silver vessels; never criticised food and always ate what was set before him.

There was a certain element of risk in offering hospitality. A 10th century Egyptian rhymester named Abu al-Qasim Husain al-Wasani wrote a lengthy comic ode on a village party to which an army of uninvited guests poured in from Arabia, North Africa, Central Asia, India and several imaginary places:

> 'They left me poorer than a chicken, nakeder of back than a snake.
> They ate 2,000 loaves of white bread, with cheese that shopowners would yearn to display.
> They ate 30 kids sharp with vinegar and saffron,
> They ate as much roast lamb and twice as much cooked in various dishes...
> They ate *madîrah* (a yogurt-flavoured stew), doubling my suffering with roast kid heads.

They ate *khashkhashiyah* (a poppyseed-flavoured stew) which lacerated my heart and stirred up my sorrow.
They ate 70 fish fresh from the river, of the largest.
They ate a middling portion of salty roasted fish thrown in vinegar and asafoetida.
They ate enough eggs and pickles to paralyze the villages of Khorasan,
They cut up quinces and apples and Raziqi dates and pomegranates,
And so much basil that I went into debt with Ahmad the fruiterer...
You may hear, o people, in the falling dusk the weeping of women and children
Calling wail and woe behind doors and walls
And saying, "Evil fortune to us because of Abu al-Qasim, who invited an army against us." '

When Muslim armies conquered Iran, however, they encountered a civilisation where the court had exulted in display dining. Herakleides of Kyme is quoted as saying a thousand animals were slaughtered daily for the Persian King: horses, camels, oxen, asses, deer and above all sheep. [3] The number of guests at the Shah's table is often given as 15,000.

The Persian court had elaborate conventions about the best of foods and their preparations. About half of a Middle Persian writing called 'The Story of King Khusrau and His Page' is a discussion of the finest dishes. As Unvala, its translator, has pointed out, this work was later known to the Arabs; a rendering appears in al-Tha'alibi's *History of the Persians* with surprisingly many of the gastronomic details intact (the lamb which has suckled from two mothers, the chicken fed on hempseeds, the pastry made from gazelle fat). The many Persian dishes in medieval Arabic cookery books and the Persian-style gourmet contests of the Abbasid Caliphs also attest to this influence.

These elements - hospitality, conviviality and gourmet display - combined in the medieval Arab feast. In the 12th century al-Hariri gave a classic description of the elements of a feast with his customary mixture of slyness and euphuistic language (the original is virtually clotted with untranslatable wordplay). The terms beginning "Father" or "Mother" are conventional expressions in the so-called *tufaili* or "uninvited guest" jargon.

'Abu Zaid said, "I think the Father of Indwelling [hunger] has kindled their stomachs to roasting, so call the Father of Assembling [the serving tray], for it is good news to all who hunger. Complement it with the Father of Pleasantness [white bread], patient at every wrong. [4] Fortify it with the Father of Lovingness [roast kid], dear to every heart, which has been turned about between burning and torment. [5] Call for the Father of Acuteness [vinegar], for how excellent a companion it is, and say, Bring hither the Father of Help [salt], for there is no help like it.

'"And if you were to send for the Father of Comeliness [vegetables: however, some commentators say the term means melted fat or gravy], it would be most comely. Be quick with the Mother of Hospitality [6] [*sikbâj*, meat stewed with vinegar, often served cold], bringing to mind Kisra. [7] Do not forget the Mother of Strengthening [*harîsah*, porridge of whole grain and meat], for how many rememberers she has, and call for the Mother of Joy [*jûdhâb*, roast meat served with a sort of Yorkshire pudding sweetened with sugar or fruit]. Then attack it; there is no objection.

' "And end with the Father of Dignity [*khabîs*, a date-flavoured pudding], which is the solace of every grief. And if you unite with it the Father of Loftiness [*falûdhaj*, another pudding, of Persian origin]. [8] you erase your name from (the rolls of the) misers." ' [9]

Footnotes

(1) Al-Jâhiz, *Kitâb al-Bukhalâ*, Dar Bairut lil-Tiba'ah wal-Nashr, Beirut 1974, pp. 138-9.
(2) Quoted in Muhammad al-Ghazâli, *The Revival of the Sciences of Religion*, al-Maktabah al-Tijariyyah al-kubra, Cairo n.d., vol.2, p.8.
(3) Athenaeus, *Deipnosophistae*, IV, 145-146.
(4) So called because it is beaten by the baker's hands and put in an oven.
(5) The references to roasting are also conventional expressions for the pangs of love.
(6) Because it was always offered to a guest, say the commentators.
(7) The Arabic form of the Persian royal name Khusrau.
(8) The names Father of Dignity and Father of Loftiness are said to refer to the costliness of these dishes.
(9) Al-Harîri, *Maqâmât*; maqamah #19, *nisîbiyyah*.

L'ORDRE DE BON TEMPS: GOOD CHEER AS THE ANSWER

by Jo Marie Powers, Associate Professor
Hotel and Food Administration, University of Guelph, Guelph, Ontario

The Order of Good Cheer is a unique feast in the history of feasting. Its significance lies in its being established specifically as a means of survival in an unknown land for men who knew that the winter would be long and bitterly cold and that many would die of scurvy. In the winter of 1606-1607, Samuel de Champlain spent his third winter in New France. Lodged in a habitation at Port Royal (now Annapolis Royal, Nova Scotia), Champlain initiated the Order of Good Cheer as the first formalized feasting and social club in the New World in an attempt to break the chain of winter illness and deaths from scurvy. The Order served also to bring together two widely differing cultures, the French and Micmac, at the common ground of the feast table. Samuel de Champlain writes of the Order:

> "We spent this winter very pleasantly, and had good fare by means of the Order of Good Cheer which I established, and which everybody found beneficial to his health, and more profitable than all sorts of medicine we might have used. This Order consisted of a chain which we used to place with certain little ceremonies about the neck of one of our people, commissioning him for that day to go hunting. The next day it was conferred upon another, and so on in order. All vied with each other to see who could do the best, and bring back the finest game. We did not come off badly, nor did the Indians who were with us." [Champlain, 1971:VI,447]

Thus in founding this feast, Champlain marked the importance of humankind's daily search for food: the need for both physical survival and for individual and communal life. This paper attempts to develop a picture not only of the foods of the feast, but of the structure and rituals of the feast.

Background

We can gain an understanding of why the Order of Good Cheer was established by looking at the series of events leading up to the winter of 1606-07. Fishing on the Newfoundland banks was the "unofficial" starting point: three to four hundred fishing vessels yearly left France for the great cod fishing grounds but they did not winter in New France [Denys 1908:259-269]. Many of these vessels carried a crew of fifty and built an extensive staging area for the salting and drying of the cod as well as lodgings for the crew on the shores of Newfoundland and Nova Scotia [Denys, 1908:269-283]. Thus, when Champlain reached Nova Scotia in 1604, he already was in possession of information about the country and the native people from fishermen who regularly traded with them [Lescarbot, 1928:4, 221]. He came to New France, however, lacking one crucial piece of information—the severity of the winters.

Long before Champlain's time, the first Frenchmen to winter in Canada, under the command of Jacques Cartier in 1535-36, were stricken down by a mysterious malady: "their legs became large and swollen, and their sinews shrank and grew black as coal, and with some all besprinkled with spots of blood almost purple." In addition, the "mouth withal became so infected and the gums so putrid that all the flesh fell away from them" [Baxter, 1906:190]. By mid-February of 1536, all but ten of the original 110 were at death's door. As the men died, and all hope seemed to fail, a captive native named Dom Agaya walked up to their ships. Ten to twelve days earlier he had been seriously ill, but now was completely cured. He told them of the remedy made from the "annedda" tree. A broth made from this tree was fed to the men every other day. The cure was immediate and appeared miraculous [Baxter, 1906:190-196].

In 1604, when Champlain was part of the exploratory expedition headed by the Lord of Monts "chiefly to populate, to manure, and to make the said lands to be inhabited", [Lescarbot, 1928:4] he knew about the disastrous plague that had visited Cartier, and the story of its cure. Champlain chose his first wintering site on Ile Sainte-Croix (now Dochet Island), however, for protection from the natives [Champlain, 1971:I,271-274].

An optimistic beginning turned into a nightmare as the men sickened and died of "land sickness" [Champlain, 1971:I,303]. As winter set in the Frenchmen were completely unprepared for the huge cakes of ice that prevented them from crossing to the mainland for fresh water and fuel [Champlain, 1971:I,306]. The cold was so severe that winter that even their cider froze, which they doled out by the pound [Champlain, 1971:I,306]. Of the seventy-nine who wintered there in 1604-1605, 35 died of scurvy.

The expedition party left Ile Ste.-Croix in July, 1605, and moved to Port Royal bringing most of the buildings with them [Champlain, 1971:I,367]. Both the habitations on Port Royal and Ile Ste.-Croix were drawn by Champlain and his drawings are our only surviving records of the settlement where the Order of Good Cheer was held (see figure

1). When the storeroom was built it had a cellar, presumably to keep the wine and cider from freezing [Champlain, 1971:I,367]. The bakeshop and kitchen were two different buildings [Champlain, 1971:I,372]. To the east of the settlement Champlain made his own personal garden, which he surrounded with streams of running water in which he put trout [Champlain, 1971:I,371]. That winter of 1605-06, twelve of the 45 men died of scurvy [Champlain, 1971:I,376].

In July of 1606, Poutrincourt arrived on the *Jonas* with fifty men and provisions, bringing along Marc Lescarbot, a young Parisian lawyer fleeing a wrong-doing in court. Shortly after arriving part of the group made an exploratory trip south, meeting with misfortune at every turn, including four men killed by the natives over a bread-baking incident. Limping back with broken rudder, nearly out of food, and dreading the ravages of the winter to come, they were met by Marc Lescarbot who greeted them on the beach with the first drama to be performed north of the Spanish settlements and which included a feasting passage [Champlain, 1971:I,438 and Lescarbot, 1928:115]. Across the waves came Neptune and his tritons, lauding the courage of "Sagamos" (native word for chief) or Poutrincourt.

> "Come, then, chefs, cooks, and boys—all you who make good cheer.
> Scullions and pastry cooks, let soup and roast appear,
> Ransack the kitchen shelves, fill every pot and pan
> And draw his own good portion for every eater man!
> I see the men are thirsty, SICUT TERRA, SINE AQUA
> Bestir yourselves, be brisk. Are the ducks on the spit?
> What fowl have lost their heats? The goose, who cares for it?
> Hither have sailed to us a band of comrades rare;
> Let portions and their hunger be matched with equal care."
> [Lescarbot, 1927:27]

This was an appropriate beginning for the winter in which it began to snow the end of December and the frosts lasted until the 12th of June, but the winter was not as severe as the previous. The drama on the waves of Port Royal set the stage for the Order of Good Cheer, founded to create good times under adverse circumstances.

Figure 1. Samuel de Champlain's drawing of the Habitation at Port Royal. The plan shows location of storeroom (C), the bakeshop (G), the kitchen (H), and gardens (I).

There is no information about menus and little about dishes served at the feast. Rather, reports of the feast emphasize the abundance of fresh meats, the ceremonies, and the beneficial effect of the Order. Documents examined for this paper include not only the two remaining eye-witness accounts, those of Samuel de Champlain and Marc Lescarbot, but also those of two other contemporary observers, Nicolas Denys and Pierre Biard.

The Structure of the Order

Lescarbot says, "there was an order established at the table of the said Monsieur de Poutrincourt" [Lescarbot, 1928:117]. The number in the Order was around fifteen: "[the Order] were every one at his turn and day (which was in fifteen days once) steward and caterer" [Lescarbot, 1928:117]. The original documents do not tell us who the Members of the Order were. This can be deduced by the customs of the time and the practices of the Order. In the spring of 1606, there were 33 survivors and Sieur de Poutrincourt brought 50 men. When the *Jonas* went back to France in the autumn of 1606, we do not know how many from the previous year were aboard. We can say that there were somewhere between 50 and 83 men (no women were aboard) at the habitation during the winter of 1606-07.

From French custom of the time the membership was most likely to be made up of the officers and gentlemen who ate at a separate table from their men. In Denys' description of the fishing establishments in the New World, the captain, beach master, pilot and doctor ate in a lodging separate from the fishermen's mess. This would seem to be in keeping with Champlain's statement that a captain should not be on "too familiar terms with his ship's company except with the officers" [Champlain, 1971:I,xiii]. Table 1 is a list of likely candidates for the Order drawn from the voyagers' accounts. While the surgeon and apothecary are included in this list, we do not know if they would have been acceptable members of the Order. In France at the time there were distinct class differences, definitely present at the dinner table. There appeared to have been some lessening of these barriers away from home.

Unfortunately, there is no indication of dining areas on any sketches of the habitations that Champlain made—of Ile Ste. Croix, Port Royal, or Quebec—to give us a clue whether separate buildings for the Order and the men were used. On the Ste. Croix drawing, a public building (where they went during the rain) is the building closest to the kitchen. The custom of the time would indicate separate dining rooms for the Order and the common men. Yet the purpose of the Order was to benefit all and the motive to survive the winter was strong. The group was of a different composition from the fishing camps, and the period of time was much longer than the six months the fishermen spent on the cod banks. In any case, even if separated at dinner, the fact that many of the common men went hunting, indicates that they felt the influence of the Order. Whether the men ate together as a group may never be known.

Issue of Natives. Lescarbot states that the Sagamos, including the powerful Membertou, Sagamos of the Souriquois (Micmac) ate with them: "But as for the Sagamos Membertou and other Sagamos (when any came to us), they sat at table eating and drinking as we did; and we took pleasure in seeing them, as contrariwise their absence was irksome unto us" [Lescarbot, 1928:119]. Native custom probably dictated that Membertou was surrounded by young unmarried men who accompanied the powerful chiefs. We do not know if they or his sons Actaudin and Actaudinech (the two whose names we have) were invited to eat with the Order [Lescarbot, 1928:129]. It is not likely that his wife or any native women ate with the Order since the custom of a tabagie (native feast) was that the women ate separately from the men [Lescarbot, 1928:222]. According to Lescarbot there were always twenty to thirty natives around the habitation [Lescarbot, 1928:118].

Table 1

CANDIDATES FOR MEMBERSHIP IN THE ORDER OF GOOD CHEER

Name	Biographical Notes
1. Samuel de Champlain	Established Order; geographer of expedition; about 35 yrs. old; later to found Quebec City and thus called Father of New France.
2. Marc Lescarbot	Lawyer, poet, playwright; Poutrincourt his law client; his *History of New France* made his fame as an historian; loved singing, dancing, laughing, and "making good cheer".
3. Jean de Biencourt (Sieur de Poutrincourt)	Leader of the expedition to Port Royal; his desire was to find a home for his family in the New York, but he died before attaining his dream.

4.	Champdoré (Pierre Augibaut)	Pilot of barque; obstinate to the point of being put in chains for running aground, but a genius for repairing and navigating (and thus forgiven his misdeeds).
5.	Robert Pont-Gravé	Son of the navigator du Pont (du Pont returned to France for winter); in an exploration south of Port Royal Robert lost three fingers in a skirmish with the Indians.
6.	Sieur de Boullet	"Sometimes" Captain of the regiment; later became brother-in-law of Champlain.
7.	Le Fevre of Retel	Young nobleman prone to seasickness.
8.	Charles de Biencourt	Eldest son of Poutrincourt
9.	Foulgeré of Vitré	Nobleman.
10.	De Noyes	Nobleman.
11.	Ralleau	Secretary to M. de Monts (de Monts had been granted a monopoly for the fur trade and a royal commission to establish settlements in New France).
12.	Master Stephen	Surgeon.
13.	Master Louis Hébert	Apothecary who grew herbs and delighted in cultivating the earth; settled in Quebec where he is considered the first farmer.

This list is a compilation of names mentioned by Champlain and Lescarbot during 1606-1607. A list of the occupants of the habitation did not survive. Of notable absence is a priest. In La Rochelle Lescarbot tried to find a priest replacement without success, not knowing that the priest in New France had died.

During the winter of the feast Poutrincourt undertook to feed some of the Micmac who were starving because of the mild winter. This does not mean that they were fed with the members of the Order. In a later volume of his memoirs, Champlain said that only chiefs ate at his table [Champlain, 1971:VI,8].

The Rituals of the Feast

Ceremonies played a crucial role in the Order of Good Cheer. These were repetitively performed as the feast was held daily throughout the winter. One man was appointed the Governor of the feast or Steward (called "atoctegic" by the Micmac) each day. Two days before his turn as organizer, the Steward went hunting or fishing and provided "some dainty thing, besides that which was of our ordinary allowance" [Lescarbot, 1928:118]. The Steward instructed the cook to prepare the food, and when all was ready, the Steward "did march with his napkin on his shoulder and his staff of office in his hand, with the collar of the order about his neck, which was worth above four crowns, and all of them of the order following of him, bearing every one a dish. The like also was at the bringing in of the fruit [dessert], but not with so great a train. And at night, after grace was said, he resigned the collar of the order, with a cup of wine, to his successor in that charge, and they drank one to another" [Lescarbot, 1928:118].

The Steward provided food for all three meals each day, and it is probable that the great banquet was at night. The French custom was to have the main meal or dinner around one o'clock and supper between seven and eight o'clock [Vence, 1978:43]. However, in the fishing camps, the men were provided with bread and drink until evening when they ate their principal meal [Denys, 1908:318]. Lescarbot said: "at breakfast we never wanted some modicum or other of fish or flesh; and, at the repast of dinners and suppers, yet less; for it was the great banquet", indicating the great feast was in the evening [Lescarbot, 1928:118].

We can assume that there was entertainment added—singing, dancing, and perhaps even drama, as was the custom of the time after feasting in France. Lescarbot himself liked a good time—during the month in La Rochelle he had so much "good cheer" that he was anxious for the ship's diet, and during the voyage over the men danced and sang [Lescarbot 1928:64,73].

We also know that at the celebrations in Port Royal, Membertou, after dancing, made long orations, during which the custom was for all the attention to focus upon the speechmaker [Lescarbot, 1928:237]. (Besides eating, a necessary part of the Micmac tabagie was smoking tobacco, dancing, singing and speechmaking) [Lescarbot, 1928:229,235]. The French enjoyed Membertou's speeches and shared his sense of humour. Most likely, passing around a pipe of tobacco would have been in order as the natives considered it rude not to accept a pipe in friendship, and the French liked the habit, too [Lescarbot, 1928:298].

The Foods for the Feast

Although it is impossible to reconstruct the menus for the Order of Good Cheer, we can identify the raw ingredients for the feast with accuracy. As well, Lescarbot and Denys both identify in their writings dishes that might have been prepared. Approximately some fifteen dishes were cooked each meal, since Lescarbot states that each man following the "atoctegic" marched out in procession "bearing every one a dish" [Lescarbot, 1928:118]. These dishes prepared came from sources ranging from shipped provisions to native supplies and local foraging and hunting. The probable dishes show a remarkable range and variety.

Ship's Provisions. Although a ship's record of provisions does not exist for the *Jonas*, Lescarbot tells us the limitations of the ship's rations: "For our allowance we had peas, beans, rice, prunes, raisins, dry cod, and salt flesh, besides oil and butter" [Lescarbot, 1928:96]. The foods were chosen to provide the most nourishment in the least space. A typical fisherman/sailor was provided with between 3,500 and 4,500 kilocalories per day at the end of the 16th century [Turgeon, 1990:8]. Also, we know that for the winter of 1606, the settlement was furnished with 45 tons of wine and "everyone had three quarts of pure and good wine a day" (1 1/2 pints by today's measure) [Lescarbot 1928:45,96]. The wine was of utmost importance on the journey over because fresh water keeps only several weeks at sea [Turgeon, 1990:4].

"Other little conveniences" [Denys, 1908:270] were brought along as well. The Captain, in the on-shore fishing camps, for instance, generally had cheese with his bread at lunch while the men had bread only. He also had vegetables from an onshore garden, and game if time permitted hunting. Live animals such as wethers (sheep), chickens and pigeons were carried on shipboard for the captain's use; they also provided eggs [Denys, 1908:318]. In Port Royal, Lescarbot said, "We had hogs which have multiplied very much. We had one wether which proved very well. We had no other household cattle, but hens and pigeons, which failed not to yield the accustomed tribute, and to multiply abundantly" [Lescarbot, 1928:274].

Lescarbot tells us of the "little conveniences", but we do not know if the Order of Good Cheer had access to them. In May of 1607, after the winter, a young man from St. Malo, Chevalier, was to have brought them "six wethers, 24 hens, a pound of pepper, 20 pounds of rice, as many of raisins, and of prunes, a thousand of almonds, a pound of nutmeg, a quarter of cinnamon, two pounds of maces, half a pound of cloves, two pounds of citron-rinds, two dozen of citrons, as many oranges, a Westphalia gammon of bacon, and six other gammons, a hogshead of Gascony wine and as much of sack, a hogshead of powdered beef, four bottles and a half of oil-of-olive, a jar of olives, a barrel of vinegar, and two sugar-loaves" [Lescarbot, 1928:128]. Unfortunately, Chevalier claimed when he reached them the animals had died and that his crew ate the rest because they thought the exploration party was dead. It is quite possible that the provisioning for this winter had more "conveniences" because it was financed by M. de Monts who had spent the miserable winter on Ile Ste. Croix in 1604.

Native Contributions. The native people in the vicinity of Port Royal were Micmac, hunters and gatherers. Rarely did they store up food for winter since they were amply provided for by nature. Pierre Biard, who lived in Port Royal in 1611-1613, described the seasonality of their food as a matter of dividing the year into thirteen moons and using appropriate food sources in each one—as, for example, seal hunting in January [Biard, 1616:78-81].

October until middle of March meant the season for wild game—beaver, otters, moose, bears, and caribou [Biard, 1616:79-80]. But even with the use of dogs, the Micmac were highly dependent upon snow—for use of snowshoes which allowed them to go over the top of the snow to capture floundering animals [Lescarbot, 1928:270]. A wet winter (and the winter of 1606 was one) was the reason the Micmac were starving [Champlain, 1971:I,447].

March and April meant the spawning of fish—first the smelt, then the herring, and toward the end sturgeon and salmon. April also brought eggs of many waterfowl. From May until fall there was never a lack of food since cod as well as other fish and shellfish were plentiful [Biard, 1616:78-81].

Moose and beaver were the primary winter sources of meat for the Micmac in this area of New France. Wearing snowshoes, they hunted moose with bows and arrows, aided by trained dogs. French guns would prove an advantage in hunting these beasts, which were much esteemed during the winter of the Order of Good Cheer. Beaver was added probably strictly through the agency of the natives, who—since the beaver does not go on land in winter—used a complicated process of cutting through ice and, by hand, grabbed the beaver from its lodge. Lescarbot considered the best and most delicate part of the beaver to be the tail, and that its flesh was good and tender, like beef [Lescarbot, 1928:269-273].

Natives were probably taken along on a hunt to insure a Steward's supply of meat. As well, they were a most giving people for the feasting. It was the native custom that the hunter who killed the animal for the tabagie ate none of it himself but gave it all to the members of his tribe [Lescarbot, 1928:271]. Lescarbot states that half of what the Micmac brought back was given to the French [Lescarbot, 1928:96].

Lescarbot certainly included natives in his hunting expeditions. A new cooking method was encountered and reported by Lescarbot during a moose hunt. First the hunters roasted the moose, making a "very dainty feast with this venison, more tender than any other kind of flesh", and then a native made a delicious broth as follows: a native quickly framed a trough with his hatchet from a tree and cooked the meat in the wooden container with red hot rocks, renewing them from time to time (presumably adding water to the tub) [Lescarbot, 1927:270-271].

The Gardens near the Habitation. Seeds of grain and garden vegetables brought from France were planted not only for the needs of the settlement, but also to determine if the land could sustain European agriculture. In fact, Poutrincourt delayed his return to France in order to harvest grain to be presented to the king. A spring planting of root vegetables was not specifically mentioned by either Champlain or Lescarbot. There was, however, a period of several months between explorations when a planting could have been made and gardens tended. Both Poutrincourt and Lescarbot are recorded as sowing grains, legumes and vegetables plus garden herbs in the autumn. [Lescarbot, 1928:43,93,95,133; Champlain, 1971:I,439].

Over the winter, bread for both explorers and natives was plentiful. We can assume that they either brought wheat or flour with them for the winter although this was not included in the list of provisions. They did not mention harvesting grain in Port Royal, but were surprised when they went to Ile Ste.-Croix to find rye as tall as a man and ready for harvest [Lescarbot, 1928:26,293]. It is likely that they had rye bread during the winter. It is also possible that they traded for Indian corn from tribes south of Port Royal (the Micmac practiced no agriculture).

The Flora and Fauna of Port Royal. For the winter of the Order of Good Cheer, Lescarbot wrote "we had an abundance of game", consisting mostly of birds, and wild animals that the Micmac caught [Lescarbot, 1928:118]. While there was no ice on the bay, the men gathered shellfish, either in their shallops or on the tidal flats [Lescarbot, 1928:285]. Besides mussels, large sea scallops, cockles and sea urchins, clams, sea snails, crabs and lobsters were abundant, although oysters are not mentioned in connection with this settlement [Lescarbot, 1928:285, Champlain, 1971:249].

Many varieties of fish were caught until winter set in, after which they caught salmon and trout through the ice [Denys, 1908:559]. In addition, game birds of all kinds were provided throughout the winter by a servant of de Monts, François Addeni [Lescarbot, 1971:278].

Lescarbot described edible flora consisting of vines, wild onions, wild peas and "good herbs" growing in the area [Lescarbot, 1928:86]. Roots (probably Jerusalem artichokes) were described as well as walnuts (possibly butternuts, the only nut tree of this kind in this region) and acorns [Lescarbot, 1928:86,351 and Biard,1616:259]. Fruits growing in the area included gooseberries, raspberries and strawberries, but there was no mention of any put away for winter use [Lescarbot, 1928:86,301]. Cranberries were gathered during the winter and made into a marmalade to serve with meats [Lescarbot, 1928:301]. Early in the spring Lescarbot drank maple sap, shown to him by the natives [Lescarbot, 1928:247].

The Dishes Prepared for the Feast

For the Order of Good Cheer Lescarbot asserts "we made as good dishes of meat as in the cook's shops that be in La Rue aux Ours" (a Paris street of shops specializing in roasted meats) [Lescarbot, 1928:118]. The Members of the Order neither did the cooking nor the baking. It is learned from Lescarbot that the stone carvers and masons became bakers, and that there was a cook who prepared the food [Lescarbot, 1928:96,118]. The only preparations that Lescarbot decribed were the beneficial nature of a *colice* (a hearty broth) made of a cock [Lescarbot, 1928:45], and good pastries made of moose and turtle doves [Lescarbot, 1928:97,118] (today in Quebec the tortière or meat pie is traditional fare). On the fishing banks, he enjoyed white sausages made from the flesh and innards of cod with lard and spice [Lescarbot 1928:80].

Nicolas Denys' description of food preparation from his observations of mariner/fishermen's lives on the shores of

New France during the summer months provides some insight into cooking practices of the time. For instance, in the fishing camps, boys served the food and worked for the steward who was in charge of the cooking for the fishermen.

Daily mariners were served a plate of boiled peas or beans boiled with oil or butter, and on Sunday, pork (assumably salt pork) was cooked with the legumes [Denys, 1908:318]. Presumably this was served daily to the Order (and it is not surprising that it became French Canada's traditional soup).

Denys provides us with considerable information about how fish and animals living in water (which they considered to be fish) were prepared. Typically fish such as cod, mackerel and halibut was either boiled, or roasted on a spit, and often served with oil and/or vinegar [Denys, 1908:318]. Fish could be cooked "in every other sauce that can be made for the sole, and the body also (is excellent) on a short boiling with good herbs and orange" [Denys, 1908:355]. Sturgeon, its flesh considered as good as beef, was carved into slices and boiled four to five hours [Denys 1908:353]. For frying fish, seal oil was considered good [Denys 1908:349]. The "four-legged fish" (and thus allowed during Lent), muskrat, otter and beaver were excellent roasted [Denys, 1908:361]. The pluck (heart, liver and lungs) were fried and black puddings and chitterlings were made from the tripe of porpoise [Denys, 1908:351].

Shellfish preparations were popular among the fishermen. Squid was roasted, boiled or fried and "makes the sauce black." [Denys, 1908:359]. Lobsters were "good eating with all kinds of sauces" [Denys, 1908:356]. Tortoise was first boiled, and the shell removed; it was then skinned, cut into pieces and made into a fricassee with a white sauce. According to Denys, "there are no pullets which are as good as this" [Denys,1908:359].

Preparations would have been influenced by cooking practices in France. The Members of the Order were very much familiar with the latest trends in dining in Paris, and they were equally familiar with the port towns, particularly La Rochelle, and preparations would certainly have followed current trends in France, limited only by availability and seasonality of raw materials. Church laws of fast and abstinence could also have influenced their menu. In their preparations, it is not likely that they used native preparations because generally, they did not care for native food because the natives never used salt or spices [Lescarbot, 1928:119].

Some mystery surrounds the dessert course. Desserts were popular in France then and this course was an integral part of the banquet. It must have taxed the imagination of the cook to create variety using only raisins and prunes. Sugar must have been scarce, if any. They might have cooked these dried fruits with the wines—particularly if they had sweet wines.

The Order's Effectiveness Against Scurvy

Since lurking in the background of any feast, as the conference title points out, is the possibility of fasting, it is appropriate to return to the central impetus of the Order of Good Cheer—combating the "imposed" fasting by the members of the exploratory party. The men of Port Royal experienced a "fast" that obviated fresh meat, fruits and vegetables from their diets for long stretches and left them easy prey to scurvy.

Caused by a deficiency of ascorbic acid (vitamin C), symptoms of scurvy appear in about eleven to twenty weeks [Carpenter, 1986:200-204]. Before this, fatigue and melancholy are signs of the onset of the illness [Carpenter, 1986: 241-42]. The disease is easily remedied by the addition of most fresh fruits and vegetables, and some raw game meats, and, recovery is rapid—reports of men able to work in 6 days to two weeks [Lind, 1753:Carpenter, 1986:200-204]. An intake of about 10 mg of vitamin C a day can prevent the disease [Carpenter, 1986:224]. The only known cure at the time was the mysterious annedda provided by the natives on the St. Lawrence [Baxter, 1906:196]. The Micmac were not aware of this tree (probably since they had no history of the disease). It is thought that the tree was the white cedar, an infusion of which contains 200 mg vitamin C per 100 g of leaves [Rousseau as cited by Carpenter, 1986:229]. This cedar was brought to France in 1542 and named "arbor vitae" or tree of life, the reason for its name and its use had been lost by the time Champlain went to Nova Scotia [Carpenter, 1986:10]. According to both Lescarbot and Champlain, the Micmac were healthy which the explorers attributed to their "sweatings", but native winter diet contained enough ascorbic acid from fresh game to prevent signs of scurvy (cooked deer liver is high in vitamin C and stewed bear meat has a small amount of vitamin C for example [Health & Welfare Canada, 1984]).

For food remedies Lescarbot discoursed on the use of "good" meat such as capons, partridges, ducks and rabbits (rather than "rude, gross, cold and melancholy meats" or those without sauces), as well as good wine as a "sovereign preservative for all sicknesses" [Lescarbot, 1928:45]. (The sick drank wine through a "pipe" [straw] as their mouths became diseased) [Lescarbot, 1928:45]. Lescarbot made a list of foods that physicians recommended be avoided that was so extensive that Lescarbot said one might starve instead [Lescarbot, 1928:37]! Other causes were suspected - air, winds, sun, waters, and the season. Spring, of course, brought a cure and Lescarbot went many times to gather young buds of herbs for his sick before the garden was ready [Lescarbot, 1928:45].

A common theme runs through the narrations of the early explorers that the primary cause of scurvy was salted meat and the lack of activity of the men. According to Lescarbot, the ones who were affected by the disease were "they that use not a stirring life, but sitting and without frequent motion, are more apt and subject to these sicknesses" [Lescarbot, 1928:42] as well as those "always grudging, repining, never content, idle, have been found out by the same disease", and those who died were of a "fretful condition or sluggish" [Lescarbot, 1928:119]. He recommended the best preservative was joy in life, taking pleasure in work, and the company of one's lawful wife [Lescarbot, 1928:47] While one would prefer to think that a good time and activity are health-giving, they are, more likely, signs of good health, and the malaise and exhaustion were warnings of the onset of scurvy. Perhaps the hunters had the first choice of game and a heartier appetite, thus consuming a sufficient amount of fresh meat (and particularly deer liver) to avert the illness.

Did the Order of Good Cheer achieve its purpose? Unfortunately during the winter of 1606-1607 there was still scurvy in the fragile outpost, but much less severe than before. Four, according to Lescarbot, and seven, according to Champlain, died during the winter and others were ill with it, but there was no mention of deaths among the Members of the Order of Good Cheer. It is likely that the needed ascorbic acid came from a variety of sources—small amounts from the fresh meats, from fresh vegetables and the cranberry marmalade, or from "little conveniences". The mild winter was certainly a factor, allowing as it did, garden salads until late in the fall and early wild herbs in the spring.

Conclusions

A major purpose of the Order of Good Cheer, to fight scurvy, had limited success, but the Order had other, unqualified successes. The winter was unquestionably pleasant, even with illnesses, and the Order met its purpose of raising morale. Lasting only a year in time, the Order had an unexpected bonus of a lasting friendship between the Micmac, under the leadership of Membertou, and the French. Telling stories, laughing together, singing, and, most of all, eating together created a bond that lasted throughout Membertou's lifetime. There was, on the part of both cultures, a strong sense of giving throughout the feasting, and this ensured the survival of both the natives and the French.

The forum of the Order helped, for a short time, to lower class barriers. The nobles served the food, unheard of for gentlemen in France, and, learned the pleasures of working with their hands by hunting and by tilling their gardens. More than anything else, their love of life and sense of adventure comes alive. I think that their view of life and the true achievement of the Order of Good Cheer, can be summarized by Samuel de Champlain's comments on the first summer he spent in Port Royal:

"This spot was completely surrounded by meadows, and there I arranged a summer-house with fine trees, in order that I might enjoy the fresh air. I constructed there likewise a small reservoir to hold salt-water fish, which we took out as we required them. I also sowed there some seeds which throve well; and I took therein a particular pleasure, although before hand it had entailed a great deal of labour. We often resorted there to pass the time, and it seemed as if the little birds thereabouts received pleasure from this; for they gathered in great numbers and warbled and chirped so pleasantly that I do not think I ever heard the like" [Champlain, 1971:I,371].

References

Biard, Pierre, "Relation of New France" (1616) in Thwaites, Reuben Gold, Ed., *The Jesuit Relations and Allied Documents, Vol.III*. New York: Pageant Book Company, 1959.

Baxter, James Phinney, *A Memoir of Jacques Cartier*. New York: Dodd, Mead & Company, 1906.

Carpenter, Kenneth J., *The History of Scurvy & Vitamin C*. Cambridge: Cambridge University Press, 1986.

Champlain, Samuel de, *The Works of Samuel de Champlain*, Vol. I-VI. Reprinted, translated and annotated by six Canadian scholars under the editorship of H.P. Biggar, published by the Champlain Society. Toronto: University of Toronto Press, 1971.

Denys, Nicolas, *The Description and Natural History of the Coasts of North America (Acadia)*. Translated and edited by William F. Ganong. Toronto: Champlain Society, 1908.

Health and Welfare Canada, *Nutrient Bar Graph, A Teaching Aid to Learn the Value of Native Foods*, Ottawa: 1984.

Lescarbot, Marc, *Nova Francia: a Description of Acadia, 1606*. Translated by P. Erondelle, 1609. New York and London: Harper and Brothers, 1928.

Lescarbot, Marc, *The Theatre of Neptune in New France*. With translation by Harriette Taber Richardson. Boston: Houghton Mifflin, 1927.

Turgeon, Laurier and Denis Dickner, "Contraintes et choix alimentaires d'un groupe d'appartenance: les marins-pecheurs français a Terre-Neuve au XVI siecle", paper presented at the XVe colloque de l'institut d'études

médiévales, University of Montreal, Quebec: May, 1990.
Vence, Céline and Robert Courtine, *The Grand Masters of French Cuisine*. Edited, with Introductory Notes, by Philip and Mary Hyman. New York: G.P. Putnam's Sons, 1978.

Beans for the Dead

by Gillian Riley

Giacomo Castelvetro, in his account of the fruit, herbs and vegetables of Italy, gives two recipes for dried broad beans, *Vicia faba*. The refined way is to remove the tough outer skin and stew the beans in water with sage or rosemary and serve them with pepper and olive oil. In the coarse version the beans are cooked whole and eaten with oil and pepper. This dish, says Castelvetro, 'is seldom eaten by gentlefolk, except on the day that superstitious papists dedicate to their dead, when custom has it that everyone prepares large quantities to give away to the poor, in the fond belief that this will relieve the excessive torments of their ancestors, languishing in purgatory.'

These *fave dei morti*, had by Castelvetro's time, the early 17th century, become a conveniently cheap way of showing respect to the dead and doing good to the poor on the feast of All Souls. By the mid-nineteenth century Gioachino Belli knew them as inexpensive sweetmeats, *ossetti da morto*. He laments in a sonnet to his favourite cousin Ursula that he is so hard up he cannot even afford to send her a few for the *Santa Befana*:

> 'Sora racchietta mia, proprio quest'anno
> che m' annate più a sangue e più a faciolo,
> non ho potuto ave' manco un pignolo
> né un ossetto da morto ar mi comanno...'

The recipe given by Vittorio Metz in his edition of a selection of Belli's sonnets, happily married to appropriate traditional Roman dishes, is similar to Artusi's *Fave alla romana o dei morti*. These are little almond biscuits in the shape of beans, or bones. Metz and his brother, when they were small, had a miserable time of it on the night of 2 November, wondering if the greedy dead would have eaten up all the huge pile of biscuits their mother had ceremoniously placed on the dining room table.

The ancient Romans, too, offered beans to their dead. The broad bean was the only bean they knew; it had been around the Middle East since about 3000 BC and associated with religious practices for almost as long. Pliny and Cicero commented on Pythagoras's prohibition of beans, '*A fabis abstineto*' and subsequent writers have commented at length on them. He also forbade his followers to eat fish or meat of any sort, fresh or dried, and to consume only fresh, tender young vegetables, roots, flowers or seeds, that needed the minimum of cooking. Eggs were allowed, but not milk or wine. Beans, he held, were of the same putrid composition as flesh, and so were as harmful. Later, writers claimed that they clouded the brain and disturbed sleep and gave rise to unwholesome and libidinous thoughts. The strange black markings on their white flowers were thought to be evil symbols. According to Pliny, Pythagoras believed that beans contained the souls of the dead, another reason for not eating them. The use of beans when casting votes gave them a political connotation, so Pythagoras may also have meant 'Steer clear of politics.'

As a young man, Pythagoras was trained with Egyptian priests, and to some extent his views on beans reflect the religious and dietary practices of the ancient Egyptians, who were said to have prohibited the cultivation and consumption of beans. But the evidence we have is not entirely clear. You can't prohibit a food that doesn't exist. The ancient Egyptian name for the broad bean is held by some authorities to be *pr* and *fel* in Coptic, which is close to Arabic *foul*. Those heaving pots of stewed beans had a name in Coptic, *metmes*, which resembles *foul medamès*, a popular dish of stewed beans in present day Egypt.

Rameses III offered as a sacrifice to the god of the Nile eleven thousand nine hundred and ninety nine jars of shelled beans. And they have been found in tombs and temples from the fifth to the twelfth dynasty. So the Gods and the masses seemed to have gone on enjoying this robust, nutritious food whilst the priesthood and upper classes endured the prohibition. Classical Roman writers commented on Pythagoras's views on beans, but did not endorse his strictures. Legumes were an important part of the Roman diet and some distinguished Roman families were named after pulses - Cicero (chickpeas), Fabius (broad beans). Beans figured in offerings of food in ceremonies for the dead, and like many other pagan rituals, these ceremonies were taken on board by the Catholic church. As late as the mid-sixteenth century the bishop of Bologna, Cardinal Gabriele Paleotti complained about the superstitious practices that were contaminating the funeral service; one of these was the habit of handing out broad beans to the congregation, with the priest's share prudently converted into cash.

A saying from Genoa
> *Ai morti, bacilli e stocchefisce*
> *no gh'è casa che no i condisce,*

refers to a time when boiled stockfish and stewed dried broad beans were staple fare in Liguria on All Saints' day. A tentative investigation of the role of other varieties of bean in Mexican celebrations of the Day of the Dead, *Todos Santos,* seems to show that beans, although a basic food in both urban and rural areas, did not have a significant role in the festivities. The offerings for the dead, on domestic and ecclesiatical altars, are festival rather than everyday food, the tamales and moles of pre-Christian cultures, not the basic bean dishes.

As we have seen the beans were later transmogrified into biscuits. In Venice they were called *ossi da morto.* One version from Salgaredo in Treviso was a hard, crunchy biscuit made of flour, yeast, butter, a little sugar and a pinch of salt. These were left to cook in the oven after the bread had come out and must have been rather tough cookies, best eaten at the end of a meal, dunked in wine or coffee. A version from the countryside was made of sugar whipped up with eggs for ten minutes with a wooden spoon, and the flour folded lightly in and baked for fifteen minutes in a very hot oven.

In the area around Verona the *ossi da morto* were made from a soft polenta, stiffened with a little flour and seasoned with salt and pepper, made up into plump shapes, tapering at each end, and baked until crisp. From Treviso comes another yeast biscuit, bread dough mixed with butter or oil, flavoured with anise and honey, moulded into bone-like shapes, about ten centimetres long, baked in a moderate oven, and then given a second baking to dry them out, as th name *biscotti* implies.

Ada Boni has a more sophisticated version of the Roman *fave dei morti,* in which almonds are pounded with sugar, mixed with flour, egg and butter, flavoured with cinnamon and grated lemon peel, formed into little bean shapes and cooked until golden. They come soft out of the oven and harden when cool.

I end this somewhat ragged survey of the manifestations of 'beans for the dead' on a diffident note. The commonsense approach is notoriously the fall-back position of the intellectually inadequate, but in fairness to Pythagoras we must admit that the prohibition of beans, in the light of the Observer's recent candid survey of the fart, is a sensible measure to be observed by any priest and congregation operating in confined quarters. The admirable Harold Magee has provided us with guidelines for the preparation of beans which helps us to understand and deal with some of the factors which create flatulence. Meanwhile another of Pythagoras's injunctions, that beans should never be prepared with salt or sea-water, is surely a sensible way of making sure we cook them soft before adding seasonings, rather than some arcane spiritual discipline.

A staple food, with strange associations, conveniently transposed from its origins in the prehistoric near East, via the funerary rituals of many different civilisations, to the repertoire of a provincial Northern Italian *pasticceria,* is a topic impossible to cover in such a brief survey. I would be grateful to receive any further information about the *fava dei morti* in any of its historic manifestations.

The First Communion Banquet

by Alicia Rios

The First Communion is a religious and social event which marks the end of early childhood for the majority of Christian children.

The Eucharistic banquet, held during the sacrifice of mass in church, is followed by a social communion, the sharing of a banquet. In Spain this celebration is becoming increasingly ostentatious as nowadays it is a symbol of economic power and social aspirations.

It is perhaps one of the few surviving ritual banquets which, like weddings, are also democratic. There are similar connotations and external signs at almost all levels of urban and rural society. Aesthetic and cultural criteria are the only differential indicators, as there is widespread uniformity with regard to the level of extravagance and disproportionate amount of money invested in the necessary clothes, banquet, service and gifts. In this initiation rite the communicants take on an important role for the first time, as interlocutors of divinity in a sacramental dialogue.

They learn the importance of their religious initiation by means of the catechism, and prepare to receive the sacraments of penance and the Eucharist for the first time. This spiritual banquet is preceded by a fast by way of organic preparation.

This event is usually described as "the happiest day of my life". It is indeed a very happy time, as it means being in the social limelight for the first time, symbolised by white, the colour of innocence, which governs the whole celebration. But above all, for the first time they are taking a leading role before God in an intimate discussion with the consecrated bread and wine, the body of Christ, inside them.

The Meaning of the Ritual

The Bible describes the aspirations of the people of Israel and their secret hope of taking part in divine life. Their history describes their effort to overcome all the obstacles in their path, guided by divine intervention and revelation. First by means of the prophets, then by the Gospel, God had been purifying their way of life, social organisation, laws, civil institutions, domestic customs and rituals and religious ceremonies, thus moving away from the hitherto common practices of the other peoples of ancient times. New principles of supernatural life were the driving force in the lives of the Hebrew people.

These moral and religious truths, destined to mould and govern human life, were perpetuated with the consolidation of the Church, which maintains the same rituals, liturgies and dogmas, and still gives out the sacraments as a sign of salvation.

The Origins of the Ritual

The ritual can be traced back to two sources:
- a) Jewish Passover
- b) The Last Supper

The Jews were living oppressed on Egyptian soil. Yahweh echoed their endless pleas and Moses was appointed as liberator and guide to lead the Hebrew people to the promised land of milk and honey. The people of Israel needed to make sacrifices to Yahweh. Moses asked the Pharaoh in vain to allow them to go to the desert for three days to make their blood sacrifices, but the Pharaoh's hard heart turned out to be an insurmountable obstacle. As a punishment, Yahweh sent plagues to Egypt to show how he could work miracles. Yahweh finally announced to Moses and Aaron the celebration of the sacrifice which started the custom of Passover (Exodus XII-XIV).

The meaning of the ritual is shown in Exodus XII, 21-29.

Following the institution of Passover, the Pharaoh urged Moses and Aaron to leave Egypt with their children of Israel, with their oxen and sheep to celebrate the sacrifice. Yahweh enacted the law of Passover and the Exodus began (Exodus XII, 43-50).

The Ritual or Sacrament

The Last Supper

Jesus Christ, the son of God, had become a man and had established the sacraments as signs of salvation through which grace, light and divine strength are received.

The Church, today, still grants salvation by means of sacraments such as the Eucharist which re-enacts the sacrifice of the Holy Mass in the Last Supper. The Epistle to the Corinthians describes the establishment of the Eucharist (Corinthians I, XI, 23-25). The Gospels give a description of the Last Supper (Matthew XXVIII, 17-29; Mark XIV, 12-25; Luke XXII, 7-23 and John XIII).

The Menu of the Last Supper

For religious reasons the dinner consisted simple of some herbs, chicory and wild lettuce, seasoned with salt and olive oil, roast lamb, unleavened bread and wine.

The herbs were eaten as an appetiser, authentic aperitifs with stimulating properties. The salt and oil were a symbol of blessing and joy. The meat, the main dish of the sacrifices and festivities, was eaten after being bled. Yahweh had declared blood to be the soul of the meat. The lamb, which was roasted, had to be male, unblemished and with unbroken legs. The unleavened bread of Moses in the Old Testament was the daily bread. In the Bible it becomes a symbol of nutrition, purity and perfection. Noah is attributed with having first grown vines and invented wine, which was not prohibited at all. Jesus Christ had shown he had a good palate in the wedding in Cana.

During the Last Supper, a non-blood sacrifice, the bread and wine are consecrated for ever as the blood and body of Christ.

Despite the frugality of the food at The Last Supper, the meeting of Jesus with his disciples around the table had the nature of a banquet with all the classical elements: a meeting based on food and drink, music and the announcement of death. The food was prepared observing the rules laid down by Moses, kosher requirements and laws of sanctity giving meals a symbolic value.

Jesus started the banquet with these words, "I ardently desired to eat with you this Passover before suffering", then he blessed the bread and wine, "This is my blood of the covenant, spilled for many". The words evoke ever greater sadness. It was the custom to drink four glasses of wine. When the head of the table, the uncrowned king condemned to the ultimate punishment, drank his wine, he was blessing the feast day and the wine itself. The other glasses were consumed while the lamb and vegetables were being eaten, along with the bread. When the Agape finished, he intoned the Hebrew ritual "Hallel" and made a heartrending toast to the whole of humanity, "That you may all love one another", and the blessing was established, the Eucharist.

The Last Supper, Sacrificial Drama

The Last Supper seals the mystic union between the Master and his disciples. The food consolidates one of its main functions, its character as a dynamic, profound link. It is an object of change which on being exchanged in the religious sacrifice is part of both the earthly world and the world beyond. The spirit of incorporation is there too: eating and drinking together the body and blood of sacrificed Christ. If, in principle, what the body takes in gives it strength, here in this supper it is also a sign of salvation, of sacrament. We see the sacred character of shared food which has the value of a pact, of an exchange. The participant in this banquet of divine sacrifice is consecrated by the act of taking part in the offering, of receiving Communion in the presence of the two consecrated species: the blood and the body of Christ in a non-bloody sacrifice. A supernatural practice which takes the participants into the supernatural. The sacred character of the food is strengthened. It is a gift from God, laden with power, and must be consumed with ritual precaution. The systems of prohibitions and prescribed rules have in fact an organising function on society, on the group, and adapt the eaters to the double metaphysical and social level. The cultural belonging to a group functions by means of its system of eating. Rituals, as the context of the sacrifice of the supper-mass, catalyse interindividual relations and establish a solid and complex network of affective and symbolic resonances between the basic food, the people eating and the transcendence of it all. In the sacrifice of the mass there is a superlative level dealing with sacrifice and the paschal lamb, suggesting the profound identity of the lamb, man and Christ, the son of God.

Jesus as the Lamb Victim

In the sacrifice of the Last Supper, Jesus becomes a victim and the others share his body. He identifies himself with the victim who is going to be sacrificed in Golgotha to save the people. This is described in the Exodus passages already mentioned, telling how the blood of the sacrificed lamb after the Passover ritual saved the Hebrews from the most terrible plague, the exterminating angel which killed the first-born children of the Egyptians, the human offspring and their animals.

Parallel to this, according to John (John 11, 50-52), later on the Sanhedrin prophesied through the mouth of the high priest Caiaphas that a man should die for the people. Jesus Christ was chosen to be the scapegoat and was identified with the mystical lamb. The difference is that in the Jewish ritual the Sanhedrin wanted to free themselves from the threat that Jesus Christ was for them with regard to the Romans, while in the sacrifice of the mystical lamb, the death of Jesus Christ was a sacrifice by God for the benefit of the world.

The mystical lamb represents Jesus Christ as a lamb. The most solemn is in the Book of Revelation, with the seven seals of the Apocalypse and a staff under the leg. The lamb appears triumphantly, like an innocent victim taking on all the sins of the world. In ancestral ritual the scapegoat was tied up and abandoned outside the town to die. With Jesus Christ as the mystical lamb, the ritual is carried out to perfection. He was taken out of the town, to Golgotha, to be sacrificed. Saint John the Baptist, the precursor, was the first to establish the association when he said: "Here is the Lamb of God; here is the one who takes away the sins of the world".

The Eucharistic Revolution of the communion or Ritual Anthropophagy

Background: the Galilee crisis (John VI, 30-38)

"The bread of God came down from Heaven and gave life to the world". A perfect sacrifice of self-immolation in which the victim is a priest and an altar. Melchisedec, the priest king of pre-Jewish Jerusalem, whose religion allowed only sacrifices with bread and wine, was an extremely remote precursor of the rejection of the traditional sacrifice of animals, lambs, oxen and doves.

In the mass the victim is also a priest and an altar, a perfect sacrifice following the ritual of the other blood sacrifices. The mass is the ritual before the blood sacrifice to be carried out hours later in Golgotha.

The Last Supper where God offers his body and blood to the Apostles by means of the species of the bread and the wine, might seem like a sacrifice in reverse, as it is God, in the guise of his son, who offers himself to be consumed by the people. It is however more classical, closer to a human sacrifice, as the son of God is also a man in relation to God the Father, who welcomes him later on when the sacrifice has taken place. The community of the Apostles prefigures the Church and starts the act of commemoration which forms the heart of their ritual, the sacrament, sacrifice, of the Eucharist. The love of men for their saviour is expressed in an act of consummation, of fervent consumption which throughout the centuries has consecrated in the eyes of the faithful the two species of the bread and the wine, the Sacred Form, the Communion Bread. The mass is the sacrifice, the central ritual, a remembrance of the passion and death of Jesus. "Every time you do this you will remember my passion and death until I return triumphant". In this context, today, the child starts out as a participant and interlocutor of divinity in the ritual of the First Communion.

The Eucharist as Food

Time and Frequency of the Eucharistic Communion

Until Pope Pius X regulated the communion of children, considering them capable of receiving the most important sacrament, frequency and timing depended on the spiritual leader. Saint Theresa of Jesus complained that she could not take communion as often as she would have wished.

It is obligatory to receive communion at least once a year, at Easter. Nowadays it is even possible to take communion twice a day provided it involves two quite different solemnities. Today the controversy about whether the Sacred Form can be chewed or touched has been overcome, and it is left up to the individual communicants to do as they please.

The reformed churches and Catholics differ on the interesting subject of the reservation. Protestants do not allow the presence of the Host to be maintained outside the sacrifice of the mass, so there can be no "reservation" of the Eucharist. They dispense with the Eucharistic cult outside the mass, and also with the classical instruments of the shrine, the Monstrance and the Exposition of the Host. Catholics can have recourse to what remains in the ciborium, which is consecrated and not consumed. The problem of the reservation is the danger and risk of sacrilege it involves.

The moment when Christ ceases to be present in the species of the bread and wine is specified as the moment when the least corruption of the species occurs. Vomit is a problem in view of the enormous sacred respect there is for the Eucharist. Contact with saliva, which has digestive powers, makes the species decay and the divine presence disappears.

The Eucharist as an Artistic Subject

The Last Supper is an intermittent artistic motif. It appears in Byzantium and in mediæval frescoes, then fades away and reappears in the 16th century.

Christ plays the leading role in the portrayal of religious drama. For religious reasons food is limited to lamb, bread and wine. The bread shown is not always unleavened as demanded by the Jewish ritual. Embroidered tablecloths are usually used to make the table look more sumptuous and attractive.

As a pictorial subject, the Last Supper is above all a portrait of various characters in mutual interaction. The material context in which the action takes place is less important than a suitable reflection on the relationships between the main characters. In paintings, the objects on the table, the furniture and the way it is organised all reflect the habits of the epoch of each artist, and a detailed study would therefore throw light on the eating habits of any particular time.

From the time of the Counter Reformation onwards, there was greater freedom with respect to the introduction of other figures – smiling, carrying plates – as well as angels, and the addition of secondary episodes shown in pictures and adjoining rooms.

The remarkable leading role of each disciple and their standardised behaviour highlights the strength of the systems of belonging, coexistence and reciprocity, while also reinforcing the community.

Chromatic Symbolism

Colour was one of the first means of transmitting thought and preserving memory, a way of representing the Logos.

The robes worn to receive the Eucharist are always white. As a symbol of divinity and the priesthood, white represents divine wisdom. It is a symbol of absolute truth, purity and eternal light. When the prophets first saw the divine being he had white hair and was covered by a snow white cloth. The white vestments of the Sovereign Pontiff are a symbol of eternal light, while in the Bible they are a symbol of the regeneration of souls and the reward of the chosen ones. In the Book of Revelation it says that the kingdom of the heavens belongs to those who have washed and whitened their tunics in the blood of the lamb.

The white vestments of the neophytes of the Church represent their innocence and celestial initiation. Wisdom, innocence, purity, simplicity, naïvety and faith are the virtues designated by whiteness.

The tunics of the disciples in paintings are usually white while Christ's is the red of love.

The most emblematic paintings portraying the Last Supper include works by Bassano, Botticelli, Bouts, Dali, Ghirlandaio, Tintoretto, Veronese and Leonardo da Vinci (see more detailed list at the end of the text).

The Development of the Celebration of the Eucharist as a Banquet

The first masses, the central ritual of the sacrifice in remembrance of the passion and death of Jesus, were not masses with the liturgy used today, but banquets. The dimension of taste was not excluded and death also featured, prefigured by the act of the communion. Neither fasting nor frugal eating were required, and each person brought food for the ceremony. Fasts were however included in the prescriptions of the Hebrews, as a sign of penitence and affliction, a sign of personal and national mourning. For centuries the Eucharistic fast began at twelve midnight on the previous day. Today there is only a fast of solid foods for two hours beforehand, but drinking and smoking are permitted.

The Banquet as a Symbol and the New Values

A new international code of standards governs celebrations and festivities in line with the new symbols of social status: mobility, speed, automation, usefulness, social facilities, efficiency and accessibility.

The emphasis on these things reveals a worldwide attitude shared by us all: rushing, luxury, excess and ostentation. A new concept of space as a festive environment is also established; another hedonistic interest, a different idea of service and a new search for decorative effects and forms. The constant feature in the celebration of the First Communion, however, is the purity of the colour white as the ideal setting, and the sacred character of sharing, the pleasure of coexistence.

The communicant, whether a boy or a girl, has taken on the characteristics of the executive and become an object designed to show off an aspiration to a fantasised social status. Their white outfits restrict their freedom, a reflection of social pressures.

We can no longer savour the aromas of cake baking and frying, nor of ironing and starch. People no longer get out the best crockery and there are no more servants in white caps. Nowadays industry supplies the rational support, and to rationalise the thirst for profit, a wide range of banquet paraphernalia has been created for an event which is meant to be individual and original.

Banquets have become gradually more restricted with regard to both the number of dishes and the amount of time spent around the table, but the spirit of the feast lives on. The organisation of an authentic banquet is an extremely complex affair and these days is hardly ever held at home. It needs to be planned and served by professionals, whose job is as difficult and delicate as that of an orchestra leader.

The Ritual of the Preparation of the Communicants

Spiritual preparation: catechesis learning beforehand to prepare to receive the sacraments of forgiveness and love. (John XX, 22-23, and Psalm 32).

Material preparation: organising the catering for the banquet, in a restaurant or at home; present list; guest lists printing invitations and commemoration cards; dress or suit and shoes for the communicant and the close family – which must be fashionable and smart – and present buying.

The Happiest Day of my Life, Today

The spiritual experience of the child: the child becomes aware that something important exists, that there is a God, whom he or she is going to receive and think about while eating the symbol of His body. By means of confession they feel whiteness in their inner selves. If they have fasted, despite the suffering, the hunger and thirst make them feel a bit lighter both physically and mentally. On digesting and becoming part of the divine message – being good, loving, forgiving, respecting, obeying – the communicants gradually become aware of the banquet of their dreams, of the unreality, of the fiction of their transformed inner selves, while still to come are the presents and the real banquet. They are aware of being in the limelight on two counts.

Social Difference and the Development of the Communion Festival from 1900 - 1990

Here are just some of the features which define the communion banquet as an eloquent marker of the changes in social and economic situations, as well as the shift in values in 20th century Spain.

The present list, guest list and invitations are horrible innovations which have gained importance in the same way as for weddings. The commemoration cards have always existed but both the reasons and the wording have deteriorated; today they are childish and fussy. The boys usually carry them in a little bag and the girls in the alms box as a memento.

The clothes: the boy's outfit has always been like the navy uniform, ranging from admiral to sailor. It has changed very little over the years, except in the case of some very modern children who wear designer tracksuits. When money was short, a white shirt was worn with a bow on the right arm.

The girl's white dress is made of a fine material such as organdie or Swiss batiste. It is long and white with embroidery, pleats, tucks and elegant trimmings. At the beginning of the century crowns of white roses were worn and the girls could dress as angels. Today, a paradoxical spirit of sobriety leads some mothers into choosing nun-like touches. The shoes are always white and brand new.

The Banquet

Up until the civil war years, middle and upper class families held a breakfast in the local school for the participants and their relatives. They would drink a glass of milk – which created a lot of phobias – and also had hot chocolate with *churros*, the traditional fried strips of dough.

At midday the family had a slap-up lunch, then went off to visit their friends, neighbours and relatives, and give them the commemoration cards. The communicants would then be given the odd coin, biscuit or sweets, which would be put in their alms boxes. In the evening there was a *merienda* for the child's friends and cousins, consisting of fancy cakes, fried confectionery like *churros* or *buñuelos*, and thick hot chocolate made in the traditional Spanish way. Everything was homemade. Before this they went to the photographer's studio to record the memorable day.

'30s – '40s. War and Post-war

Hunger, scarcity, poverty. Social differences. Welfare. No special clothes. Communal breakfasts in the welfare institutions. No luxuries. In the visits to friends and relatives the children were given a dried fig, some almonds or pine nuts.

'50s – '70s

Smaller houses. Progressive materialism and laicisation in life. The fancy cakes were bought at the baker's. Savoury foods were included in the tea, and also vanilla and chocolate icecream. As a sign of the end of the crisis the luxury of the clothes and external signs of wealth were increased. The photos started to be taken at home. Some people made home movies.

'80s – '90s

The ecclesiastical liturgy is now less serious: Spanish is used instead of Latin; there are guitars and secular music in the church. Fasting has been abandoned and communion is taken by hand. The communion service takes place later in the day, and afterwards the communicants either go straight home – in the upper classes and more well-to-do families – where a banquet awaits, served by the best catering company, with every conceivable luxury, or they go off to a large restaurant which specialises in communions, banquets and weddings. There are usually between 35 and 75 people at the meal, which starts around 2.30 and goes on until 5.30 or 6.00. The children are no longer the central figures, but the pretext. Other children are not invited because all the children from one school take communion on the same day.

The scene: maximum theatricality with exorcist decoration. The height of elegance is bought for the duration of the celebration: candles, waiters and the best crockery. Everyone dresses up to the nines for a serious bout of people-watching. The super-ego and the mask merge together in an extremely lively Zarzuela operetta. Sometimes there is an orchestra to supply discreet background music. There isn't any dancing as the guests would then get in the way of the waiters.

The operation culminates, to the loud accompaniment of the orchestra, with the presentation of the cake: three tiers, all white, covered with chantilly cream and flowers, and crowned by a little figure of a boy or a girl. The initiate cuts the cake with an ornate sword from Toledo, then kisses his parents and greets the guests.

The final stage of the ritual begins with applause, cigars and all the after-dinner drinks imaginable. The move away from religious values has reached the extreme of holding civil communion ceremonies, without either sacraments or religious content. It is just a party for the sake of it.

Bibliography

Augé. M. 'Aimer, manger, mourir'. In *L'honnête volupté*. pp. 6-8. Lettre Internationale, Paris: E. V. R. S. H. 1989.
Bellini. M.(Ed.) 'An imaginary museum, The Last Suppers'. In *Album, Annuario di progetto e cultura materiale*. Vol.1, Progetto Mangiare, pp. 220-227. Milan: Electa 1981.
Biblia, Sagrada. Version by E. Nácar, A. Colunga, Madrid: B. A. C. 1954.
de Brito Rezende, L. C. 'Le festin de soi'. In *L'honnête volupté* pp. 35-39. Lettre Internationale, Paris: E. V. R. S. H. 1989.
Anonymous. *El Encuentro. Iniciación y a la Penitencia a la Eucaristía*. Secretariado Diocesano y Ediciones Paulinas. Madrid-Huelva 1988. 29th ed.
de Garine, I. *Alimentation et Culture*. I. E. D. E. S. Recherche: Paris: 1978.
Koupernik, C. 'Du Goût'. In *L'honnête volupté*. pp. 12-14. Lettre Internationale, Paris: E. V. R. S. H. 1989.
Portal, F. *El Simbolismo de los colores*. Madrid: Edición de la tradición unánime, J. Olaneta, 1989
Portinari, F. 'Et si les dieux mangeaient'. In *À MANGER DES YEUX. L'esthétique de la nourriture*. pp. 11-17. Boudry – Neuchatel: Les éditions de la Baconnière, 1988.
Soler, M. C. *Banquetes de Amor y Muerte*. Barcelona: Tusquets-Los Cinco Sentidos. 1981

Iconography

Bassano, J. *L'Ultima Cena*. Galleria Borghese, Rome.
Botticelli, S. *Madonna of the Eucharist*. Bridgeman Art Library, Boston.
Bouts, S. *Last Supper*. Church of Saint Pierre, Louvain.
Dali, S. *La cena. El Sacramento de la Ultima Cena*. National Gallery of Art, Washington.
de Foix, Margaret. *Book of Hours – The Last Supper*. Victoria and Albert Museum, London.
Del Castagno, A. *La Cena*. Convent of Sant' Apollonia, Florence.
del Sarto, A. *La Cena*. Abbey of San Salvi, Florence.
Duccio di B. *L'Ultima Cena*. Museo dell' Opera Metropolitane, Siena.
Ghirlandaio, D. *L'Ultima Cena*. Convent of San Marco, Florence.
Ghirlandaio, D. *L'Ultima Cena*. Convent of Ognisanti, Florence.
Giotto di B. *L'Ultima Cena*. Alte Pinakothek, Munich.
Gothic Retable. 15th Century. Detail – *La Santa Cena*. Monastery of El Paular, Madrid.
Goya, F. de. *La Santa Cena*. Museo Provincial, Cádiz.
Juanes, Juan de. *La Ultima Cena*. Museo del Prado, Madrid.
Leonardo da V. *L'Ultima Cena*. Santa Maria delle Grazie, Milan.
Romanesque Retable. 13th-14th Century. Detail of *La Santa Cena*, Archangel Gabriel, Soriguerola, Urtx, Gerona.
Serra, Jaume. 14th Century retable from the Monastery of Sigena. Museu de Arte de Catalunya, Barcelona.
Tintoretto, I. *L'Ultima Cena*. San Giorgio Maggiore, Venice.
Tintoretto I. *El Lavatorio*. Museo del Prado, Madrid.
Veronese, P. *La Cena in Casa di Levi*. Galleria dell' Accademia, Venice.

A Perfect Feast ?
Preventative Medicine and Diet in Medieval France.

by Brenda S. Rose.

Ayla Algar, a Turkish writer commenting recently [1] on Edward Fitzgerald's nineteenth century translation of the celebrated Persian poem the *Rubaiyat of Omar Khayyam* [2] makes certain observations. Algar suggests that readers though aware of the fact that Fitzgerald's work was not a full and literal translation of the original text have assumed (wrongly in his opinion), that it closely followed it. For example, he points out that in the second line of what is probably the most frequently quoted quatrain of the poem the translator substituted one phrase for another. Fitzgerald's version reads as follows,

> "Here with a loaf of bread beneath the bough,
> A flask of wine, a *book of verse* and thou
> Beside me singing in the Wilderness
> And Wilderness is Paradise snow."

but writes Algar the second line in a true translation of the Persian should read.

> "A flask of wine, a *leg of lamb* and thou"

This would have been no more than an interesting anecdote if it were not for the fact that Algar's remarks were printed at a time when I had been examining medieval thinking on the relationship between food and health, and in a little known French medical treatise of the thirteenth century, I had found a list of dietetically ideal foods: bread, wine and lamb.

In his article Algar also suggests that by altering the imagery in the way that he did, Fitzgerald,

> "missed the point that in Persian culture the enjoyment of food was an important part of aesthetic and sensory enjoyment"[3].

The implication of this is that what constituted the ideal of aesthetic and sensory enjoyment ie. bread, wine and lamb to a medieval Persian seems to a modern Western reader an incongruous, unromantic collection of foods.

My intention in this paper is therefore to explore this list of ideal foods. I shall consider the ways in which the assertion is to be understood, by setting the list within the wider medical and dietetic context of the Middle Ages. It is my hypothesis that the identical choice of ideal foods made by a physician writing a text-book in thirteenth century Europe, and by a cultivated Persian poet writing at the end of the twelfth could have stemmed not from mere coincidence but from current dietary opinion.

In the Middle Ages food choices were clearly closely linked to maintaining or promoting good health, a fact of which educated members of medieval society would have been acutely aware. The evidence is limited but there are pointers. Firstly, Muhammed ibn al-Hasan ibn Muhammed ibn al-Karim al-Katid al-Baghdadi, the author of an Arab cookery treatise written in 1226, [4] on acknowledging in his book that in his view the noblest of all pleasures is food, also writes

> "... food is the body's stay, and the means of preserving life. No other pleasure can be enjoyed, unless a man has good health, to which food is ancillary ..."[5]

Secondly, this view is re-inforced in a contemporary European medical text which states:

> "Fortior est meta medicine certa dieta" [6]

I intend to explain how knowledge of the important role diet played in the prevention of illness, as conceived by Arabic specialists in the Islamic world, spread not only as far as European intellectual society but how it filtered down until it also reached a wider, interested public. I propose to look at examples, circulating in French medieval society, of a certain type of health book which outlined a regime an individual would be advised to follow to avoid illness and to live well. These books devote a section to dietetic information included in which is a classification of all foods. From an examination of the relevant material I hope to discover how medieval physicians perceived food and diet, what criteria they used to measure the qualities of foodstuffs and what constituted an ideal food in medieval terms. Finally, I propose to look more closely at the three ideal foods which constituted *the perfect feast* the wine, the bread and the lamb, hoping to discover what, if any, additional features they possessed that prompted doctors to describe them in the way they did.

Before undertaking an examination of some of the principles underpinning medieval dietetic medicine, it is essential first of all to look at some of the fundamental aspects of medieval medicine in general in order to see how all these concepts fitted into medieval man's holistic view of Nature, and his belief in the interrelationship not only between the animal, vegetable and mineral kingdoms but with the intellectual and spiritual worlds too. It must be understood too, that all medieval medical advice is placed in a philosophical context, focusing on the interaction of man and the universe. Ideally, to avoid illness and to preserve good health, man and the universe should be in harmony and balance not only within themselves, but also with each other.

Briefly, medieval medical doctrines themselves were firmly rooted in the theories of the Ancient Greeks especially those of the second century philosopher and physician Claudius Galen. The medieval concept of the harmony of the universe is founded directly on the Gallenic theory that the universe is composed of four elements formed by the union of unknown matter with four qualities, namely heat, cold, dryness and moisture. The four elements produced from this union are earth, air, fire and water. Galen also believed that at least two contrary qualities lent their characteristic features to these elements. Earth for example is cold and dry, fire hot and dry, air hot and moist and water cold and moist. Since these qualities are present in Nature they must also correspond with the climatic differences of the seasons. Heat and moisture are the dominant qualities of Spring, heat and dryness those of Summer, dryness too predominates in Autumn along with cold which with moisture is also dominant in Winter. Galen attributed a combination of these four qualities to all objects including man, the organs of his body, the food he ate and the diseases that befell him.

The notion of qualities, however, is a vague concept and Galen and the Greek physicians sought more tangible ways of explaining the phenomena of illness and disease. They describe harmony in man in terms of the four cardinal humours or vital body fluids, namely, blood, yellow bile, black bile and phlegm all of which could be seen or felt by the human senses.

Each of these humours was said to be dominant during a particular season of the year and to be influenced by it. Blood was hot and moist like Spring, the season in which it dominated, yellow bile was hot and dry and was predominant in Summer until the cold and dryness of Autumn prevailed and during which time black bile was dominant in the body. Phlegm the coldest and the most moist of the four humours increased in Winter. Its increased presence was evident by the rise in the number of phlegm related problems such as coughs and colds.

The permanent predominance of one or other of these four cardinal humours (not pathologically but physiologically i.e. still within the norm) was believed to be responsible for producing four, different, distinct human temperaments, natures or constitutions. Galen described these four different temperaments according to the dominant humour thus: *sanguine* (blood = hot and moist), *choleric* (yellow bile = hot and dry), *melancholic* (black bile = cold and dry) and phlegmatic (phlegm = cold and moist). The predominating humour was believed to influence an individual's mental and physical well-being. Galen did believe that there was such a thing as a perfect temperament for maintaining good health, one which by its nature could be called temperate. In other words, one which was moderately hot and moderately moist. He did, however, recognise that this was the ideal and that to avoid illness it was essential to maintain the humoral balance established as the norm within each of the four constitutional types since it was when this balance was disturbed that sickness occurred.

To Galen and the Ancient Greek Masters good health then was a matter of establishing the correct balance of the elements, the four qualities and the four seasons in harmony with an individual's own temperament.

Among several factors believed to influence this balance and harmony, food and drink were of prime importance. Galen placed great emphasis on the curing and prevention of illness by diet. He applied his doctrine of the four humours to all foodstuffs and in his *De Alimentorum Facultatibus* [7] he attributes humoral qualities to all foods and describes them in terms of their degree of heat, cold, moisture or dryness. Each food, according to Galen had its own temperament which, in turn, had its own particular effect on the mind and body of the person who was to eat it. For example, a particular food could create a superfluity of certain humours and a subsequent inbalance of the body fluids in a person of a similar temperament, thus causing ill-health. This same food, however, could restore a deficiency of those particular humours in a person of a different temperament, thus correcting any inbalance in him. Ideally, each of the four constitutional types should be prescribed diets most suited to their particular temperament i.e. diets which would help to maintain rather than disturb the humoral balance of their particular group. Thus healthy individuals known to be of a melancholic temperament that is pre-dominantly cold and dry should avoid a diet with an excess of foods which temperamentally were also predominantly cold and dry.

Galen's dietetic writings along with his other medical works were eventually examined and subsequently interpreted several hundred years later in the tenth and eleventh centuries by three leading medical authorities, in particular, of the Arab world. Firstly, two major works of an Egyptian born doctor, Isaac the Jew, [8] written at this time were primarily concerned with diet and were rooted in Gallenic philosophy. Secondly, another Arab authority, Rhazes, [9] an erudite Persian philosopher and physician, like Galen laid great emphasis on dietetic medicine. If a cure can be effected by diet, then there is no necessity for other forms of medication, was part of his philosophy. Much of what he wrote can also be traced back to Galen. Finally, the theories of Galen were codified in the eleventh century by the great Persian Physician and teacher Avicenna. [10] A large section of Avicenna's book the *Canon of Medicine* [11] is in fact an exposé of Galen's dietetic principles. Avicenna's Canon is considered to be one of the most influential medical text books ever written and it was so highly regarded by European medieval medical science that when it was translated into Latin in the twelfth century [12], it formed the basis for at least half the curriculum at the great medical schools of Salerno and Montpellier.

Although the Arab science of dietetics based on Gallenic tradition remained primarily the province of the universities, the principles underpinning it were disseminated until they filtered down and became accessible not only to learned doctors but also to learned laymen. Educated people like Omar Khayyam and Muhammad ibn al-Hasan may have been able to look at original treatises for themselves, or they may have had access to less specialised and more general types of medical books which are known to have been circulating in contemporary society. These books were in fact detailed health handbooks containing comprehensive guidelines for the practice of preventative medicine. They contain borrowings from the great medical writers but their work has been simplified. Various versions of these books appeared, apparently levelled at different sections of an interested society. Some are known to have been written in Arabic. Others in Latin, the language used in medieval Europe for serious didactic works, were written by physicians and teachers at European medical schools, perhaps, for less informed colleagues or for knowledgeable lay persons. [13] Others, written in vernacular prose, were produced by court physicians often at the request of their royal or aristocratic patients eager to have some form of health education. A third type, written in verse, give their advice in easily remembered aphorisms. Guides of this type would have probably been popular with the layman since they sometimes contained an additional commentary explaining everything in medical and non-medical terms. Yet a fourth, an illuminated version, presented its information in a series of detailed pictures of scenes from everyday life with only the minimum of written information. This visual approach may have been adopted especially for those readers with neither the time nor the expertise to wade through more complicated works but who wished to see at a glance what they could do to preserve their health. All these versions contain basic dietetic information along with other general advice on how the individual should best conduct himself in order to live well and remain in good health. The fact that good health in the Middle Ages was considered to be the personal responsibility of the individual may account for the arrival of these health guides.

I have examined three examples of different manuals directed towards a non-medical public and produced between the thirteenth and fifteenth centuries. One, written in French prose, is the earliest known medical text to be written in that language. It is called *Le Régime du corps de maître Aldebrandin de Sienne* and dates from 1256. [14] The second, the *Tacuinum Sanitatis* is an Italian fourteenth century illuminated manuscript with a short accompanying text in Latin. [15] The third, dating from the fifteenth century is called *Le régime tresutile et tresproufitable pour conserver et garder la santé du corps humain.* [16] It is the first French translation of a version of the *Regimen sanitatis salernitatum* with a commentary attributed to Arnaldus of Villanova. The *Regimen sanitatis salernitatum* is a poem written in Latin verse and dates from the twelfth or thirteenth century. It is, in fact, a compendium of the medicine taught at the great medical school at Salerno.

Each of these manuals presents a regime for the individual to follow in his daily life if he wishes to stay in good health. Their advice though founded on different precepts is much the same as any doctor today would offer a patient who sought advice on how to pursue a healthy life-style. While emphasis is placed on personal hygiene and the importance of regular washing, plenty of fresh air, exercise and rest, the role of a sensible diet in this regime is particularly stressed. By far the greatest section of each book is devoted to dietary matters presumably because it was thought that diet played a major role in the promotion of good health. All the dietary advice too, as we shall see, has its origins in Arabic medicine. Both the French manuals refer specifically to the works of Isaac, Rhazes and Avicenna so presumably their authors expected their readers to have heard of these men and be familiar with their ideas even if they had not studied them at first hand. The Latin text also of the *Tacuinum Sanitatis* is said to be an abbreviated translation (probably by Gerard of Cremona) of the work of Ibn Botlân, [17] an eleventh century Arabic doctor, known to have written many works on medicine and health. At the beginning of the text the author pays tribute to the great Greek and Arab physicians of the past for their indispensible wisdom.

Though the dietary advice in all three of the manuals is basically the same, and I have drawn extensively on all of them for my information, I have at times relied most heavily on Aldebrandin's book. This treatise was a commissioned work and designed to provide comprehensive knowledge for an intelligent, interested but uninformed society. Thus it contains great detail which is of particular help to the modern reader. Its author, Aldebrandin, was chief physician at the court of Saint Louis and he tells us in the preamble that he is writing his book at the request of the king's mother-in-law, Beatrix of Savoie, Comtesse de Provence. The Comtesse, Aldebrandin informs us, is aware that his reputation as a fine physician extends beyond France. She too values his advice, in fact above that of all others and to such an extent that she wishes to have it written down in a comprehensive handbook to take and consult on her travels, an indication in itself of Aldebrandin's prestige. Seemingly, the Comtesse would rather consult his written advice, in preference to a personal consultation with any one of a number of equally well-informed and eminent physicians who must surely have been in permanent residence at the courts of her other daughters, the Queens of England and of Germany.

Aldebrandin goes to some length to assure "cil ki ce livre verront et orront" [18] (he obviously intended his book to reach a wide audience) of the reliable nature of his work. It is he says the carefully researched work of a professional, familiar with the works of the great writers of medicine and philosophy. The fact that he insists that his manual is not the product of a quack or charlatan, suggests first of all, that non-professional and therefore possibly inaccurate, unreliable information was available in handbooks written by lay persons and not by qualified doctors. This insistence on the authenticity of his work suggests too that there existed in the Middle Ages, no less than at the present time, a deep distrust by the medical profession of the layman who trespasses into the field of therapeutics. Finally, it can also be assumed that Aldebrandin's manual is both an accurate and thorough reflection of current medical ideas, since he would be unlikely to risk putting his reputation in jeopardy by producing an inferior book that would not be equally respected both by lay people and medical colleagues.

Aldebrandin's book is divided into four sections and it is part three which deals exclusively with diet. The author does, however, devote two short chapters at the beginning of his book to advice about eating and drinking in general and it is from them that we can draw some useful information. For example, he insists that those who wish to safeguard their health through diet must know three fundamental things:

> "La premiere cose si est savoir et connoistre le complexion et le nature de totes coses qu'il covient user por mangier, et de celui qui le recoit.
> Li seconde si est de le quantite des viandes selonc cou ke on doit prendre pau ou asses.
> La tierce si est de garder l'usage et tenir selonc cou que on a acoustume a mengier". [19]

Though the second and third points are self-explanatory, Aldebrandin obviously feels the first point is worthy of some elucidation. Everyone, he says must know the temperaments or natures of all things and know that they are hot and moist, hot and dry, cold and moist and cold and dry. Equally, everyone must know that the four distinct matching temperaments of man who consumes these things are sanguine, choleric, phlegmatic and melancholic. It is, he adds "le commandement des auteurs de physique" [20] that to keep healthy one must know how a food of a particular nature relates to an individual with the same nature. The use of the word *commandement* suggests that this knowledge was not only advisable but essential if one wished to remain in good health. The individual had to be armed with this information because the majority of foods were believed to be capable in some way of disturbing humoral balance within the body and precipitating ill-health.

There are, Aldebrandin informs us in these two prefatory chapters, only three foods that the individual can safely eat. These perfect foods are by nature, temperate: unlike all other foods they do not run the risk of disturbing humoral balance within the body and cannot therefore precipitate ill-health. They are, he says:

> "*li pains* ki est bien cuis et bien leves et fais d'un jor, et fais de boin forment pur et net
> *char d'aignel* d'un an,
> *boin vin* ki ait boine odeur et boine saveur et boine coleur" [21]

Aldebrandin emphasises the importance of this advice by repeating that a diet composed of these three foods is the only one that can be safely adopted to ensure the continuance of good health. All other foods were seen then as potential health hazards. Only *li pains, l'aignel* et *boin vin*:

> "sont les propres coses a la nature de l'oume garder qui est bien sains, et totes autres coses qu'il convient user a l'oume ne sont mie ausi propres". [22]

It is in the whole of section three of his treatise that Aldebrandin will explore the view of human dietetics which underpins this first and most basic of recommendations.

Foods were assessed not only temperamentally but nutritionally as well. The nutritional value of a food was measured by the humours it produced. Humours here refer to the fluids produced in the body during digestion. Rich foods producing thick humours were considered to be the most nutritious though the most difficult to digest. Lighter foods producing thinner fluids though nutritionally less valuable were more easily and readily absorbed by the body. Foods were seen to have therapeutic as well as pathogenic properties. They could cure illnesses as well as cause them. It was essential to know which foods should be eaten to counteract the ill-effects produced by eating certain other foods.

The true purpose of Aldebrandin's book though is to prevent illness rather than cure it. He considered it preferable therefore to recommend diets combining foods that were perhaps nutritious but harmful with other foods known to have an antidotal effect on the dangers less suitable foods could produce. While striving to maintain the humoral balance of moderately warm and moderately moist, considered the ideal one for good health, it was to be remembered that seasonal variations had also to be considered since they also influenced humoral balance. Thus it was advisable to eat cold foods in summer and hot foods in winter. A final dietary rule to observe in this regimen for health is food order. Light, less nutritious but very quickly digested foods were to be eaten at the beginning of a meal and heavier richer ones were to be taken after. The theory behind such practice being that it was unwise to have in the stomach at one and the same time foods which could not be digested at the same rate, since this could cause stomach distension resulting in pain and flatulence.

No doubt realising that to truly avoid illness the medieval reader needed encyclopaedic knowledge of the natures and properties of all foods, Aldebrandin devotes a series of eight chapters in section three of his book to a systematic analysis of all the foodstuffs, presumably known to him. Each type of cereal, beverage, meat, vegetable, fruit, fish, herb and spice is rigorously examined.

We have already seen that Aldebrandin used the Galenic tradition of attributing two predominent but contrary qualities to all foods. Additionally, each of these qualities is measured, independently, in degrees, numbered on a scale of one to four, according to the intensity of its presence. [23] Thus a food which is described as hot in the fourth degree is seen to have a greater volume of heat within it than one which is hot in the first degree. Since each quality is measured separately, a food could, for example, be hot in the first degree but dry in the second. This variance in the strength of the qualities in foods of a similar temperament suggests equally a variance in the curative and harmful effects of such foods. The beneficial effects of each food is listed along with the detrimental ones and the best ways of neutralizing these.

It would be impracticable to list here all the foods and their relevant details as cited in *Aldebrandin, Le régime tresutile* and the *TC*. Out of necessity, I have had to be selective, commenting in a general way on the various main groups of foods and detailing only where a point serves to underline the way in which diet was used as a means of preventative medicine in medieval France.

Following the order in which the foods are cited in Aldebrandin's régime, the first group to be scrutinized is cereals. Most cereals are temperamentally cold and dry. If possible they should be excluded from the diet of all healthy persons, since though nourishing, they lay heavily in the stomach, are difficult to digest and cause abdominal pain. Thorough cooking or mixing with either milk, almond oil or animal fat (24) would reduce any harmful effects or remove them. According to Aldebrandin cereals: "valent as maladies removoir plus qus a sante garder" [25] particularly if eaten by those suffering from an excess of heat and humidity.

The one cereal not included in this general description is wheat the most temperate of all the grains and the most suited to the nature of man. It seems however, that even the nature of wheat can be affected by external influences, for example by its age, its greenness or even the soil in which it has grown. Those who are to eat it must make sure that it is the best available, perfectly ripe, and of a good colour, halfway between white and red. Even bread made from fine white flour ground from the best approved wheat must not be eaten freshly baked. It had to be not only well cooked and well risen but also one day old to ensure that it had had time to cool down thoroughly after baking, since the heat it absorbed during cookingwould have disturbed albeit temporarily the humoral balance of its own nature which in turn could affect the health of anyone who ate it.

Of all beverages, water is the most basic, and its nature, just as the philosophers describe it, says Aldebrandin, is obviously very cold and very moist. It major dietary function is to carry food to all the organs of the body and to dilute and reduce any unhealthy heat created in the body by warm foods. Only odourless, colourless, sweet tasting water from pure running stony streams or alternatively rain water that has been collected and kept in hygienic conditions can safely be drunk. Small sips mixed with a little rose water and taken with food can aid digestion but too much can have the adverse effect.

Wine was considered the finest of all drinks. The best should be white, bright and clear and because by nature wine was temperate and so like man's own nature, it did not disturb the humoral balance within him. If taken in moderation, never on an empty stomach but always with food, according to ones need, capability and accustomed use, all its effects were beneficial. It engendered good blood, gave one a good colour, a sweet smell and all the other virtues of a strong and healthy body. Some philosophers, says Aldebrandin believe it is good and healthy advice to get drunk twice a month because too much wine induces urination and perspiration and through them the body is purged of superfluities. This is not advice Aldebrandin adhers to, an excess of wine in his opinion affects the brain, provokes apoplexy and causes paralysis.

Of all foods, meat is said to nourish man most by fattening and strengthening his body. At the same time it could also be responsible for causing him many health problems, some of which could be avoided if the meat is accompanied by a drink of good wine.

Pork, the coldest and most humid of all meats though nourishing, is only a suitable food for those who are by nature choleric. It should not be eaten by those who have a phlegmatic or melancholic temperament since it will encourage a superfluity of bad humours in them which in turn could cause gout, severe leg pains, paralysis and all related disorders. To reduce or remove the dangers, pork should be eaten roasted and seasoned with mustard. As a result much of its excess humidity would be absorbed by such a relatively dry cooking process and the addition of a hot spice would raise its coldness to a more temperate level. [26]

Neither beef, mutton nor goat were to be particularly recommended. Though nutritious enough they were all considered relatively indigestible and their detriments were believed to far exceed their values.

Of the meat of non-domestic animals, venison (if from a young beast) and wild boar could be eaten with few ill effects but venison that had been "well-hung" produced an excess of black bile in the body and caused all who ate it to become melancholic and bad humoured.

Among domestic fowl, chicken and capon were considered : "Les plus delectables des chairs volatiles pour restaurer et gouverner nature humaine". [27]

Not only were they by nature warm and moist but they were also easily digested and they produced few superfluities thus doing little to disturb humoral balance. They also had the most marvellous capacity to dilute in exactly the right proportion the various humours in the human body. They were therefore an excellent part of any meal that included in its choice of foods, those which were known to produce humours of a particularly thick consistency.

Pheasant was the most prestigious of all game birds. Its flesh: "selon tous les medecins est bien convenable a nature humaine et la viande des princes et des grans seigneurs" [28].

Galen, apparently preferred partridge because it stimulated the brain, increased perception and sharpened the memory. Like chicken, both could be included in the diet of the healthy since they were nourishing and their dangers were minimal. These could be removed by accompanying pheasant with a sauce in which there was plenty of cinnamon and cardamon and by cooking partridge with leavened dough.

Of all these meats, however, only lamb (29) from a yearling beast (that is from one that was no longer milk fed since ths flesh of a milk reared animal would be too viscous) was considered most suited to man's nature. It had the virtues of being temperamentally moderately warm and moderately moist and, therefore, would not disturb humoral balance by producing superfluous or bad humours; it did not remain long nor rest heavily in the stomach and was easily digested.

All fruit and practically all vegetables were, surprisingly, to the modern dietician detrimental to health. They were included in the medieval diet more for their antidotal properties than for their nutritional worth. Certain fruits were tolerated either as appetite stimulants or as digestive aids. For example, cherries and peaches, eaten with fragrant wine at the beginning of a meal on an empty stomach had the advantage of softening the stomach in preparation for other foods. Pears and apples served as useful digestants if eaten at the end of a meal and provided they were cooked in mature wine with sugar and spices to warm them up a little and neutralize their harmful effects. Melon because of its excessive cold and humidity was said to be the most dangerous of all foods. To neutralize its dangers it had to be eaten at the beginning of the meal, accompanied by a hot spice such as pepper to counteract its coldness.

The almond because of its relatively warm, moist temperament and virtuosity was an almost indispensible item in the medieval diet. Eaten with wine it prevented drunkeness, served with harmful fruits it acted as an antidote, eaten at the end of a meal it became a digestant and it could be crushed for its oil or mixed with liquid to form milk.

Fish, though easily digested, was thought to have little nutritional value and because of its great coldness and high humidity it was believed to produce a superfluity of phlegmatic humours in the body. However, religious fast days were responsible for the high consumption of fish. Fish was an important item in the medieval diet at least two days out of each week and during the whole of Lent, when it was forbidden to eat meat. It is worth noting that both sea and fresh water fish had to have:

> "les chairs blanches, non visqueuses mais de legiere separations, et de substance subtile, et *de bonne odeur*, et qu'il ne soyent pas de legiere putrefactions, et *de bonne couleur* et qu'il soyent de eaue courante"

This seems contrary to received opinion that the fish eaten in medieval times was stale, smelly and in an advanced state of putrifaction. This misunderstanding may have arisen because it was considered unwise to eat *very* fresh fish. It was advisable if:

> "on les garder ainsi par auculns jours jusque autant que la chair commence a mollifier sans putrifaction"

Salted fish was not good if it had been preserved for any length of time, because it diluted and liquified the humours to an excess and as a result could cause fainting and collapse. Sea fish was preferable to the fresh water varieties. Its flesh was harder, less viscous therefore better for the health even if more indigestible. Freshwater fish was permissible provided it came from fast running streams unpolluted by city waste. Fish from stagnant pools was forbidden since it caused immediate death to those who ate it.

From these pertinent comments then it can be seen that medieval dining was fraught with danger. Food as we have seen was either helpful or hazardous to health. To remain healthy one had to watch vigilantly over what one ate and drank. The correct diet played a major role in the prevention of illness and in encouraging the body to cure itself.

To commit to memory the therapeutic and pathogenic properties of all known foodstuffs would have been a formidable and impossible task. Kings and princes are known to have had in their households personal physicians whose responsibilty it was to advise their royal patients on all dietary matters. Others relied on the written information available in handbooks of the type that I have examined. If, however, no advice, verbal or written was available or close at hand it would not have been difficult to remember that at least three foods could safely be eaten which in no way were detrimental to health. These foods were of course *bread, wine* and *lamb*.

My conclusion will of course by now be apparent. I have suggested that Aldebrandin was no original writer. His views on diet can be traced back through a long tradition of dietary advice ultimately to Galen. Galen, however, had in turn been interpreted and embroidered by Arab medical authorities. If Omar Khayyam chose bread wine and lamb for his perfect feast, it must be probable that this choice had something to do with current dietary opinion transmitted to Persian intellectual society, as it had been to that of Europe, from the sophisticated world of Arab medicine.

Finally one question still remains unanswered: what qualities did these three foods possess that distinguished them from other foods and prompted Aldebrandin to choose them as the only ones that were temperamentally suited to the nature of humans? His choice could not have been based on Galenic tradition because Galen chose veal not lamb as the ideal meat for man. Is it just a coincidence, and I put this forward as the merest hypothesis, that in other traditions bread, wine and lamb are seen as fundamental foods? In Christian tradition for example, bread and wine are consecrated at the Eucharist and in the Greek Orthodox Church on Easter Sunday, the Resurrection is commemorated by the ceremonial slaughter and cooking of a lamb. Bread and lamb play an important role in Arab culture too, as indeed did wine until Mohammed had a change of heart and condemned its use in the seventh century. Even more interesting though is their significance in Judaism. Aldebrandin's dietetic advice is taken chapter for chapter not directly from Galen's work on food but from one of the most important and comprehensive treatises on food and diet produced in the Middle Ages, the *Dietes particulieres* of the tenth century Egyptian physician, Isaac the Jew. In Jewish ritual and tradition, the role played by *bread, wine* and *lamb* is paramount. Jewish devotion to bread and wine runs right through Jewish law and literature. The Sabbath begins with an act of "Blessing and Thanksgiving" over a cup of wine and a loaf of bread made from the finest of white flour. Four cups of wine must be drunk at the Passover, two at weddings and one at circumcisions. A symbolic roasted shankbone of lamb is placed on the table during the Passover meal in commemoration of the Paschal lamb that Jews were told to sacrifice on the eve of the exodus from Egypt. The dietetic writings of the great Avicenna are known to have been influenced by the dietary laws of his own religion. Is it therefore unreasonable to propose that Isaac the Jew's were also, and that Jewish dietary rules shaped his view that bread, wine and lamb were ideal foods and ideal foods make a perfect feast?

Serendipity

by Alice Wooledge Salmon

Lured by the promise of a peaceful, escapist hotel adjoining 'the largest palm forest in Europe' and billed as 'absolutely first-class' by a usually reliable guidebook, we taxied 24 km from Alicante to Elche. Alicante, provincial capital on Spain's Costa Blanca, is dusty, raffish, gnawed by the howl of motorbikes and utterly delightful in its domed and bedizened sea-front buildings of circa 1910, its harbour-embracing Explanada paved with mosaic waves, its strolling, preening, cosmopolitan population of every conceivable type and age.

Elche, alas, was another matter. The supposed earthly paradise proved a holiday camp, in spirit, of dark and uncomfortable bungalows - put to shame by magnificent palms, bougainvillaea, hibiscus, and jasmine, but otherwise compatible with a garden stocked by the cheapest poolside furniture, with frequent, importunate litter bins painted screech orange or clamorous yellow and green, with inescapable outdoor Muzak, and a standard of cooking which, far from offering the 'most flavoursome dinners we ever had in Spain' (that guidebook once more), left us mute with chagrin. Breakfast, in a country overflowing with good fresh produce and first-class oranges, offered tinned fruit and bottled juice.

None of this came cheap, and we prowled the streets of Elche, man, woman, and daughter restless with disillusion. That promise of 'flavoursome dinners' had kept the red Michelin at base in Alicante, while we vainly searched Elche for something at least possible: restaurants with menus translated into four languages accompanied by appropriate national flags were rejected as readily as those whose baleful lighting and martyred raw materials put me in mind of the USSR. Hunger growled.

Then I remembered Alfredo Navarro. Earlier, we had wanted to drink the sweet *horchata* made from 'tiger nuts' - or *chufas* - consumed in the region of Valencia where Elche is found and the tiger nuts grow. Our daughter, who had lived in the town, showed us its main square and Helados la Nueva Ibense, a spruce *horchatería* selling ice cream and the white, translucent liquid. It was chilled, refreshing, rather cloying, reminiscent of coconut and the *horchata*'s origins as, formerly, the Moors' almond milk, sweetened and perfumed with orange-blossom essence.

We had drunk slowly, dunking between draughts - as Valencianos do - a soft, cake-like *farton*, while Alfredo Navarro, fifty-ish proprietor of la Nueva Ibense, described how he daily soaks and grinds the *chufas*, adds water, sugar, and cinnamon, takes pride in this delicate job and his stream of regular custom.

'Alfredo,' I said, 'is the man to consult.' When we found him and put the question, he expanded discreetly with the pleasure of being sought to advise on a matter so vital as where to eat 'simply, authentically, and well'. With sober deliberation, Alfredo discussed the merits of the town's choice, weighing this against that until 'El Granaino' emerged as the just measure. 'A special address,' he said, via our swiftly-translating daughter, 'where everything served is good.' But did we mind? - the address was distant.

Distance was no object. We crossed bridges, turned corners, lost our way and importuned strangers who, with typical Spanish courtesy, escorted us to the door.

El Granaino - 'the man from Granada' - felt immediately right. Beyond a *tapas*-serving bar was the L-shaped restaurant: stucco walls, ceramic-studded above tiled dado; beamed ceiling hung in the corner with tiny red peppers - looking, en masse, like a Rastafarian's braided locks - with *jamón serrano* (salt-and-air-cured ham from the Andalucían mountains) and a large dried fish above sideboard stocked by fresh produce, diverse sausages, a large bottle of fruit preserved in spirit. Fresh fish waited on ice at a bar beside the kitchen, tables wore white cloths atop blue and white checks, and the place looked prosperous, expectant, dedicated to the serious sort of cooking for which we were hungry.

We produced Alfredo's name and were amiably received and seated. Our waiter brought *tapas* and freezer-iced *copitas* - frosting furiously on contact with the ambient temperature - and opened a fresh half of chilled la Ina. The sherry was elegant, with almond bouquet and a salty snap that married admirably the house-dressed olives - *aceitunas aliñadas* - their stems intact, their mottled flesh cracked, better to receive the lemony cure which did not mask an agreeable, innate bitterness. What is absent from so much exported sherry was present, as usual, in an Andalucían - by origins - restaurant: the sherry young, served properly chilled and absolutely fresh, its delicacy unmolested by the half degree or so of alcohol added for overseas sale, its almond fragrance and suggestion of brine tactfully escorting the salt and tang of the home-cured olive. Delectable. The waiter brought small squares of bread, lightly toasted and dribbled with olive oil; still warm from the grill, they were simply described as *tostadas*. These were details of perfection.

The menu pleased us. 'Salad of quail with mustard sauce', 'peppers stuffed with anglerfish and prawns', 'scrambled eggs plus wild mushrooms and brains', 'loin of hake with clams', 'pigs' chaps braised in red wine' were considered and declined in favour of *gazpacho andaluz*, the fancifully-named *dikitiflay*, and *berenjenas a la crema*. The *gazpacho* was thick, cool, and correct, with all appropriate trimmings carefully prepared, the *dikitiflay* proved a sort of spring roll, enclosing ham and cheese and sizzling still from the deep frier, and my own *berenjena* - a favourite *entrada*, not just for the sound of its name - was deftly done: sautéed chopped flesh of aubergine, onion, ham and prawns wrapped in long-cooked *béchamel*, returned to the aubergine 'half-shell', strewn with cheese and baked. Each of these *entradas* was delicious without swagger.

The *tour de force* was to follow. *Pata de choto al horno*, our waiter explained, meant leg of baby kid, marinated in wine, olive oil and lemon, with black peppercorns, garlic, pine nuts and rosemary, baked fast in a hot oven. We had seen whole kid on sale in Alicante; such a dish, tonight, for my husband and me, eclipsed alternative choice. Each ate the flesh of a slender thigh and shank, exterior virtually caramelised, the long-fibred, well-done meat (as befits milk-fed animals) tender, succulent, suffused with flavour. This was a poem of a dish, discreetly accompanied by roast potatoes and tomato grilled with garlic.

With this, we drank a 1980 Vega de la Reina from Bodegas Vega de la Reina, S.A., a red wine of the mainly white-producing Rueda hectares in the province of Valladolid. The name 'Vega de la Reina' and its substantial price on El Granaino's list suggested Vega Sicilia, the grand red of 'heroic heights' (as described by Hispano-specialist Jan Read) from the nearby Ribera del Duero; was this, we wondered, some more affordable junior cousin? Not, said Read when later consulted, a cousin at all, but a red esteemed in its own right, the grapes 80% tinto fino - a variant of tempranillo, the principal black grape of Rioja - with cabernet sauvignon, malbec, and merlot, the wine aged 2-4 years in oak and not widely-known beyond Spain. La Reina started round and sweet in the mouth, grew rich and mellow, with a long, grapey finish. A distinguished bottle. The sweet delicacy of the kid made for much mutual flattery between beverage and beast.

Alfredo's 'special address' was busy by 10 pm - our 8:30 arrival artlessly early, by Spanish social standards - with long tables of the animated citizens of Elche, service to whom, as to us, was quiet, efficient, and friendly. From ample glass jugs, icy beer surged into large, stemmed glasses, the beer foaming into heads and looking, to *cerveza*-hating me, dashingly quaffable. The beer-drinkers ordered huge platters of *surtido de Ibericos*, a selection of ham, cured pork, and pork sausage supplemented, in Elche, which is close to the sea, by *salazones*, the salted and dried fish and roes - of tuna, skipjack, swordfish, grey mullet, herring, and spotted dogfish, among other marine life - that Valencianos adore.

They ate straw-thin asparagus, sliced into lengths and fried piping hot with garlic in oil - we hadn't noticed these soon enough - while we finished the meal with half-moons of *melón*, the pale, orangy-green-fleshed honeydew, sold cheap and abundant in Spanish outdoor markets, tasting truly honeyed in Spain and almost of nothing when carried home from the London Safeway or Waitrose.

We paid a modest bill for this memorable, hard-won dinner. It had come like manna in the wilderness, almost a revelation, certainly a feast of excellence.

And just before Christmas a year and a half later, my *esposo* and I returned for more. Giddily escaping some family obligation, we bussed this time from Alicante to Elche, through the saturated colours of a golden afternoon in Mediterranean mid-winter, to have Saturday lunch at El Granaino.

There were the same courteous welcome and constant regard for detail, the again delectable *pata choto al horno*, the 1980 Vega de la Reina once more lending its muted-oaky abundance to the succulent sweetness of kid.

We preceded the *choto* with *surtido de Ibericos*: that 'supply' or 'stock' of *chorizo* sausage, pork loin or *lomo*, and *jamón serrano*, all made from the black-foot Iberian pig - the choicest in Spain - which, one is told, roams free in the mountains northwest of Seville, feeding on acorns and chestnuts that impart distinctive virtues to the dark and well-marbled flesh.

We have an unsated passion for the meat of this salty, gamey, fine-fleshed beast in each of its manifestations; we relished these and then slid gastronomically - still savouring a slice of *chorizo*, a sliver of ham - into *asadillo de pimientos*: a plateful of 'little roasted things', in this case, red and green strips of sweet pepper with tiny squares of salt cod, served under chopped garlic and olive oil with many *tostadas*, just-grilled.

The vivid and well-judged flavours, the contrasts of salt, sweet, suave, and piquant, the crunch of one against the melting qualities of another, the sedate conviviality at surrounding tables, the snatched three hours of eating and drinking again 'simply, authentically, and well' - the sheer *fun* of the whole adventure! - renewed and extended the feast of excellence. A feast confirmed and a feast continued that will draw us back to Elche as long as the brothers Martínez García, attentive owners and chef, so honour the discernment of the wise Alfredo Navarro.

Inspired by El Granaino's 'little roasted things', I prepared the following for the Symposium's luncheon:

Asadillo de pimientos

A small piece of *bacalao* (salt cod)
Milk, water, bay leaf, thyme
1 1/4 kilos red and yellow sweet peppers
6 large cloves garlic, peeled
Cold-pressed, extra-virgin olive oil
Small toasts

Soak salt cod for 24 hours in several changes of cold water. Place in a small pot, just cover with equal quantities of milk and water; add a bay leaf, a sprig of thyme, bring liquid to the boil, simmer *bacalao* for 10-12 minutes. Drain, remove all skin and bones, flake fish into small pieces, rinse well in cold water, drain, and reserve.

Wash and dry peppers; roast beneath the grill, turning frequently, until peppers' skin is charred and their flesh tender. Peel away skin and discard, remove stems and seeds and cur peppers into narrow strips.

Place these, together with finely-minced garlic, in an attractive dish. Cover with olive oil, strew with flakes of salt cod, and serve with small toasts, freshly made.

Serves 6.

In the city of Valencia, I have eaten this under the names of *esgarrat* ('cut into small strips') or *barrejat* ('mixed') in Valenciano. The same thing with aubergines and onions added to the peppers was described as *escalibada con bacalao*.

The Golden Spice from Ancient Persia

by Margaret Shaida

"There is Saffron and it is the best in Nature; it grows in several parts of Persia, but they esteem that above the rest which grows by the side of the Caspian Sea, and next to it is that of Hamadan."

Travels in Persia, 1673-1677, Sir John Chardin

Festive foods are usually rare and expensive. Indeed, it is their very rarity and expense that make them a treat to be enjoyed on special occasions. It is on this basis then that I have placed saffron amongst the most festive of spices - and therefore a "feasting" subject - because, at a million dollars a ton, it is the most costly item of agricultural produce in the world.

Saffron comes from the valleys and plateaus of the northern mountain ranges of the ancient Persian Empire, a region today encompassing eastern Turkey, Iran, Afghanistan and Kashmir, and it consists of the dried stigmas of the crocus flower (*Crocus sativus*). Each bulb produces one or two blossoms, and each blossom only three feathery female stigmas which must be carefully gathered by hand and dried. As it requires some 400,000 stigmas to produce one kg of dried saffron, it can be seen that the production of saffron is a labour-intensive and costly activity.

Saffron can be harvested from the same bulbs for no more than nine years, the first year yielding only 10-15 kgs per acre, the second year - the best yield of all - giving 30-40 kgs per acre, and from the third to the ninth year, 20-25 kgs. After the ninth year, the land must lie fallow for seven years. This is a long time in a country of nomadic tribes, and could explain why different regions of Iran have variously been famous for their high quality saffron. Today, while the finest saffron comes from Qum, 95% of Iran's total production comes from Qayeri in the eastern region of Khorasan.

Iranian production and export has dropped over the last ten years, due in part to the revolution and in part to a number of devastating earthquakes which have damaged the crop. At the same time, Spain has increased its production, and Europe's consumption is now largely satisfied by the Spanish crop. Per capita consumption of saffron in the world in 1985 was 0.014 grams per annum.

The History

In ancient Persian texts, there were 13 different words for saffron, one of which was *carocam*, which in Old Persian meant rainbow or "multicoloured". The Greek carocus and Latin crocus are certainly derived from this. Another was *Zahfaran*, which must clearly dispel the common belief that "saffron" is derived from the Arabic *za'faran*. Quite the reverse is true of course.

One of the earliest references to saffron as a fragrant spice is in the *Song of Solomon* (1000 BC). It is known too that Darius the Great of Persia (500 BC) instructed his governors to ensure that saffron was planted throughout the far northern regions of the Persian Empire (in Caucasia). By 100 BC, saffron was even being exported from Persia to China, along with cucumber, onions, jasmine and the vine. Rome of course also imported its saffron from Persia.

By at least 500 B.C (and probably much earlier), saffron had spread from Persia to India in the east and Greece in the west, where it was equally esteemed. Because of its expense, saffron has always been a symbol of wealth and elegance. The ruling classes of the ancient empires each used it to enhance their food, dye their robes and perfume their banqueting halls. In India, following the death of the Buddha, it was ordained that the robes of the élite class of Buddhist priests would forever be dyed with saffron; in Egypt, Cleopatra is said to have used it for her complexion, while the Greeks strewed their courts with it on festive occasions. Nero ordered the Romans to sprinkle the streets of the city with saffron water to honour his return to Rome. Conspicuous consumption was the order of the day.

The aristocrats of ancient Persia not only dyed their robes and perfumed their halls, they also benefited from its medicinal properties. It was considered a splendid tonic for the heart and to alleviate melancholy, though its effects could be reversed if used to excess. Too much saffron could produce a state of alarming euphoria and even death from compulsive laughter. A hint of its fragrance on the other hand induced sleep, and the bedding of the wealthy was frequently dyed in saffron to create a soporific ambience. It was also rubbed into the skin to give off a pleasing aroma.

It was even used as an ink by Khosrow Parviz, a Sassanian king who so disliked the smell of hide that he imported paper from China and used saffron mixed with rosewater for his ink. (It has long been said that Persia took chess from

India and paper from China, but gave saffron and rosewater to both.)

In the golden age of Persian medical research in the 11th century, it was noted that when baby birds suffered from jaundice, their mothers would bring a stone back to the nest which apparently cured them. In an attempt to discover the nature of the stone and its healing qualities, Persian scientists used to daub baby birds with saffron water to fool the mother into thinking her chicks had jaundice - in order that they could follow her to the source of the miracle cure stone.

Culinary Uses

But it was in gastronomy that saffron made the most lasting impression in Persia and the rest of the world. It is the only spice that adds colour, flavour *and* fragrance to food. While specific reference to the use of saffron in Persian dishes in ancient times is hard to come by (because one of the first acts of each conqueror - from the Macedonians to the Mongols - was to burn up the libraries), it is nevertheless possible - and fun - to indulge in a little speculation.

It is known for instance that saffron first filtered through to Europe via the Greeks and the Romans as early as 600 BC. It is also known that the Persians first conquered the Greek settlement of Phocaea (near present-day Izmir) in 600 BC, forcing many of the local inhabitants to flee westward along the shores of the Mediterranean. They finally established a western outpost by the name of Massilia (modern Marseilles). From here, despite the distance, they maintained extensive contacts with their brethren and conquerors in Phocaea for at least four more centuries. In 200 BC, the Persians, the Phocaeans and the Massilians joined together to defend Phocaea against the invading Romans.

And it is known that there are some striking similarities between two otherwise very dissimilar dishes: that is, the most famous soup of the seashore, the French *bouillabaisse*, and the rather less famous but equally delicious soup of the desert, the Persian *abgoosht*.

Is it too fanciful to suppose that these frequent contacts led to the inclusion of the expensive saffron in the otherwise economical *bouillabaisse*? And why is it, I wonder, that *abgoosht* is the only Persian soup to be eaten as two courses: the broth being taken like a consomme, while the solids are pounded into a coarse paste to be eaten separately with bread. Is this an example of a meeting of culinary minds, of ancient exchanges and influences at work? Well, this is all taking us rather far from saffron as a festive spice...

In any event, the use of saffron diminished in Europe with the decline of the Roman Empire. The lack of a large ruling class of wealthy and leisured aristocrats during the Dark Ages no doubt depressed the market, and it wasn't until more than 500 years later when it was re-introduced by the Arabs that its cultivation began to blossom again in Europe, specially in Spain, Italy and the south of France.

The Arabs were much taken with saffron and with the sophistication of the Persian cuisine. Many of the dishes prepared in the kitchens of the Caliphs of Baghdad were Persian in origin, and of course they often included saffron for colour and flavour: *Sikbaj* and *Zirbaj*, which both feature in the 13th century Baghdad Cookery Book, each include saffron and each are clearly Persian dishes, for example.

The Arab conquerors, like Darius the Great a thousand years before them, made sure that saffron was planted in the sunny fertile regions of their extended empire. Thus, saffron found its way back into Europe once more, and its arrival on the shelves of the kitchens and chemists of the Renaissance period was greeted with enthusiasm. The centrepiece of many a medieval feast was a joint of meat or poultry endored with a paste of saffron and egg yolk, a method popular in the Safavid court of Isfahan. There is little doubt that the inspiration for *risotto* (Italian saffron rice) is from the old Persian for rice, *araz*,.

Saffron was even grown with considerable success in England despite the chill, damp climate. Culpeper noted in his *Complete Herbal* in the 17th century that while "it grows in various parts of the world, but it is no better than that which grows in England". Its culinary use in England was largely concentrated in cakes and buns. The leading centre of saffron production in England was at Saffron Walden in Essex, and Mrs Leyel noted in her *Herbal Delights* that saffron crocus could still be found growing wild near Derby and Halifax in the 1930s.

However, wild saffron in England (or autumn crocus, as it is sometimes called) does not produce the heavy aromatic and colourful stigmas of the saffron cultivated in hot, dry, sunny conditions.

Its costly rarity has often led to imitation and adulteration over the centuries. So widespread and lucrative was the practice in 15th century Germany, that offenders were burned and buried alive. Even today, the practice (though not the punishment) continues, and it is still unwise to buy powdered saffron, which is susceptible to dilution.

There is incidentally one other famous dish in the world where saffron makes an appearance: the Indian *beryani* of the Moghul emperors, baked saffron rice. It comes as no surprise to find that this dish also originated in Persia. A branch of the Mongol (or Moghul in Persian) conquerors of the 12th and 13th centuries who had settled in and ruled over Iran, moved to northern India in the 16th century. After a couple of centuries in Iran, they had become totally Iranianised: their religion was Islam, and their culture, language and food entirely Persian. The glories of the Safavid court of Isfahan survived in the Moghul court of India. The Indian *pilaf* comes directly from the Persian *polow*, while *beryan* means "baked" in Iran.

Saffron Today

Despite the fact that saffron is now grown commercially in a wide belt around the world (from California through to Spain, southern France, Italy, eastern Turkey, Iran, Kashmir and China), the Iranians believe that the finest and most aromatic saffron comes from the sunny plateau of central Iran, and certainly the deep golden colour and concentrated rich fragrance of Persian saffron are hard to beat.

In view of the expense, it is as well that only very little is required in any single dish. It is used together with rosewater to enhance a number of desserts, pastries and icecreams, and makes a frequent appearance as a garnish in a number of savoury dishes and soups. But it is the rice dishes, flavoured and coloured with the costly saffron, that are the most famous foods of entertainment and feasting in Iran (and in northern India too.) (Sometimes, safflower - an inexpensive substitute - is used in restaurants, to give a properly festive appearance to rice dishes, but it lacks the delicate fragrance and flavour of true saffron, and is not recommended.)

Rice, incidentally, is not the food of the common people in Iran, except in the northern provinces of Gilan and Mazandaran where it is grown. For most Iranians it is the food only of high days, holidays and entertainment. No guests would be entertained without at least one dish (and often several dishes) of steaming fluffy rice. It is this habit which has probably given rise to the quite false belief that rice is the staple diet of Iran. It is not.

And because rice is not the starchy filler of the labouring classes but a prized delicacy of festivity and celebration, most Persian rice dishes are enhanced with the addition of saffron, which is thus an important ingredient in the Persian kitchen. It is always on hand, and many housewives grind up the stigmas into a fine powder which they store for convenient use. Half a teaspoon of ground saffron blended with a few teaspoons of water will produce a rich golden liquid enough to transform a simple rice dish into one of rich splendour fit for any king - or guest.

The following rice dish, suffused with saffron and garnished with almond and pistachio slivers, is very often served at working class Persian weddings and other festive occasions. Despite its basically simple ingredients, it is a lovely dish of elegance and fragrance, and makes a gleaming centrepiece on any festive buffet table.

Haveej Polow (Rice with Carrots)

1 lb (450 grams) Basmati long grain rice
6 tablespoons salt
Vegetable oil
2 lbs (900 grams) carrots
2 oz (50 grams) granulated sugar
6-8 teaspoons liquid saffron (see below)
Peel of three oranges (or about 2 oz/50 grams)
3-4 chicken breasts
1 medium onion
1-2 oz Butter

1. Soak the rice in a plentiful amount of well-salted water for at least three hours.

2. Peel and slice the carrots into fine julienne strips. Fry in oil over a medium heat for 10 minutes, stirring constantly. Stir in the sugar, 2 teaspoons of liquid saffron and 2-3 tablespoons of water, cover and cook for 4-5 minutes until liquid is reduced. Put to one side.

3. Peel the oranges thinly (best done with a potato peeler to avoid pith) and cut the peel into julienne strips. Cover with cold water, bring to the boil and strain. Repeat twice more to remove all bitterness. Put to one side.

4. Peel and coarsely chop an onion into a saucepan, put the chicken breasts on top, add a little salt and pepper and a couple of tablespoons of water. Cover and cook very gently on a low heat for an hour or more until very tender.

5. Bring well-salted water to a rapid boil in a large saucepan. Strain the rice and pour into the bubbling water, and boil for 2-3 minutes. After 2 minutes, test to see if rice is ready: the grains should be soft on the outside, but still firm, though not brittle, in the centre. Strain immediately and rinse with tepid water. Toss rice gently in the colander to loosen up the grains.

6. Return the rinsed out saucepan to heat and add 5-6 tablespoons oil and 2-3 tablespoons water to cover the bottom of the pan. Heat till sizzling.

7. Sprinkle in one layer of rice, then sprinkle about a quarter of the carrots and orange peel, then a further layer of rice, then more carrots and orange peel. Repeat twice more, building the rice up into a conical shape and finishing with a layer of rice.

8. Poke two or three holes through the rice to the bottom with the handle of a wooden spoon (to release steam). Wrap the lid in a clean tea-cloth and cover saucepan firmly.

9. Keep on a high heat for 2-3 minutes until rice is steaming, then reduce heat to low and leave for at least 30 minutes more. This can be kept warm and fresh on the very lowest heat of all for a further hour.

10. Place saucepan on a cold wet surface and leave for a minute or two.

11. While waiting, melt the butter and put aside for garnish.

12. Remove lid, and lightly mix a skimmer of rice with 2-3 teaspoons liquid saffron in a small bowl. Reserve for garnish.

13. To dish up, gently toss and mix the rice and ingredients with the skimmer, then sprinkle lightly onto a warmed dish, heaping the rice in a symmetrical mound. Garnish with the saffron rice, and pour the melted butter all over to give it a sheen.

14. Finally remove the crusty bottom and serve on a separate plate.

15. Remove the onion from the chicken pieces and roll in the remaining liquid saffron until a pale golden colour. Serve on a separate plate, or arrange around the rice on the dish, or bury within the rice.

Liquid Saffron

Saffron should be kept in an airtight container in a dark dry cupboard. Persian housewives who use it with some frequency often grind 30 or 40 stigmas with a few grains of sugar into a fine powder in a small (clay or marble) mortar and pestle. Mix half a teaspoon of ground saffron with tepid water, teaspoon by teaspoon, until it is well blended, completely dissolved and a deep golden colour. The colour will intensify if it is left for half an hour or so. If the ground saffron is mixed with boiling water it can be kept in a jar for several weeks.

Books consulted in the Preparation of this Paper

Abrishami, Mohammad Hassan, *Recognising Saffron*, Tehran, 1985 (in Persian)
Culpeper, Nicholas, *Complete Herbal*, 17th century (reprinted by Foulsham, London)
David, Elizabeth, *Spices, Salt and Aromatics in the English Kitchen*, Penguin, London, 1970
Leyel, Mrs, *Herbal Delights*, Faber & Faber, London, 1937 (reprinted 1987)
Nourollah, *Substance of Life*, Isfahan, 1642 (in Persian)
Westland, Pamela, *The Encyclopaedia of Spices*, Marshall Cavendish, London, 1979
The Baghdad Cookery Book (translated by A.J. Arberry, Islamic Culture, 1939)

Feasts in the Archaeological Record

by Paul Stokes

It is my intention to show how archaeology and the archaeologist along with others in associated fields of study, such as anthropology and palaeontolgy, can be of use to the food historians in their quest for information on past food trends. This is purely my own personal view and may not be that expressed by those more expert in the field of archaeology.

What is, and why look at, the Archaeological Record?

Archaeology is the study of man's past by means of material remains. These remains are obtained by excavating the ground. This type of evidence is not normally obtainable by any other method. The soil can be said to be like an historical document and like all other documents it needs to be deciphered, translated, and interpreted, before it can be used. There are said to be three main objectives that need to be attained by the archaeologist once material has been excavated. They are :-

a) Describing of the life of past societies.
b) Place them within a temporal and spatial framework.
c) Attempt to explain how the society functioned, and, if it changed, why.

It is here, in the interpretation of the materials found, where the food experts can start work and play their part in achieving the objectives by explaining the meaning of what was found or not. Between the time of the cessation of a site's occupation and its excavation, a great deal of the evidence can and does disappear. The loss of material varies greatly from site to site. There are a great number of variables that can alter the archaeological record. These can be such things as:- climate, humans, animals, use of site after its abandonment, etc. The greatest losses are in the organic materials. These decay unless the conditions of preservation are particularly favourable. Ideally, the conditions must be either very wet, very cold or very dry. It is this loss that Gordon Childe in his book *A Short Introduction to Archaeology* (1956 p10) compares to pages featuring perishable objects that have been torn from a fat mail-order catalogue covering a great quantity of material goods. A very slim volume remains.

How can Archaeology be of use?

Archaeology's main role in historical cookery is one of back-up for historical text, a physical reinforcement of the documentary evidence; or, in prehistorical time, as that of primary resource. Modern archaeological techniques are advancing, with new, or adapted, scientific methods, to help the archaeologists in their quest for knowledge of human past activities. It is possible to collect from some, but not all, sites, evidence of both plant and animal remains. This has led to growth in specialist areas of study such as palaeoecology (the study of ancient animals and plants in relation to their environment); palaeoethnobotany (the study of plant remains, gathered or grown, associated with ancient man); and archaeozoology (the study of animal remains from archaeological contexts), to name but a few.

Unfortunately, it was and still is quite normal for archaeologists to base their findings on what others have done before, not questioning what they saw and found, but this practice is now being questioned by some, and this, in turn, is bringing about a change in the style and content of reports. Most excavation reports used to contain page after page of illustrations of sherds of pottery and little else. This was because broken fragments of pottery are the most common find on all post-Neolithic sites, since they are virtually indestructible, and are easily seen, and thus were easily recoverable. Recently this trend has changed. Some pottery is now undergoing reassessment. The use of the vessel used to be determined by means of shape and style. Now, by extracting the trapped residues from the fabric of the vessel, it is possible to say what its last contents were which can throw light on its use. More emphasis is now being placed on other materials such as bone, and other organic items, along with the microscopic and trace elements left in the soil. A good example of this new type of report is, the Council for British Archaeology's Report number 50 - *Archaeology of Barton Court Farm, Abingdon*, 1984, Miles, D.(Ed.).

What are Feasts and why are they held?

I will not dwell on this subject for long, as I expect other papers will answer this in far greater detail and better than I can. The dictionary gives feasts as 'A rich and abundant repast'. But what for? Feasts are normally a celebration of an event or time, mostly communal, but we must not overlook the style of feasting associated with the Billy Bunter type throughout history, to whom feasting was just the enjoyment of food and drink for its own sake or for gluttony.

A rich and abundant repast by its very nature will leave traces of evidence, be it non-edible parts of the meal such as the containers, bottles and pots etc. or the waste such as the bone, seeds, stones or cess pit material. They are all positive evidence and as such can be detected archaeologically from time to time. To these and other finds I will return shortly. Food, reproduction and death, are the common features of humanity; all three play a part in celebrations and feasts; all three are clearly represented within the archaeological record. The role feasts play in society are more than merely that of providing sustenance: they have great cultural and political significance, they have and still are used to maintain and create interpersonal bonds. Thus, feasts, and also fasts, were and are important social events.

Most standard text books about food will give the occasions for feasting as follows:

- Particular religious festivals and events.
- Times of year such as New Year, mid-winter/summer, spring or times of sowing and harvesting the crops.
- Life-cycle events, fertility, birth, puberty, weddings, death, etc.
- Provisioning the dead for an after life and paying homage to ancestors.

The foods used for feasts would vary with the status of the feast, from foods that were scarce, of high quality, or difficult and time-consuming to prepare, to the ordinary every day foods which might perhaps be served in greater quantities. The more unusual and lesser used foods may, if found, indicate a feast, especially if they are accompanied by other materials associated with a particular feast.

The Evidence within the Archaeological Record

I have been somewhat selective in the next part of my paper, taking examples from different periods of time and geographical areas covered by archaeology to try to give as broad a picture as possible. My toing and froing through time and peoples is not in chronological order.

The areas and types of material that could be of use are also very large and varied ranging from skeletal remains of humans and animals, pits, middens and cess pits, microscopic pollen, seeds, to pots and containers and through to pictorial and written material.

The first possible record of a feast is some 1.7 million years old. It is in the form of fossilised bones from Koobi Fora in Africa, the bones showed that the individual, a young female, now known as KNM-ER 1808, the Nairobi National Museum Number for her, died of hypervitaminosis of vitamin A, possibly brought about by a large amount of liver in her diet, possibly over a short period. which would not have been normal. A ritual, treat, or feast? Who can tell?

Before the times of the written records we can only make intelligent guesses as to the meaning of what is found. But with the aid of ethnographical studies elsewhere in the world, it may now be possible to be a little more realistic in interpreting what was found.

The mass slaughter of animals within prehistory, is another example, of selective eating, where it is only possible to speculate as to why it was done. Whole herds of animals were driven over cliffs and then only selective parts of the animal appear to have been removed, leaving the rest. This type of practice is thought to have been connected with some sort of feasting. It took place in both the new and old worlds.

One of the most notable areas where the archaeological record is rich, is Egypt, a very arid country where organic material survives well. Here buried in the tombs with kings and nobles are the remains of elaborate feasts. Most excavations were carried out earlier this century and thus are not recorded in the same way as they would be now, but saying that, they were meticulous. A large number of reports and books have been written on the subject, the last Cooks Books catalogue contained the following book, Emery, W.B. *A Funerary Repast in an Egyptian Tomb of the Archaic Period*; a report of excavations made during 1902-4 by John Garsing B. Litt, MA, FSA on tombs of the fifth dynasty, near Beni Hassan and the Speos Artemidos, describes such a find. An extract reads as follows:

'*Number of jars and pottery, sealed with caps of mud which had contained the drinks offered at the time of the funeral while other simple pottery dishes indicated the usual provisions of bread and other eatables...*'

It would appear that the British Museum has one of the largest collections of pots from Egyptian tombs. Also commonly found were models and mural paintings of sacrificial slaughters at which, the greatest part of the animal was handed over to friends assembled around the graveside to feast upon at the end of their day's work. In modern Egypt some still hold a commemorative sacrifice at the tomb's side.

Written material from time to time turns up in archaeological excavations in and around Egypt; these are normally made of papyrus. One such manuscript, from the time of the Romans, contains the information as to what feast was held, when, what number and type of animals were to be sacrificed and eaten, and to what gods they were to be offered. This type of document along with other written material is quiet rare.

In Britain it is somewhat rarer to discover written material, the most important so far discovered also come from a Roman context, from Vindolanda, just south of the line of Hadrian's Wall. These are the oldest pen-and-ink documents so far known from Northern Europe. Amongst the letters and routine documents, all written in ink on wafer-thin leaves of wood, was a notebook containing a list of foodstuffs coming into the fort, with their prices. The list shows a wide range of both local and imported foods and drinks. Some clearly were to be used during religious festivals for the time covered in June.

The ancient practice of offering food and drink to the dead in their tombs, is not restricted to the Egyptians, it appears to be universal. Offerings to the dead in Bronze Age Crete, are depicted on a sarcophagus of c. 1400 B.C., from Hagia Triadha, showing a scene consisting of people offering containers, possibly containing drink and two calves being brought for sacrifice.

An Iron Age chieftain's burial found in Welwyn Garden City, contained a large number of Roman wine amphorae, and many more items connected with food and wine, almost certainly the provisioning for a feast in the after life. This practice continued through the Roman period. Sometimes pipes through which libations could be poured into the sarcophagus or cinerary urn were common, such as the reconstruction in the National Museum of Wales, Cardiff, of a burial of late first century. In the Roman world such pipes would have been used during a feast held in February for the family dead, known as *Parentalia*. Virgil writes that upon such occasions the family would proceed to the grave bringing offerings of water, milk, honey, oil, and the blood of black victims, decking the tomb with flowers. Another was the festival of the dead, the *Lemuria*, held in May, here black beans were offered by householders to the hungry and mischievous spirits to persuade them to go away. In Rome the food was for the dead only. It was considered a great impiety for the survivors to partake of the offering. The Roman tomb also had its *culina*, a kind of kitchen only for the use of the dead. If neglected, the dead became noxious spirits, but if revered, tutelary deities. Those who brought nourishment were loved by the departed. Thus sometimes large deposits could build up. Remains of these may be found during excavations. A funeral feast, or *Gustatio* consisted of eggs, vegetables, mussels and other shellfish served with mulsum, a mixture of honey and wine, would appear to have been eaten by those who attended the funeral. Within the famous Sutton Hoo burial mound, there was found, a so-called pagan feasting-set, with equipment for the preparation and service of food and drink, and for hand and face washing. There was also an axe-hammer for the slaughtering and jointing of meat for the feast.

In April this year a joint excavation by the Institute of Cornish Studies and the Cornwall Archaeology Unit excavated six artificial mounds in a churchyard. The mounds covered the graves of prominent sixth century Britons almost certainly associated with nearby Tintagel. Whilst excavating, the archaeologists found signs of a bonfire and wine amphorae made in Asia Minor, suggesting that during the interment at the graveside funerary feasts were held in the cemetery.

An earlier culture in Europe, the Beaker people, known only by the shape of their vessels which are found in their graves, also appear to have buried their dead with foodstuffs. The analysis of residue from a beaker found in Ashgrove, Fife in 1973, suggests that it contained mead.

Grave worship was also practised in China. Here it consisted of foods presented at the graves; though potentially edible, they were not soaked, seasoned, or cooked; most of them were dry and unpalatable. These offerings, consisted normally of twelve small bowls of foodstuffs; commonly included foods were dried mushrooms of various sorts, dried fish and meat, dried noodles, and dried bean curd. This practice is no longer carried out, paper is now substituted for the real foods (and other goods).

Feasts for the dead, are possibly one of the most detectable within the archaeological record.

What part feasts did play in trade and contact with other societies, are they detectable? The answer is yes, they are detectable, but why or what part imported goods played in feasts is unclear. So too is the question of cost. One view for discussion is, that feasts were an economic drain, causing people to eat products that they were unable to afford.

Briefly I want to consider the evidence for fasting.

The only evidence that might be recoverable is that of the monastic fasts, not a true fast. They did not go without food but only changed what they ate. Twelfth century literary references to fast-day dishes, may be backed up with finds of such remains, as bones and scales of fish, and other bones from what was considered non-meats such as frogs and beavers; of rabbits, only the developed foetus was allowed. Eggs were also allowable. Just recently, at an excavation in Guildford, Surrey, large quantities of egg shell and fish scales were recovered from a kitchen midden, from a site next to the castle. Until all the contents have been examined we can only consider them possible remains of a fast-day.

Fasting, as the abstaining from food, can not be detected archaeologically. By its very nature it is a negative activity and therefore leaves no evidence. Even long term fasting, leaves no detectable evidence in the skeletal remains of humans.

A brief conclusion

Food is detectable within the archaeological record, that found in a prehistorical context can only be guessed at, and somewhat subjectively placed into the category of a feast if the remains were out of the ordinary. Other areas where information can be gathered is wide and varied, and it may only be of use if one takes a holistic view of archaeology and all its associated and specialist fields of study. The detection of feasts is possible, by:

- determining what pots and containers were used for.
- looking at all food remains, even the microscopic and defecated material.
- determining the food available, how much and how easily obtainable and compare with that used.
- checking to see if there was any evidence for gatherings and whether any rituals had been performed.
- examining the skeletal and mummified remains of humans, in particular the stomach contents, diseases and nutritional abnormalities.

Feasts and Fasts. As described, documented and illustrated in the Johnson & Wales University Culinary Archives and Museum, Providence, Rhode Island

by Louis I. Szathmary

Priscus Rhetor, a historian and orator, [1] attended a dinner (circa 450 A.D.) at the Royal Court of Attila, the "Scourge of God," and reported a detailed description of his experience.

Now, when we review the works of historians on Eastern monarchs, it is no great surprise to realize how elaborate, how civilized a feast was in the court of a ruler known as "barbarian," "heathen," or "uncivilized."

According to the report in *"Eyewitness to History,"* [2] at the Attila feast the logistics were designed, prearranged, orchestrated, and implemented, from the size of the tables, the number seated at each, the distance from each other, the size of the drinking vessels, that they were gold and silver for guests, and a plain wooden bowl for Attila, down to each morsel of food at every serving.

As a participant in a feast given by the City of Chicago to honour the visiting Emperor of Japan, I noted that it was conducted under similar prearranged protocol as the dinner for Attila.

At the Culinary Archives and Museum of Johnson & Wales University in Rhode Island, extensive information about feasts and fasts is available for students, faculty, and others interested in the psychology, history, sociology, nutrition, and gastronomy of the two extremes of eating.

The idea of a feast precedes recorded history. Our ancestors throughout evolution ate, apart from regular daily fare for sustenance, meals which were very different in their scope and magnitude on certain occasions, as well as meals which were extremely restricted in size and selection at other times.

One can only assume that the hunter partook of a much larger meal after a successful kill. And the gatherer who lived from what Mother Nature provided without the help of agriculture also could enjoy larger meals when fruits of tree or bush ripened unexpectedly and our wandering forebears found themselves with an abundance of fruits.

And conversely there were days of fast brought on not by design but necessity. The bad luck of the hunter or gatherer, the empty hooks and nets of the fishermen forced certain meal times into fasts.

As society started to evolve, the family and the clan shaped loosely knit groups into organized entities. Moral considerations and economic necessity of community life developed the earliest forms of religion, with feasts and fasts beginning to follow certain rules and rhythms.

People realized that through the year there were times when there was an abundance of edibles worthy of celebration - a feast. While at other times there was little or nothing available, and individuals, to serve the interests of the group, had to give up or restrict certain foods,and through such voluntary or enforced abstinence, meals turned into fasts.

Humans all over the globe adapted quickly to the reality that feasts and fasts are necessary to community life, and each culture developed its own rules and customs for feasts and fasts.

From oldest times,dishes, utensils and accessories were made for regular daily use or for feasts and festive occasions. And if the fasts had special requirements, such as taboos on certain foods, this was communicated in some way to the group.

For instance, at the Johnson & Wales Museum, we have fragments of altar cloths from a Coptic Christian society at Fayum in Egypt, dating back as early as the 2nd century A.D. These fragments were supposed to be used on fast days, depicting water animals such as fish, and frogs, which were permitted to be eaten on fast days. Supposedly, they were used to inform believers what could be eaten on the day when the cloth was on the altar.

Serving plates and drinking vessels for feast days were prepared from precious metals and richly decorated with semi-precious stones, while utensils and containers used for a fast were made of clay or wood, but retaining the forms of the everyday dishes and feast dishes.

In our Western civilization with its origins in Judeo-Christian moral standards and Greco-Roman philosophy, the fast has been a virtue for thousands of years as a part of self-denial. Interestingly, in non-Western societies, where self-denial was no virtue, where the deities didn't demand sacrifice of piety or abstinence, feasts and fasts still appear to be characteristic parts of food patterns.

I suspect that the reason for this was basically that the feast was a necessity because it prevented spoilage of the food which could not be preserved. Similarly, the fast was a necessity because at certain times of the year some foods were simply not available.

Slowly, these origins of the "unusual meals" were forgotten, and most of the documentation at Johnson & Wales depicts only the outward links of the feasts and fasts with their reasons for celebration or commemoration.

Upon examination of the manuscripts and books, we find that food for celebrations is described as festive. Characteristic of this type of meal is that the ingredients are more selective, the portions larger, the preparation more elaborate, and the table setting, utensils and accessories are designed to add to the significance of the occasion.

If you compare books written about Greek and Roman festivities with descriptions of medieval coronations or other joyful occasions, you will find that even if there are differences in certain secondary aspects, the meal itself is always similar in its primary manifestations.

The "main course," the "*pièce de résistance*," is always a whole roasted animal — lamb, goat, suckling pig, or, occasionally, a calf. At coronations not one but several whole steers or oxen are prepared, beginning sometimes a couple of days before the celebration.

Whole roasted birds were carried to the table *en plumage*, in the glory of their feathers. The birds were shaped and baked in symbolic forms; the side dishes prepared more for eye appeal than for eating quality. While for fasts, the food itself is often in the form of a soup or a thick cereal to be consumed with just a spoon, perhaps right from the vessel in which it was prepared.

The meals for feasts are the types which turn into religious tradition like Christmas and New Year's Eve dinners and Easter Sunday breakfast; or of national significance as Thanksgiving; or family feasts marking the birth, marriage, or even the death of a family member.

The Johnson & Wales collection is extremely rich in Thanksgiving material, including original copies of Thanksgiving declarations by governors of many of the states; illustrations from contemporary magazines, books, greeting cards, handwritten and printed recipes, restaurant menus, and many other items linked to the national holiday.

Our Christmas and Easter collections are close behind. Among several thousand cookbooks and in even more thousands of issues of American periodicals, we have an astonishing number of holiday references, from Christmas cakes and Yule logs to Easter eggs and lamb.

Food for the fast days has its own deep traditions. The Roman Catholic church for centuries required its members to abstain from meat on Fridays. Although the United States never was a Catholic nation, and Roman Catholicism was a small, albeit strong group, the "fish on Friday" routine became a part of American life from Colonial times on, perhaps as much for reasons of economy as for belief.

If not fish, then cereals and vegetables were the Friday bill-of-fare for households throughout the country. Although the church of Rome has lifted the call for meatless Friday, it still exists very strongly throughout Western civilization. Even cookbooks written in recent years still carry meatless dishes, perhaps partially for health reasons. Meat consumption, especially red meat, has been declining significantly.

Not only in text and pictures, a large reference source available at the Johnson & Wales collection is in the form of utensils and other food-related objects.

Among the most noteworthy is a collection of about 100 sterling silver and silver-plated skewers used to decorate cold and hot servings during the Georgian, Victorian, and Edwardian eras. Among the skewers, some of which are from France, the most intriguing are those shaped like animals or animal parts, to identify the ingredients of decorated patés, balotins, galantines, and other dishes. So, it was obvious that a silver hare skewer would be used on the hare or rabbit pate; an elk would adorn a joint of venison; and a fish would decorate a coulibiac.

In both household and institutional table settings, the objects used at feasts are distinctly different from everyday table settings. In the past 100 years or so, large numbers of special Christmas chinaware appeared on the market, as well as linen and accessories, exclusively for the festive Christmas dinner. Likewise Thanksgiving created its own tableware in the United States.

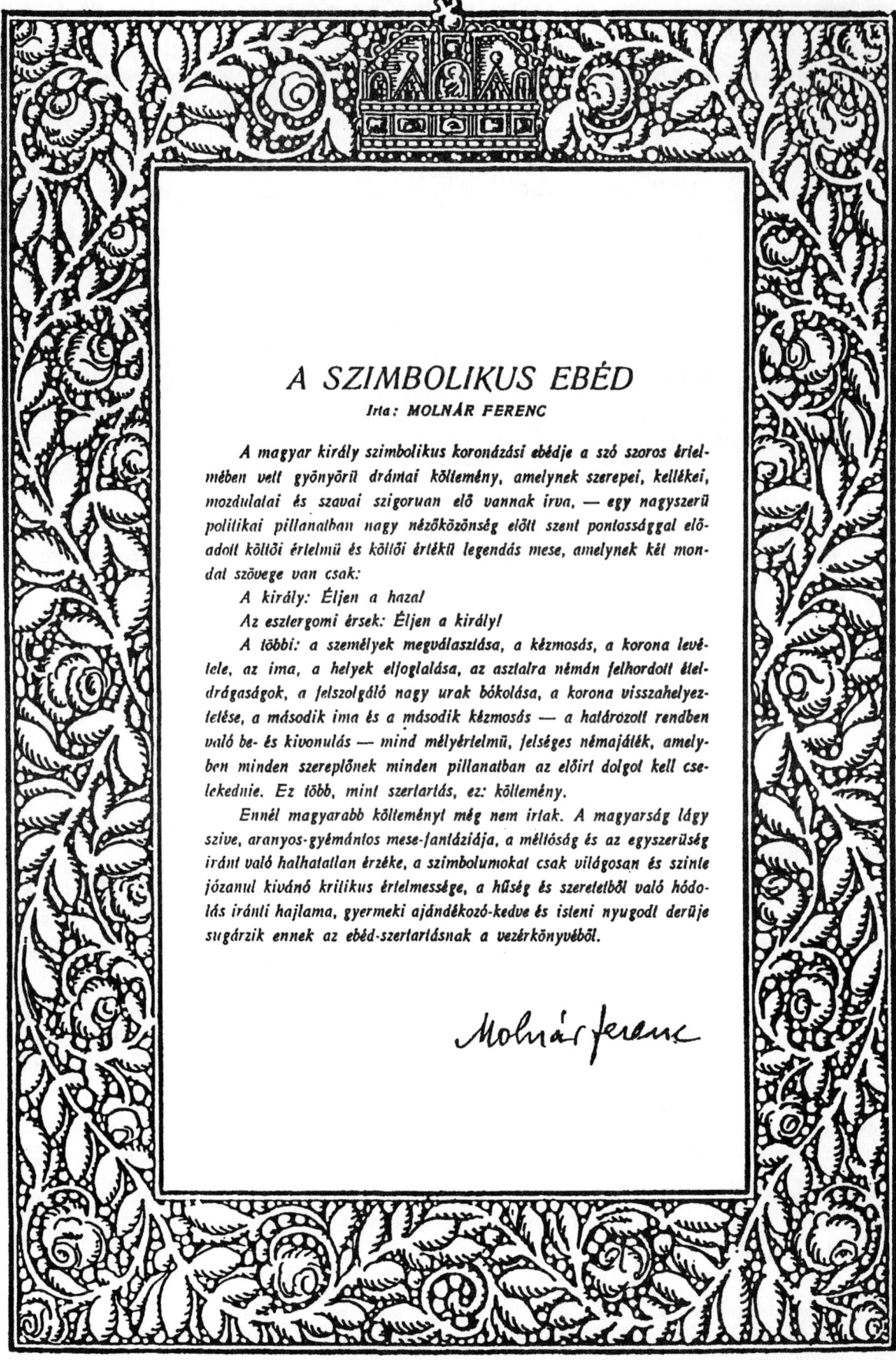

Frontispiece of *Koronazasi Album*, Erdekes Ujsag, Budapest, 1917.

Fasting is not limited to the food itself. Religious fasts in most faiths require not only simple food, but simple accessories and simple presentation.

At Johnson & Wales many books, periodicals, and clippings deal with fasting. It is worthwhile to mention an article in the May 1912 issue of the *Ladies Home Journal*, "How I Fasted Fifteen Days," by Bertha Damaris Knobe.

The author, who described herself as a "professional working woman" living in New York City, and being about 30 years old, relates how she felt on the verge of a nervous breakdown, which could possibly lead to suicide, because of her eating habits, which were very much the ones of upper society in New York, "the eatingest place on earth."

In desperation, she landed in a "fat farm," where, under a doctor's care, she completely stopped eating for 14 days, with no intake except two quarts of water daily.

She claims a miracle after two weeks, physical and mental. She became a new person with bright rosy glow replacing her sickly yellow skin. Then she resumed eating, at first only the juice of three oranges a day, then including eight glasses of milk. In six weeks she gained "precisely 30 pounds."

At Johnson & Wales there are dozens of similar case histories from medieval times to the present, as well as vivid descriptions of unusual feasts and really out-of-proportion meals.

Perhaps one of the strangest combined both feast and fast into one symbolic meal. It was the coronation dinner of the last King of Hungary, Karl IV, who was Emperor of Austria as Karl I. He was crowned in 1916, upon ascending the throne of Franz Joseph. Karl's wife, Empress and Queen Zita, and their first-born son, Crown Prince Otto, attended the dinner in Budapest.

At Johnson & Wales, there's a magnificent book in which Franz Molnar, the noted playwright, describes this dinner step by step. [3]

"The room in the royal castle in Buda was set in an extremely festive way," he writes. When the ruling monarchs of the day assembled for their ceremonial procession toward the dining room, Molnar relates, Prince Otto, who was four years old, walked, by mistake into the royal box of the King of Bulgaria. The King lifted up little Otto, and members of the royal family, already seated on the main floor, rose to pay homage to the next ruler of the Austro-Hungarian monarchy.

Finally, the royal couple arrived. They walked to the ceremonial hand-washing basin, where, after pulling off their gloves, a few drops of water were carefully poured on their fingertips, and then dried with exquisite towels.

Then Karl and Zita walk to the royal table which is set for only six – the ruler, his wife, and the four highest officials of the realm, two from the church, and two civilians. At the nod of the royal chief steward, the plate carriers, all high-ranking nobility from the best families of Hungary, bring up, one by one on magnificent gold platters, the 19 courses of the meal. Here is the precise listing:

The roast of homage
Pheasant en plumage
Parfait of chicken à la Reine
Paté of goose liver with truffles
Salad of assorted poultry
A light whipped paté of venison with white truffles
Coronation ham
Quail en gelée
Stuffed roast sirloin of venison
Pork roast à la Hortobagy
Ducks roasted on the spit
Turkey roasted in a medieval manner
Young rooster roasted
Brook trout from the Tatra Mountains
A fruit jelly from Tokay
Assorted small pastries
Fine bonbons
Assorted fresh fruit
A homage basket for the Crown Prince

Each member of the Upper House of the Hungarian Parliament carries a platter, stops for a few seconds in front of the royal couple, slightly bowing, then marches on with his platter until all 19 are gone. No one has had a single bite of the food.

Then the King stands with his crystal goblet filled with Tokay wine raised. In the silence of the room, "where you could hear a feather fall to the floor," as Molnar describes it, the King toasts: "Long live our country."

For a moment the silence prevails, and all in the room, as one, respond: "Long live the King."

Gun salutes sound from the hills over the castle. Everyone takes a sip of wine, starting with the Queen. At this moment, the last of the 19 food carriers is slowly walking out of the room with the magnificent sweet basket created by the royal pastry chef from marzipan, pulled sugar, and pastillage, and filled with the favourite sweets of the 4-year-old Crown Prince.

The Archbishop gives the short after-dinner prayer, thanking God. The royal coronation banquet is over. From the sumptuous 19-course dinner, not a single bite was consumed. All will be transferred to plain metal platters and brought to a building where badly-wounded victims of the ongoing First World War are under care.

In this symbolic meal, feast and fast merged their metaphysical meanings. The King, when he takes upon himself the responsibility of ruling, gives up for the glory of God, and for the benefit of the country, by fasting at the greatest feast of his life.

References

(1) Priscus, in Dindorf (ed.), *Historici Graeci Minores*, trans. B.K. Workman, in *"They Saw It Happen in Classical Times,"* Blackwell, Oxford, 1964.
(2) Carey, John (ed.), *Eyewitness to History*, Harvard University Press, 1988.
(3) *Koronazasi Album*, Erdekes Ujsag, Budapest, 1917.

TWELFTH NIGHT

by Greta Verdin

'Today we are liberated from darkness and are illuminated by the light of divine knowledge'. (Epiphany hymn)

Queen Elizabeth and her court were dressed in white and an epiphany service, conducted by the Lord Bishop of London with magnificent music, took place in the Chapel Royal. The queen would offer gifts - gold for the King, the Father, frankincense for the the Holy One, the Holy Ghost, myrrh for the mortal man, the Son. The queen dined in state in the Great Chamber of Whitehall with the Muscovy ambassador, Grigori Ivanovich Mikulin. He describes the Epiphany celebration at the Chapel, the noble officers, the procession of ladies, the wonderful ceremony, healths and entertainments at the state dinner and what the queen said when she when she waxed merry, but he does not record the food at the feast. The dining hall was hung with tapestries of gold and there was a great court cupboard full of vessels of gold. The viands were borne by knights. The queen washed her hands in a silver ewer. She drank to the Czar of Russia and passed the cup to the ambassador.

After the feast in the Great Hall Queen Elizabeth entertained a certain Virginio Orsino. He tells of a paradise full of fair shows and music and of rooms perfumed with cassia and amber. He also writes to his Duchess of a pleasing comedy with great variety and music and dances. Lesley Hotson in his book *The First Night of "Twelfth Night"*, suggests that this comedy was Shakespeare's play. Duke Orsino had been presented by his Duchess, Flavia, with twins and Shakespeare may have woven his story around two twins to honour the Duke and the reference to Orsino's sea battle may be a glancing reference to the Duke's campaign against the Turk.

The Great Hall at Whitehall was ninety feet long and the audience probably sat round the actors who performed in the middle of the hall. The open central stage was set with scenic houses to represent Olivia's house and the Duke's court. Elizabeth had requested a play of courtly love with music and dancing to celebrate the Saturnalia, the ancient feast of liberty. Perhaps this is why Viola embraces the role of servant to Orsino but is transformed at the end of the play into 'Orsino's mistress and his fancy's queen'. Maria, the maid servant, is the Lord of Misrule and develops the plot against Malvolio and is rewarded by becoming wife to Sir Toby. Malvolio, the steward, aspires to become Olivia's lord but is subdued to the level of a madman and the dark prison house. The Saturnalia was sanctioned by Christians as combating self-love and perhaps in Malvolio's fall we see pride punished and self-knowledge achieved.

Mr. Hotson suggests that in writing the play Shakespeare offered a portrait in Olivia of the Queen in her youth when she too mourned a dead father and brother and refused marriage. Olivia certainly has great power in the play, but it is Viola-Cesario who possesses the spiritual authority associated with the feast of Epiphany. She and her brother, Sebastian, journey across the sea and perhaps bring illumination to Illyria. Olivia is redeemed from her mourning and woos Sebastian. Duke Orsino is transformed from being love's martyr and recognises the beauty of Viola's devotion and service and chooses her as his bride.

Many people still honour the feast of Epiphany by following the Elizabethan custom of baking a Twelfth Night cake in which a pea and a bean were hidden. The lucky people who find the pea and the bean become King and Queen. A recipe for this can be found in Hilary Spurling's account of Lady Fettiplace's Twelfth Night cake.

Bibliography

Hotson, Lesley. *The First Night of "Twelfth Night"*, Rupert Hart-Davis 1954.
Spurling, Hilary. *Elinor Fettiplace's Receipt Book, Elizabethan Country House Cooking*, Viking Salamander 1986, 137.

Feasts in Jordan and the Transkei

by Kathie Webber

Feasts combine eating with entertainment. Feast times are sociable and give the host the chance to display his wealth, status, taste and style. Feasting should be pleasurable.

Feasts are given in celebration and although they vary widely throughout the world, their form is always governed by traditions and local mores.

Travelling hopefully, I have always assumed that a feast is not to be missed. My discoveries have not always been delightful. This is an account of a feast that was sumptuous, delicious, over-abundant and hugely enjoyable, and a feast that wasn't.

Mansaf in the Desert

Invitations to feasts, as I have said, are not to be turned down so when, on a visit to Jordan, I was to be a guest of a Bedu sheikh, (a wealthy and urbane citizen of Amman since his adulthood but with many family members still desert dwellers), I brushed up on my knowledge of Arab customs. For the pleasure of his guests my friend had organised a mansaf, a desert dinner, in his traditional black goat's hair tent in the desert near to Petra. Arab custom dictates that women eat after the men and so the desert dinner could not be truly authentic for we were a mixed party, but for the evening the women were accorded honorary male status.

Simply described, the mansaf is a huge communal platter of rice with meat on top and variations of the dish occur throughout the Arab world. The kind of meat differs, so do the additions and accompaniments depending on the country, the culture and the wealth. The meats I have eaten include kid and goat, camel, lamb and mutton. Sometimes buffalo is used but I have yet to taste it.

Rough-cut chunks, cooked until the meat falls off the bones, are put on top of mounded rice which can be plain or studded with fruits and nuts and enriched with spices and colourings. Turmeric, cardamom, allspice and cinnamon are the most favoured spices and for perfuming, saffron and rose and orange flower waters are used. Further east, cumin and coriander are preferred and cloves and dried limes make their appearance. Dates, fresh or dried, are included and when the host leads a less itinerant lifestyle, the benefits of supermarket shopping are apparent, often as a garnish of huge quantities of almonds. I particularly enjoyed a mansaf of kid and turmeric-flavoured rice, sprinkled with pomegranate seeds, the finished dish, borne in by two servants, looking like an antique, jewel-studded and gilded shield. Some kind of sauce is poured over once the communal platter has been placed in position on the carpet and this can vary from the melted tail fat of the lamb used for the dish to a watered down labneh (a yoghurt preparation).

Driving in a collection of four-wheeled vehicles through the wadis of Lawrence of Arabia's desert, we arrived at the camp of black goat's hair tents, the largest one of which was open on one side and lined, walls and floor, with Jordanian rugs, but other than these and a few bolster-type cushions was empty of furnishings. Several guests had already assembled, the men dressed in the long Arab robes with curved and ornate daggers in their belts. On their heads each wore the square cloth or kuffiyah headdress held in place with double gold or silver cords which, nowadays, are an elegant reminder that these were once the plain ropes with which the desert-dweller hobbled his camel.

Dinner is eaten sitting cross-legged on the carpets. The sheikh sat with us, another departure from tradition as custom says he should stand to one side while his guests eat. Our feast began with a ceremonial washing of hands; warm water from a large battered kettle was poured by a servant over the hands of each of us in turn, the dribbles caught in an equally battered bowl. We shook off the water drops and when all were clean, prayers were said, acknowledging "God the Merciful and Compassionate…"

The mansaf was carried in on one huge brass tray which had been lined with shirak, the large handkerchief-thin wholemeal bread of this part of the Middle East. Piled on it was the rice, coloured and perfumed with saffron and rose water and on top of the rice, pieces of lamb on the bone and strewn over all, cinnamon bark, dried fruits and golden fried pine nuts and almonds. Another servant brought in an old and blackened saucepan and in front of us poured the contents - scented clarified butter - over the dish. Throughout the meal, servants dribbled thinned labneh over the rice, adding a pleasing, almost elusive, sharpness to the buttery richness of the other ingredients.

Not only does the Muslim religion dictate that eating is done with the right hand and preferably with the first three fingers, but also that the fingers that go into the communal dish must not touch the mouth or any other part of the body during the meal. Eating in the Arab manner is difficult for the uninitiated; the wise practise beforehand. Between thumb and the first two fingers, a little rice and meat should be formed swiftly and cleanly into a small ball resting on top of the thumb, like a coin prior to tossing it. This food ball should be flicked into the mouth in such a way that the fingers never touch the lips and no grain of rice is dropped. It is bad manners for food to come above the second joints of the fingers and, it follows, gross to use the complete hand in the communal dish. The whole operation, when raised to it from birth, is clean and very skilled. The beginner often makes as much mess as any baby left alone for the first time with a plate of blancmange and a spoon.

To be a guest of honour is to discover other mores. Favoured pieces of the meat, testicles, eye balls, at worst (to us), to succulent pieces of the choicest parts of the muscle, at best (again to us), may be pushed across the pile of food or placed in front of you and should not be refused. To be most favoured is to have your host form some exquisite little portion of food into a ball ready for your enjoyment. The meal should be accompanied by much lip-smacking and at least one good well-rounded belch to prove that you have eaten well and to compliment the host on his hospitality.

When it was obvious that we had all eaten enough and the tray had been removed, the hand-washing servant returned, followed, once we were again clean, by other servants who stooped into the tent bearing dishes of dates, and small pastries, some stuffed with date paste, others with chopped pistachio nuts, still others with dried apricots, sticky with sugar syrups and honey.

At the end of the meal Allah was praised again, and the coffee, a sweetened, dark drink flavoured with ground cardamom seeds, was brought in and poured into tiny handleless cups. Three cups is considered the polite intake and at any time after that you can indicate that you have had sufficient by gently shaking your empty cup from side to side. The host has done his duty - he has fed you well. The guest's duty throughout the feast is to provide good conversation and lots of it. The Arabs are a sociable people who will converse for hours.

Meanwhile, the tray that we had eaten from was refilled and those who had served us sat down to eat. When they had eaten, the tray was once more piled with food and the women and children ate.

Preparing a mansaf is a day's work for several servants or, when simplified, two or three hours for one person, but for entertaining large numbers it is unparalleled. When cooked, the work of the cook/hostess is almost finished, because the meal will keep hot for long periods and there is little serving to be done. And in the tradition of the desert, the mansaf can end simply with fresh dates and rich coffee. The recipe that follows is my own version put together from some of the best of those I have eaten.

Mansaf

(for six)

3lb (1-1/2kg) shoulder lamb on the bone, or kid meat
salt and pepper
2-4oz (50-100g) clarified butter
3oz (75g) pine nuts
3oz (75g) flaked almonds
2 large onions, not too finely chopped
1/2 teaspoon (2.5ml) ground allspice
1 teaspoon (5ml) ground cardamom
few pieces whole cinnamon bark
6oz (150g) goat's milk yoghurt

Ask your butcher to chop the meat through the bone into 12 pieces. Clean them and put them in a large pan with enough water to just cover the meat and bring the pan to the boil, skimming as required. When clear and boiling, add salt and pepper, cover and simmer gently for the best part of an hour.

Meanwhile, heat the clarified butter in a pan and fry first the pine nuts then the almonds until golden brown, keeping them moving so that they colour evenly. Remove, letting the fat drain back into the pan and then fry the onion slowly until it is translucent. Stir in the allspice, cardamom and cinnamon and cook the mixture for a few minutes more before adding it to the simmering lamb. Continue cooking with the pan uncovered so that the liquid reduces and after about another 1/2 hour, or when the liquid is reduced enough for you to think of it as a sauce rather than a cooking liquid, stir in the yoghurt. Continue simmering slowly until the liquid is thick and the lamb is falling off the bones. Check the seasoning.

To serve, mound rice on a large dish, lift the meat from the pan and arrange it on the rice, then pour on as much sauce as the dish will take to begin with. You don't want to saturate the rice. Any remaining sauce can be poured over the rice as the meal progresses. Finish by sprinkling the mansaf with the pine nuts and almonds.

Note: If you have to use cow's milk yoghurt because of the unavailability of goat's milk yoghurt, add it almost at the end of the cooking time because of its tendency to curdle easily. Once added, do not let the mixture boil.

Installation of a Chief

While working on a story in South Africa and travelling from Durban southwards via the Wild Coast, my husband, Magnum photographer Ian Berry, and I decided to detour through the Transkei, one of the autonomous tribal homelands, to stay at the Holiday Inn at Umtata. Gambling is illegal in South Africa, legal in the homelands, so naturally there is much traffic to and from hotels which have gaming rooms. We approached an unprepossessing low-lying concrete structure, but stepped into a miniature Las Vegas. The ground floor, gaudily decorated and over-bright with chandeliers, was packed with one-armed bandits, coloured lights displays and patrons both black and white, dressed as flashily as their surroundings in satins of peacock and crimson, sequins and feathers, gold Rolex watches and shiny ostrich and crocodile skin shoes - all the trappings of wealth.

The following morning, our lust for losing money slaked, we were back to work and at the Government Information Office, learned that there was to be an installation of a Chief of one of the local Xhosa tribes. It would involve a twenty-four hour delay in the Transkei, but it sounded as though the story would be worth it.

Instructions from Africans of how to get to places are vague and are likely to include statements like 'travel for three days', which translate to mean the time taken on foot. Once out of the capital, and after about an hour's driving in the suggested direction, we began to see tribal members streaming towards a point somewhere in front of us from all directions over the surrounding hills, confirmation that we were going the right way. Nearer still, we turned a corner and pulled up behind three cars full of local dignitaries and the Chief to be. This was his cavalcade and promptly we were invited to join it, an extra car could only add to the Chief's standing among his people.

In convoy we bumped along, following the dust cloud which totally obscured the other vehicles. A couple of miles further, the procession turned on to a large open grassy area where a small canopied stage had been erected. I don't think we knew what to expect but this was disappointing. The Chief's and other dignitaries disappeared; we separated, I to scout round and take notes, Ian to photograph.

Discovering a large pot of the missionary-eating variety set on a good fire of wood sticks, I asked what was to be cooked and was shown a goat tethered nearby under a tree. I cannot report on the ritual killing of the animal; I kept away from the area until I could be sure it was ready for the pot. Meanwhile, the crowd streaming across the hills began to thin and the crowd around the stage thickened, good humoured and jostling, and dressed in their best and most festive clothing. The women's ankle-length skirts were of brightly patterned local cloth wound round and round their waists, their blouses plain and store-bought. On their heads they had fashioned turbans from strips of cloth and most favoured red. The men, although dressed in shirts and trousers, western-style, were blanket-wrapped in the local custom. Mothers used their blankets to tie their babies to their backs. And everyone waited.

As the waiting time extended to two hours and more, those sitting around the stage began singing, a thrilling sound of voices in natural harmonies - the African equivalent of 'Why are we waiting', we supposed. By this time, the goat, chopped randomly from end to end, although the entrails had been carefully removed in total length before the chopping, had been thrown into the warm water and the pot was stoked to get it seething. It seemed that the meat was given no benefit of seasoning or flavouring whatsoever. After about an hour, the intestines were carefully laid in the grey scummy water and cooked for a while, before being lifted out on a stick, inspected, and allowed to singe a little in the flames now leaping up around the pot. They were put back into the pot and cooking continued.

Alerted to the beginning of the proceedings by the high eerie sound of the women ululating in honour of the Chief, we hurried to the stage. There was no tribal dancing, no singing, other than the spontaneous outburst earlier, and no mock warlike clashes between groups of youths. The installation was a low-key affair. The Chief made a few speeches, as did other dignitaries and, in less than an hour, the ceremony was over. When asked to join the feast, I accepted and squatted on the ground in readiness. Ian, having seen the boiled goat, tried to explain that we had another engagement.

His instinct was right. The meal when it was proffered was almost indescribably unpleasant to look at. It didn't smell very good either. The greyly-boiled meat, sitting on the plates with its liquid (bereft as I thought of seasoning or flavouring), was topped with a portion of the choicest part, those intestines, and served with a spoonful of mealie (sweetcorn) and some green leafy vegetable.

After our first taste we became quite skilful at 'accidentally' dropping bits of food for the scavenging dogs, and hiding the rest under the green vegetable leaves. What bits we managed to eat we felt lucky to keep down. The feast finished with a pudding of tinned fruit cocktail (and this in a land of super-abundant fresh fruit) with thick and lumpy custard of the Bird's variety and throughout the meal, orangeade to drink, the Quosh bottles proudly displayed.

It is interesting to note that expensively-bought and not very good Western-style foods in tins and bottles were a feast for the new Chief and the local worthies, as well thought of as, say, the marrons glaces or vintage Champagne we treat ourselves to for Christmas. I couldn't be sure of this, of course, but I did notice that we were the only ones not eating with relish.

And now for the boiled goat recipe...

Of Sugar and Porcelain
Table decoration in the Netherlands in the 18th Century

by Joop Witteveen

When the Ancien Régime in Western Europe came violently to an end in the French Revolution and the Napoleonic wars, the privileged status of the nobility and the higher clergy ceased to exist as well. With it disappeared a way of feasting, developed by the nobility in the course of almost eight centuries into a very complicated ritual. In this ritual, table decoration played an important role in banquets and in the 18th century the decoration had taken on a specific shape. In this paper I will focus on the 18th century Dutch table decoration, and on what it meant to the people who joined those tables.

Good sources for examining decorations are pictures and descriptions of the feasts and its decorations because the actual decorations, usually made of transient materials, have not been preserved. Pictures of feasts and decorations from all over Europe have been collected in two recent studies. 'Baroque Table Decorations' by Stephan Bursche and 'Household Silver, 16th till 19th century' by Alain Gruber [1]. Both books deal with the 16th to 18th century. Many pictures, especially those from the 18th century, represent scenes from the Imperial court at Vienna. There are also pictures from France, Italy, Sweden and several German principalities. Remarkably enough, England is not mentioned.

All the pictures, be they from the Middle Ages, the Burgundian period, or from the time of Louis XIV or Empress Maria Theresa, show a similar scene: a buffet loaded with golden and silver dishes, ewers, tankards and goblets. Over a period of at least six centuries princes had their gold and silver forged into these beautiful and awe-inspiring objects. They displayed their possessions both on the buffet and on the tables; golden plates and dishes on the princely table, silver ones on the other.

Table Decoration of Sugar

Not only dishes of precious metals were placed on the tables, but decorative elements also. At a wedding banquet of a Burgundian duke numerous counterfeited exotic animals stood on the tables, hung about with baskets filled with all kinds of comfits [2]. These sweets were to be eaten after the meal [3].

In the same period, the second half of the 15th century, it appears that in Italy, the table decoration was made of sugar. In the summer of 1473, Eleonora of Aragon, the daughter of the king of Naples, travelled to Ferrara to marry Ercole I d'Este. On her way she visited Rome and dined with the two cardinals della Rovere, cousins of the reigning pope. The entire table decoration for this meal was made of sugar: a statue, almost life-size, representing Hercules fighting with monsters, a serpent winding around a mountain made of sugar and a castle of sugar decorated with flags. Ten ships filled with acorns all made of sugar decorated the table, the acorn being the heraldic emblem of the della Rovere family [4].

At this banquet of the Rovere cardinals it is already clearly visible how the table decoration will develop: depicting representations of classical gods and heroes (as allegories of the prince and his princely qualities), the coat of arms and the devices of the prince and princely architecture. In the course of time the Renaissance, the Baroque and Rococo will shape the table decorations after their own ideals.

The Italian habit of using sugar as raw material for table decorations spread all over Europe, slowly at first but picking up rapidly in the 16th century when the production of sugar started in the Caribbean and in Brazil. Until the French Revolution at the end of the 18th century, sugar remained an important raw material for table decoration.

Desserts

In contrast to what one might expect, 18th century table decoration was not on the table throughout the meal. It was brought in just before the last course, the dessert, hence the similar name for the decoration: "dessert".

The edible dessert consisted of confitures, candied fruits, creams, jellies, ices, pastry, cookies, rare fresh fruits like pineapples and savouries like pickled gherkins, olives, anchovies and radishes [5]. All this was arranged around the table decoration in the right order and in a strict symmetry, just as was customary for the other courses of the banquet.

A special craftsman - not the cook - prepared the desserts. The *"chef de l'Office"*, as he was called, was specialized in preparing all what was needed, decoration included. Recipes for *l'Office* or dessert making can be found in specialized cookbooks such as *'Nouvelles Instructions pour les Confitures (...) avec la Manière de bien ordonner un Dessert'* by Massialot [6] or in the famous but very rare *'Le Cannamelliste Français ou Nouvelle Instructions Pour Ceux qui Desirent D'apprendre l'Office (...)'* (The French cannamelliste, or a new instruction for those who wish to learn the Office) This book was written by a Sieur Gilliers, *chef de l'Office* and distiller of his majesty the King of Poland, Duke of Lorraine and Bar. The employer of Gilliers was the father-in-law of the French king, Louis XV. The book was published in 1751 in Lunéville near Nancy at the author's own expense [7]. Some of its illustrations are reproduced in Bursche's *'Tafelzier des Barock'* [8] and in Barbara Wheaton's *'Savouring the Past'*. But Wheaton does not mention Gilliers at all [9].

It must have been a whim of lady Fortune that in the Republic of the United Provinces of the Netherlands a number of good illustrations of 18th century table decorations has been preserved, along with ample descriptions. These decorations do not originate from the court of the Stadholder but from feasts of rich citizens. Good occasions for such feasts were the celebrations of the bicentennials of the Leyden [10] and Utrecht universities [11], the wedding-feast of an Amsterdam burgomaster, or the meals organised for political purposes by fractions supporting the Stadholder - or by their adversaries [12]. The *chefs de l'Office* who made these decorations were neither employed by the court of the Stadholder nor by the nobility. They were independent pastry cooks in various Dutch cities. About 1750, the Amsterdam pastry cook, Gerrit van den Brenk, published a handbook, describing his recipes and explaining the techniques used for making table decoration, titled: 'A Dialogue between a Lady and a pastry cook - Confiturier'. This handbook became rather popular, by 1760 already four editions had been published [13].

What did the Table Decoration look like?

The 18th century table decoration was designed after the princely pleasure- palace surrounded by its formal gardens. In the Netherlands only a few of such palaces existed, though much smaller in size than those in France or Germany. But the Dutch society offered other models for table decoration: the country houses and gardens of the rich.

Amsterdam merchants owned country houses with gardens in the newly reclaimed Watergraafsmeer, just outside Amsterdam. The gardens of these country houses served as models for the Dutch pastry cooks. They had either seen the gardens themselves or the illustrations of them in a book depicting these houses and gardens (plates A, B) [14]. Rather small in size, the soil being flat without any natural or artificial differences in height, these enclosed gardens were intimate and private.

So were the table decorations. Though the enclosures by walls or hedges are omitted, the decorations give no illusion of extensiveness, but suggest clarity and intimacy. This effect was created by placing the garden on a legged plateau, mounted with gold or silver coloured borders. The plateaus were made of mirror-glass [15], which was very practical. The dessert was the last course of a supper, often served at dusk. Candlelight was then needed and the brightness of the light was increased by means of large mirrors. The light reflected by the glass plate of the plateau gave the impression that the decoration was also lit from below, which added to the artistic appearance.

A Golden Wedding

On June 28, 1757, the Amsterdam Burgomaster, Gerrit Hooft and his wife, Hester Hinlopen celebrated the 50th anniversary of their wedding [16]. The dessert for the festive supper was built on such a mirror-glass plateau. The edible part of the dessert was placed around the decoration and consisted of many fruits. Not only the fruits in season but also peaches, cantaloup melon, but pineapple, grapes and "all that can be produced by the art of the forcing. One got the impression that summer and autumn had merged into just one season", the chronicler wrote about this feast. He was convinced that the statues in the decoration rightly reflected the qualities of those who were honoured with the feast and the occasion on which it was celebrated [17].

The centre-piece of this decoration (plate C) was a temple - ten feet long, seven feet high and three feet broad - comprising of eight gilded columns on pedestals of sugar. These pedestals were decorated with musical instruments in bas-relief, which indicates that they were cast in a mould. The roof of the temple represented a cloud made of (probably) spun sugar. The floor of the temple was sprinkled with coloured sugar forming a tapestry which was decorated with flowers and plants, the number 50 being woven in its borders.

On both sides of the temple was a terrace-like elevation on which the names and the coats of arms of the burgomaster and his wife were sprinkled in coloured sugar. On both ends of the decoration there were similar statues of water and river gods, resembling the sculptured river gods on the edges of the ponds in the real gardens. The river gods represent the Amstel and the Y, (the river and the harbour of Amsterdam), which is indicated by images of sprinkled coloured sugar at the feet of the gods [18].

Triumphal arches were placed between the terraces with the coats of arms and the river gods. The arches were three feet high and made of sugar, and in them statues of the Amsterdam patroness and Minerva were placed.

The chronicler of this feast tells us once more that the decoration is made of sugar and that along its edges crystalline arches and beautiful figures of Saxon porcelain were placed. Distributed over the garden were parterres (rocaille shaped flower beds), and the usual garden decorations like putti, vases, urns, trees pruned in the shape of pyramids, balustrades and hedges of Taxus leaves.

Inside the temple and in the garden were many statues, representing the qualities of the burgomaster and his wife. In front of the temple stood Hercules with his club, the unwavering, audacious hero who all by himself performed the Twelve Labors. He was considered to be the personification of the prince and subsequently of the burgher-prince, the burgomaster of Amsterdam. Hercules guarded the temple with the statues - all like Hercules fifteen inches high - of the virtues Gratitude, Reason, Generosity, Merit, Love, Fidelity, Vigilance and Concord. On the roof of the temple Illustriousness can be seen. At her side is a Youth with crown and sceptre pointing to Heaven and an old winged man with an hourglass, being Time.

The decoration for the wedding anniversary of Hooft and his wife made a strong impression. Not only had it been pictured and described in detail, it also was exhibited for three days on the premises of the maker, the Amsterdam pastry cook, Adriaen Kok. Many people who held high offices came to see it [19].

Pastry and Dessert Makers

In 1757 Kok was already pastry cook for more than 25 years. He created the detailed and ingenious dessert at the installation in 1751 of Stadholder William IV in Vlissingen [20]. Well-to-do citizens also used to order their desserts from Adriaen Kok.

A description of an Amsterdam wedding in 1750 tells us that the mothers of both bride and groom, together with the young couple, went to the shop of Mr. Kok to choose statues for the dessert. On the wedding day the dessert was exhibited in the house of the bride and many people came to have a look at it. At night it stood on the table amidst fruits, confitures and other sweets, a light burning in the temple. At the moment the light gave out the bride was brought to her sleeping room, as custom required [21].

Not only Amsterdam had fine dessert makers, the university cities Leiden and Utrecht had them as well, so had the seat of the government, The Hague. Of their work, descriptions and pictures have survived, such as those of the beautiful desserts made by Pieter van Gelleke in The Hague (plates D and E) [22] for the feast given by the Austrian ambassador Baron Reischach on the 19th of January 1746. The occasion for the celebration was the coronation of the Emperor Francis I, the husband of Maria Theresa, Empress of Austria. Van Gelleke made four desserts, three for a table of twenty-four persons and one, the greatest and the principal one, for seventy persons. The coat of arms of the Austrian Emperor, the crowned double eagle, played a prominent part in the decoration. The principal table was even made in a special shape to make it represent the double eagle. On the pictures of the four desserts one can clearly distinguish a temple in the centre of a formal garden, embellished with triumphal arches, statues, vases, pruned trees and hedges [23].

The Statues

The building of the dessert was made in close cooperation with the commissioner. He chose the themes and the statues.

That the 18th century table decoration or dessert was popular in the Netherlands can be illustrated with a scene from the satirical play 'A Mirror of our Merchants', by the in Holland well-known playwright Pieter Langendijk. The play criticizes the Dutch merchant who no longer seeks new markets, but prefers to speculate on the Stock Exchange in stead, risking to loose his capital. This modern merchant has given up the old morals and follows "the French way of living". The principal character of the play, Lightheart, is one of them. Celebrating his birthday, friends have been invited for the evening meal, and a dessert is ordered.

In the second scene of the first act where the principal character is introduced, the pastry cook is arranging the dessert.

Lightheart asks the pastry cook Sweettooth:

"Tell me, which symbols do you show at this meal?"

Sweettooth answers:

> "The Tower of Babel made of white sugar will be in the middle of the lake, according to an illustration in Flavius Josephus' book, the Jewish historian.
> Your name and age will be written in gold over the entrance.
> The lake is surrounded by caves inlaid with shells.
> Venus will sail in it in her shell and whales are swimming around.
> You will see Neptune, taming the sea with his trident.
> Two East-India ships will sail in it, bound for Batavia, manned with sugar bankrupts.
> The names of the ships are the Phaeton and the Icarus, sculptured in the Town Hall".

Lightheart:

> "Is this your invention ?"

Lightheart's father, who does not at all agree with his son's life style, appears to have ordered this dessert. This infuriates Lightheart who exclaims:

> "When you put that on the table, I will smash it to pieces, all your sugar dolls and ornaments.
> It is a lampoon, it hurts my decency.
> ....
> Say master Sweettooth, can't you transform it?
> You have got so many statues".

Sweettooth answers that if he were to change it into a temple of Mercury, he would have to work on it until night. But Lightheart tells him:

> "Well, then do so" [24].

Lightheart is understandably angry about his father's intervention regarding the dessert and wants to see the Tower of Babel, centre-piece of the decoration and symbol of the pride of the human race, to be replaced by a respectable temple of Mercury, which refers to his trade only. Although the description of the decoration is satirical and the symbolism of a negative nature, all the elements of a (Dutch) dessert are present. The centre-piece is a temple, placed in a lake surrounded by grottos made of shells. Statues of classical gods refer symbolically to the person who offers the feast. Ships bound for the East Indies symbolize the Dutch merchants of the East India Company as well as those who leave the country for the colonies after their bankruptcy. It is no coincidence that these ships bear the names of the sons of Greek gods, Phaeton and Icarus, who were brought down by their pride. The author of the play even specifies the sculptures of Phaeton and Icarus placed over the entrance of one of the offices in the Town hall, to which one had to go to report a bankruptcy.

In describing a table decoration the playwright Langendijk succeeds in depicting the main character. Using means normally employed to praise the host as a person of great stature, he lets the father turn the meaning of the table decoration into the opposite.

Because of all the different themes the pastry cooks were obliged to have a great collection of statues at hand to satisfy the various demands of their customers. When in Langendijk's play Lightheart asks how Sweettooth is going to decorate the table, the latter answers :

> "Like I have done in The Hague for Ambassadors and other Lords. I have got thousands of statues kept in fine English glass" [25].

The pastry cooks indeed had a great number of statues in stock, along with a large collection of moulds. In the 'Amsterdam Newspaper' of the 26th of January 1732, Adriaen Kok announced that he had all kind of new moulds available and that he is able to supply "all kinds of fine sugar statues" to every shopkeeper or private person in town as well as abroad [26].

The descriptions of the desserts make it clear that a garden with a temple in its centre - no matter how the design may vary - forms the scene in which the statues perform the silent play of meanings.

How did the pastry cooks find the models for their statues? A clear answer is found in Van den Brenk [27]: in model books. The *"Iconologia"* by the Italian Cesare Ripa (Rome 1593) is the most important one. In the 17th century this book was most often used by the painters of allegories, a much higher valued art form than still-life or genre-painting. Ripa describes how the allegories had to be painted and what attributes and colours had to be used. In 1644 a Dutch translation was published [28], several editions followed. The numerous statues in the dessert of burgomaster Hooft can all be found in Ripa's book. The sculptured decorations in the Amsterdam Town hall as well are derived from it. The playwright Langendijk makes an allusion to these decorations in his description of the dessert. The model for the Tower of Babel in this same dessert came from an illustration in an other book "The Jewish Histories" by Flavius Josephus.

Van den Brenk's handbook is very brief on the making of moulds for the statues. "Have them made from wood, or just buy them", is his laconic advise [29]. We already saw Adriaen Kok advertising that he had new moulds in stock. Obviously craftsmen made such moulds, consisting of two halves, one for the front of the statue, the other for the back. The statues were made of a mixture of very finely grained sugar and gum tragacanth. This mixture forms a dough that can easily be kneaded and will become hard when dried and it is also edible. One half of the mould is filled with the dough and a same amount of it is placed on top. Then the other half of the mould is placed over it and both halves are strongly pressed together. The statue is then removed from the mould and put aside to dry. When dried it is not yet complete. Lacking are the attributes which give it its exact meaning. From the remaining dough the attributes are shaped and pasted on the statue with a watery solution of gum tragacanth [30].

Ripa's book mentions which attribute belongs to a certain representation and which colours are needed. Gold leaf was sometimes used and also eaten because it was thought to be wholesome.

Porcelain

When in the first quarter of the 18th century the production of porcelain in Europe had been invented, the sugar statues had to compete with the porcelain ones. As the sugar statues were made of a cheap material the porcelain ones were preferred, because of their high costs and rarity. Feasts before the French Revolution had to be ostentatious, and a display of rare and costly items was almost obligatory.

In the table decoration of the golden wedding of the Amsterdam burgomaster statues of Saxon porcelain had their place. Temples too were made of this new material. Between 1730 and 1760 Johann Joachim Kaendler was the greatest designer in the porcelain manufactury in Meiszen in Saxony. His designs of figures represented a whole new world of images. These statues no longer referred to the past, but depicted contemporaries in elegant Rococo dress and gestures. Such figures found a place in the gardens of the table decoration. He made temples of porcelain as well, some of which have been preserved [31]. Van den Brenk, who in his handbook described so well the craft of making desserts of sugar lamented in the introduction to the chapter on table decorations 'nowadays many statues and figurines are made of Saxon porcelain, whereas sugar statues are hardly used any more' [32]. Porcelain finally replaced sugar.

References

1. Bursche, Stephan: *Tafelzier des Barock*. München, Editions Schneider, 1974.
   Gruber, Alain: *l'Argenterie de maison, du XVIe au XIXe siécle*. Fribourg, Office du Livre, 1982. German edition: *Gebrauchssilber des 16. bis 19. Jahrhundert*. Fribourg, Office du Livre, and Würzburg, Editions Popp, 1982.
2. De la Marche, Olivier: *Mémoires d'Olivier De la Marche, Maître d'Hotel et Capitaine des Gardes de Charles le Téméraire* edited by Henri Beaune and J. d'Abremont, 4 vols, Paris, 1883-1885, vol III: pp 165-66.
   Cartellieri, Otto: *Am Hofe des Herzogen von Burgund*, Basel, Benno Schwabe, 1926, pp 172-77.
3. Witteveen, Joop: Rose Sugar and other medieval Sweets, *P.P.C.* 20. London, Prospect Books, 1985, pp 24-5.
4. Chledowski, Kazimierz: *Het Hof van Ferrara* (the Court of Ferrara). Translated from the Polish by B. Fogelfang. Amsterdam, 1927: p 73. Chledowski's source is:
   Gandini, L.A.: *Tavola, Cantina e Cucina della Corte di Ferrara nel Cuattrocento*, Modena, 1889 (not seen).
5. *De Volmaakte Hollandsche Keukenmeid* (The Perfect Dutch Cook), onderwijzende Hoe men allerhande Spijzen, Confituren en Nagerechten (...) gezond en smakelijk kan toebereiden, Amsterdam, Steven van Esveldt, 1748: p 146.
6. *Nouvelle Instruction Pour Les Confitures, Les Liqueurs Et Les Fruits*. Avec la Manière de bien ordonner un Dessert, & tout la reste qui est du Devoir des Maîtres d'Hôtels, Sommeliers, Confiseurs, & autres Officiers du Bouche. Suite du Cuisinier Roïal & Bourgeois. Egalement utile dans les Familles, pour sçavoir ce qu'on sert de plus dans les Repas, & en d'autres occasions. Paris, Chez Charles de Sercy, 1692.
   (The author of the Cuisinier Roïal is Massialot).
7. Gilliers: *Le Cannameliste français* ou nouvelles instructions pour ceux qui Désirent d'Apprendre l'office, rédigé en forme de dictionnaire, contenant les noms, les descriptions, les usages, les choix et les principes de tout ce qui se pratique dans l'office, l'explication de tous les termes dont on se sert; avec la manière de dessiner et de

former toutes sortes de contours des Tables et de Dormants. Enrichie de planches en taille douce. Par le sieur Gilliers, Chef de l'Office, et Distillateur de Sa Majesté le Roi de Pologne, Duc de Lorraine en de Bar; Nancy, de l'Imprimerie d'Abel-Denis Cusson, au nom de Jesus et se vend à Lunéville chez l'auteur, 1751. Avec 13 planches gravés.
The word 'Cannameliste" has been coined from "canne à sucre" (sugar-cane) and "mel" (honey).

8. See ref. 1
9. Wheaton, Barbara Ketcham: *Savouring the Past*. The French kitchen and table from 1300 till 1789. London, Chatto & Windus, 1983: p 187.
10. Fock, C.W. and Ekkart, R.E.O.: De confiturier Jan Honkoop en het dessert op 8 februari 1775. *Leids Jaarboekje, Deel 68*, Leiden, 1976: pp 80-110.
    K, A.J.C. van der, Een kostbaar Suikerwerk, *De Oude Tijd*, Haarlem, A.C. Kruseman, 1870: pp 246-7.
11. Vries, D. de: *Nauwkeurige Beschrijving van alle Plechtigheden, Vreugdebedrijven enz.*, Zo ter gelegenheid van de honderdvijftigste Verjaring van de Utrechtsche Hoge Schole op den 31 May 1786 gevierd, als van den promotie met kap. Utrecht, 1786 (not seen).
12. Grijzenhout, Frans: *Feesten voor het Vaderland. Patriotse en Bataafse Feesten 1780-1806*. Zwolle, Waanders, 1989.
13. Brenk, Gerrit van den: *t'Zaamen-spraaken tusschen een Mevrouw, Banketbakker en Confiturier*, 4 parts, Amsterdam, Erven de weduwe Jacobus van Egmont, about 1750.
14. Brouërius van Niedek, H: *Het Verheerlijkt Watergraafs- of Diemermeer*, with copperplates by Daniel Stoopendaal. Amsterdam, 1725, Folio.
15. van den Brenk Part II: p. 22.
    Beschrijving der voornaamste Vreugde-Bedrijven in 's Gravenhage ter gelegenheid van de krooning van Zijne Keizerlijke Majesteit Franciscus I enz. enz., La Haye, aux dépens d'Antoine de Groot et Fils, MDCCXLVI.
16. *Nederlandsche Jaarboeken*. Elfde Deels, Tweede Stuk. Amsterdam, F. Houttuyn, 1757: pp 569-80.
17. Nederlandsche Jaarboeken: p 571
18. According to van den Brenk similar end pieces of the table decorations were typical for the Dutch style of decorating, in which it differs from the French style. Part IV: p 24.
19. *Nederlandsche Jaarboeken*: p 579.
20. Huët, Daniel Theodor: *Inhuldiging van Zijne Doorluchtige Hoogheid Willem Karel Frederik Friso (...) als Erf Heer van Vlissingen op den Vden van Junij MDCCLI*. Amsterdam, Isaak Tirion, 1753.
    This book has a detailed description, unfortunately it is not illustrated.
21. Eeghen, S.H. van: Een Amsterdamse Bruiloft in 1750. *Jaarboek Amstelodamum 1958*, Amsterdam, 1958, pp 142-88.
22. Schimmelpenninck - Hartman, E.C. and Zonnewijle - Heyning, C.E.: Achttiende-eeuwse Tafelversiering van Suiker. *Leids Kunsthistorisch Jaarboek 1985*, Delft 1987 (pp 437-51): p 445.
23. *Beschrijving der Voornaamste Vreugde-Bedrijven*.
24. Langendijk, Pieter: *Spiegel der Vaderlandsche Kooplieden*. Edited by G.A. van Es, Zutphen, W.J. Thieme, 1979: verses 10-43.
25. Ib: verses 18-19.
26. Schimmelpenninck: pp 441, 445.
27. van den Brenk: Part II, p 15.
28. *Iconologia, of uytbeeldingen des Verstands, van Cesare Ripa van Perugien (...) waer in verscheiden afbeeldingen van Deughden, Ondeughden, Genegentheden, Menschelijke Hertztochten, Konsten, Leeringen, Sinlijckheden, Elementen, Hemelsche Lichamen (...) en alle andere ontallijcke stoffen, met haare verklaringen werden verhandelt (...) uyt het Italiaans vertaelt door D.P. Pers*. Amstelredam, by Dirck Pietersz Pers, Boekverkooper op 't Water (...) in't Jaer 1644.
29. van den Brenk, Part II: p 15.
30. Ib.: pp 15-6.
31. Bursche, illustrations no. 304, 305, 306.
32. van den Brenk, Part II: Tot de Leezer (Introduction).

PLATE A

REIGERSBURG, uit het Kabinet naer het
Huis toe te zien.

Vüe de REIGERSBURG Cabinet
vers la Maison.

PLATE B

MEERGENOEGEN, van de voorpoort door
de bloemverken en Triumfboog naer
achteren toe te zien.

Vüe de MEERGENORGEN, du Coté du Jardin
& de l'Arc de Tiomphe.

PLATE C

AFBEELDINGE van het DESSERT der VIER VOORNAAMSTE TAFELS van het FESTYN, door Zyne Excellentie den Heer BARON VAN REISCHACH, Rooms Keyzerlyken Minister in den Haag, gegeven den 19 January 1746, ter gelegenheid van de VERKIEZING en KROONING van ZYNE ROOMS KEYZERLYKE MAJESTEIT.

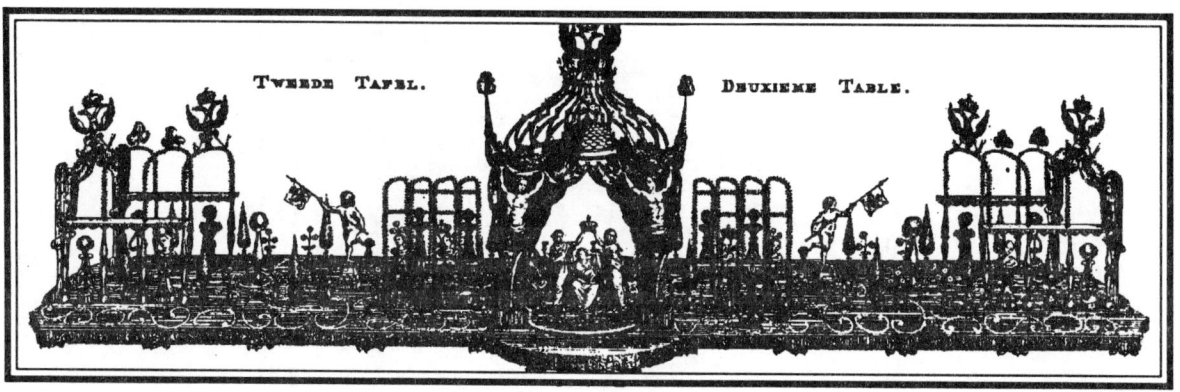

PLATE D

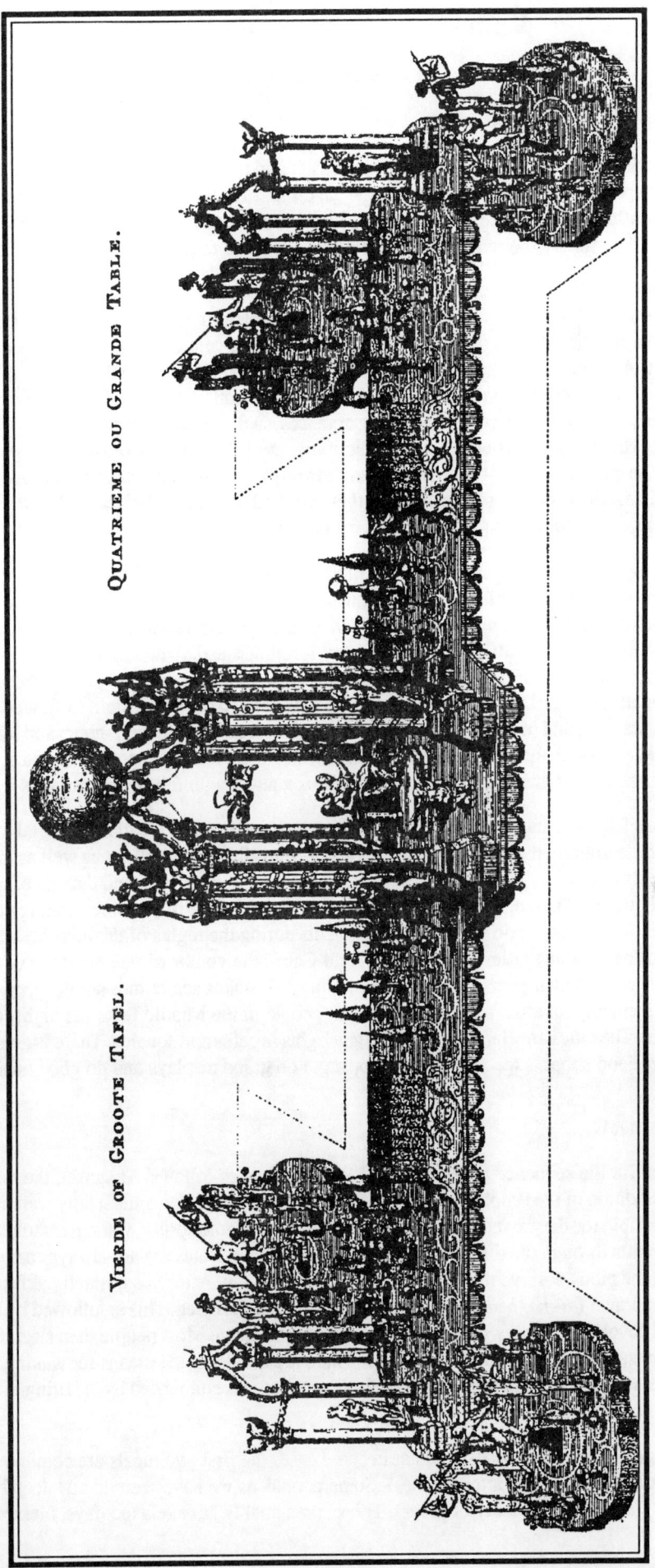

PLATE E
VIERDE OF GROOTE TAFEL - QUATRIEME OU GRANDE TABLE

Ramadhan: Fasting and Feasting

by Sami Zubaida

Every ritual fast ends with a feast. Lent is followed by Easter and its special foods. The supper after the fast of Yom Kippur turns into a special feast. Ramadhan has the special distinction, however, of repeating the fast-feast cycle each day for a lunar month. As such, there is an elaborate culture, both culinary and social, surrounding the month of Ramadhan. First, let us survey the religious specifications and ritual requirements of the month.

Ramadhan is a holy month to Muslims. The Quran was revealed during this month. Fasting the month is one of the five major duties of a Muslim. The month begins with the sighting of the new moon (the Muslim calendar being lunar). Following Ottoman practice, this is usually indicated by the firing of a cannon. The fast begins at daybreak the following morning. At sunset, also marked by the firing of a cannon or some other public signal, the believer is obliged to break his or her fast. He or she can then eat and drink all night until daybreak. The fast is rigorous: no food and no drink. Religious schools differ on certain minor observances, such as whether it is allowed to wash out one's mouth with water, taking extreme care, of course, not to swallow any, or whether one can brush one's teeth or swallow excess saliva, and so on. Certain categories of people are exempt from the fast: the sick, those who must travel, pregnant and menstruating women. All except the seriously ill are then required to fast on other days, after Ramadhan, to make up for the days missed, as are those who break the fast for one reason or another.

In addition to fasting, the Muslim must also strive to higher levels of piety and virtuous conduct to mark the holiness of the month. Conflicts and antagonisms between Muslims must be resolved or forgotten. Visiting and sociability between relatives and friends on the nights of Ramadhan are thought to promote peace and reconciliation (or at least this gives conviviality a religious rationale). Believers are forbidden sexual intercourse or any sexual contact during the hours of fasting, though not during the night. In general, Muslims are enjoined to voluntary restraint over pleasures and indulgences at all times during the month. The believer is not expected to abstain from work during the days of fasting, though in practice, and in most places, there is a general relaxation in work hours and long siestas. Only the poor have to continue working for their daily bread at the normal rate. Pious folk spend long hours, especially between the night meals, reading the Quran and discussing religious matters with fellow worshippers in mosques.

These requirements for piety and abstinence, however, are contradicted by the general social tendency to feasting after a fast. People sleep little, if at all, during the nights of Ramadhan. They all eat as well as they they can afford, in two or three meals (as we shall see) and in between. Some devout persons spend the rest of the time in religious pursuits in the mosques or at home. But many spend the nights in conviviality at home, visiting others, or in the cafes and public squares. The cafes put on special entertainments during the nights of the month, such as story tellers or singers and musicians. In some cities, like Baghdad and Cairo, the youths of one quarter pay a collective visit to another where they engage their peers in competitive games, the stakes sometimes are the provision of sweetmeats to the assembled company. In most places and for most people in the Middle East, the nights of Ramadhan are a continuous festival. The cities are alive at night with gay lights in cafes and squares. There is music in the air and the smells of cooking. Food shops, especially sweet shops, put on grand displays and do good business.

The Sequence of Meals

The religious ideal for the sequence of the nights of Ramadhan is as follows. At sunset, the fast is broken (*iftar*), according to to a tradition of the Prophet, with some dates or the water of Zamzam, a holy well in Mecca. The latter, of course, is impossible for the great majority, who may substitute some spring water. Ramadhan, being a month in a lunar calendar, shifts through the differrent seasons over the years. Dates are not always easily available. All that can be said is that the pious observe the tradition in so far as they can. After this initial breakfast, the believer must perform the sunset prayer (*al-maghrib*). After the prayer a full meal is eaten. This is followed by hours of sociability and/or prayer and devotion, during which sweets and snacks are eaten. Most people then sleep for a few hours, but must waken before sunrise to eat a final meal, *suhur*. There are usually some means for waking people for *suhur*, a cryer or a drummer walking through the streets. At sunrise, sometimes announced by the firing of a cannon, all eating and drinking must cease.

This sequence is generally followed, except that in some cases the first two meals are combined into one, and the prayer either omitted or performed after the meal. Some people, as we have seen do not sleep but spend the hours between iftar and suhur in conviviality or prayer. Those, presumably have relaxed days, blessed by some hours of sleep.

Literary Representations

The festive air of the month, the special atmosphere it generates at night, are naturally the stuff of nostalgia, fantasy, and poetic imagery. Literary representations of the month abound. I have chosen here a particularly vivid illustration of the features of Ramadhan in a novel by Nejib Mahfouz, *Khan al-Khalili*. This is set in Cairo during the years of World War II. The central character, Ahmad Akef, is an unmarried middle aged civil servant, living with and supporting his parents in a flat in the central part of old Cairo, near the mosque of al-Hussain. Akef earns little and is careful with his money. The approach of Ramadhan is the occasion of gentle banter with his parents about provisions. Ramadhan, argues the mother, has its rights as well as its duties. We soon discover that the 'rights' consist of food provisions. At the mention of *kunafa* and *qataif*, popular sweetmeats in Egypt as elsewhere in the Middle East, Akef is swept by a wave of nostalgia and relents. The father then intervenes to underline the necessity for a small quantity of pine nuts and raisins for the stuffings, and half a roll of *gamar-eddin* for breaking the fast. Gamar-eddin refers to sheets of dried apricot paste, which can be eaten as it is, but for Ramadhan is usually made into a drink taken first thing at *iftar*. Another discussion then develops over how much meat is needed per week to sustain those fasting, concluding that meat must be eaten two days out of every three. The mother spends the few days before Ramadhan in cleaning up and preparing the kitchen and putting down stores of flour, sugar, fats and oils, onions, spices and so on, for Ramadhan, we are told, is the month of the kitchen as much as it is of fasting.

Ramadhan is announced at the sighting of the new moon. In the evening the minaret of the Hussain mosque is brightly lit with strings of lights. Groups of people wander around the quarter beating drums and shouting in rhyme 'fasting, fasting, ordered by the Qadhi of Islam', and are greeted by boys and girls shouting, singing and ululating, gaiety and excitement spreads through the quarter. Akef's father, however, is nostalgic for the Ramadhans of his youth, which were naturally even better. The night was alive with song and conversation and play. And at the time of suhur, he and his companions would descend on the specialist food shops of the quarter for a meal of cowheel and heads, followed by a smoke of the water pipe at al-Hussain cafe.

On the first day of the fast, Ahmad Akef has a difficult time, missing his morning coffee and cigarette. He spends the working day at the ministry yawning, half asleep. He goes home at noon and falls into a deep sleep, waking one hour before sunset. He washes himself, then wanders around the apartment. He passes by his father's room and finds him intent upon his prayers and devotions. He then passes by the kitchen and fills his nostrils with the aromas of food. His gaze pauses at a large platter filled with salad vegetables of parsley and rocket, carrots and onions and tomatoes, glowing green and pale red. This delights his heart and intensifies his appetite. His patience and resolve almost collapse when he sees the large pot (*sultaniya*) of *foul* (Nile beans, a kind of fava, one of the staples of the Egyptian diet). He then passes by the dining room and sees the table set with rounds of bread and a cup of water at each place, and a pile of radishes in the middle. He can stand it no longer and goes back to his bedroom to read the daily newspaper which he has saved up precisely for this moment. Having finished reading it, he still has to wait half an hour till the time of iftar. He looks out of the window and sees all the shops and tradesmen closing down, fathers returning home to be greeted by their noisily impatient children. Then came the wonderful moment awaited by all, when the sound of the cannon is heard, and the sweet chant of the muezzin from the neighbouring mosque. The three of them then gather around the table, gratify their thirst with a deep drink of the liquified gamar-eddin, then fall upon the foul and finish it quickly. The father then remarks that it would be better to leave the foul till after in order to be able to eat other things with appetite, and the mother responds laughing that that is what is said every year. However, they still have plenty of room in their bellies for green beans, stuffed peppers and fried meat. We should keep in mind that this is a relatively poor family, going through the difficult period of the war years.

Akef leaves the house after dinner and repairs to the local cafe for a session of conviviality with his circle of men of the quarter. This ends at midnight, when Akef, a serious and virtuous man, goes home to read till the hour of suhur. Some of his companions, however, have other ideas for the night, like smoking hashish, or amusing themselves at a house of ill repute. The men who commit these sins in the holy month are not necessarily lacking in religion. The ebullient Muallem Nunu, with four wives and an army of children in one apartment, one of the worst offenders with hashish and women, observes his prayers and fasts, and is ever hopeful of the mercy of God for miserable sinners who trust in Him. The only atheist in the group is an ardent Marxist who looks down with contempt at these manifestations of decadence of the old order.

The Foods of Ramadhan

The only thing that can be said in general on this subject is that there are few special dishes for Ramadhan. What distinguishes the Ramadhan table, like any feast table, is the muliplicity of dishes. Let us first survey these few specific foods. As we have seen, a tradition of the Prophet favours breaking the fast with dates. This tradition seems to be widely observed in the Arabian Peninsula and the Gulf countries, where there is, in any case, an extensive date culture.

Elsewhere, the emphasis on dates varies with piety and the seasons. The drink of gamar-eddin, which occupied such an important part on the iftar table of the Akef family, is traditional in Egypt and Greater Syria, where this confection originates. However, this drink seems to be more widely appreciated throughout the Arab world in more recent times.

For the rest, every city and region seem to have their own iftar table, consisting of feast versions of their normal foods. But there are common themes. In most places the fast is broken with a cold drink. We have noted the pervasiveness of gamar-eddin. Traditionally, however, many places favoured milky drinks: fresh milk and dates in Morocco; dates and soured milk in Libya. In Bahrain the drink is fresh lime juice. In Yemen they have a hot drink made of coffee husks called *gisher*. Another common feature is a rich soup. There is the famous *harira* of Morocco, a soup of lamb broth with a variety of pulses, vegetables, fragrant herbs and/or meat, depending on season, region and level of prosperity. It is paralleled in Iran by a very similar *ash*, with the addition, for Ramadhan, of dried fruit. A plate of green herbs and fresh vegetables, as we saw in the Akef household is also a common feature throughout the Middle East and North Africa, its composition depending on the season.

In addition to these common features, we have a variety of local dishes, the richer the better. Stuffed vine leaves and vegetables, but often cooked with meat fat and *samen* (clarified butter), roasted and stewed meats, fried fish, traditional in Egypt for the last night of Ramadhan, various *brik* (pastries stuffed with egg, tuna or cheese and deep fried) in the North African countries, and so on. The emphasis is on richness and variety, in so far as these can be afforded.

Then there are the sweets, the items of food that arouse the richest memories and nostalgias of the month. And what a great variety of sweets are offered and eaten during the nights of Ramadhan? Baklavas and kunafas and qatalf and halwas, made at home or bought ready made, with a variety of garnishes and stuffings of nuts, dried fruits, syrups and honey, sweetened cheeses, dates, and in many places, a thick cream variously known as *kaymak* (Turkish) or *qishta* (Arabic), often made from buffalo mik. These are eaten at the end of the iftar meal, and often continued through the night to lubricate the conviviality.

The Suhur Meal

Almost everywhere the traditional suhur meal was a large, rich, meaty affair. We have noted the nostalgia of Akef's father for the old days, in which he and his companions concluded the Ramadhan night with a suhur of cowheel and head meat. In Fez, Morocco, there is a tradition of eating *khlei'*, a 'confit' of mutton and/or camel meat preserved in fat. In Baghdad and southern Iraq, they ate rice and lentils with meat broth for suhur. However, of late, and in line with modern ideas about food and health, these customs are changing. Most people now report eating an ordinary breakfast for suhur, consisting of bread, butter, cheese, jam, and maybe eggs and *mahalabiyya*, a thick milky sweet.

The end of Ramadhan brings *Id al-Futur*, the feast of breaking the fast, three days of feasting, with many characteristic foods, especially sweets for each region. This is the subject for a different paper.

Dinner on Saturday evening

by Lisa Chaney and Harlan Walker

Lisa Chaney and Harlan Walker devised the dinner with the object of trying to show English food - and of a kind not usually encountered. Here is the menu followed by the recipes with some comment on their origins.

Oxford Symposium on Food & Cookery 1990.

Dinner - Sat. 22nd September

MENU

Soop Meagre [1]

☆ ☆ ☆

Boiled Mutton [2]
Carrots
Turnips
Onions
Potatoes

Sauce for Mutton [3]

☆ ☆ ☆

Snow Cheese [4]

Dessert Biscuits [5]

☆ ☆ ☆

Devils on Horseback [6]

☆ ☆ ☆

Coffee
Port

☆ ☆ ☆

Seed Cake [7]

The Recipes

1. A Soop Meagre

This recipe is taken from the delightful and scholarly *Cookery of England* by Elisabeth Ayrton, a book which has done more than most to increase our knowledge of English food. She says that it comes from 'an early nineteenth-century unpublished manuscript', but both its title and content suggest the origin is much earlier. Here is the text she quotes followed by her adaptation that the chef used:

'Take spinnage, sorrel, chervil and lettuces chop them smale then brown some butter and put in your herbs, keep them stirring that they do not burn, then have ready boiling water, and put to it a very little pepper, some salt and an onion stuck with cloves and a French roll cut in slices, and some pistachio nuts blanched and shred very fine and let all boil together. then beat up the yolks of 6 or 8 eggs with a little white wine and a piece of lemon, mix with your broth and toast a whole French roll and put it in the middle of your Dish and your soop over it if you choose you may garnish your dish with poached eggs and spinnage'

> '1/2 lb. (240 g.) leaf spinach
> 6 or 8 leaves of French sorrel
> 1 tbs chopped chervil
> 3 lettuces
> 6 oz. (180 g.) butter
> salt and pepper
> 1 onion stuck with cloves
> 2 oz. (60 g.) butter
> 2 oz. (60 g.) flour
> 2 glasses white wine
> 2 oz. (60 g.) pistachio nuts, chopped fine
> yolks of 3 eggs
> 2 tbs double cream
> 1 tbs finely chopped mixed parsley and thyme
> 1 small French loaf, sliced crisply toasted

'Wash, chop finely and mix together the spinach, sorrel, chervil and lettuces. Melt the butter in a large saucepan and turn all the leaves about in it, letting the butter just begin to colour, but only just. Fill up with a quart (1 litre) of boiling water and simmer gently for 30 minutes after adding the onion and salt and pepper.

'Pour the soup into a large bowl, remove the onion and cloves, and make a roux in the saucepan with the butter and flour. Gradually pour and stir the soup into it and add the nuts and the wine. Simmer stirring well for 2 or 3 minutes. Beat up the egg yolks with the cream and, just before serving, remove soup from heat and stir them into it. Stir well so that it is smooth and creamy, but do not let it boil or it will curdle.

'Place a slice of toast in a warmed bowl for each person, pour on the soup, sprinkle with parsley and thyme, and serve quickly.'

From *The Cookery of England* by Elisabeth Ayrton, Andre Deutsch 1974, p. 325.

2. Boiled Mutton

We did not give the chef any particular recipe. There are instructions in every eighteenth or nineteenth century cookery book - even Mrs. Beeton's are reliable. Here is Eliza Acton.

'TO BOIL A LEG OF MUTTON'

'Trim into a handsome form a well-kept, but perfectly sweet leg of mutton, of middling weight; wash, but do not soak it; lay it into a vessel as nearly of its size as convenient, and pour in rather more than sufficient cold water to cover it; set it over a good fire, and when it begins to boil, take off the scum, and continue to do so until no more appears; throw in a tablespoon of salt (after the first skimming), which will assist to bring it to the surface, and as soon as the liquor is clear, add two moderate-sized onions, stuck with a dozen cloves, a large faggot of parsley, thyme, and savoury, and four or five large carrots, and half an hour afterwards, as many turnips. Draw the pan to the side of the fire, and let the mutton be simmered *gently* for two hours and a half, from the time of its first beginning to boil. ...If stewed *softly*, as we have directed, the mutton will be found excellent dressed thus; otherwise, it will but resemble the unpalatable and ragged looking joints of fast-boiled meat, so constantly sent to table by common English cooks.

Any undressed bones of veal, mutton, or beef, boiled with the joint, will improve it much, and the liquor will then make excellent soup or bouillon.'

From *Modern Cookery* by Eliza Acton, Third Edition 1845, Longman, Brown, Green and Longmans, p. 226.

The vegetables served with the mutton should not of course be the ones cooked with it.

3. Sauce for Mutton

> 82
>
> Cosin ED Sauce for Boyld Chicken Lambe of Veal
>
> Take half a pint of Whitewine; a Ladle full of strong broath; 2 or 3 Anchovies; a little Nuttmeg sliced; one blade of Mace; two or three slices of Lemmon or in the time of the Year you may add green Grapes or Gooseberrys; beat it up thick with good butter; you may garnish y'meat with parsley or spinnage boyl'd green & shred; pour it over your meat; & if you use it for Mutton add a handfull of Capers.

From a 17th century manuscript in the possession of Lisa Chaney.

4. Snow Cheese

The 1591 recipe for the 'Dish of Snow' and the 'Snow' recipe from the same C17 MS, which follow, are ancestors of Elizabeth David's early Victorian MS. "The 'Snow' looks wonderful when decorated as instructed in my manuscript" (LC). Lisa would be most interested in any early (especially unprinted) accounts of this dish.

> **To make a dish of Snow**
>
> Take a pottle of swat thick Creame, and the white of eight Egs, and beate them altogither with a spoone, then put them into your Creme with a dish full of Rosewater, and a dish full of Sugar withall. then take a stick and make it clean, and then cut it in the end four square, and therwith beat all the aforesaid things togither, and euer as it ariseth, take it off, and put it into a Cullender, this don, take a platter and set an Apple in the midst of it, and stick a thick bush of Rosemary in the Apple. Then cast your Snow vpon the Rosemary & fill your platter therwith, and if you haue wafers, cast some withall, and so serue them forth.

From *A Book of Cookrye* by A. W., London, 1591.

> *No 48*
> *Sis Duke.*
>
> **To Make Snow**
>
> Take a quart of Cream: & the whites of 15 eggs: & some Rose-water: & sugar enough to season it; beat them together with birche twigs: & as any froth riseth take it off with a spoon; then pare away the crust of a manchet; set it in a dish; stick a branch of Rose-mary in the middle of it; lay the froth in the ~~bread~~ dish on the bread; guild the Rosemary & hang some Strawberrys; Rasberry's or currants on it; & stick wafers in the snow.
>
> You may lay this snow on a Sillabub or on any made Creame.

From Lisa's 17th century manuscript.

Here is Elizabeth David's recipe that we actually used:

> 'Three quarters of a pint of double cream
> 4 oz. of caster sugar
> 1 lemon
> ["I usually put nearly two medium sized ones"-LC]
> 2 egg whites

'Pour the cream into a large bowl; stir in the sugar, the grated peel of the lemon, and its strained juice. Have also ready a round sieve or a cheese mould standing over a plate and lined with a piece of muslin wrung out in cold water.

'Whisk the the cream mixture until it stands in peaks. Don't overdo it or it will turn to a grainy mess. Fold in the stiffly whipped egg whites. Turn into the lined sieve. Leave to drain overnight. Turn out on to shallow dish.

'Serve the snow cheese with plain wheaten biscuits.'

From *Spices, Salt and Aromatics in the English Kitchen* by Elizabeth David, Penguin Books, 1970, p. 216.

5. Plain Dessert or Wine Biscuits

'Rub very small indeed, two ounces of fresh butter into a pound of flour, and make it into a stiff paste with new milk. Roll it out half an inch thick, and cut the biscuits with a round cutter the size of half-a-crown. Pile them one on the other until all are done; then roll them out very thin, prick them, and lay them on lightly-floured tins, the pricked side downwards: a few minutes will bake them, in a moderate oven. They should be very crisp, and but slightly browned.'

…'flour 1 lb.; butter, 2 oz.; new milk about 1/2 pint.'

From *Modern Cookery* by Eliza Acton, revised edn., Longman, Brown, Green & Longmans, 1855, p. 560.

In fact Barbara Yeomans, who baked them, added a very little sugar - to flavour rather than sweeten.

6. Devils on Horseback

We did not give the chef a recipe for this as any English chef knows it. This is how Mark Walker, the chef at Saint Antony's did it.

Take large prunes, soaked and stoned, and stuff them with good quality mango chutney. Then sprinkle them with plenty of cayenne pepper and wrap them with a slice of back bacon, which should be fairly fatty. Grill gently so that the bacon becomes crisp, but not burned. Serve on toast - two 'devils' per person.

7. Seed Cake

Seed Cake.

4 ~~5~~ Eggs
6 oz. Fresh Butter
6 ~~½~~ lb. Fine Castor Sugar
8 ~~10~~ oz. Fine Flour

¼ lb. Citron ~~Peel~~ ⎫ grated lemon
¼ lb. ~~Orange~~ Peel ⎭ rind
6 oz. Almonds ground
Some Carraways

Cut the peels in thin, flat slices; blanch and split the almonds. Put the butter and sugar in a basin, and beat till they become a cream; then add the yolks and flour, time about—1 yolk and 1 table-spoonful of flour— beating all the time; then beat the whites up very stiffly, and stir in; then all the fruit, and mix thoroughly; put into a papered and buttered cake-tin. Sprinkle carraways all over the top, and bake for 1 hour.

From *Choice Cookery, La Bonne Cuisine* by Mrs. Black, William Collins, Sons & Co., n.d. [c. 1890].

This cake is richer and less dry than usual for a late 19th century recipe because of addition of almonds. The annotations to the quantities were already there when Lisa acquired the book. She sticks to them, as did the chef. We believe that, as has been normal from the 17th century onwards, most of the caraway seeds should be mixed in with the fruit with just a few sprinkled on top, though surprisingly the recipe does not say this. Because of the almonds this is a richer cake than Jane Grigson's (*English Food*, Macmillan, 1974), but they are interesting to compare.

Welsh Foods and Drinks Offered at Lunch on 23rd September

by Gilli Davies

Cheeses

Pant-ys-gawn. Goat's milk cheese, pasteurised. Vegetarian Society approved. Clean mild taste. Fries well. [Tony Craske, Abergavenny Fine Foods Ltd., Mamhilad, Gwent NP4 8RG. Tel:0873 880844].

Pencarreg. Mould ripened soft cheese; made with organically produced milk. [Welsh Organic Foods Ltd., 20/21 Llambed Industrial Estate, Lampeter, Dyfed SA48 8LT].

T'yn Grug. Farm made, vegetarian; organic unpasteurised milk from mixed breed herd. Cheddar type, matured at least six months. [Dougal Campbell, c/o Welsh Organic Foods Ltd. Tel: 0570 422772].

Felin Gernos. Traditional brined Caerphilly; unpasteurised cow's milk. [Gillian Bond, Maesllyn, Llandyssul, Dyfed SA44 5NB. Tel: 023975 362].

Nevern Dairies. Traditional farm Cheddar. Pedigree Friesian cow's milk, pasteurised, matured nine months. [Andrew Thripland, Glasdir Farm, Nevern, Dyfed. Tel: 0239 820354].

Caws Caron. Firm goat's cheese, unpasteurised, vegetarian rennet. [John Jones, Tregaron Foods, Station Road, Tregaron, Dyfed SY25 6HX. Tel: 0974 298944].

Teifi Farmhouse Cheese. Organic Gouda style, semi-hard, unpasteurised cheese made with vegetarian rennet. [John Savage-Onstwedder, Glynhynod, Ffostrasol, Llandyssul, Dyfed SA44 5JY. Tel: 023975 528].

Acorn. Farmhouse ewe's milk cheese, vegetarian rennet and pure salt. 100% halal. [Karen Ross, Little Acorn Products, Mesen Fach Farm, Bethania, nr. Llanon, Dyfed SY23 5NL. Tel: 097423 348].

T'yn Rhos. Unpasteurised cow's milk Cheddar type, matured over twelve months. Not for retail, only to farmhouse visitors! [Lynda Kettle, T'yn Rhos Farm, Seion, Llanddeiniolen, Caernarfon LL55 3AE. Tel: 0248 670489].

Butter

Rachel's Dairy Farmhouse Butter. Hand churned from full cream milk from organically reared Guernsey cows. [Rachel's Dairy, Brynllys Farm, Borth, Dyfed SY24 5LZ. Tel: 097081 489].

Bread

Wholemeal bread (made from organic 100% wholemeal flour), white bread and bara brith. Kneaded by hand and baked in a traditional faggot oven, lit daily at 4 a.m. The oven was moved from Aberystwyth to the Welsh Folk Museum. [Chris Aston, The Bakery, Welsh Folk Museum, Saint Fagans, Cardiff. Tel: 0222 569441].

Beer

Felinfoel Double Dragon Beer. [Felinfoel Brewery Co. Ltd., Felinfoel, Llanelli, Dyfed SA14 8LB. Tel: 0554 773357].

Water

Ty Nant spring water, mildly carbonated. The design of the blue bottle received the British Glass Federation's First Class Award for design excellence for 1989. [Ty Nant Spring Water Ltd., Lampeter, Dyfed SA48 8LT. Tel: 0570 423601].